The Jewish World
of Yesterday

1860-1938

The Jewish World of Yesterday

1860-1938

Texts and Photographs from Central Europe

Edited by Rachel Salamander

With essays by
Schalom Ben-Chorin, Marcel Reich-Ranicki,
Joachim Riedl, and Julius Schoeps

Photographs selected by Christian Brandstätter

Translated from the German by
Eileen Walliser-Schwarzbart

RIZZOLI
NEW YORK

First published in the United States of America in 1991 by
RIZZOLI INTERNATIONAL PUBLICATIONS, INC.
300 Park Avenue South, New York, NY 10010

Copyright © 1990 by Christian Brandstätter Verlagsgesellschaft
m. b. H., Wien

Library of Congress Cataloging-in-Publication Data

Jüdische Welt von gestern, 1860–1938. English
The Jewish world of yesterday, 1860–1938 / edited by Rachel
Salamander : texts by Schalom Ben-Chorin . . . [et al.] : pictures
selected by Christian Brandstätter.

p. cm.
Translation of: Die jüdische Welt von gestern, 1860–1938.
Includes bibliographical references and index.
ISBN 0-8478-1415-7
1. Jews–Germany–Pictorial works.
2. Jews–Germany–Intellectual life.
3. Germany–Civilization–Jewish influences.
4. Jews–Austria–Pictorial works. 5. Jews–Austria–Intellectual
life. 6. Germany–Ethnic relations. 7. Austria–Ethnic relations.
I. Salamander, Rachel. II. Ben-Chorin, Schalom. III. Title.
DS135.G33J8213   1991
943'.004924 – dc20
91-52794
CIP

Printed and bound in Austria

FOR MY FATHER

At the graves of their parents
children weep
for the hopes placed in them.
R.S.

CONTENTS

CONTENTS

FOREWORD

*T*he past lives only in us. It is our memory that gives it historical reality, making images and words from the past into an aspect of present-day consciousness . . . : Old gravestone in the Jewish cemetery of Kolin (northern Bohemia).

*I*n considering Jewish life and history from a European standpoint, it is necessary to bear in mind that the remaining Jewish population is small. Its strength to support and sustain liturgical rites are diminished. Consequently, when a large city wishes to honor its Jewish population, it is usually in the form of building a Jewish museum. But the wish to do something – at least for the past – immediately encounters obstacles there, too. It is virtually impossible to infuse a museum with life; original pieces to be put on display are rare. Thus what we usually find are copies of domestic crafts that all too clearly elicit cultural enjoyment of a second-hand variety. But are we to forgo tradition completely for the sake of cultural authenticity?

And what about the selection of pictures and texts intended to provide a survey of the Jewish world of central Europe from 1860 to 1938?

In the nineteenth century, written records were joined by a new and major kind of documentation, the photograph. Apparently as authentic as life itself, a medium could suddenly begin to capture more than just spectacular events and personalities. The camera takes intimate, essentially insignificant details of an otherwise unheeded daily routine and makes them into pictorial sensations. Chance circumstances, even trivialities, suddenly achieved the status of visually immortal testimony to their time. These photographs are printed realities of past lives, admittedly torn out of context. And this context is what we must seek to reconstruct, for these images can never be more than fragments, endless details capable of infinite expansion. By capturing a part they forfeit the whole, and that means we are forced to rely on additional sources for our reconstruction.

We fall back on written records, on literary and biographical documents and chronicles. The gaps left by the pictures begin to fill. Even if the two sources, text and picture, cannot totally complete the pattern, they can illuminate a crucial aspect of Jewish history: there was no more a Jewish world of yesterday than there is a homogeneous Jewish world of today.

As the rest of society consists of many societies, so Jewry is composed of many Jewries. Contrasts abound: here the vitality of the traditional eastern European way of life, there the requisite refinement of the assimilated Jewish upper class. Here those who fastidiously consign their shtetl origins to oblivion and go to the cities to escape from poverty and find refuge from pogroms, there those who no longer feel at home anywhere, neither among the Orthodox nor those who have national ideas, and plaintively bewail the loss of the authentic selves they have just shaken off. They know that, without falling into romanticism, what once was can never be recreated again. What was unquestioned and self-evident to their forefathers is no longer self-evident to even the first generation of descendants and, as a standard that is no longer lived, is lost. The great, modern Hebrew novelist S. J. Agnon once described the loss of cultural and religious tradition approximately as follows: the grandfather loved the Torah, the son wrote about love of the Torah, and the grandson wrote only about love.

So shall we ignore these documents of bygone times and comfort ourselves with the insight that the past can never be apprehended as it really was? If our reason for preserving these records is a present need rather than an obligation to the past, we will tolerate their imperfect presentation.

It is a Jewish tradition to preserve what was and acknowledge the claims of the dead, for that is the way to keep them and their works alive.

When European Jewry was annihilated, the visible signs of its existence were also destroyed. Not imbuing the little we have left with immediacy would mean giving up this vanished world for good.

It might be objected that the people shown in the photographs were hopelessly lost. That is true. But they did not know then what we know now. A further possible objection: showing them on fine, glossy paper is splendor in the wrong place; it evokes idylls where there were none. But mourning the irretrievability of this obliterated world cannot mean retrospectively shaking the ashes of future disaster over a time that has not yet experienced that disaster; it cannot mean presciently depriving the doomed of their personal concerns, yearnings, and glory.

The past lives only in us. It is our memory that gives it historical reality, making images and words from the past into an aspect of present-day consciousness. Thus does history come alive in us, and through us become the present. How these documents of the past are shown is secondary. The people who speak in the texts, the people who look at us from the pictures are being given back their names and with that their individuality. That is why in the Jewish prayer for the dead we always mention the person we are remembering by name.

Schalom Ben-Chorin
THE JEWISH FAITH

*I*n the eighteenth century, the German philosopher Moses Mendelssohn still referred to Judaism as "my nation," whereas in the nineteenth and first third of our own century Jews tended to favor a religious definition. Sometimes the term "Jewish" was even replaced by "Mosaic" or "Israelite," though admittedly only in central and western Europe, whereas eastern Jewry remained aware of its national character, if only because it had a colloquial language of its own, Yiddish.

In Germany, the "religious" ideology was cultivated by the Centralverein deutscher Staatsbürger jüdischen Glaubens (Central Association of German Citizens of Jewish Faith); in Austria, the Union österreichischer Staatsbürger jüdischen Glaubens (Union of Austrian Citizens of Jewish Faith) represented a similar world view.

Isaak Breuer, spiritual leader of the radical Jewish Orthodox faction in Germany, commented ironically on German citizens of Jewish lack-of-faith, a phrase that often characterized the situation accurately.

Nineteenth-century German Judaism generated the three basic trends that still mark Judaism today, at the end of the twentieth century: Orthodox, Reform, and Conservative Judaism.

The term 'Orthodox' is not used here to mean the highly traditional Judaism of eastern Europe as it evolved in the popular religious mys-

What sustained the Jews through all their hardships? The first thing to name would be the Sabbath, about which there is a saying: "More than the Jews have kept the Sabbath, the Sabbath has kept the Jews" . . . : Cracow Jew on his way to the synagogue. 1904

ticism of Hasidism and, above all in Lithuania, the Talmudic scholarship of the Mitnaggedim. The Neo-Orthodoxy that wanted to combine worldly western education with strict adherence to Jewish law was founded in Frankfurt am Main under the aegis of Samson Raphael Hirsch.

Radical reform as envisioned by Abraham Geiger found little echo in Germany. Only the Jewish Reform Congregation in Berlin steered a truly radical course, whereas the majority of congregations and synagogues in

Germany and Austria had a more moderate, Liberal inclination, which lives on among the "Conservatives" in the United States.

While eastern Jewry was cultivating Jewish scholarship in the yeshivas (institutions for Talmudic study), academic rabbinical seminaries were being established in Germany: the Liberal Hochschule für die Wissenschaft des Judentums (Academy for Jewish Scholarship) in Berlin, the Conservative Jüdisch-Theologisches Seminar (Jewish Theological Seminary) in Breslau (and in Vienna), and the Orthodox Hildesheimersches Seminar in Berlin.

But it was the religious services, more than the theological differences, that revealed the disparities between the three movements.

Simple "shuls" for prayer and study yielded to imposing Moorish and neo-romanesque synagogues, even among the Neo-Orthodox, who competed with the Liberals when it came to the visual representation of an affluent Jewish bourgeoisie.

Organs became a regular fixture in Liberal synagogues. Though this raised the aesthetic standard of services, it also led to a degree of alienation because of its echoes of Christianity, particularly Protestantism.

Rabbis and cantors wore robes, and sermons in German became an integral part of Sabbath and holiday services. The folkloristic form (or formlessness) of eastern European shtetl Judaism survived only at the fringes of this official, institutionalized religion.

Jewish piety in any form is characterized by bipolarity, the two poles being the congregation (synagogue) and the home. Lived Judaism cannot be restricted to the synagogue, it flourishes first and foremost within the family. The true culmination of Sabbath Eve, for instance, is the festive Sabbath meal at home, after the Friday night synagogue service. Mother has already blessed the Sabbath candles, Father chants or recites the blessings over the wine, the bread and the Sabbath. Parents bestow the age-old Priestly Blessing on their children: "May the Lord bless you and guard you; May the Lord shine His countenance upon you and be gracious to you; May the Lord display kindness toward you and grant you peace."

The Jewish home stands literally under the word of God, for affixed to the doorpost is the mezuzah, which invokes blessings on the house and contains the fundamental Jewish profession of faith: "Hear O Israel, the Lord our God, the Lord is ONE."

The festivals of the Jewish year do not revolve around the synagogue any more than the Sabbath does, apart perhaps from the High Holidays in autumn (New Year and the Day of Atonement). But the next holiday, Sukkot, the Festival of Tabernacles, once again centers around the family, who must spend at least mealtimes in the sukkah, or booth, for seven (if they are in Israel) or eight days (in the Diaspora).

The spring holiday of Passover (the Jewish Easter), too, is far more family- than synagogue-oriented. The first evening, known as the Seder (Seder = order of the home festival), is celebrated with a home liturgy that lasts until late into the night and includes symbolic foods, ritualized

dialogues, and songs. It inspired the fifteen-year-old Heinrich Heine to write his ballad "Belshazzar": "Midnight was approaching . . ."

While the male element dominates in the synagogue, it is the Jewish woman who is responsible for family life, from the kosher kitchen to planning religious holiday celebrations.

There are many holidays throughout the Jewish year: the High Holidays in autumn; the three Pilgrim Festivals (the name originated in the time of the Temple in Jerusalem, a place of pilgrimage); Passover; the Feast of Weeks and the Feast of Tabernacles; the Maccabean feast of Hanukkah in winter, during which the candles in the menorah (seven-branched candelabrum) reflect their cozy light in the windows of the home; and the joyous Purim festival, the Jewish carnival, in the early spring.

From cradle to grave, a Jew's life is governed by tradition. If Schopenhauer spoke of the "world as will and idea," then Judaism is the world as law and custom.

The archaic character of the religion manifests itself in patriarchal dominance. Eight days after a boy is born, he is circumcised as a sign of God's covenant with Abraham.

Although there is no corresponding introduction into the covenant for girls, the Jews of western Europe, interestingly enough, had the custom of "holekresch," when the infant girl was lifted up in her basket and her Jewish name publicly announced.

At the age of thirteen years and one day, the Jewish boy becomes bar mitzvah: he attains religious adulthood and becomes a full member of the religious community. Among the German Jews of the Emancipation and Assimilation era, bar mitzvah became a major synagogue and home festival; Liberal congregations also introduced a collective confirmation

festival for girls during the Feast of Weeks.

Even non-traditional Jews generally wanted more than a civil wedding ceremony and requested a festive rabbinical wedding under the canopy, with a shared cup of wine.

Funerals are marked by their stark simplicity. A plain coffin consisting of six planks, the same for rich and poor, is the final resting place of the dead. The little bag of soil from Eretz Israel (Palestine) that was often placed in it reflected the strength of the ties to the Holy Land.

Jews all over the world tended their cemeteries faithfully. Temporary burial was unknown. The cemetery was called "the eternal house," but also "the good place."

In his 1938 poem "Der Gute Ort zu Wien" (The good place in Vienna), Franz Werfel wrote: "Do you forget the command / That binds you, Israel!? / In the lands that hate you, you must leave / Your graves as footsteps."

And that is precisely what happened. In many former centers of twentieth-century Jewish life, graves, if they were not destroyed by enemies' hatred, are all that remain of what was once the presence of Israel.

But what has sustained the Jews through all the hardships of persecution? The first thing to name would be the Sabbath. Achad Haam, a twentieth-century Jewish cultural philosopher, once remarked: "More than the Jews have kept the Sabbath, the Sabbath has kept the Jews."

Sadly, German Judaism often forgot the Sabbath. Faith could no longer be taken for granted. Environmental influences and other forces alienated the spirits and souls of assimilated Jews from the heritage of their fathers.

But it was precisely in this situation that German Judaism acquired a profile of its own. Jewish thinkers rooted in both worlds, in Judaism and the European spirit, gave a face to post-assimilatory Judaism. We are thinking here of such people as the Marburg neo-Kantian Hermann Cohen, whose posthumous work *Religion der Vernunft aus den Quellen des Judentums* (Religion of reason from the sources of Judaism) created a Jewish ethic and represented a synthesis of Jewish and Kantian thought.

We are thinking of the last great German rabbi, Leo Baeck, who worked out a valid Liberal theology of Judaism in *Das Wesen des Judentums* (The essence of Judaism); of Martin Buber, who offered a masterful illustration of internalized Hasidic religiosity in German linguistic garb with *Ich und Du* (I and Thou); and of Fritz Rosenzweig, who collaborated with Buber on the Bible translation *Verdeutschung der Schrift* (Germanization of the Scriptures) and, in his own main work, *Der Stern der Erlösung* (The star of redemption), took Hegel as his point of departure and advanced to a new way of thinking.

Only the history of early medieval Spanish Judaism and the Hellenistic era of Philo of Alexandria shows a comparable synthesis of the spirit of Judaism and its environment.

*T*hen came Thursday, a very busy day, for that was when preparations for the Sabbath were begun. The dough for the bread – the white barches and the sweet corn malaj – has to be mixed. The women rush around breathless and flustered, borrowing a piece of sourdough or some wood, or asking for advice – everything at once and all at the last minute.

From Thursday to Friday, they work through the night kneading dough, heating the oven, peeling potatoes. The various dishes are already cooking on the stove, and it is time for baking: bread, challah, sweet corn malaj; the potato bread, known as mandaburtschinik, that is already hungrily devoured on Friday and tastes so delicious with butter or cream cheese.

On Friday everything is washed, polished, and tidied away. The older children wash and comb the little ones' hair with petroleum; petroleum is a good remedy against lice. In the living room, the fragrance of freshly baked bread and roasted meat combines with the smell of petroleum. In the late afternoon it is almost time to put the schalet in the oven; the oven is hermetically sealed and carefully cleaned. The earthen floor is whitewashed with a thin layer of lime, then a green stripe is painted along the very bottom of the walls. The table is set in white; the polished brass candlesticks gleam, and there are little plates for everyone; everyone has his or her special place at the table, in order of age and precedence. The male members of the family have already gone to pray . . . In the meantime Mamma has blessed the candles, always interspersing prayer with personal conversation; she has always spoken to God like a grown daughter to her father, reminding him of his responsibilities and duties. It is the same every week.
Alexander Granach

Judaism is more than a matter of faith, it is above all the way of life practiced by a community shaped by faith.
Gustav Janouch

It is the peculiar and creative element in Jewish optimism that every belief is regarded as a responsibility; this idea entered into the world as the Jewish idea.
Leo Baeck

When I think back to the years of my youth in the large Jewish town of Minsk, one very unusual figure stands out among the images crowding in: an elderly Jew of unusually slender, delicate build, with an extremely long grey beard that had once been black, a very prominent forehead and deepset eyes that, once seen, are never forgotten. This man was called Reb Jajnkew-Mejer (hardly any-one knew his last name) and he held the post of assistant rabbi in a minor synagogue. Despite his modest post he enjoyed the sort of respect otherwise accorded only to very fam-ous and very learned rabbis. This reputation was in no way based on erudition, normally the most important quality of an eastern European rabbi; it derived solely from his unusual, in part holy way of life and from a unique office that he performed of his own accord.
He was the censor – in the ancient Roman sense of the word – and considered it his noblest task to supervise the observance of the Sabbath: he sternly saw to it that on Fridays the Jews stopped working as early as possible and closed their shops, and that on Saturday evenings they returned to their businesses as late as possible. The Jewish Sabbath begins at dusk on Friday and ends when at least three stars have appeared in the sky on Saturday evening. So every Friday afternoon, long before dusk, Reb Jajnkew-Mejer got into a cart that the carter or the congregation made available to him at no charge, and began his rounds through the streets, stopping in front of every Jewish business, knocking at the door and calling: "Yidden, it's time to observe Sabbath!" His authority was so great that everyone immediately closed his store or workshop. At the end Reb Jajnkew-Mejer drove out to the freight depot and sent all the Jewish shipping agents and their employees home. Even the Russian stationmaster fell under the strange spell the man cast: he always had an armchair carried out onto the platform for him. When the last Jew had left the station, Reb Jajnkew-Mejer went to the ritual bath and then to the synagogue.
Alexander Eliasberg

Shortly before the Sabbath begins, the woman of the house lights the candles.
<u>Right</u>: Waiting for the Sabbath. Ca. 1920

The holidays and the Schabbes (Sabbath) were the highlights of our meager existence. In the Orthodox Jewish milieu the Sabbath is a unique celebration of great ethical value. The Talmudists surrounded the day with many series of "fences around the law" to protect the core, the Sabbath, for which the Lord is continually offered prayers of thanks, from violation. This day is held so sacred that "Mechallel Schabbos," profaning the Sab-bath, is one of the gravest sins a pious man can commit. (In Biblical law profaning the Sabbath is punishable by death.) The "fences around the law" were created to ensure that absolutely no work could be done on this day, a day dedicated to rest and contemplation. For instance, although making music cannot be regarded as work, musical instruments may not be played on the Sabbath so that professional musicians will never be forced

into the position of having to work. To make sure that no heavy burdens are carried, carrying any object, even a pocket watch, is frowned upon. The pockets of one's clothing must be carefully emptied on Friday evening; not even handkerchiefs are permitted to re-main there, they must be tied around the neck or arm to lend them the appearance of a piece of clothing. The poor saved all week to be able to "make Schabbes." Mutual assistance to enable everyone to celebrate the Sabbath with the appropriate dignity was a sacred commandment . . .
Friday is already a half-holiday. The house-wife, who has to prepare ahead for Friday and Saturday, has a great deal to do and works hard at it. The husband, too, no matter how learned or wealthy he may be, does not find it beneath his dignity to lend a helping hand in the kitchen, to make himself useful

An especially good meal is eaten on Sabbath. After the gefil-te fish and soup, there is usually boiled chicken. Many of the poor eastern Jews saved up all week for the chicken. Sometimes the pros-pect of "Schabbes" was the only thing that made life bearable.
<u>Right</u>: The Sabbath chicken. Ca. 1920

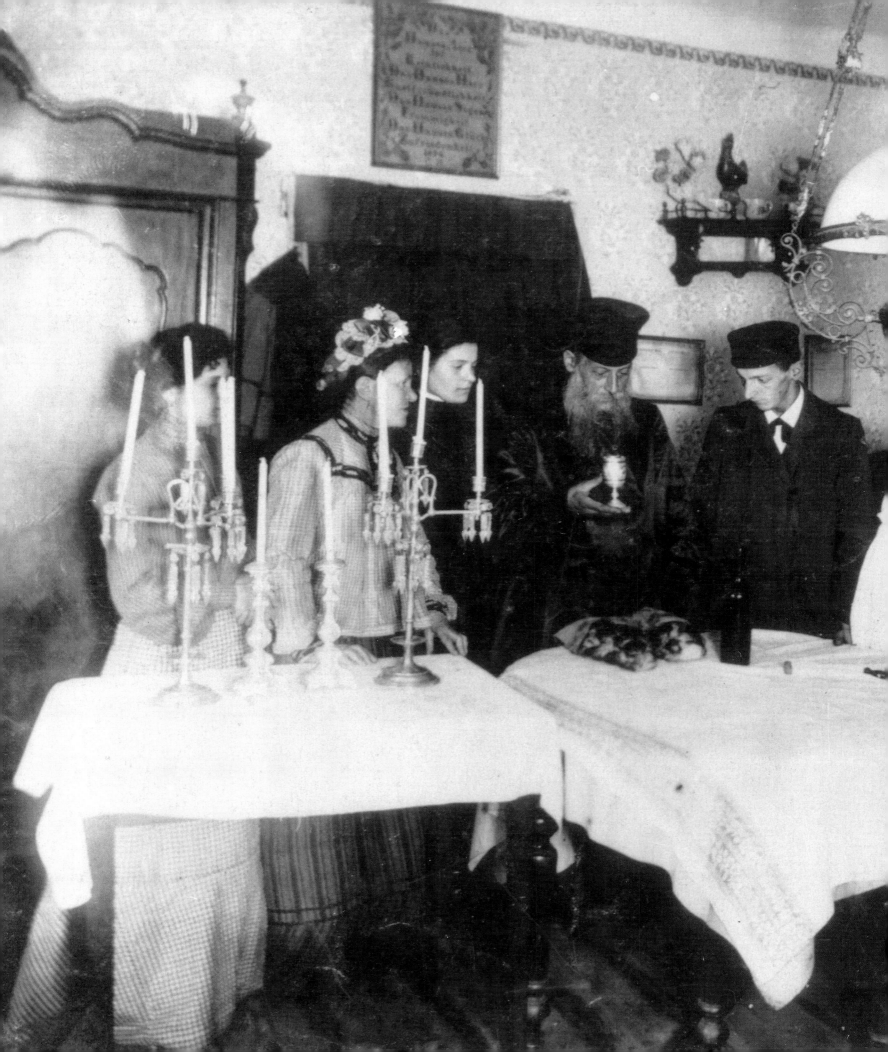

Pious Jews may travel on-ly 2,000 steps on the Sabbath. Nothing could be so important that one would dare let it desecrate the day of rest.
Right: Polish Jews in kaschkets (brimmed caps). Ca. 1910
Left: Reciting Kiddush: welcoming the Sabbath at the table on Friday night. 1906

"in honor of the Sabbath," for tasks such as these are pleasing to God and will be rewarded in Heaven. He goes shopping, polishes the silver or the candelabra, chops wood; in short, he strives to render a variety of services. There are many chores to be done, and they must be started in good time, for even the white Sabbath bread known as "challah" is baked at home . . .
On this day even the poorest Jew has a white tablecloth on his dinner table and eats fish or meat, sometimes even fish and meat, and a dessert, the "zimes." Pike prepared the kosher way is a specialty, and it really is a delicacy; even unbelievers love it. There was also a schnapps to season the Shabbes meal. Wine was too expensive and subject to ritual usage, and our bad beer does not appeal to anyone. Even as little children we were given a glass of schnapps, which we sopped up with white bread . . .
The woman of the house is particularly busy in the afternoon; everything has to be finished so the Sabbath will not take her by surprise, for when it comes, all work must cease.
The municipal steambath is heated up in good time: the bath attendant walks through the streets of the Jewish quarter shaking a birch whisk in his raised right hand and calling loudly, "Jews to the bath!" – Immediately all the men put down their work, fetch themselves fresh linens, and hurry to the bath. The whole community meets there. A tiered construction is set up in the steam room; the top step, which is the hottest place, is where the men of consequence sit and discuss community interests and personal matters as well as lofty political issues . . .
In the late afternoon the men hurried home again from the bath, their wet sidecurls straggling down next to their ears like dripping rattails. Quickly they put on their Schab-

bes gaberdines and hastened to the synagogue. The pious wear Schabbes garments made of black silk or satin, the less pious, ones of black cloth. A man who laid claim to erudition, a so-called "good Jew," or the Rev himself might also dress in black or brown velvet.
Jehudo Epstein

Sabbath effectively eliminates the differences that exist because of the work people do. The artisan, too, becomes his own master. Having one's weekly rest on a specific day puts the worker and his master on equal footing . . . And the ghetto Jew casts off all the hardships of day-to-day life with the lighting of the Sabbath candles. All indignities were shaken off. God's love, which gave him the Sabbath every seventh day, also gave him back his honor and human dignity in his low-ceilinged hut.
Hermann Cohen

31.IV.33

Considering the suffering that pervades the whole historical life of the Jew, it is surely a wonder that he could continually maintain such equanimity, such a genuine humor, without which he would never have been able to lift himself again and again from the deepest humiliation to proud heights. The Jewish holidays have brought about this wonder for him.
Hermann Cohen

The holiday that we children felt most strongly, even though, being very small, we couldn't take part in it, was Purim. It was a joyous festival, commemorating the salvation of the Jews from Haman, the wicked persecutor. Haman was a well-known figure, and his name had entered the language. Before I ever found out that he was a man who had once lived and concocted horrible things, I knew his name as an insult. If I tormented adults with too many questions or didn't want to go to bed or refused to do something they wanted me to do, there would be a deep sigh: "Hamán!" Then I knew that they were in no mood for jokes, that I had played out. "Hamán" was the final word, a deep sigh, but also a vituperation. I was utterly amazed when I was told later on that Haman had been a wicked man who wanted to kill all the Jews. But thanks to Mordecai and Queen Esther, he failed, and, to show their joy, the Jews celebrated Purim.
The adults disguised themselves and went out, there was noise in the street, masks appeared in the house, I didn't know who they were, it was like a fairy tale; my parents stayed out till late at night. The general excitement affected us children; I lay awake in my crib and listened. Sometimes our parents would show up in masks, which they

then took off; that was great fun, but I preferred not knowing it was they.
Elias Canetti

This festival had broad political significance, commemorating the Exodus from Egypt and liberation from slavery, but it also celebrated spring and was the most joyous of all festivals. Provisions were made to furnish parents and children with new clothes and head-coverings for the coming season, which fit in well with the beginning of spring and contributed to a contented, cheerful mood.
Long before Easter, spring-cleaning began all over the town.

Poverty is, unfortunately, accompanied by grime and dirt; and in our town the poverty was great. A thorough cleaning from time to time was vital. All the houses were cleaned from top to bottom, inside and out, and the walls were stripped and white-washed. Metal dishes were polished till they gleamed and then "kashered," which means made kosher for "Pessach," the Passover, as everyday dishes and silverware are not allowed to be used during Passover unless they have been specially prepared. Rich people had an extra set of Passover dishes carefully stored away and never used during the rest of the year. Those who did not, had to have their ordinary set "kashered."
Jehudo Epstein

Matzoh, unleavened bread, recalls the Exodus from Egypt, which took place in such haste that there was no time for the bread to rise.
Left: Producing and packing up matzoh in Berlin before the Passover festival. Photograph by *Roland Lewy*. 1936

The week-long festival began in the evening with the Seder. Around the long, extended table sat the thirty children from the orphanage, my father's family and invited guests. Father particularly liked to invite his students, many of whom had no relatives in Berlin. So we were a party of approximately fifty reliving the Exodus from Egypt in memory once again. Father sat at the head of the table in a big broad armchair with additional snow-white, down-filled pillows on it. For on this night one must recline and sit comfortably – after all, there is a great deal of wine drunk during the narrative, not unrestrainedly, but to accompany specific passages. Father wore his white shroud, for although Pessach is a joyous festival, man must always be pre-

One of the customs observed on Rosh Hashana (September/October), the festival of the New Year, is to go to a river bank to throw breadcrumbs into the water (tashlikh) and pray for the current to sweep away one's sins. Rosh Hashana is the first of the Ten Days of Penitence ending with Yom Kippur. The traditional greeting on Rosh Hashana is "l'shanah tovah tikatevu v'taychataymu," may you be "written and sealed for a good year" in the book of Divine Judgment.
Left: Tashlikh on Rosh Hashana in Munkacz (Hungary). Photograph by *Abraham Pisarek*. 1930

pared to stand before God on the Day of Judgment. On his head he wore a white silk kippah trimmed with a broad border of elaborate silver embroidery. As he sat there in his broad armchair, his face illuminated by the tall candles in the heavy silver candlesticks, it was a Biblical figure we saw, returned to us from ancient times. Before him lay the Haggadah, printed in large Hebrew letters on parchment-like paper. Some of them were already quite discolored because during the recitation of the ten plagues God visited on the Egyptians, the little finger of the right hand must be dipped into the filled wineglass for each one and then allowed to drip onto the pages of the book. As the years pass, the wine that has seeped through lends the book the appearance of a document centuries old. In a small but pleasant voice, Father sang the traditional melodies he had learned in my grandparents' home. But that was not enough for him. When one of the students, most of whom came from countries in eastern Europe, knew a different melody to the same text, father would not rest until we had all learned it. And so a very long while might be spent over a single passage before the narrative could be taken up again.
Josef Tal

On Rosh Hashana we sometimes accompanied our Orthodox friends to the river bank, where they threw breadcrumbs into the water. This ritual, known as "tashlikh," symbolizes the hope that during the Ten Days of Penitence, genuine contrition will wash away man's sins as the river washes away the breadcrumbs.
Philip Seligsberger-White

When people go home from the synagogue after the Rosh Hashana Eve service, they greet their friends with the words "l'shana tovah tikatevu!" (May you be inscribed for a good year.) At home after the Kiddush and the Motsi, a piece of apple dipped in honey is eaten as a symbol of hope and a "good and sweet new year." In some regions it is the custom to eat from the head of a fish or a ram on Erev Rosh Hashana as a symbol of being at the beginning and not the end.
Manfred Swarsensky

I had already seen them beside themselves with praying. That was on Yom Kippur, a day known in western Europe as the "Day of Reconciliation" – all of the western Jew's readiness to compromise is expressed in this term. But Yom Kippur is not a day of reconciliation, it is a day of atonement, a hard day, whose twenty-four hours contain the repentance of twenty-four years. It begins at four in the afternoon on the eve of the holiday. In a city populated predominantly by Jews, this greatest of all Jewish holidays seems to pervade the air as would a heavy thunderstorm approaching a frail boat on the high seas. Suddenly the lanes are dark because the glow of candles bursts from all the windows, and the shutters are fastened in anxious haste – and bolted so indescribably tightly that one thinks they will only be opened again on Doomsday. It is a general farewell to worldly life: to business, to joy, to nature, and to food, to the street and to the family, to friends and acquaintances. People who only two hours ago were walking around in everyday clothing with everyday faces hasten transformed through the lanes towards the house of prayer in heavy black silk and the terrible white of their shrouds, in white socks and loose slippers, heads bowed, prayer shawls under their arms. And the silence that is amplified a hundred times in a town of otherwise almost oriental noisiness hangs heavy even over the lively children, whose cries are the strongest accents in the music of daily life. It is time for the fathers to bless their children, for the women to weep over their silver candlesticks, for friends to embrace, for enemies to beg each other's forgiveness. The Angelic Choir is summoning to the Last Judgement. Soon Jehova will open the big book in which all the sins, punishments, and fates of the year are inscribed. Now lights are burning for all the dead. Others are burning for all the living.

On Sukkot (September/October) every household constructs a sukkah, or booth, to recall the temporary booths of the Israelites during their wanderings in the desert. The sukkah, which should serve as the family's home during the eight-day festival, is built outdoors if possible; its temporary roof must allow the stars to shine through.

Opposite page, below: Hungarian house with open segment of roof, in accordance with the laws applying to sukkahs. Ca. 1914

The dead are only a step away from this world, the living only a step from the next. The great praying begins. The great fasting began an hour ago. Hundreds, thousands, tens of thousands of candles burn next to one another, behind one another, incline towards each other, merge into great flames. From a thousand windows bursts the wailing prayer, punctuated by soft, quiet, otherworldly melodies, echoing the lesson of celestial song. Shoulder to shoulder they stand, the people in all the houses of prayer. Some throw themselves to the floor, remain there for a long while, then rise to sit on stone slabs and footstools. Suddenly they leap to their feet, their trunks swaying, their legs running back and forth interminably in a tiny space, like ecstatic sentinels of prayer. Whole houses are filled with white shrouds, with the living who are not there, with the dead who have come to life. Not a drop of water to moisten parched lips and refresh throats that wail in anguish – not into this world, but into a higher world. They will not eat today, nor will they eat tomorrow. It is terrible to know that today and tomorrow no one in this town will eat or drink. Suddenly they have all turned into ghosts, sharing the attributes of ghosts. Every little grocer is a superman, for today he wants to reach God. They all stretch out their hands to touch the hem of His garment. There is no difference between them now: the rich are as poor as the poor, for no one has anything to eat. They are all sinners, and they are all praying. Frenzy overcomes them. They reel, they rave, they whisper, they hurt themselves, sing, call out, weep; heavy tears roll down their old beards and hunger vanishes before the pain of the soul and the eternity of the melodies the enraptured ear can hear.
Joseph Roth

On this holiest and highest of Jewish holidays, the pious beg forgiveness for all the sins they have committed during the past year and mortify themselves before God by abstaining from washing and eating. For twenty-four hours, even through the night, the faithful remain together in the synagogue, praying ceaselessly during the uninterrupted service. Most of them are in their white shrouds, which have a depressing effect and add to the solemnity of the occasion – a day especially to remember the dead.
Philippine Landau

Judaism is a religion of atonement; to the meaning of life it gives thus its completing chapter. Two old Rabbinic sayings express this thought as follows; "The purpose and aim of all creation is atonement" . . . The day of atonement became the sacred centre of the year, its most important religious holy day.
Leo Baeck

The fragrance of exotic fruit [before the Feast of Tabernacles in autumn] is a memory of my earliest childhood – for several days an old man swept into our apartment morning after morning, the cool autumn air in his wake, and handed my father twigs, a palm frond, and what looked like a kind of lemon but was called an "ethrog." My father hastily shook the palm frond, put the ethrog to his nose and sucked in air, and said a blessing – upon which the stranger quickly ran off again, for he had many other apartments to visit and render the same enigmatic service. It was a remnant of the ceremonies of the Feast of Tabernacles, which in an "enlightened" family, retained a shadowy existence for a few short years before vanishing completely.
Max Brod

Above: Sukkot preparations. Ca. 1930

Simhat Torah, the festival of rejoicing in the Law, takes place one day after the end of Sukkot. It marks the end of the annual cycle of Torah readings and begins a new cycle.

Above: Choosing flags for children. Photograph, *Studio Kuszer*, Warsaw. Ca. 1930
Right: Hanukkah. Photograph by *Abraham Pisarek*. Ca. 1935

Once a year we children are allowed to make merry in the shul. From evening on we pant from the boisterousness of the hakkafot. The shul is packed full of people. There is no place in which to get away from the boys. Even little girls come to the men's section for the hakkafot, and together with the boys they crowd around underfoot. The lamps seem to burn with a new flame. The holy ark is open, the scrolls of the Torah are carried out of it, one after the other. All of them are cherried up in little holiday mantles. The shul is glorified like a holy temple. Men dance and stamp with the scrolls of the Torah in their hands. We children dance and stamp with them.
Like little wild creatures we run around the lectern, jumping up on it at one side, jumping down at the other. The wooden steps groan under our feet.
We push and chase one another; each of us wants to run around the lectern as many times as possible. We are not given time to touch or stroke its carved handrail, not even to catch our breath. The rattles shake in our hands, the shul is filled with their noise. The paper flags whistle, flutter after us, and tear in the wind. The shames hides in a corner. He fears that we will push the walls apart. Now it seems that the books on the stands are begin-

ning to slip. He begs us: "Children, will there
be no end of this? We've had enough! You'll
upset the whole shul!"
Bella Chagall

*T*here is nothing in our homes and houses of
prayer to recall those victories but a little
light, to which one will be added daily for
eight days, and a quiet celebration in the
peace of the home. For when we celebrate
Hanukkah, it is not the victories of the
Maccabees that we celebrate but the resump-
tion of the Temple service, the lighting of the
menorah. The Hannukah light only suggests
the meaning of the Maccabees' victory and
the means and secret of that victory. "Not by
might, and not by power but by my spirit,
says the Lord of hosts" (Zech. 4:6).
Max Grunwald

*T*he first light was kindled and the origin of
the festival related: the miracle of the lamp
that burned so unexpectedly long and the
story of the return from Babylonian exile, the
Second Temple of the Maccabees. Our friend
told his children what he knew. It was not
much, but it was enough for them. When the
second candle was lit they retold it to him,
and as they spoke he found everything they
said, though they had it all from him, totally
new and beautiful. And every day from then
on he looked forward to the evenings, which
were becoming brighter and brighter. One
candle after the other rose from the menorah,
and the father joined his children in their
reverie over the little lights. Ultimately it
exceeded what he could or wanted to tell
them because it was still beyond their grasp.
When he had decided to return home to his
people and openly to affirm this return, he
had merely thought he was doing something
honest and reasonable. That he would find
fulfillment of his longing for beauty along the
way he would never have suspected. And
what happened to him was nothing less than
that. The menorah in its growing radiance
truly was something beautiful, and its presence inspired to lofty thoughts. So he went
and, with practiced hand, sketched a design
for a menorah he wanted to give his children
the following year.
Theodor Herzl

23

The next thing I can see is the Feast of Circumcision. Many more people came into the house. I was allowed to watch during the circumcision. I have the impression that they deliberately let me look. All doors were open, even the house door, a long covered table for the guests stood in the living room, and in another room, facing the bedroom, the circumcision took place. It was witnessed only by men, all standing. My tiny brother was held over a basin, I saw the knife, and particularly I saw a lot of blood dripping into the basin.

My brother was named after my mother's father, Nissim, and they explained that I was the eldest and was therefore named after my paternal grandfather. The position of the eldest son was so greatly emphasized that I remained conscious of it from that moment of the circumcision on and never lost my pride in it.
Elias Canetti

Dr. Baeck spoke about "holy joy." He went out from the fact that the boy being confirmed was called up "to the Law," that he was a "bar mitzvah," which other peoples must view as a restriction of his freedom, for the world generally considered "being accountable to the law" necessary but hardly "pleasant." He explained that taking up the burden of the Law and joyfully "boasting in its glory" was a peculiarity of Judaism, for it was the Law that gave man his essential human freedom and it was through the Law that he rose above base creatures. This joy was no "abandoned merriment," however, it was the uplifting holy joy that he, Dr. Baeck, beseeched God to bestow on me, the "bar mitzvah" boy, in this important hour.
Conrad Rosenstein

The boy's new position as an adult member of the Jewish community is demonstrated to the assembled congregation by his recitation of the blessing over the open Torah on the Sabbath of, or following, his thirteenth birth-

For the thirteen-year-old boy, bar mitzvah means attaining the age of religious responsibility. During the Reading of the Law in the synagogue, the boy is called to read from the Torah for the first time. Preparing for bar mitzvah also includes learning to put on phylacteries (tefillin), which are worn across from the heart on the left arm and on the forehead.
Above: Family bar mitzvah. 1906

One of the most important commandments in Judaism is circumcision, berit milah, which seals the covenant with God. The male infant is circumcised and named on the eighth day of his life. The ceremony is followed by a big celebration.
Left: Family celebration on the day of circumcision. Ca. 1910

The Talmud recommends that serious thought be given to whether a man and woman who are to wed are well matched physically, emotionally, and with respect to their backgrounds and views. Though marriage is considered a divine commandment, divorce is permitted if it "fails." There are various types of weddings, the most frequent ceremony being held under a canopy (huppah) symbolizing the home the couple will share.
Right: Outdoor wedding ceremony under the huppah. Photograph by *Abraham Pisarek*. 1935

accomplishment if, in addition, the boy makes a siyyum ("completion of the study") on a tractate of the Talmud . . . and at the festive repast given by his parents in honor of the day, "bentsches" the Birkat ha-Mazon, the Grace recited after meals, from memory.
Leopold Neuhaus

day by the Jewish calendar. He is "called up" to the Torah; he is, as we say, ole latora (he goes up to the Torah) and receives an aliyah. The "bar mitzvah," who is called up by his Hebrew name, sometimes reads a parashah (section of the Torah) or the whole siddrah (the weekly portion for that particular Sabbath) himself . . . It is considered a particular

*I*n the meantime the bridal procession had begun to move. In front the musicians, scratching away mercilessly on their fiddles, then the bride, accompanied by her own and the bridegroom's mother, behind them all the female guests.
In front of the temple, the procession's destination, the men were already grouped around a canopy that had been erected outdoors. A small, round, motionless white mass that might from the distance have been taken for a sack of flour rose from the ground under the canopy. It was Moschele. In view of the solemn act that was about to take place, Moschele had been dressed in a snow-white coat. He pressed his handkerchief even harder to his eyes to protect his gaze from falling on the mass of women streaming towards him;

there they were, against all normally observed rules of decency, pushing ever closer to his chaste self. Then – a thrill of heat surged round his heart – someone stopped right in front of him. His hand brushed a gentle, tingling body, his breath took in the waft of another breath. There she was! The unknown, mysterious, enigmatic creature at whose side he was to go through life from now on. According to law he should at this point have lifted his bride's veil and examined her face for the first time. After all, who would buy something sight unseen? How easily the little woman one intended to lead home might turn out to be malformed, a monster, and that would be the end of the poor man's happiness . . .
But in his present bewilderment Moschele saw and heard nothing. Mechanically he placed the ring on the bride's finger, mechanically he mumbled: "Behold, with this ring are you sanctified to me according to the laws of Moses and Israel." Only when the glass had shattered under his foot (when the wedding ceremony is over the groom breaks a glass by stepping on it) and the musicians had struck up the wedding march amid exultant congratulations did he awaken from his reverie.
Jacob Fromer

Above: Wedding of Käthe Sternfeld and Samuel Wilhelm von Freudiger in Budapest. 1931

Right: Wedding procession with musicians (klezmorim) through Unterbergstrasse in Eisenstadt (Burgenland, Austria). 1934

*T*he Jews wrapped their dead in "tachrichim," shrouds, laid them on a plain black bier, covered them with a plain black cloth and then the friends of the deceased carried the bier to the cemetery on their shoulders, taking turns calling out: "May justice walk before it!" Passers-by relieved the tired men of their burden, for helping to carry the dead to the funeral is very pleasing to God. There were no clergy in attendance and there was no display of pomp: rich and poor, all were buried with the same lack of ostentation. The same plain black bier and the same plain black cloth for everyone. The burial of a man of standing was recognizable only by the mourners. As a result of this austerity death was something profoundly solemn and harrowing. A procession of this kind, a "lewaie," and the loud, slow cry of the pallbearers, "Zedek lefònow jehàlech," always had a horribly chilling effect on me. It unsettled and intimidated me. For a long time I was haunted by the image of what I had seen. The dead were mourned by their closest relatives for seven days; the mourners sat on the floor or on low stools, ate and drank as little as possible, and were allowed neither to wash nor to cut their hair.

Jehudo Epstein

A positive command enjoins upon the judge the duty to judge righteously, as it is said: "In righteousness shalt thou judge thy neighbor" (Lev. 19:15). What is meant by a righteous judgment? It is a judgment marked by perfect impartiality to both litigants, not permitting one to state his case at length and telling the other to be brief, not to show courtesy to one, speaking softly to him, and frown upon the other, addressing him harshly.

If one of the parties is well clad and the other ill clad, the judge should say to the former, "Either dress him like yourself before the trial is held or dress like him, then the trial will take place."

One of the litigants must not be allowed to be seated and the other kept standing; but both should be standing. It is, however, within the discretion of the court to permit both to be seated. But one must not occupy a higher seat and the other a lower one; they are to be seated side by side.

The Code of Maimonides. The Book of Judges

*H*e sat in shullate at night studying. The large room was nearly empty. Most of the artisans had already gone home. The Talmud students had withdrawn to adjacent rooms, which were smaller and better heated. It was cold and dark in the large prayer room, with its grille-enclosed women's gallery, and its large windows. Only the hesitant little flames of a few candles fought desperately against the sea of darkness. The eternal light by the Torah ark seemed to be swallowed up in the shadows. Before the little wax candles on the large table sat a few old men and late visitors. They were studying, voices drowsy, or slumbering, their heads resting on their books. The benches round the single stove, which was supposed to warm the room but had already gone out, were populated with a confused clutter of bundles and shadows of sleeping beggars who were spending the night in the shul. Two or three were still awake, some of them had fallen asleep sitting up. The darkness near the box not far from the bookcase was so dense it was almost palpable; it was as if the souls of all the dead of the shtetl were crouching there, like a flock of birds with their heads under their neighbors' wings. Jechiel pulled the wax stump he had brought along out of his pocket, lit it on a burning candle, and sat down at the table to review a passage. He had not yet had time to pick up a book today. And when, in the grey dawn, he stood next to the poor, simple people, whose cries of distress and heart-felt pleas heated the walls of the basement shul, he was transported to another world. The floor, the four walls, the ceiling receded, and Jechiel floated in a sea of cloud . . . No longer was God an abstract concept. He was a living Being, whose nearness he could feel, with whom he could speak. Jechiel asked Him for nothing, he delighted in His presence. How happy he was to be able to stand so close to God and tell Him how greatly he delighted in Him, how deeply he loved Him.
Schalom Asch

*T*o the stranger all houses of prayer look alike. But they are not, and in many the divine services are different. The Jewish religion knows no sects, but it does have various sect-like groups. There is an inexorably strict and a more lenient Orthodoxy; there are a number of "Ashkenazic" and "Sephardic" prayers, and textual variations in the same prayers. There is a very clear difference between the so-called enlightened Jews and those who believe in the Kabbalah, the followers of the various tsaddiks, each of whom has his own Hasidic group. The enlightened Jews are by no means unbelieving Jews. They simply reject any form of mysticism, and their firm belief in the miracles related in the Bible cannot be shaken by the skeptical view of the miracles of the Rebbes of the present. For the Hasidim, the tsaddik is the intermediary between man and God. Enlightened Jews need no intermediary. In fact, they consider it a sin to believe in an earthly power capable of anticipating God's wisdom, and they are their own intercessors. Yet many Jews, even if they are not Hasidim, cannot remain unaffected by the wonderful aura that surrounds a Rebbe, and in times of distress unbelieving Jews and even Christian peasants will betake themselves to the Rebbe to find help and comfort.
Joseph Roth

*W*hatever eastern Jewish families practiced in the way of religion radiated a certain warmheartedness. One had the feeling that religion was reality to them. As so many of them did not possess German citizenship and as they were certainly not proud of Poland, their native land, with its never-ending anti-Semitism, it is perhaps understandable that Judaism, in other words the Jewish religion with all its laws, customs, and traditions, represented their true inner home. But that alone does not explain their warmheartedness, for it was embedded deep in their personality. In contrast to this strongly emotional, inner warmth, the Judaism of the German Jews was cold, an intellectual-emotional phenomenon at best, as I found particularly well typified by my teacher Isaak Heinemann in Breslau. The top hat German Jews wore to the synagogue signified more than a custom, more than self-imposed respect for God. It was evidence of a kind of rigidity of the heart.
Emil Schorsch

*T*his is the most general sense of revelation: that God comes into relation with man.
Hermann Cohen

*A*mid the utter hush of the assembly, the cantor intones the ancient Kol Nidre prayer. He is squat, has a white beard, a white coat, a prayer shawl over it. He wears a skullcap, it is made of velvet, embroidered with gold threads. The prayer shawls of the other men are simple and plain. A few wear elaborate ones with silver embroidery. The cantor has begun very softly. He chants the same prayer once again, louder. And now, for a third time, in a full lamenting voice.
This chant ushers in the evening, intensely and powerfully. The people do not seem consistently anxious and agitated. Here and there, I see them chatting. The small choir gets into gear; the teenagers and young men sing from memory. The cantor conducts them himself; during the singing, he caresses this boy or that, nodding to them. Then comes a passage that forms the climax of the evening. The white-bearded man, as a preparation, has drawn his prayer shawl all the way over his head. Others in the room do likewise. The cloth drops down over his forehead; he squeezes the cloth together under his chin. And what I then hear, what he then sings is an echo of the wailing and yammering that I heard at the cemetery this morning. But now it's in the chant. In this ardor, the man sucks himself in just as he has drawn himself into his shawl, in an ardor that moves everyone. He truly weeps, he truly sobs. Sobbing has become singing. Singing borne by sobbing. The song sinks into its primal element. He trills; his voice drawls down level by level. Then, desperate and pleading, he throws it high again, it sinks back, woeful. And again

he throws it high. The weeping overflows into the women's gallery. Like the man, who never yields in his yammering and urging, who intensifies them, the women, overhead, give in completely. Their weeping grows louder, stronger, drowning out his weeping. Ultimately, a truly anxious universal weeping has spread out, reverberating through the room. The men rocking in their prayer shawls sing, deep and dismal. The head of the bearded old man is still bent back, his eyes are shut. His tears flow visibly down his cheeks. Then he grows stiller. Solemn chants come, also strange and joyous songs. And in the end, when everything is over and they are leaving, someone launches into a song. And old and young, male and female join in: the proud, hopeful "Hatikvah," the Zionist anthem.
Alfred Döblin

I saw that this little town was full of red-haired Jews. Several weeks later they celebrated the Festival of the Torah, and I saw them dance. It was not the dance of a degenerate race. It did not merely express the strength of a fanatic faith. It was surely a kind of health finding its occasion to burst forth in religiosity. The Hasidim took each other by the hand, danced in circles, let go and clapped their hands, threw their heads rhythmically right and left, took hold of the Torah scrolls and danced them in circles like girls, pressing them to their breasts, kissing them and weeping for joy. There was erotic passion in their dancing.
I found it deeply affecting that a whole people should offer up its sensuality to its God and make the Book of strictest laws its lover, that it could no longer distinguish between physical desire and spiritual pleasure, but united the two. Their ardor was physical and spiritual: their dance divine worship, their prayers sensuous excess. The people drank mead out of large jugs. Who invented the lie that Jews cannot tolerate alcohol? Half admiration but half reproof as well, it expresses mistrust of a people reproached with never losing control of themselves. Yet I saw Jews lose control, not after three tankards of beer but after five jugs of heavy mead, and not at a victory celebration but because they were rejoicing that God had given them laws and knowledge.
Joseph Roth

Sunday was the day of preparation for the Day of Atonement. Before Evening Prayers, nearly the whole congregation had, as usual, gathered in Rabbinergasse, before the home of the Chief Rabbi, their beloved teacher and spiritual leader. The old man appeared. A tall figure, eyes blazing and undimmed, flowing beard of silvery white, he was wrapped in a magnificent tallit that revealed his snowy shroud only in front. His effect on the assembled crowd was profound. As soon as they saw him, the mass of people parted and he passed through, bestowing his blessing right and left. Those who stood closest to him kissed the hem of his garment, and everyone greeted him with reverent blessings. At the Altneu Synagogue the crowd fell back. The parnas and the president of the congregation had fetched him at his home and accompanied him. Now he entered the brightly lit synagogue with them, first touching the doorpost with his hand and then putting his fingers reverently to his lips. The Altneu Synagogue is one of the oldest and strangest of buildings.
Inside it is rectangular, longer than broad, the ceiling resting on two mighty pillars. These flank a platform, the almemar, which has three steps leading up to it and is enclosed by a low, marble-faced wall topped by a railing. The almemar is not in the center of the synagogue, it stands somewhat closer to the Ark of the Covenant. A huge flag hangs above the almemar, extending from one end of it to the other.
That evening the synagogue was, as usual, gloriously lit, and wax candles burned in all the lamps hanging from the high ceiling. In addition a number of man-sized, white candles had been placed around the almemar and along the walls of the synagogue; matching the white shrouds of the praying men, they contrasted magnificently with the deep black of the walls and ceiling.
Salomon Kohn

spiritually united. Few other nations are as centered in religion and spirituality as this one. Jews had an easier time of this than others, they didn't have to tussle with politics, revolutions, wars, border improvements, kings, parliaments. They were relieved of such concerns two thousand years ago, by the Romans. *And the Jews didn't really complain. It didn't make them sit by the waters of Babylon and weep. Their focus was always on the temple. They needed the state only for the temple. The proper temple stands only on Zion.*
Alfred Döblin

What an impressive nation Jews are. I didn't know this nation; I believed what I saw in Germany, I believed that the Jews are the industrious people, the shopkeepers, who stew in their sense of family and slowly go to fat, the agile intellectuals, the countless insecure unhappy refined people. Now I see that those are isolated examples, degenerating, remote from the core of the nation that lives here and maintains itself. And what an extraordinary core is this, producing such people as the rich, inundating Baal-Shem, the dark flame of the Gaon of Wilno. What events occurred in these seemingly uncultured Eastern areas. How everything flows around the spiritual! What tremendous importance is placed on spirituality, on religion! Not a minor stratum, an entire mass of people –

*T*hen I reach the temple, a large fenced-in building with a round dome. Well-dressed gentlemen and ladies step into various doors. It's like Tlomacki Street in Warsaw. The man with the prayer shawl in the vestibule is wearing a real concierge cap, and it also says "portier" (concierge). Two glass doors: the room is chock-full all the way to the doors. Total silence. The bright clear singing of the choir. These prayer rooms reveal a difference of worlds. Only occasional whispers in the throng behind the benches; the center aisle is also filled. The room is a large wide circle, and lo, it has three genuine tiers with a balcony, it's built like a real theater. The tiers are empty; a tiny number of women in very fine modern clothes are sitting in the first one. The men crowd downstairs, soldiers among them. In front, the clergymen stand in black coats, each wearing a round skullcap with a button. The man in the middle is the cantor. Splendid, splendid singing. I've come here only to see and then leave, for I despise what the liberals of all persuasions call "divine service." But then he sings. I don't understand what he sings, but it's the finest artistry. What trills, what coloraturas he produces, how he shapes the tone. Everyone stands and listens. And it's not mere art, the art of concert halls; there is such a thing as religious art, even if it's not as sublime as religious non-art. The praying begging praising emotions express themselves here with a thin veneer of civilization. He sings in the lofty foreign tongue. Now the concierge goes wild, he makes room in the center aisle. The singing cantor comes down with the rabbis. They carry the Torah, wrapped in red velvet, around the seats, and the singer rejoices and laments as he walks. From all sides, the men stretch out their hands to touch the red velvet, to kiss the Torah.
Alfred Döblin

*I*n the baroque era, eastern European synagogues developed a characteristic architectural genre, with a fortress-like exterior and frescoes usually decorating the interior. In the seventeenth and eighteenth centuries, the Polish authorities increasingly interfered in Jewish internal affairs, reserving the right, among other things, to prescribe the site and style of synagogues. As their peripheral location made the buildings particularly vulnerable to arson and other outrages, such as the 1648–1650 pogrom under the Cossack Bogdan Chmjelnicki, stronghold-like construction seemed an obvious choice, while the frescoes inside the synagogues were products of the vivid baroque imagination. A curiosity: the synagogue of Zolkiev was built in 1687 under the patronage of King Jan III Sobieski and bears the name "Sobieski Schul" in his honor.

Left: Synagogue of Zolkiev (Galicia). Ca. 1910
Opposite: Synagogue of Przemysl (Galicia). 1905

*A*fter traversing this turbulent world, where all the hustle and bustle of the street crowded in, one heard the soft thud of the strangely heavy synagogue door shutting and was immediately seized by the holiness and solemnity of the place. The heart of the child that had entered, still dazzled by the light and noise of everyday life, was gripped, too. One was enfolded in a different world: its alien quality, its dissimilarity to anything ordinary, its holiness captivated, elevated and touched the heart with an almost painful solemnity.
Philippine Landau

It could hardly have been three hours since he had left the synagogue. Now that he entered it again, it seemed to him as though he had returned there after many weeks, and he stroked with a tender hand the lid of his old prayer desk and celebrated a homecoming with it. He lifted the lid and reached for his old, black, heavy book, which felt so at home in his hands that he would have recognized it instantly, without hesitation, among a thousand similar books. So familiar to him was the leathern smoothness of the binding, with the round, raised little islands of tallow, the encrusted remains of innumerable candles burned long ago; so familiar the under corners of the pages, yellowish, porous, greasy, thrice curled by a decade of turning them with moistened fingers. Any prayer that he needed at the moment he could turn to immediately. It was buried in his memory with the smallest feature of that physiognomy which it carried in this book, the number of the line, the character and size of the print, and the exact colour tone of the page.
Joseph Roth

As I have already indicated, the synagogue was a second home to me when I was a young pupil. I often fled into its comforting twilight, even when no service was being held. I thought up my own prayers, in which I always entreated God to fulfill a concrete wish.
Oskar Kosta

35

In line with neo-romantic and historicist trends, nineteenth-century synagogue architecture took over elements from earlier periods and displayed a variety of stylistically imitative components. Neo-Moorish, neo-romantic, and neo-gothic buildings embody the search for appropriate form. The Frankfurt synagogue had stood in the ghetto, i.e. on Judengasse (Jews' Lane), since the Middle Ages. By the mid-nineteenth century it was in such ruinous condition that it had to be torn down. Reformed circles commissioned the architect Georg Kayser to build a synagogue for Liberal worship on the same site from 1855 to 1860. The interior was pervaded by Moorish elements, intended to symbolize bonds with religion and the Orient. The neo-gothic features of the façade reflected membership in the German nation. The so-called Neue Synagoge in Berlin, Oranienburger Strasse, was completed in 1866 under the supervision of August Stüler, according to plans by the architect Eduard Knoblauch. Its consecration on September 5 may be regarded as a symbol of the formal equality of the Jews in Prussia and was attended by such dignitaries as the Prime Minister, Otto von Bismarck. The synagogue, destroyed on November 9/10, 1938, seated 3,000 worshippers and was considered one of the most magnificent in Europe.

Left: Judengasse synagogue in Frankfurt. 1860
Right: Synagogue on Oranienburger Strasse in Berlin. 1870

The synagogue on Oranienburger Strasse even had an organ. Pious Jews were actually not allowed to listen to organ music, but naturally it made everything much more solemn and festive. And praying in synagogues had a totally different character, too. The women sat in decorous silence, placidly looking down at their prayerbooks. (The men's section was much quieter than a "Betstube" [prayer room], too.) It was precisely this decorous silence that did not appeal to me on my occasional visits to a synagogue. I missed the authentic, genuine feelings. German Jews were hardly ever found in "Betstuben." The atmosphere was too alien to them.
Gittel Weiss

37

Left: Interior of the synagogue on Oranienburger Strasse in Berlin. Ca. 1935

The synagogue on Fasanenstrasse played a decisive role in Jewish life in the imperial capital. It was, so to speak, the symbol of "how far" emancipation had enabled the Jews in Germany to go. The "Jewish Reform Congregation" may have been mentioned more often than this synagogue. Yet the Reform Congregation was not a symbol, nor was it "typical"; it was an extravagance in so far as it consciously abandoned Jewish tradition in order to emulate the ways of the church. Sunday replaced the Sabbath and Hebrew prayers were totally discarded. The style of service was modeled on Christian worship. None of this was true of the synagogue on Fasanenstrasse. There the tradition created a generation earlier was upheld; the form may have been modern, but with the time-honored contents.
Conrad Rosenstein

The one new building we looked at in Berlin was the synagogue, with its magical Sabbath lighting; we also attended the service. The new design produces a monumental effect; the service, too, is uplifting. But the latter has its opponents, and from unexpected quarters at that. Sal, for instance, told me . . . that there was no way to know what religion was actually represented there. In these people's opinion, a service of this kind does not have a specific character of its own. But they do not realize that a character that takes over the best aspects of all other characters is also a character. And that is the task of the new Judea.
Louis Mayer

Although some synagogue reforms are to be welcomed, they will no longer be of any help to those who are striving for them, for they largely . . . originated "sub specie emancipationis," from an aesthetic perspective, with a furtive eye to the tastes of the incidental non-Jewish visitor. The prayer rooms of our forefathers and eastern brothers are too noisy to fulfill our aesthetic demands, but they are filled with warmth and intimacy. Here no one brings anything to the synagogue, and that is why no one can get anything there either.
Gustav Sicher

but there was a great deal chanted in Hebrew, to beautiful music: some of the chants have come down from very early times, perhaps as far back as David. The chief Rabbi chanted a great deal by himself, without music. The congregation alternately stood & sat down: I did not notice any one kneeling.
Lewis Carroll

We followed the example of the congregation in keeping our hats on. Many of the men, on reaching their places, produced white silk shawls out of embroidered bags, & these they put on square fashion: the effect was most singular – the upper edge of the shawl had what looked like gold embroidery, but was probably a phylactery. These men went up from time to time & read portions of the lessons. What was read was all in German,

The building is most gorgeous, almost the whole interior surface being gilt or otherwise decorated – the arches were nearly all semicircular, tho' there were a few instances of the shape sketched here – the east end was roofed with a circular dome, & contained a smaller dome on pillars, under which was a cupboard (concealed by curtain) which contained the roll of the Law: in front of this was a reading-desk, facing east, & in front of that again a small desk facing west – the latter was only once used. The rest of the building was fitted up with open seats.
Lewis Carroll

Right: Synagogue on Levetzow-strasse in Berlin-Tiergarten. Ca. 1912

Left: Hannover synagogue (built in 1870). Ca. 1900

To Rabbi Wolf of Zbarazh, one of his five sons, Rabbi Mikhal once said: "When I had risen in prayer, and was standing in the hall of truth, I begged God to grant me that my reason might never proceed against his truth."
Martin Buber

They stood in the candle-lit house of prayer; the soft singsong with which young men accompanied their study of the Talmud disturbed the zealous debaters as little as did the playing children, whose noise was tolerated even more readily because some of them had only recently lost a father or a mother. The orphan boys had to repeat the prayer for the dead three times a day, loudly, clearly. And if the text was too difficult for them, someone would help them along word for word. Singsong and children's noise and, not infrequently, a loud argument – none of this bothered the debaters, for they were absorbed in discussing everything, their own affairs and those of the wide world. Whether talking about themselves or the others, the "great ones," they always seasoned their plaintiveness with self-irony, their bombast with mockery. On Sundays, these men did not know how they would get their families through the new week, and on Thursdays, they racked their brains about finding the wherewithal to prepare for the Sabbath. These destitute men, who usually married too young and fathered children incessantly, were not poor in spirit, for they knew they would be part of the "olam haba," the afterlife to which they would be admitted after dying. And if the Messiah arrived first, then the "next world" would open to them that much sooner.
When I think back to those Jews, whom I saw daily until the age of ten in the streets, the marketplace, the houses of prayer and study, then I recall two noises: sighs, lots of sighs and moans, but also laughter, kindly or derisive, yet always loud laughter, with sighs and moans soon joining in. Every bon mot ("gitvertl" in Yiddish) was instantly taken up, repeated, and relished, until it was finally replaced by a new one. Aside from the bon mots, these men often quoted wise, deep, and very astute statements. Hasidim brought them from the courts of their "tsadik," the miracle-working rabbi, to whom they traveled again and again. Or else they quoted books and articles, mostly by Hebrew writers, or apocryphal utterances attributed to one "sharp mind" or another.
Manès Sperber

Right: The rabbi, the highest spiritual authority. Ca. 1910

Opposite page: Village elder in Carpatho-Ruthenia. Photograph by *Roman Vishniac.* 1938

On Saturday I happened into a Hasidic shtibl . . . The songs were the main attraction; I have never heard anything like it. They do not need an organ – such rapturous enthusiasm, young and old all together.
Franz Rosenzweig

Once when Rabbi Mordecai was in the great town of Minsk expounding the Torah to a number of men hostile to his way, they laughed at him. "What you say does not explain the verse in the least!" they cried. "Do you really think," he replied, "that I was trying to explain the verse in the book? That doesn't need explanation! I want to explain the verse that is within me."
Martin Buber

Thus it has gone for many years. Rebbe Ascher-Baruch grows old but his Torah does not abandon him. As his strength was, so it is now. Night has a single purpose: study. There has, however, been one small change. His wife has begun to select only thin candles for him. For she says: The hands of my Asher-Baruch, he should live to a hundred and twenty, have grown heavy and his fingers tremble, perhaps they cannot hold thick candles anymore. – Otherwise nothing has changed. – Rebbe Ascher-Baruch is Rebbe Ascher-Baruch and light is light. – And as it shone in the past, so it shines now. Night after night he sits, studying by candle light . . . But his strength cannot last forever! As all men are stricken, so is Rebbe Ascher-Baruch stricken, and as all men die, so did he die. Rebbe Ascher-Baruch died, old and sated with life. Night after night he had sat, all night he had sat and studied. His mouth had not stopped studying until the day he died.
Samuel Josef Agnon

41

*What form of Judaism is foreign to us?
Judaism is so diverse and its development has
been so varied that we will probably always
succeed in finding some form that suits our
temperament. Judaism is based on history and
has fortunately combined and preserved all
the phases it has gone through down the ages.
There is nothing in Judaism whose contrary
cannot be found there as well.*
S. Bernstein

*Berlin, October 4, 1862. I was at the
Reformed Synagogue with August, Eugen,
and Ottilie last night. However far my
thinking and striving may go, you know I
have a need to affirm that I am part of the
whole, and I want the children, who have to
suffer at school and in the streets because they
are Jews, to gain a certain intimacy with their
religious community. The service made a
great impression on them. I once again had
the strange realization that a free ethical
congregation would be the place for me. Only
the silent prayers affected me. The way
everyone soundlessly speaks the same words
for himself is a silent bonding of spirits that
produces a profound thrill of emotion. Otherwise everything was alien to me, despite the
beauty of the liturgical responses. For us who
grew up in the old traditions, only the old
melodies and words would awaken the poig-
nant sounds of our youth . . .*
Berthold Auerbach to Jakob Auerbach

Opposite page: Cracow rabbi at prayer. Ca. 1910

Above left: Zacharias Frankel (1801–1875), Chief Rabbi of Dresden and Leipzig, Director of the Jewish Theological Seminary in Breslau. Ca. 1871

Above center: Viennese rabbi with his wife. Ca. 1865

Above right: Leopold Stein (1810–1882), leader of the Frankfurt Jewish Reform movement. Ca. 1865

Below left: Jisroel Szyldewer, Hasidic preacher and "Baldarschn" in Staszów (Poland). 1923

Below center: Robert Kaelter, rabbi in Danzig. Ca. 1910

Below right: Cantor in Damboric (Bohemia). Ca. 1920

They have assimilated. They no longer pray in synagogues and houses of prayer but in boring temples, where the services become as mechanical as in any better class of Protestant church.
They have become temple Jews, which means: well-bred, clean-shaven gentlemen in frock-coats and top hats, who wrap their prayer books in the editorial of the Jewish newspaper because they think they will not be as easily recognized by the editorial as by a prayer book. In the temples the organ can be heard; the cantor and the preacher wear headgear that makes them look like Christian clergy.
Joseph Roth

Left: Cornerstone-laying ceremony for the Neue Synagoge in Kremsier (Moravia). Under the canopy, three rabbis: Dr. Frankl-Grünn, Dr. Freimann, and Dr. Reach. 1908

Right: Neue Synagoge near Karlsplatz in Munich. Ca. 1890

Right: Laying the cornerstone for the synagogue on Bornplatz in Hamburg on March 23, 1905. The ceremony was attended not only by the Chief Rabbi and the congregation of the new synagogue but also by members of all the other synagogues and Jewish institutions. 1905

45

The Sephardic community in Vienna numbered approximately one thousand. It also owned a building in Leopoldstadt, the "Casa Sefardi," to house its various religious associations.
Left: The Turkish-Jewish temple in Vienna-Leopoldstadt, Zirkusgasse 22, was built in the Moorish style in 1885/86 according to plans by Hugo von Weidenfeld.
Ca. 1890

Above: There were many small houses of prayer in the large cities. In Vienna, for example, this shop (left) served as a synagogue. Above the entrance there was a sign reading "Sephardische Synagoge 'Gemeinde Jakobs'" (Sephardic synagogue/congregation of Jacob).
Photograph by *Abraham Pisarek*.
Ca. 1930

*T*he eastern Jewish population living around Grenadierstrasse had their "Betstuben," their prayer rooms. These had to be within walking distance of the homes of the pious, for on Sabbath and the holidays, one was not allowed to drive or ride to the house of God. There were always two rooms, one for the men and one for the women. The division according to gender is strictly prescribed. The prayer rooms were unadorned. Orthodox

Jews are not allowed to have pictures where they pray. And certainly not portraits, for it is written: "You shall not make for yourself a sculptured image, or any likeness . . ." The believers sat or stood crowded together (particularly on the High Holidays). And there was a strong, passionate devotion to God, at least among the women.
Gittel Weiss

*T*he Jewish families from eastern Europe had established three so-called "shtibl," prayer rooms where their special religious customs were observed. The Jewish families from Lithuania assembled at the first shtibl, the Polish Jews went to the second, and the Galicians to the third. This separation is not difficult to understand considering how important slight differences in pronunciation, recitation, and melody were for the prayers. When the prayer leader began a familiar melody, the whole congregation would hum along.
Emil Schorsch

Right: Synagogue (left) in Mattersburg (Burgenland, Austria).
Ca. 1925

This connection of plain living with industrious study, with a study that is not exaggeratedly called titanic, gave and preserved for Jewish life that peace, firmness, superiority, and sublimity without it could not have withstood misery and persecution for thousands of years.
Hermann Cohen

Herr Oppenheimer and his son, both of them hunchbacks, were Torah scribes: conscientiously, painstakingly, letter by letter, word by word, they covered the parchment scrolls of the Pentateuch, from which the cantor reads out the daily passage during the divine service. It took months to complete a single scroll. But the Jewish congregations had little demand for new Torah scrolls, so the family was forced to run a small grocery store to earn some additional income. They took in boarders for the same reason.
Julius Frank

Left: David Elye, the sofer (scribe) of Annopol. Sofers wrote Torah scrolls, tefillin, and mezuzot. 1912

Below left: Studying Talmud in the bet midrash of the old age home in Vilna (Lithuania). Photograph by *Moryc Grossmann.* 1937

They asked Rabbi Levi Yitzhak: "Why is the first page number missing in all the tractates of the Babylonian Talmud? Why does each begin with the second?"

He replied: "However much a man may learn, he should always remember that he has not even gotten to the first page."
Martin Buber

When the Baal Shem had a difficult task before him, he would go to a certain place in the woods, light a fire and meditate in prayer – and what he had set out to perform was done. When a generation later the "Maggid" of Meseritz was faced with the same task he would go to the same place in the woods and say: We can no longer light the fire, but we can still speak the prayers – and what he wanted done became reality. Again a generation later Rabbi Moshe Leib of Sassov had to perform this task. And he too went into the woods and said: We can no longer light a fire, nor do we know the secret meditations belonging to the prayer, but we do know the place in the woods to which it all belongs – and that must be sufficient; and sufficient it was. But when another generation had passed and Rabbi Israel of Rishin was called upon to perform the task, he sat down on his golden chair in his castle and said: We cannot light the fire, we cannot speak the prayers, we do not know the place, but we can tell the story of how it was done. And, the story-teller adds, the story which he told had the same effect as the actions of the other three.
Gershom Scholem

The prayer room of the great Gaon. I hear his name often – the great learned Jew of Wilno a century ago. Stairs leading from the courtyard up to a large warm wooden room. The "bimah" is at the center; men in street clothes and prayer shawls bustling on it. One clutches the Torah scrolls, which are wrapped around two wooden sticks; he lifts them up toward the room. Another steps up, takes hold of the Torah, rolls it up solidly, ties it up. Meanwhile, liturgizing. Elderly men with very sharp, brooding expressions sit at wide tables, propping their heads over their books. Others converse softly, leaning back, scratch- ing their white beards. Small groups read a single book together. Here, there are more individual lecterns than in that large hall. Few people walk about. Their eyes are glued to the books.
Alfred Döblin

<u>Right</u>: In the house of prayer, where men gathered to study and pray. Ca. 1920

Heder was the traditional elementary school where boys studied Scripture and Talmud. The melamed (teacher) taught them from the time they were four or five until their bar mitzvah.

Left: Yitzchok Erlich, caretaker of the heder in Staszów (Poland). Ca. 1920

Opposite page: A melamed and his pupils at heder. Lublin (Poland). 1924

"*Heder*" – the word means "room." It refers to the Jewish elementary school, usually run by a destitute man, an "air person," in a single room, where his wife and countless children lived, ate, and slept. The pupils were at least three years old and seldom more than six. Later, they studied under a qualified teacher in some heder that was more like a classroom, but seldom like a class. I didn't want to go to heder, partly, no doubt, because I was very spoiled at home, but chiefly because of the endless poverty and depressing ugliness. For the first time, I learned that most children did not eat their fill, that they suffered from skin ailments that disfigured their faces. I experienced revulsion at an early age and discovered that it was accompanied by fear, by an anxiety, that was hard to grasp. In order to get me to the heder without actually forcing me, they hit on the idea of having the teacher's factotum, the so-called "belfer" (assistant), carry me there on his back. A belfer was usually a young man who was incapable of doing anything and could expect nothing out of life. Once he told me that I should treat him like a horse. He capered about, galloped, whinnying rather woefully. Since he was my mount, I had to feed him, of course. I was glad to feed him because I usually had no appetite, and I was delighted to empty my pouch, making it look as if I had eaten my lunch. But I also enjoyed letting my "horse" think that his playacting had enticed me into giving him my food.
Manès Sperber

*W*henever Zusya met a Jewish boy, he blessed him with the words: "Be healthy and strong as a goy."
Martin Buber

51

The yeshivah (Talmud academy) is an institution for scholarly and rabbinical training. The principal is known as rosh yeshivah, the student as bachur (Yiddish: bocher).

Left: Polish yeshivah bocher. 1860/70

Right: Yeshivah bocher. Before 1904

Leibke lived in any era but our own. He did not know life and the world. His parents worked hard for their only son, but he did not ask how. They procured the best teachers for him, provided him with all possible comforts, but he did not ask where they took the money from. They often worried because times were hard, but he did not listen and did not know he should be listening. The sighs of his father or mother could not tear him out of his world.
David Pinski

Right: Traveling to the yeshivah. Photograph by *Abraham Pisarek*. Ca. 1930

Perhaps we met in a word that was never spoken between us, but which keeps crossing my mind when I think about him. It is the word "learn." Both of us were filled with the dignity of learning. His mind and my mind had been aroused by early learning, by an immense respect for learning. However, his learning was already completely devoted to human beings; he needed no pretext – neither the expansion of a field of knowledge, nor alleged usefulness, purpose, planning, in order to "learn" people. At this time, I, too, seriously turned to people; and since then, I have spent the greater part of my life trying to understand human beings. Back then, I had to tell myself that I was doing so for the sake of some bit of knowledge or other. But when all other pretexts crumbled, I was left with the excuse of "expectation": I wanted people, including myself, to become "better," and so I had to know absolutely everything about every single human being. Babel, with his enormous experience – although he was only eleven years my senior – had long since gotten beyond this point. His desire for an improvement of mankind did not serve as an excuse for knowing human beings. I sensed that his desire was as insatiable as mine, but that it never caused him to deceive himself. Anything he found out about human beings was independent of whether it delighted or tormented him, whether it struck him to the ground: he had to "learn" human beings.
Elias Canetti

Below: A yeshivah bocher holding the opening speech from the balcony of his yeshivah. Photograph by *Abraham Pisarek*. Ca. 1930

Above: The large lecture hall at the yeshivah of Lublin, an institution with a great tradition. Photograph by *Abraham Pisarek*. Ca. 1930

The corpse of a pious Jew lies in a plain wooden box, covered with a black cloth. It is carried by four Jews walking very quickly along the shortest route – I do not know whether the law prescribes this or whether it happens because a slow gait would double the burden for the pallbearers. Corpses are virtually raced through the streets. The preparations have taken one day. The dead may not stay on earth longer than twenty-four hours. The lamentations of the bereaved can be heard throughout the town. The women walk through the streets, wailing their pain at every stranger. They speak to the deceased, murmur endearments, beg for forgiveness and mercy, heap them with reproaches, ask helplessly what they are to do now, aver that they no longer want to live – and all this in the middle of the street, hurrying along, while inside the houses faces look on indifferently, strangers go about their business, cars drive past, and shopkeepers try to attract customers. Heart-rending scenes take place at the cemetery. The women do not want to leave the graves, they have to be subdued; consolation looks more like subjugation. The melody of the prayer for the dead is of an exquisite simplicity, the funeral service is short and almost fierce. The throng of beggars compet-

Right: Cemetery in Eisenstadt (Burgenland, Austria), which had a Jewish community since the fourteenth century. Photograph by Bruno Reiffenstein. Ca. 1920

ing for alms is large. For seven days the nearest relatives of the deceased sit at home on low stools, walk around in their socks, and look as if they were half-dead themselves. In the windows a small, dim watch candle burns before a small piece of white linen, and the neighbors bring the mourners hard-boiled eggs, the food of those whose pain is round, with no beginning and no end.

Joseph Roth

Left: Cemetery in Lublin, one of the principal centers of eastern Jewish life from the end of the fifteenth century. Ca. 1895

Right: Mourning women (kloge-rins) at the cemetery of Brody (Galicia). It was customary in the month of Elul (August/September) to visit the graves of relatives and for very pious Jews to pray for "everlasting peace" for the weak and the sick. There were professional mourners to improvise prayers in Yiddish. Ca. 1910

Joachim Riedl
HOME OF HARDSHIP, HOME OF LEARNING

*T*he sewing machine rattles, the iron stands on the pastry board, he takes people's measurements on his marriage bed. Who would go to such a tailor?
Joseph Roth

Opposite page: In Galicia and Poland, married men, whether Hasidim or not, wore a shtraymel (a velvet hat trimmed with sable or marten) over their kippah.
Ca. 1930

Above: Zelig, the tailor from Wolomin (Poland). Ca. 1925

Sometimes it seemed as if time had stopped. They lived in a closed, self-contained world, a world so complete within itself that on a certain day in ancestral times it had ceased turning; gradually becoming slow and sluggish, it had finally stood still and wanted to move no further. A hundred years was nothing. What happened in the rest of the world raced by like clouds in a sky hanging low over the land. The mud clung heavily to their feet. Poverty had been inherited from their fathers, to whom it had already been passed down from generation to generation. Three times a day the people died of hunger. Life weighed heavy as lead.

No one doubted the law that God Himself had given to man. There were 613 rules. They regulated every weekday and every holiday; they even kept dreams in check. There were rules for how to slaughter a chicken, how prayers were to sound or how to put on one's shoes in the morning. The hasty eye saw only pathetic, disheveled creatures, sinking ankle-deep into the morass that was the street and desperately struggling to survive. It did not see these people's dignity. Yet even the most wretched of them was unfaltering; though he might quarrel with fate, there was never a moment in which his profound faith abandoned him or he stopped giving thought to the strict discipline it demanded. After all, God lived amid the people, and their redemption was as certain as it

was only a matter of time; every day of want brought them closer to the promised goal. But if someone took flight from the community, his family crept into mourning for three days.

It was the home of the *Luftmenschen* ("air people"), called this because they seemed to obtain their livelihood from of the air. The home of the "see-traders," who did business with everything one could see. The home of the Hasidic masters, whose wisdom was so magnificent that it dazzled all who did not dare to look them in the eye. The home of the tsaddiks, the saintly and righteous. The home of fools, philosophers, and storytellers. The home of hardship and the home of

rapturous joy of life. The shtetl that was home to eastern European Jewry was not a geographical place; it was the center of the world, the universe of a trust in God that was as old as mankind itself.

"The Jewish community has remarkable trust in God, it lives with the burden of two thousand years of history on its shoulders," wrote the pioneer of Yiddish literary criticism, who concealed himself behind the pen name Baal Machschabbot: "It lives apart from the surrounding world like an island in the ocean. The members of this community are tied to one other, eternally linked with one another. The Jews live in constant fear that they might, God forbid, break out of the narrow cage into which their ancestors squeezed them, and they are inclined to renounce even those pleasures of life that Jewish law allows. They continually bring themselves under a new yoke. They have ears only to listen to the reading of the Law, eyes only to subject the holy texts to critical study, voices only for the cry: Hear, O Israel. They regard themselves as the Chosen People and they live worse than dogs . . ."

Poland had been considered a country of refuge since the first Jews settled there around the turn of the millennium. They were driven out of Germany, Italy, and Spain; Catholic princes confined them to ghettos to please the God of Christianity; when plague, famine, or other ravages beset a country, superstitious mobs slaughtered them and burned down the quarters where they lived. Consequently many Jews fled east. The Polish princes and kings defended the newcomers against the Catholic Church and the population. Casimir the Great built his Jews a town of their own near the Cracow Residence.

It was the golden age of eastern European Jewry. The celebrated Rabbi Moses Isserles taught in Cracow and produced a comprehensive, universal code for the Polish Jews. Studying went on everywhere, a dense network of schools and academies covered the land. Long before it was common in the civilized west, the eastern European Jews had developed a system that guaranteed education for all.

This efflorescence did not last long. Rebellious Cossack hordes drowned it in the blood of tens of thousands of Jews; with the decline of their empire before their eyes, the Poles became more hostile. As the Enlightenment dawned in the West, the Middle Ages began in the East. Now Jewish mystics went preaching from town to town and false messiahs tempted the bewildered Jews. One of them, Jacob Frank, led thousands of them into the bosom of the Catholic Church.

The centuries of tolerance were over. Some 600,000 Jews lived in the kingdom of Poland at the time, and most of them sought refuge in the pious traditions of their people, which they had neglected in better times. They left the large cities, moved to the country and formed Law-revering, insulated communities in villages and small towns.

The world of the shtetl was a haven, a consequence of moving closer together, a spiritual fort. From the very beginning it signaled withdrawal and oppressive backwardness. The shtetl Jews had renounced the

world, they had stopped fighting for recognition. They encountered every new blow of fate with God-fearing humility; they prayed and fasted more and more, and people drew ever closer together. It was into this narrowness that the charismatic Baal Shem Tov brought his message of hope: the Jews should celebrate their faith, open their hearts to God instead of merely studying; they should be permeated with holiness and demonstrate this holiness with ascetic joy. Up to the very end, the shtetl Jews remained faithful to these Hasidic teachings. The more oppressive their distress, the more rapturous their exultation; the more unyielding the persecution, the stronger the faith in their hearts.

Poland was battered and partitioned. The Russian czars, who had raked in the lion's share of the spoils, forced their Jewish subjects to settle on a narrow strip of land, 500,000 square kilometers between the Baltic and the Black Sea; in 1897 there were almost five million Jews living there. In this "Pale of Settlement" the shtetl was transformed into a cosmos withdrawn from the rest of the world. Threatened by misery and pogroms, at the mercy of a hostile world around them, the Jews possessed no weapon but their faith in God; and the Mameloschen, their Yiddish language, knew no words for all the different murderous tools with which they were pursued. The western concept of history was of no consequence to them. They had their own history, an eternal, unchanging cycle that would last unaltered until the coming of the Messiah. For the inhabitants of the shtetl, writes Maurice Salomon, "the Bible [replaced] the daily reading of the latest news in the paper."

"In a certain sense the Jews had no social problems as long as they isolated the rigid religious Ortho-

doxy from the outside world," observed Isaak Berlin. They lived in a pre-bourgeois, pre-industrial society, sustained by an archaic order, a patriarchy of holy erudition. The living space of the shtetl wedged itself into the interstices of the outdated agrarian structures of eastern Europe. As most Jews were prohibited from owning land, they supported themselves by trade and artisanship, tenanting small shops and working as day laborers – and lived by their wits. "Theirs was both a community and a society," writes historian Irving Howe, "internally a community, a ragged kingdom of the spirit, and externally a society, impoverished and imperiled."

The shtetl was doomed from the outset. Dogged immutability bore in itself the seeds of slow decay, withdrawal led to isolation, oblivion and death.

It resembled the "eastern Jewish face" that Arnold Zweig described: "Bowed but untiring, the Jew carries his past with him. Bearer of God's burden that he is, he inclines his strong shoulders and, knees bent, strides slowly towards the goal he has been set – carrying the past into the future." But there was no future where only desperate, radical defensiveness prevailed, where there was nothing but the past. In the shtetl the future meant the end of the past.

Only once the shtetl had ceased to exist was it mourned and transfigured in melancholy memory into an idyll of misery. Already the Jewish avant-gardists in revolutionary Russia had had to go in ethnological search of their roots. In 1925 the director of the Moscow Jewish Theater, Alexander Granovsky, a student of Max Reinhardt's, filmed one of Scholem Aleichem's many stories about the fortunes of the Jewish Sisyphus, that eternal *Luftmensch* Menachem Mendel. When the Muscovites went to the nearly archetypical shtetl of Berdichev in the Ukraine to shoot the film, they found a virtual ruin and carefully had to reconstruct the centuries-old street. As the only film to immortalize the unretouched reality of life in the shtetl, *Jewish Luck* was to become a virtual documentary.

"The town itself is a jumble of wooden houses clustering higgledy-piggledy about a market-place . . . [and] is as crowded as a slum." That is how Maurice Samuel describes the world of Scholem Aleichem, which comes to life once more in the silent film: "The streets . . . are as tortuous as a Talmudic argument. They are bent into question marks and folded into parentheses . . . They run into cul-de-sacs like a theory arrested by a fact; they ooze off into lanes, alleys, back yards . . ."

Who builds and maintains the roads of Poland, the Rabbi of Rizin, a proud prince of the Hasidim once asked a visitor. "The Jews." – "And who should know more about highways and byways?" exclaimed the Riziner joyfully.

The roads *out of* the shtetl led all over the world. The roads *inside* the shtetl led in a circle. Of death.

And so Itzik Manger, who had trod them all, wrote: "I am the road to destruction, / the blonde death in the sun, / the brown strain of the shepherd's pipe, / the tired sunset glow. / My brother, do not follow me, / to pass down my road is to pass away . . ."

Left: Market day in Rawa Ruska (Galicia). 1910

Left: Market day in Rawa Ruska (Galicia). 1910

Right: Market day in Kremieniec, one of the oldest Jewish settlements in Russian Poland. Photograph by *Alter Kacyzne*. 1925

What did the Jews themselves think of the shtetl? Did they know how ugly their houses were, how unsightly their poor clothes? Naturally, they lacked any possibility of comparison for most of them never traveled more than twenty miles away, perhaps once or twice, before they died. They didn't like the surrounding countryside; in their eyes, the thatched huts of the Ukrainians were a lot uglier than their own houses. Moreover, they avoided those villages as much as possible, because they rightfully feared hostility. Nevertheless, the shtetls were not ghettoes; indeed, they were the very opposite, both in essence and by definition. A shtetl was not an appendage within lawful precincts to a Christian community, it was not an alien body, discriminated against within a higher culture. On the contrary, it was a clearly defined autonomous community with its own culture – amid poverty and ugliness and surrounded by enemies of the Jewish faith. The shtetl was a center, and the Jews saw the Slavic villages as peripheral agglomerates whose inhabitants, mostly illiterate, had no relationship to the world of the intellect. In all its misery, the shtetl was a tiny civitas dei, amazing in mind and spirit, centuries behind the times in certain respects, sometimes repulsive, and yet admirable, because the lives of these people were ruled by their truly exemplary devotion to a relentlessly demanding faith, daily, nay, hourly, down to the slightest detail. The Jews in the ghettoes of Venice, or Rome, or Worms remained a minority in their home cities, exiled and discriminated against. But the Jews in a shtetl formed a majority, they were at home. Their gentile neighbors,

the Polish aristocrats, for instance, might be powerful and wealthy and look down on them. But the Jews were convinced of their own superiority. They had no sense of inferiority whatsoever about being Jews, and thus they didn't have the slightest desire to conceal who and what they were or to become like the others.

Normally, two families lived together, sometimes in a single room. The arguments of the women, who had to cook on the same stove, the screams of the children – all this noise could be heard out in the street, day and night. Unhappiness was always made public; happiness often remained private, but it was urged on everyone else whenever parents could boast about their offspring. Children were scolded loudly; they were even cursed and, almost in the same breath, showered with the most affectionate words.

Most of the houses had only one story and seldom more than two small rooms and a kitchen; they were made of wood and the roofs were shingled. These homes were crowded together, as if each were seeking protection with the others. The streets seldom ran in straight lines, for every house looked as if it were trying to be different, at least in its shape. It all seemed right out of a town planner's nightmare.

There was no gas, no electricity, no sewer in the shtetl, and naturally no indoor plumbing. There were just a few wells, where the Jews obtained their water. Carriers delivered it to those families that could afford them, and the Jews kept it in large barrels inside their homes. The poor had to get water themselves.

Manès Sperber

"So what kind of a business do you have now?" – "Who has a business?" – "What do you live on?" – "Oh, is that what you mean. I manage." – "But on what?"
"The Holy One, blessed be He! When He gives, a man has." – "But He doesn't throw it down from Heaven!" – "Oh, yes, He does! Do you know what I live on? Just work it out: I need a fortune – at least four rubles a week! Besides my own apartment the house brings me about twelve rubles; nine rubles go out for interest, about five rubles for repairs. What's left? A two-ruble hole in my pocket at least." His tone turns proud: "Money I haven't got, thank God! I don't, and neither do any of the other Jews standing here, not one of them! Except maybe for a few Germans in the big cities . . .We don't have money! I never learned a trade, my grandfather didn't sew boots! Still, if it's God's will, I can live, and have for almost fifty years now. And – if a man has a daughter to marry off, she gets married off, and there's dancing all the same!"
"What are you, Kurz?" – "A Jew like any other Jew." – "What do you do all day?" – "I study, I daven . . . what does a Jew do? When I finish breakfast I go to the market . . ." –
"What do you do at the market?" – "What do I do? What there is to do. Yesterday, for instance, I happened to hear that Joine Borik wants to buy three goats for a poriz; early in the morning I'm already with the second poriz, who once said he had too many goats. So I help Joine Borik make the deal, and both of us, the Lord's name be praised, get one and a half rubles."
"So you're a broker?" – "What do I know? When I think of it, I buy a measure of wheat sometimes." – "Sometimes?" – "What sometimes means? When I have a ruble, I buy." – "And when you don't?" – "I get myself a ruble!" – "But how?"- "What do you mean, how?"
And it takes me an hour to find out that Lewi-Jizchok Bärenpelz is sometimes a dayyan and sits on the courts of arbitration, then he works partly as a broker, but here and there he sells things, too, oh, and he does a little matchmaking on the side, and sometimes, when it occurs to him, he even runs errands.
And from all the "occupations" he names and doesn't name, he scrapes together a living for his wife and children, and even for his married daughter, because her father-in-law is a poor devil!
Jizchak Leib Peretz

<u>Right</u>: The market square in a Galician shtetl. Ca. 1910

<u>Above</u>: Shtetl inhabitants in front of their home cum shop. Ca. 1910
<u>Below</u>: "Small Goods and Yeast": a grocery store, with the proprietors family and customers. Ca. 1915

<u>Right</u>: Jewish family in eastern Slovakia. Photograph by *Abraham Pisarek*. Ca. 1930

Left: Daughters were a problem in the shtetl: their fathers had to find a good match for them. Ca. 1915

When Jechiel Meier came into the world, narrowness stepped up to his cradle and never left him again. From his very first day, he had to use his elbows to fight for the tiny bit of space his sinful body needed in the infinite space of the universe . . .
He was born in one of those little lanes where low houses pitch over one another. The first impression Jechiel Meier received of our earth was: too narrow. The little room in which he first saw the light of day was crammed with beds and tables. Wherever he moved, he bumped into a bedstead. Every corner of the room was occupied. Wherever Jechiel Meier went, wherever he stood, the space he needed was already taken up by something else. All his life he never slept alone, his body was always pressed up against another body, a relative's or a stranger's. Even in earliest childhood he had to fight for the space he needed on the family bed. His two brothers, Gedalje and Shlojme, who slept with him, squeezed him against the wall; he did the same to them. Throughout the night the three brothers, whether asleep or awake, fought with their bodies for space on the bed. Only slumber made peace among them and the three so intertwined that they seemed to become a single body.
At heder, with the teacher at Bible school, there was narrowness again – on the bench, crushed among a crowd of boys, sat Jechiel Meier. Even the holy house of prayer was narrow. The walls were damp with heat. The boy stood near the door with his father, hardly able to breathe. His weekday was narrow and his Sabbath was narrow. It was a constant fight for that bit of space his little body needed day and night . . .
Only once did he experience the world as big, broad and long. Oh, the vastness – how often he thought of it, pondered it, longed for it, hoped he could live in it one day!
Schalom Asch

Such was the serenity and kindness in that smile that it dominated even the power of the flat, melancholy, alien landscape through which I was driving.
Joseph Roth

The majority of Jewish families were desperately poor. The father was away from home from early in the morning until late at night. Either he had regular work and toiled for twelve, fourteen or even sixteen hours a day, or he was a "Luftmensch" and lived from hand to mouth, a small-time merchant, broker, and commission agent all rolled into one. He ran from customer to customer, shop to shop like a wild animal scrambling for a morsel of food. But the father was not the only one to slave away like this; the mother shared his lot to a very high degree. With few exceptions she not only took care of the household but also worked outside the house, doing other people's laundry and gardening. Sometimes she gathered berries. She went to the goose-herd's field to collect feathers or plucked them from slaughtered poultry, all to fill pillows. The latter occupation was reserved for late at night, when the children were asleep and the wick of the one and only lamp had been cleaned and screwed very low. That was the lot of the average woman. The lot of the grocer's wife was even worse. From crack of dawn till late into the night, sweating in the oppressive summer heat or shivering in the bitter winter cold by her little clay stove, she was chained to her shop. Thus poverty, whip in hand, loomed large over Jewish parents, constantly goading them along the treadmill of life and separating them from their children.
And a lack of children there never was.
Schemarja Levin

Right: Grandfather and grandson on the road between Warsaw and Otwock. Photograph by *Menachem Kipnis.* 1928

Above: Crooked wooden houses and numerous children were part of the typical face of the shtetl: street in Wladimir Wolynsk (Poland). 1914

Below: Summer afternoon in a Galician shtetl: one of the garments worn by eastern Jews was the caftan, which, at least during prayer, was belted. 1900

Opposite page: A pious man dons tefillin (phylacteries) to pray. The two leather boxes, worn on the left arm and the head, contain four Biblical passages. The Talmud says that "whoever has tefillin on his

head, tsitsit (fringes) on his garments and a mezuzah on his door is protected." During prayer, a tallit (prayer shawl) is also worn. Ca. 1914

The little town lies in the middle of the flatlands, not a hill, not a forest, not a river to bound it. It simply fades away into the plain. It starts with little huts and ends with them. The huts yield to houses. This is where the streets begin. One runs from south to north, the other from east to west. The market is at the crossroads. The railroad station is at the very end of the north-south street. Once a day a passenger train arrives. Once a day a passenger train departs. And yet many people have things to do at the station all day, for they are merchants . . .

The station is fifteen minutes away on foot. When it rains, walking is impossible because the macadam is so bad that the street is soon under water . . . The eight coachmen are Jews. They are pious Jews and do not cut their beards; but as they can do their jobs more easily in short jackets they do not wear long gaberdines like their fellow-believers. On the Sabbath they do not drive.

The town has 18,000 inhabitants; 15,000 of them are Jews. Of the 3,000 Christians, some 100 are merchants and traders, 100 are civil servants, one is a lawyer, one the district medical officer, and eight are policemen. There are in fact ten policemen, but, strangely enough, two of them are Jews. I do not know exactly what the other Christians do. Of the 15,000 Jews, 8,000 earn their livings as shopkeepers. They are small-scale grocers, larger-scale grocers, very large-scale grocers. The other 7,000 Jews are artisans, laborers, water-carriers, scholars, rabbis, cantors, beadles, teachers, scribes, Torah scribes, tallit weavers, doctors, attorneys, civil servants, beggars and the shamefaced poor, who live on public charity, gravediggers, circumcisors, and tombstone masons.

The town has two churches, a synagogue, and about forty small houses of prayer. The Jews pray three times a day. If they did not have so many houses of prayer – where people not only pray, but also study the Talmud – they would have to make their way to the synagogue and back to their homes or shops six times a day. There are Jewish scholars who study at the house of prayer from five in the morning until twelve at night, like European scholars at a library. They only come home for meals on the Sabbath and holidays. If they have neither fortune nor patrons, they live on small donations from the community and occasional religious tasks, for example, leading the prayers, teaching, or blowing the shofar on the High Holidays. The family, the house, the children are taken care of by the wives, who eke out a living selling corn in summer, naphta in winter, and sour pickles, beans, and baked goods.
Joseph Roth

The two little towns of Barnow and Buczacz
are only five miles apart, but a deep gulf
separates their inhabitants. Although they are
equally uneducated, equally poor, equally
scorned, although they wear the same clothes
and pray to the same God, they serve Him in
totally different ways.

The Jews of Barnow are "Hasidim," bigots
and zealots, wild, bizarre fanatics, who vacil-
late oddly between cruel asceticism and lavish
indulgence. They regard themselves – hence
their name – as the "saintly ones" among the
Jews because their revelation comes from
other, deeper sources: those of the "Kabbalah," particularly the "Zohar." Buczacz, on
the other hand, is the home of "Mitnaggedim," hard, sober people who chiefly honor
the Bible and the Talmud only in so far as it
elucidates the Bible. In fact, the validity of
the Talmud is not, and cannot even be,
binding for any sect because there are few
subjects on which this encyclopedic work does
not contain very diverse opinions. Cool, practical people, the Mitnaggedim somehow manage to live by the laws of their faith, but they
consider the Ten Commandments more important than anything else; they try to find
the most natural possible explanations for
miracles and otherwise have a distaste for any
kind of superfluous speculativeness . . .

As faith inspires the eastern Jews in all they
think and do, and is the basic source and
ultimate purpose of all aspiration, the Jews of
Barnow and Buczacz are indeed fundamentally different. In Barnow there is a great deal
of fasting but also of celebrating; in Buczacz
life moves along a measured, regular path. In
Barnow, the live-long day is spent debating
scholarly questions, and work and usury are
reserved for the breaks in between. The
Buczaczer devote themselves to crafts and
trade; they exhibit greater diligence and a
bourgeois sense of honor, less respect for
intellectual activity and less readiness to make
sacrifices for poverty and scholarship. The
Barnower are eccentric and passionate, the
Buczaczer are considered hard and calculat-
ing. Equal piety and equal pressure from
outside admittedly obliterate these distinctions at first glance; the Pole or Ruthenian
hardly notices that a different spiritual atmosphere reigns in Buczacz than in the other
towns of the district, just as the Silesian
"Water Polack" does not quite see the discre-
pancy between a Moravian Brethren community and a Protestant industrial town. The
knowledgeable person cannot help noticing it.
Karl Emil Franzos

*H*asidism derives its uniqueness and greatness not from a doctrine but from an attitude; it is an attitude that promotes community and is by nature dependent on community.
Martin Buber

*I*n the Hasidic message the separation between "life in God" and "life in the world," the primal evil of all "religion," is overcome in genuine, concrete unity.
Bound to the world, receiving and acting, man stands directly before God – not "man" rather, but this particular man, you, I. Hasidism sets the undivided wholeness of human life in its full meaning: that it should receive the world from God and act on the world for the sake of God.
Martin Buber

*F*rom far away, from darkest Russia, from the remotest backwaters of Galicia, from the historical settlement areas of the Orthodox Jews, from holy Moscow, from Warsaw, Cracow, Petersburg, Kiev, Odessa – from everywhere in the east that there are Jews they came streaming, the countless Orthodox rebbes with their disciples, the pious "Hasidim" with their wives and children, and countless other admirers of the Chief Rabbi of Sadagora, to join in his family celebration and turn it into an Orthodox street festival. The Friedmann family, in which the title of Chief Rabbi is passed down from father to son, indisputably enjoys an international reputation; for Orthodox Jews, it represents a kind of voluntarily recognized religious dynasty. And the wedding celebration for the Rabbi's son and a Russian

millionaire's daughter was truly princely. Princely because of the magnificence of the open-air wedding procession, princely because of the hospitality lavished on both invited and uninvited guests, and princely because of the crowd of many thousands, who stood themselves sore all round so that they could watch the ceremony. Whole hosts of curious city people, the Czernowitzers leading the way, flocked there and contributed striking nuances to the already colorful scene: glittering officers' uniforms, costly silk ladies' gowns, light men's clothes and imaginatively crumpled Panama hats, and a cheerful crowd of Czernowitzers normally found at outdoor brass band concerts had settled on the wooden stands put up for strangers come to watch.
Czernowitzer Allgemeine Zeitung (Czernowitz General News)

There is wealth in Rebbe Ascher-Baruch's house and Torah in his heart. He is a great scholar and a rich man. Wisdom and wealth together. That is why his house is so spacious and taller than all the other houses in the town, although the owner of the house walks with a stoop, bent under the yoke of the Torah. And this is the arrangement of the house: downstairs the store, the winter room, and the kitchen. And upstairs in the gable room sits Rebbe Ascher-Baruch, at his studies and pious exercises, pondering over the Torah day and night. In the meantime his virtuous wife works industriously with her hands, buying and selling, carrying on her business, feeding her children decently, and raising them to study, marry, and do good deeds. And between one customer and the next, she supervises the housemaid. And Rebbe Ascher-Baruch sits in his gable room, at his studies and pious exercises; he does not indulge the follies of temporal life, he does not bother about business — such was the custom in Israel in those days.
Night after night he sits by the light of the candle, all night he sits and studies. The candle is not in a silver candlestick, not in a lead candlestick, not even in a clay pot; it is wedged between his fingers. Torah weakens the scholar, and sleep overcomes the man drowsy from learning. He wakes up again and musters his energy to begin serving his Creator again.
Samuel Josef Agnon

Opposite page: In the courtyard of the Rebbe of Munkacz (Hungary), Chajim Eleazar Shapira. Photograph by *Abraham Pisarek*. Ca. 1930
Left: Palace of the Rebbe of Czortkow (Galicia), Moische David Friedman. Ca. 1900
Above: The Hasidic master of Góra-Kalwarja (Galicia) during a visit to Vienna. 1932

The town is full of life, and there is great excitement among the Hasidim. The famous tsaddik from B. has accepted his followers' invitation and come to N. for Rosh Hodesh. Throngs of people crowd into the house where the distinguished guest has taken up residence: old men whose thoughts are trained on the next world; youths struggling in this world; men apprehensive because they cannot feed their families; women trembling for the health of their children; rich people afraid the times might change; poor people hoping to be delivered from penury; scholars thirsting for new teachings; the simple-minded, who, it is hoped, will be illuminated by the sight of the tsaddik; the pious, who dream of higher worlds; sinners, who want to salve their consciences — each wanting to be admitted to the Rebbe's presence, each making his request vehemently or pleadingly, proudly or humbly, the tone corresponding to the temperament.
R. Niemirower

105

There are many tsaddiks living in the east, each with his own followers, who consider him the greatest of all. The title of tsaddik has been passed down from father to son for generations. Each holds court, each has his regiment of guards, Hasidim, who have free run of his home, pray with him, fast with him, and eat with him. When he blesses, his blessing is fulfilled. When he curses, his curse is fulfilled and visited on a whole family. Woe betide the skeptic who denies him. Happy the believer who brings him gifts. The Rebbe does not keep them for himself. He lives more humbly than the lowest beggar. He eats only to keep barely alive. He lives only because he wants to serve God. He lives on little morsels of food and a few drops of drink. When he is seated at the table among his own, he takes a bite from his richly filled plate, a sip from his glass and then passes his plate round the table. Every guest eats his fill from the Rebbe's food. The Rebbe himself has no bodily needs. To him, enjoying a woman is a sacred duty, and a pleasure only because it is a duty. He must beget children so the people of Israel can multiply like the sand on the shore and the stars in the sky. Women are always banished from his closest surroundings. Eating, too, is not so much nourishment as thanks to the Creator for the miracle of food and the fulfillment of the Commandment to eat of the fruits and animals – for He has created everything for man. Day and night the Rebbe reads in holy books. He knows many of them by heart, so often has he read them. But there are millions of pages in every word, in every letter, and each page proclaims the greatness of God, a subject no one can ever learn enough about. Day after day they come: people with a dear friend who is ill or with a dying mother; people threatened with imprisonment, or people pursued by the authorities; people whose sons have been declared fit for military service so they can march for strangers and fall in a foolish war for strangers. Or those who have barren wives and want a son. Or those who are faced with a major decision and do not know what to do. The Rebbe helps and mediates, not only between man and God but between man and man, a far more difficult task. From far afield they come to him. He will hear the strangest stories in the span of a single year, but no case is so labyrinthine that he has not heard one even more complicated. The Rebbe is as wise as he is experienced, and his practical intelligence is as great as his belief in himself and the fact that he is one of the Chosen. His advice is as helpful as his prayers. He has learned to interpret the sacred texts and God's commandments in such a way that they do not contradict the laws of life and that no loophole remains through which a disbeliever might slip. A great deal has changed since the first day of the Creation, but not God's will, which expresses itself in the basic laws of the world. No compromises are necessary to prove this. It is only a matter of understanding. Anyone who has experienced as much as the Rebbe has, has transcended doubt. The stage of knowledge is behind him. The circle is closed. Man is a believer again. The surgeon's arrogant science brings death to the patient, the hollow wisdom of the physicist leads the disciple astray. He who knows is no longer believed. He who believes is believed. Many believe him. The Rebbe himself makes no distinction between those who faithfully fulfill the written commandments and those who are not quite so faithful, not even between Jew and non-Jew, or between man and beast. Whoever comes to him can be sure of his help. He knows more than he is permitted to say. He knows that above this world there is another one, with other laws, and perhaps he even senses that in this world prohibitions and commandments are meaningful while in another they are meaningless. His concern is the observance of the unwritten but all the more valid law.

They besiege his house. It is usually larger, brighter, and wider than the homes of the other Jews. Some tsaddiks can genuinely hold court. Their wives wear costly dresses, have maids to order about, and own horses and stables: not for enjoyment's sake but to provide an appropriately dignified setting.
Joseph Roth

He who has attained the highest degree of spiritual solitude, who is capable of being alone with God, is the true center of the community, because he has reached the stage at which true communion becomes possible.
Gershom Scholem

Opposite page:
Cracow Jew. 1904
Right: Hasidic Rebbe Urbach emigrated to Palestine and became known as the "rabbi of the pioneers." 1924

Left: Ezrielke, the schammes (synagogue beadle) and Schabbes-klaper of Biala (Russian Poland), knocking on window shutters to announce the beginning of Sabbath. Photograph by *Alter Kacyzne*. 1926

Above: The schammes of Wisokie Litewskie (Poland). 1924

Right: Cracow Jew. 1904

*T*he Jew, in spite of all his most base daily occupations, has, as a rule, at the same time been a scholar. As a scholar, he could become a wise man, and as a wise man the basic mood of the Jew could become contentment with this earthly lot.
Hermann Cohen

*T*o make sure that enough Jewish men assembled for morning worship . . . a boy ran to the houses with Roman numerals and knocked the es-tata signal with a wooden mallet. On Saturdays, when it was forbidden to pick up tools, the boy would shout "In Schul!" at the doors. For the Jewish temple is also a school. It is assumed that the pious will go there throughout their lives to seek instruction and advice that will help them pursue the true and exacting path they have chosen.
Norbert Frýd

*T*his wonderful man taught the vast power of the soul, the omnipotence of the soul. They made him a tsadik, a superhuman, a mysterious being who saves others, works miracles. Even rabbis followed him. He taught joy and merriment, ardent prayer; sorrow struck him as reprehensible. Pure thought, feeling were everything for him; praying in the forest and amid the sheaves of grain was also good. These people called themselves the pious, the Hasidim.
Alfred Döblin

A heightened, intensified, impassioned form of this type of Jew is represented by the Hasid. His ideal is the deification of man, and he seeks to create Heaven on Earth. The bridge that leads man to God is prayer. That is why the Hasid tries to express his purified sensibilities, all his thoughts and wishes through prayer, which must set him spiritually ablaze. The prescribed prayers are far from enough for this purpose. He often goes beyond the letter, sweeps away the form that cannot hold the fullness of his soul, and falls into religious ecstasy. Like a yogi in a trance, he jumps, dances, sings, whistles. As he believes that only a joyous soul can soar up to God, he considers melancholy the greatest evil and does his best to keep cares, grief, and sadness at arm's length. Kabbalah and Hasidic literature are what he likes to study best. In daily life he proves unselfish and sensitive. If he is poor, he goes to a friend who is better off and gladly shares his table. If his family is in need, a collection is taken for them. If a poor man has a daughter to marry off, the rich provide him with the necessary dowry. Because it is a deadly sin to humiliate one's neighbor, he gives in secret. If a thief wants to rob him, he pretends to be asleep so as not to humiliate him.
Artur Landsberger

T hese Jews, refugees from their own blood wherever they go, no longer know anything about Judaism. And the Christians know even less about it. They do not know that a Jewish father considers it the greatest honor for himself and the greatest good fortune for his daughter if he finds her a scholar as a husband. This father is more than happy to slave away to feed his son-in-law, daughter, and grandchildren, for his house has been ennobled by becoming the home of unselfish reflection, study, knowledge, and wisdom. Many marriages among Jews who still deserve the name are made by the rich man taking the poor philosopher into his home as his son-in-law. And in the democracy that is characteristic of the Jewish people and has been instinctive since time immemorial, nobility can be attained by neither property nor power; it derives only from the spirit. But is there anyone at certain cosmopolitan salons who would know anything about that?
Felix Salten

If it only occurred to Nachman to sell his little house, he would immediately stop being a Worobjowker; then he would suddenly become a newcomer, a stranger. This way at least he had his own little corner, his own little house, and in front of the house, a garden. The garden is taken care of by his wife and daughters, and when God grants a good year, there are vegetables all summer, and sometimes there are enough potatoes to last till almost Passover. But you cannot live on potatoes alone. You need some bread to go with the potatoes. And bread he does not have. So he has to take his stick and walk through the village to see if there isn't business to be done somewhere. And when Nachman walks through the village, he never comes home empty-handed. He buys everything he can get his hands on: scrap iron, a pot of millet, an old sack, or a skin. The skin is stretched, dried, and then taken to town, to Avrohom-Eliohu the furrier. And there is money to be made – or lost – on all these little deals: that's what a man is a merchant for! "A merchant is like a hunter!" says Nachman, who likes to use a "goyish" saying now and then. And Avrohom-Eliohu the furrier, a Jew with a bluish nose and fingers as black as if they had been dipped in ink, laughs because Nachman is such a village rustic that he even uses "goyish" sayings now . . .
Scholem Aleichem

Whenever Rabbi David of Lelov came to a Jewish town he gathered all the children around him and gave each a little whistle. Then he packed them into the big wagon he used for traveling, and drove them all over town. The children whistled with might and main the entire time, and the entire time Rabbi David's face was wreathed in smiles.
Martin Buber

A few old men have twirled earlocks; from behind, in their heavy, skirtlike caftans, they look like women. When they step across puddles, they lift their caftans like women. Very many of the ones standing here have dreamy expressions; they look somnolent.
Alfred Döblin

Women were by no means in the same position as, for instance, in the Orient. They often ran businesses single-handed, almost always worked in their husbands' shops, and were thus in total contact with the outside world. However, the rules of decency demanded that the sexes be strictly separated; this meant that women even had their own section of the synagogue to pray in. At festive events, men danced with men and women with women. The rules of decency also demanded that every woman who set store by the reputation of a "Jische znue," a virtuous woman, avoid anything in her clothing and behavior that might be interpreted as provocative. According to one of the Talmudists, the very sound of a woman's voice is already lascivious. The pious man did well not to look at any member of the female sex at all so as to be sure of avoiding temptation.
Jehudo Epstein

Above: Playing children in Maciejowice, one of the oldest shtetls in the Polish province of Lublin. Photograph by *Alter Kacyzne.* Ca. 1928

Right: Children in the market square of a Galician shtetl. Ca. 1910

Opposite page: Water pump at the fish market in Otwock near Warsaw. Photograph by *Alter Kacyzne.* Ca. 1928

*I*magine how these mothers in the East used to live and how thousands of them still live today. The men sit in the "bet midrash" studying, the children sit in the "heder" studying, and the mothers work. The Jewish mother has a small shop and sells, the Jewish mother goes from house to house and peddles, the Jewish mother stands at her market stall from early morning until late evening to earn a few meager groschen to buy bread for her large family. She also takes care of the house, cooks the meals, does the laundry, dresses the little ones and keeps them clean. When she finds the time to do all this and where she takes the time to endure it all is a mystery. And yet enabling her husband and sons to study is her greatest pride and gives her life meaning. Though poverty has left her rough and coarse, she still manages to muster the tender affection and gentleness it takes to be a Jewish mother.
Egon Jacobsohn/Leo Hirsch

*Y*esterday it occurred to me that I did not always love my mother as she deserved and as I could, only because the German language prevented it. The Jewish mother is no "Mutter," to call her "Mutter" makes her a little comic. . . .
"Mutter" is peculiarly German for the Jew, it unconsciously contains, together with the Christian splendor Christian coldness also, the Jewish woman who is called "Mutter" therefore becomes not only comic but strange.
Franz Kafka

In their ghetto the Jews are artisans and laborers; they are porters and blacksmiths, locksmiths and carpenters as often as they are watchmakers and jewelers. Wherever in their exile they are permitted to have contact with the soil, they are hard-working farmers, cattle-breeders, and winegrowers. The estates in Hungary that were managed, tenanted, or owned by Jews prove this. And a certain Prince Urussow, who in the eighties was governor of the Ukraine, a region where the Jews were allowed to own land, writes with amazement in his memoirs about the Jews as farmers and winegrowers, their results as the latter a match, according to him, for any winegrowing done along the Rhine. As a Russian of the ruling classes, this prince and governor is no friend of the Jews, and yet he feels it would perhaps be advantageous to allow the Jews to settle in other regions of vast Russia and inspire the sluggish Russian peasants by their example. And he says all this with an astonishment totally devoid of good will.
Felix Salten

The village of my birth is called Wierzbowce in Polish, Werbowitz in Yiddish, and Werbiwizi in Ukrainian. It is located near Seroka. Seroka is near Czerniatyn. Czerniatyn is near Horodenka. Horodenka is near Gwozdziez. Gwozdziez is near Kolomea. Kolomea is near Stanislau. Stanislau is near Lemberg . . . About a hundred and fifty Ukrainian families lived in our village of Werbiwizi, and there were four Jewish families among them. All of them lived by tilling the fields. The Jews also ran little grocery stores on the side, and one of them had leased the village inn from the owner of the estate. The village had two hills; on one of them stood the little wooden church with its onion dome, on the other lay the estate. The little chatas in the village had straw roofs, brown and black with soot from the chimneys that let in the rain. One could always tell by the smell of the smoke whether the neighbors were cooking meat. The stables, barns, and farm-workers' quarters on the estate also had straw roofs. Only one house was white, and had a flowerbed and a roof shingled with wood. The estate belonged to the Polish estate owner and was alien to us. There was a wall between the estate owner and the village. Theirs was an alien world. He, his wife, his children, even his employees did not mix with the village. They spoke a different language, too. Polish.
Alexander Granach

Above: A peasant couple from Bukovina. Ca. 1910

Opposite page, above: Peasants in western Galicia. Ca. 1920

Opposite page, below: Jewish peasant and his wife in "their own" field in eastern Slovakia. Photograph by *Abraham Pisarek*. 1933

The soil of eastern Galicia is black and succulent, and always looks a bit sleepy, like a huge fat cow standing there good-naturedly letting itself be milked. Eastern Galician soil gratefully returns a thousandfold what is put into it without needing to be particularly flattered with fertilizer and chemicals. It is profligate and rich. It has thick oil, yellow tobacco, grain as heavy as lead, tranquil old forests, rivers, and lakes, and, above all, healthy, attractive people: Ukrainians, Poles, Jews. All three look similar, despite their different habits and customs. The people of eastern Galicia are clumsy, good-natured, a little lazy, and as fertile as the soil. Wherever one looks there are children. Children in the yards, children with the animals, children in the fields, children in the barns, children in the stables, children! As if they grew on trees every spring, like the cherries. Spring in the Galician village is the time for calves, piglets, foals, chicks, and little squealing bundles, those little people: children.
Alexander Granach

Nor were these village Jews simply small shopowners and peddlers, all of them were farmers besides and did the farmwork with their own hands: pastures, fields, and barns. They have a common working rhythm, and they share the same cares. The women give birth every year or two. The men drink their glass of beer together in the evening. Everyone is invited to everyone else's wedding, and the young people dance together, whether at carnival or Purim.
Fritz Frank

Landscape that invented me

water-limbed forest-hairy the blueberry hill honey-black

Songs fraternizing in four languages in a divisive time

Dissolved the years flow to the riverbank of the past
Rose Ausländer

No rag was too dirty, no shard too broken for him to examine and put in his pack. Whatever he saw had commercial value: he bought rags, skins, feathers, bones, scrap iron, pulses, cracklings, semolina, barley, flour, poultry, anything he could. He bargained, persuaded, pleaded and, when he paid, carefully ran the kreutzers between his fingers, turning them over and over as if he hoped some of the copper would stick to his fingers. Nothing that moved in the village eluded Itzig. He preferred to pay in goods rather than money; in his pack he had a little oilcloth bag containing string, ribbons, pins, buttons, leather straps, small round mirrors, pieces of silk, and whatever else he could purchase with the little money he had.
Jan Herben

But in general the poverty of the Jewish population was frightening. A great mass of people who did not have enough to eat were crowded together in these provinces. They literally tore the morsels out of each other's mouths, and it was a battle for their daily bread in the truest sense of the word. The only thing most of these people lived on was, as they themselves put it, that little bit of "Bitochen" (trust in God). Many, like my father, had no specific occupation; they resorted to all sorts of jobs, and that they were able to survive was sheer coincidence. The day began trusting that God would help somehow, and they went to bed trusting that tomorrow, too, would bring His help. If need be they hoped for a miracle, as the "Moschiach," the Messiah, might appear any day, any hour. This desperate trust in God sustained them in their poverty. Need taught these people to pray; it sharpened their wits. And it lent them the resourcefulness to extract at least a tiny profit, no matter how small the opportunity – an ability that understandably did not increase their popularity among the Christian population.
Jehudo Epstein

Left: Butcher shop for "apostates" in Kazimierz, the Jewish section of Cracow. The sign recommends such goods as Polish sausage, salami, tongue, and ham. 1900

Right: Ringplatz in Oswiecim (Auschwitz), Galicia. Photograph by Jacob Hennenberg. Ca. 1906
Left: Shop selling caps and dishes in Russian Poland. Ca. 1910

We had all kinds of beggars: the "bashful" ones, who only wanted a loan, which they could never repay – not even the usually tiny sums that one could scarcely refuse them, not the flour and not the potatoes. Then there were the professional beggars, locals and intinerants, who usually appeared in groups, especially when well-to-do families married off a child or buried a relative. There were the poor who starved and froze silently. They lived on "miracles," which always came, though sometimes too late; a small remittance from a relative, an inheritance that brought them a few crowns, or the greatest, most hoped-for miracle: the children moved abroad and kept sending their needy parents tiny sums of money.

No matter how many people went hungry, no one starved to death. It was said that members of the community woke the rabbi early one morning lamenting: "Something terrible has happened. Someone has died of hunger right in our midst. His dead body was just found in his home."

The rabbi replied, "That can't be true. Why, it's impossible. Would you or you have refused to give him a piece of bread if he had asked for it?"

"No," they said, "but Eliezer was too proud to ask for anything."

"Well, then don't say that someone has died of hunger in our midst. Eliezer perished because of his pride."

Some people were indeed that proud, but they were few and far between. Most people just barely scraped by until they got help from their children, in America, or until they died of a lung disease or heart attack.
Manès Sperber

If the Jewish shtetls still existed today, they would belong, for me, only to a remote past. But since they were destroyed, so thoroughly wiped out that nothing of what they were or could have become can reach into the future, Zablotow now belongs to my present. It is at home in my memory.
Manès Sperber

In the ghetto, the life of the Jewish community was self-contained and encompassed everything – not only religion, but custom, law, language, and family life, all in one . . .
Interaction with the non-Jewish world ranged, so to speak, under the category of "foreign policy."
Adolf Böhm

I really miss the figure of the forceful Jew in your play [Das neue Ghetto]. It is not true that all the Jews in the ghetto you describe walk around bowed or inwardly spent. There are others – and they are the very ones the anti-Semites hate most.
Arthur Schnitzler to Theodor Herzl

My father was an orthodox Jew, in love with German culture, philosophy, and poetry . . . He was always wanting to read German literature and German periodicals with me. He had himself, in his youth, published essays in the "Neue Freie Presse," the best-known Viennese newspaper; had been correspondent of the Warsaw "Hazefira," the first daily to appear in the Hebrew language; and had also written a little book in Hebrew about Spinoza, with the Latin title "Amor Dei Intellectualis." Spinoza was one of his heroes; Heine the other. My father also had a great respect for Lassalle, but the highest intellectual ideal for him, apart from Hebrew writers, was, of course, Goethe. I did not

Left: Street scene in Kolomea (eastern Galicia). 1914
Below: Street life in the Jewish quarter of Lodz, the second largest Jewish community in Poland. Ca. 1930
Opposite page: Entrance to the Jewish quarter of Cracow. Photograph by *Roman Vishniac.* 1938

share my father's partiality for German poetry. I was a Polish patriot. Mickiewicz and Słowacki were incomparably dearer and closer to me. For this reason I never learned the German language thoroughly either. My father often used to say to me: "Yes, you want to write all your fine poetry only in Polish. I know you will be a great writer one day" – for my father had quite an exaggerated idea

of my literary talent, and wanted me to exercise it in a "world language." "German," he would say, "is 'the' world language. Why should you bury all your talent in a provincial language? You have only to go beyond Auschwitz . . ." – Auschwitz was just near us, on the frontier – "you have only to go beyond Auschwitz, and practically nobody will understand you any more, you and your fine Polish language. You really must learn German." That was his ever-recurring refrain: "You have only to go beyond Auschwitz and you will be totally lost, my son!" Impatient as I was, I often interrupted him: "I already know what you are going to say, father – You have only to go beyond Auschwitz, and you will be lost." The tragic truth is that my father never went beyond Auschwitz. During the second World War he disappeared into Auschwitz.
Isaac Deutscher

Three hundred fifty thousand Jews live in Warsaw, half as many as in all Germany. A small number of them are strewn across the city, the bulk reside together in the north-western sector. They are a nation. People who know only Western Europe fail to realize this. The Jews have their own costumes, their own language, religion, manners and mores, their ancient national feeling and national consciousness.
Alfred Döblin

Jewish women pass through the crowd; they wear black wigs, small black veils on top, a kind of flower in front. Black shawls. A tall young man in modern clothes with his elegant sister looks strange; he walks proudly, with a skullcap on his head. Families converse in the street; two youngish men in clean caftans with their wives in modern garb and piquant Polish makeup. A boy in a sailor's suit is with them, his cap says "Torpedo." A Polish policeman directs vehicular traffic in the roadway. This contiguousness of two nations. Young girls stroll arm in arm, they don't look very Jewish, they laugh, speak Yiddish, their clothes are Polish down to the fine stockings. They amble erect. The shoulders of the men are slack, their backs crooked, they shuffle.
Alfred Döblin

Achad Haam once formulated it like this: the western Jew has achieved his outer freedom at the expense of his inner freedom; the eastern Jew may not possess any outer freedom but is still himself. When the ugly, not overly clean "Yid" wrapped in his tallit jubilated or sobbed, he still knew that he was a descendant of Abraham, Isaac, and Jacob. In him resided the jubilant cry of the Hasidim, the fervor of the tsaddikim – the mystics of the Zohar – and the wisdom of the Gemara: the cross-section of a whole history.
Conrad Rosenstein

We German Jews are a spiritual proletariat, whereas the Polish Jews, who live in proletarian conditions, are aristocrats of the spirit.
Franz Rosenzweig

Warsaw had the largest Jewish community in central Europe (32% of the population). There was both a small assimilated upper class, and a broad proletarian and petit bourgeois stratum, most of whom were merchants and artisans.

Opposite page: Market day in the Warsaw ghetto. 1906

Above: Street scene in the Warsaw ghetto. Ca. 1910
Below: A Sabbath stroll in the Jewish quarter of Warsaw. 1906

Left: The Jewish town hall on Meiselgasse in the Prague ghetto; at the left, the Altneuschul Synagogue. Photograph by K. Bellmann. Ca. 1890

Below: Street in the Prague ghetto. Photograph by K. Bellmann. Ca. 1890

The old synagogue . . . was located in the Jewish district. The steel wire that had once separated this part of the town from the outside world had been cut. But a prison atmosphere still pervaded the narrow streets. Outside, the artistic beauty of bygone times flourished, here age was only an ugly infirmity. Cramped, airless lanes criss-crossed like wrinkles on a weathered face. Narrow houses jutted out like loose teeth in a wilted jaw. The poverty of both religions crowded into this grey corner, which is why the odd grocer's shop witi its dusty inventory was open on a Saturday.

The Jews celebrated. Dressed in their best clothes, they stood in the entrances of their junk shops, talking and gesticulating energetically with their hands and bodies, and shouting across the road to one another.
Auguste Hauschner

Prague is the city of queer characters, daylight ghosts and eccentrics. Sometimes, in the morning twilight, figures scuttle about that might have sprung from Meyrink's "Golem"; there, a living grasshopper vaults around the corner in big leaps; Haschile, the grinning fool, jogs by unsteadily, his torso tilted forward; Herr Grünwald of the velvet jacket, *the long cravat, and the thick, towering hairpiece, carries his violin-case past. A hunchback, lame man, madman. Out of the chaos of alleys, crannies, arcades, passages – that one can peep out of like a mocking apparition and, cocking a snook, quickly escape – creep primordial creatures.*
Anton Kuh

At the beginning of the redevelopment campaign in the early 1890s, there were 128 buildings in the Josefstadt. They were partitioned, some of them into as many as thirty sections.
Joseph Teige

A monstrous case of this kind of partitioning is sections A and D of house number 213. The first of these parts contained, on the ground floor: a kitchen, a room, a shop, a cellar, a toilet, a small room, and a woodshed, with use of the hall and the courtyard. The second had two cellars, stairs to the second floor, a passage, a toilet, a room, a closed-off hall, a kitchen, three further rooms, and the stairs to the third floor, which had a hall, a toilet, two rooms, a kitchen, four further rooms, the stairs to the attic and the whole attic over the house toward the lane, with a share of the hall and the courtyard. These sections belonged to fourteen co-owners at the same time, including some unsettled legacies and several participative shares that were, from a bookkeeping standpoint, expressed in, so to speak, incredible fractions.
Emil Svoboda

On March 28, 1885, the Municipal Sanitation Council of Prague decided that the lower part of the old quarter and the Josefstadt were to be torn down. The reasons were "the high mortality rate and frequent cases of infectious disease, the large number of sanitational and structural impediments, blind sewers, overpopulation due to architectural congestion, a large number of wretched, overcrowded, unsanitary apartments, the majority of which consist of one room, a lack of fresh air in densely clustered buildings, plus a lack of good drinking water; furthermore the circumstance that this district lies in an area that is often flooded." The redevelopment program began in 1895.
Joseph Teige

Above: "Flying Coffeehouse" in Prague. 1905
Left: Judengasse in Nikolsburg (Moravia). Photograph by Bruno Reiffenstein. Ca. 1920

In us all it still lives – the dark corners, the secret alleys, shuttered windows, squalid courtyards, rowdy pubs, and sinister inns. We walk through the broad streets of the newly built town. But our steps and our glances are uncertain. Inside we tremble just as before in the ancient streets of our misery. Our heart knows nothing of the slum clearance which has been achieved. The unhealthy old Jewish town within us is far more real than the new hygienic town around us. With our eyes open we walk through a dream: ourselves only a ghost of a vanished age.
Franz Kafka

Do you know that nice anecdote about the two Jews standing in front of the Rothschilds' family vault? After gaping at its marble splendor for a while, one of them nudges the other and sighs pensively: "That's what I call living!"
I think I have discovered the key to Prague in this cemetery declaration. There is no city in the world where what is buried is more alive or decay more cozy. Past and present are equally responsible for the familial odor wafting from the narrow jumble of lanes. At noon a dead ancestor sits down at the table, too.
Anton Kuh

*M*any *return. Even more stay away. The eastern Jews have no home, but they have graves in every cemetery. Many become rich. Many become important. Many become creative in a foreign culture. Many lose themselves and the world. Many remain in the ghetto, and only their children will leave it. Most of them give the west at least as much as it takes from them. Some give it more than it gives them. In any case, all of those who sacrifice themselves by seeking out the west have the right to live there.*
Joseph Roth

Left: Entrance to the ghetto in Eisenstadt (Burgenland, Austria); in the foreground, the barrier chain, which was not allowed to be crossed on the Sabbath. Photograph by Bruno Reiffenstein. Ca. 1920

Above: In the Warsaw ghetto. Photograph by *Roman Vishniac.* 1938

The water carriers are organized in an interesting way. There are 14 of them in Kolomea, but they are not workers, they are entrepreneurs. Each of them has a wagon with a long barrel, four buckets and an old nag he can call his own; that is the basis of his income. From Saturday evening till Friday afternoon he drives around and brings "fresh water" to people's homes. Two buckets cost 1 kreutzer and monthly deliveries cost 40–70 kreutzers, depending on the quantity required. Every water carrier has a bucket carrier working for him, whom he pays 50 kreutzers a day. The water carrying trade in Kolomea is lucrative because there is no competition. The 14 entrepreneurs have divided the town into 14 districts; no one would think of invading anyone else's territory. That way each one possesses a monopoly in his area; but he does not exploit it, prices remain fixed. The bristle sorters and the tallit weavers, with their "Einigkeit" (Unity league), are the only ones to have actual trade unions. A Jewish socialist leader says it is impossible to organize the other Jewish workers along social democratic lines. Some, like the bakers, petroleum refinery workers, and match-makers are too deeply rooted in the factories where they have worked from generation to generation; others, like the coachmen, are afraid of the authorities. But even where trade unions exist, not every worker joins. The bristle sorters have an excellently organized union, perhaps the best in all Galicia; it has a small amount of capital and is turned into a productive cooperative when its members go on strike. That is the only reason the members of this trade have succeeded in obtaining such singularly high wages. The

Left: Water carrier in Staszów (Poland). 1935
Below: Ferryman on the Weichsel River near Kazimierz, the Jewish suburb of Cracow. Ca. 1910

tallit weavers' case is different. The older ones among them are interested in neither unions nor politics. Sometimes the men who sit at the looms twelve hours a day, treadling away and pushing the shuttle back and forth between the warps to earn 5 to 7 gulden a week are extremely old. The younger ones, however, are social democrats. That is what they call themselves, that is how they feel. But it is hard to find out from them what the ultimate goal of social democracy is. They may never have heard or read about it, for most of them are illiterate. The social democratic agitators *among the Jewish workers usually specialize in criticizing the established order, and the people they address are more than ready to listen. In Kolomea and elsewhere the Jewish workers with socialist leanings offer a colorful mixture of political and social ideas that can hardly be reconciled with official party policy, but they all agree on one thing: they want shorter working hours and better wages. "We are badly off, we want to live better – after all, we work," said one of them.*
Saul Raphael Landau

The stranger will immediately recognize, among the teeming masses in Judengasse, a class of people whose appearance differs from the others; whereas almost all Jews wear ordinary clothing, they are dressed in coarse linen or sailcloth, and have bundles of rope hanging down over their shoulders. They stand or sit idly in the street and converse in the crudest slang. These are the Jewish "corner-standers," the street porters. They are regarded as members of the lowest and most uneducated class of people, and no one wants to be in contact with the trade. More than any other nation, the Jews are proud of their ancestry, and a Prague Jew is a genuine aristocrat. It is true that the porter is coarse; the intellectual advances of the time have passed him by without a trace. But for that he is absolutely honest. You can hand fortunes in gold and jewels over to him, send him here or there with them, and he will take them where you want him to, not a sliver missing. You do not need to go along; just say to what house he is supposed to bring the goods entrusted to him and he'll take them there, often waiting many hours for you, so he can hand them over and receive his wage . . .

A hard life, isn't it? And yet there are misers who make deductions from a poor porter's meager demands. On Sabbath and holidays you will not recognize him. Nicely dressed, his beard carefully clipped, a silk "tallit bag" in his hand, he strides gravely through the lane to "shul," where he has a reserved seat and plays an important role. In the afternoon he drinks his black coffee at the "Roter Adler," then takes his wife for a walk on the glacis or in the "canalischer Garten," behind "Lämmel" and "Jerusalem." Maybe he has even started indulging in a little politics lately, thinking about "beautiful emancipation," and calling out: "I, too, am a citizen!" And right he is. Who carries more burdens in the state than he?
Georg Leopold Weisel

It could have been worse, and there are no limits to how much "better."
Scholem Aleichem

The conspicuous mass of old, white-bearded men. Lots of dirty, raggedy caftans. They gaze from pale, yellow, bearded faces. An intense commercial life on the sidewalk and the roadway; many also lean against the building walls, their expressions are very calm, muted. Five utterly shabby men sit in a row outside a house entrance, ropes tied around their waists: porters. Yiddish newspapers are hawked. Men emerge from the huge deep shops, toting sacks. How horribly tattered they are, boots with dangling soles, sleeves ripped out, seams bursting. A boy leads a man with white dead eyes; they beg. An old greasy woman accosts the passersby, holding out her hand. Three elderly Jews sit in front of a government "papierosi" shop, chatting, smoking. How many stand around, look around, waiting, waiting, waiting. A gust of wind blows frequently; then their long black coats fly open, exposing their white ritual fringes. A small fat man with a huge knotted rope around his waist stands in front of a shop window, his beard black, his face learned. His greasy caftan and his trousers are rags. Some people wander in small slow crews.
Alfred Döblin

Right: Porters waiting for work in front of the Stadttheater in Vilna (Lithuania), a center of the Jewish workers' movement. Ca. 1916

I am in the embarrassing position of having to call people proletarians against their will. To some of them I can concede the idiotic, mitigating appellation invented in western Europe "spiritual proletariat." They are the Torah scribes, Jewish teachers, tallit makers and wax candle makers, ritual slaughterers, and minor religious officials. They are, shall we say, confessional proletarians. But then there are the hosts of the suffering, the crushed and the scorned, who cannot find solace in faith, class-consciousness or a re-volutionary attitude. This category would, for example, include water carriers in small towns, who fill water-butts in the homes of the affluent from early till late – for a meager weekly wage. They are touching, naive peo-ple, and they possess an almost un-Jewish physical strength. Their social equals are the moving men, the porters, and many others who live by day labor – but all the same by labor. They are a healthy breed, brave and kind-hearted. Nowhere is kindness as closely allied to physical strength, is coarseness so alien to rough employment as in the Jewish day laborer.
Joseph Roth

Right: The schadchen (marriage broker). Photograph by *Roman Vishniac*. Ca. 1935
Below: "Tevye, the Milkman" – Scholem Aleichem's character was no mere product of the imagina-tion; he could be found in every shtetl, just managing to scrape through somehow. Ca. 1910
Opposite page: Klezmorim, the traditional Jewish musicians: group from Rohatyn (Galicia). 1912

The matchmaker asks: "What do you re-quire of your bride?" – Answer: "She must be beautiful, rich, and educated." – "All right," says the matchmaker, "but I make that three matches."
Sigmund Freud

Like other Jewish country teachers, my father was also a matchmaker, a "schad-chen," for the usually small Jewish country communities had so few eligible marriage partners that it was not easy to find a suitable Jewish spouse.
Willi Wertheimer

Almost everyone in the small town knew the little, haggard Jew generally called "Herschko the musician." He was a tiny man with a bashful look in his eyes, eyes set so deeply in his spare face that they seemed about to sink into their sockets. His character was like his eyes: bashful and withdrawn. A fiddler by profession, he had come here several years earlier and started an instrumental group. There were five men apart from him. Two of them played the fiddle, one the double bass, the fourth the flute, and the fifth the big drum, the triangle, and the cymbals. But Herschko was the soul of the band; he gave it rhythm, sound, and backbone. His five men treated him with loyal affection, gentle veneration, and silent admiration, for Herschko was an artist in his profession. When he played the violin, homely little Herschko seemed to grow with each note until he towered far above his listeners. The busiest season for the band was winter. There were firemen's, veterans', and casino balls, plus numerous private dances. Weddings were the most lucrative, but they were rare events here, so the band's income was fairly meager, and the musicians were forced to have a second occupation next to their artistic one.
Lorenz Scherlag

The melodies are long, the body gladly gives itself up to them. Because of their ceaseless flow, the best way to respond to them is by swaying one's hips, raising and lowering one's arms while breathing regularly, bringing the palms of one's hands to the temples, and carefully avoiding contact.
Franz Kafka

Once the rabbi of Berditchev saw a drayman arrayed for the Morning Service in prayer shawl and phylacteries. He was greasing the wheels of his wagon. "Lord of the world!" he exclaimed delightedly. "Behold this man! Behold the devoutness of your people. Even when they grease the wheels of a wagon, they still are mindful of your name!"
Martin Buber

David Leb Magdeburger was a customer-goer. Do you know what that is? No! – All right, let me explain. At the time of our story, the Jews in Austria, Bohemia, but above all in Prague depended almost exclusively on trade. "Customer-goers" were a special category of businessmen. They were traveling peddlers who did not keep merchandise, in stock; they bought only what they needed for their customers, and brought them everything they required directly to the door. The goods they delivered were paid for partly in kind and partly in small monthly or weekly installments. A true customer-goer had to procure all conceivable manner of things, and when he got on well with his business associates, he was their friend, advisor, sometimes even their moral counsellor. If the father of the house needed a winter coat, the mother earrings, or the son a silver watch, it was the "house Jew"- that is what his Christian business associates called him – who had to obtain it all, accepting on account, at modest prices, several old nightgowns, a hoarse spinet, a broken-down hunting rifle, a long discarded copper laundry tub, probably a few mousetraps or other more or less useful objects, and receiving the rest in weekly installments.

Where the customer-goer was not only the house Jew but a friend of the family as well, his help was also called upon in very different situations. Say, for instance, there is a young widower from the upper new town who comes courting Babi, the pretty daughter of Karbatsch, a well known inhabitant of the old quarter, clearly expressing his wish to marry her. If the girl's parents wanted to make discreet enquiries about her suitor, the house Jew was often used for this friendly spying service. He went to many houses and always had a chance to hear this and that; but what made him particularly well qualified was that he was perfectly harmless and un-biased. He would never be in a position to want to acquire the matrimonial candidate he was reporting on for his own daughter, sister, or niece. Had anyone even mentioned the idea of a mixed marriage at the time, he would safely have been regarded as totally mad.

Industrious, active, and energetic, a customer-goer was on his feet from early Monday morning until early Friday evening. His business activities ceased before sunset on Friday evening. On Saturdays he was a king – in his own house.

Salomon Kohn

Ground down by poverty and persecution, shaken by pogroms, numbed by an archaic Messianic faith, torn between hopes held out by Zionism on the one hand, and revolutionary socialism on the other, Eastern European Jewry was hovering over the precipice. The Jewish "Luftmensch," economically unproductive and rootless, struggled helplessly yet tenaciously for survival, and survived as if by miracle.

In his fantasy he raised himself above the realities of his existence and scaled dizzy heights of wish-fulfillment only to be hurled down again and again in rude awakenings. The Jewish imagination sought to escape reality or to make life fluid, bright, unpredictably miraculous; and Jewish humour and self-irony cried and laughed over the constand clash between hopes and realities.
Isaac Deutscher

Then there were the "Luftmenschen," as that classic Jewish writer Scholem Aleichem so delightfully described them. They had no occupation, they had no money, but they had "ideas."

Sometimes they made money on them, and sometimes they went broke. For if someone had the idea of selling a particular commodity, say underwear, then a dozen of these Luftmenschen pounced on the article, and all of them went broke. But they quickly found another "idea."
Mischket Liebermann

<u>Left</u>: Galician porters. Ca. 1910

95

The little streets and lanes around the old synagogue in Lemberg form a small town of their own. Here time seems to have stood still for a hundred years. Only rarely does the sun penetrate these narrow, winding lanes. The houses are old and the courtyards dirty and gloomy. And each courtyard is a street in itself, with crumbling buildings and wondrous, bent gables that, in the dark, look like crouching monsters. One hardly dares walk erect for fear that the old walls might tumble down at any moment . . .

These houses are inhabited from attic to cellar by poor Jewish families. They are all in trade. Their small dark shops are filled with all sorts of things: a colorful jumble of household utensils and furniture, books and children's toys, hats and shoes of all shapes, old clothes in all hues and sizes, livery and uniforms that have seen better days. Anything in town that has become decrepit or unusable is brought here, and no piece is so bad that it will not find a buyer.

The street is a perpetual fair, with one stand after the other. Jewish women, with scheitels or dirty scarves on their heads, the old and the prematurely aged, sell fruit, vegetables, and baked goods at the cheapest prices. Next to the hawkers sit the shoemakers, hunched over their work. Further along, a bookseller with old magazines, prayerbooks and penny dreadfuls. Throngs of buyers and brokers jostle each other among the stalls. Jews with dusty, dirty faces push their way through the crowds. They are wearing threadbare, old top hats and carrying tattered umbrellas . . .

Cripples and beggars let out wails of frustration as they try to make headway in the crush . . .

At the street corners stand shoe-shine men, porters, and Jewish beggar boys in torn caftans, their faces pale and hungry.

Day after day the battle for survival is waged here . . .

How little they make, these people whom fate has gathered here in one tiny spot. They sweat and slave only to appease their hunger. Earning a few kreutzers makes them happy and restores their vigor. Here sits a woman with apples. Her inventory may be worth one crown. She has to live on what the fruit brings in, and she does not leave her place all day. Neither heat nor cold could drive her away . . . A little further on a man is selling ices, "one kreutzer a spoonful." Others are hawking buttons, brushes, shoemaker's wax, boot polish, and matches . . . A woman is carrying around a jug of lemonade, calling out, "Who needs refreshment! A Cal! A Cal! A long life! Cold, but good for a poorly throat! A long life for only one kreutzer . . . !" A boy stands on a box. Cupping his hands around his mouth like a megaphone, he keeps shouting: "Haaaandkerchiefs . . . ! Three kreutzers apiece . . . ! For big noses. For little

noses! Haaaandkerchiefs! Only three kreutzers!"

The peddler-filled lanes echo the babble of street cries . . . Haggard women, pale emaciated children, careworn men drag heavy pails, baskets, boxes . . . They extol their wares in all keys and try to outdo and outscream each other . . . They hurry through life as if pursued, in constant fear of tomorrow . . . All day they toil, untiring, uncomplaining . . . No one has a proper occupation . . . Today they drive a fruit cart, tomorrow they sell old clothes . . . That is how the lanes bustle with activity from early till late – until Saturday comes. Saturday is the holy day of rest for these harried people. On that day they are human beings . . . They sleep and eat and discuss what is going on in the world . . .
Hermann Blumenthal

A peddler carries soap, suspenders, rubber articles, trouser buttons, and pencils in a basket strapped to his back. He takes his little shop round with him to various cafés and inns. But it is advisable to think first whether it is a good idea to stop at this or that place.
Joseph Roth

In the seventies of the last century there lived in Prague a young schnorrer named Popper. He did not want to work, he lived on charity and as a minjanman. The rich Jews of Prague calculated that it would be cheaper for them to buy him a ticket to America, a one-time investment. North America was to be spared; Prague shipped sheet-metal to South America and Popper traveled along to seek his fortune in Argentina.
Leo Brod

T raveling peddlers and "Luftmenschen" . . .
Above: A chair-mender from Vilna (Lithuania). Ca. 1900

Below: Street peddler from Warsaw. Ca. 1900
Opposite page: Tailor (left) and secondhand-goods dealer from Cracow. 1904

I arrived in a small town in eastern Galicia on a Sunday night. There was a main street with very unprepossessing buildings. Jewish tradesmen live in this town, as do Ruthenian artisans and minor Polish civil servants. The pavement is uneven, the roadway an imitation of a mountain range. The sewer system is inadequate. In the side streets, washing hangs out to dry – striped and checked, red and blue. Shouldn't there be an odor of onions, dusty domesticity, and mustiness hanging in the air?

No! The obligatory promenade was beginning in the main street of the town. The men's clothes were of an unselfconscious, sober elegance. The young girls swarmed out like swallows with darting, unerring grace. A cheerful beggar asked for alms with dignified regret – he was so sorry to be forced to incommode me. Russian, Polish, Romanian, German, and Yiddish could be heard. It was all like a small branch of the big world. And yet this town has no museum, no theater, no newspaper. But for that it has one of the "Talmud-Torah schools" that produce European scholars, writers, and philosophers of religion; and mystics, rabbis, and department-store owners.

Joseph Roth

Left: Naftali Grinband, watchmaker in Góra-Kalwarja (Galicia). Photograph by *Alter Kacyzne*. 1928

*I*t was uncannily black and colossal. His beard, his smooth, blue-black beard, could not have been said to frame his hard, brown, bony face. No, the face seemed virtually to grow out of the beard, almost as if the beard had been there before the countenance, and had waited for years to frame it and grow luxuriantly around it.
Joseph Roth

*J*ews know about the thirty-six tsadiks.
These are not rebbes, but anonymous righteous men in the populace. They are not allowed to reveal themselves, and no one guesses who they are; they can be cobblers and tailors. The world rests on these silent hidden thirty-six righteous men. If they didn't exist, the world would go under. Whenever one of them dies, another is born.
Alfred Döblin

*T*he existence of Jewish artisans is also denied in the West. In eastern Europe there are Jewish plumbers, carpenters, shoemakers, tailors, furriers, coopers, glazers, and roofers. The idea of countries in the East, where all the Jews are tsaddiks or merchants, and the Christian population consists solely of peasants, who share their homes with their pigs, and of gentlemen, who are always off hunting and drinking – these childish notions are as ridiculous as the eastern Jews' dream of western European humanity. There are more poets and thinkers among the eastern Europeans than there are tsaddiks and merchants. And even tsaddiks and merchants by profession may be poets and thinkers – a combination that does not, for example, seem to come easily to western European generals.
Joseph Roth

*W*e know that our forefathers were very like the men we find in the cities of Lithuania, Poland, and Galicia today; no, in fact the latter lived in the Frankish hill country and German plains like us. Today we speak different languages, think different thoughts, live a different Judaism, eat different foods, measure by different standards, and have received one part of our soul from Europe, trading in part of our Jewish one. It has formed not quite five generations of us, this European destiny and its freedom, its new air, its wonderful artistic values, its integrating and expropriating breath; and then it took the direst of distress to bring us to our senses, distress of the heart, distress of memory, distress of the countenance. For out of the strict, ascetic, and forward-looking countenance of the Jew, that witness to the impotence of time, and out of the national essence drawn from an indestructible will, it had made the bloated, amorphous, mediocre, grotesque mask of the merchant of a northern Levant, predestined to disappear into the eternal sameness of all big cities . . .
The old Jew from the east, however, retained his face. It looks out at us from Mendel's stories, that face: the face of a guileless dreamer, whose purity could be purchased only at the cost of renouncing ordinary activities and the happiness of ordinary activities.
Arnold Zweig

There was a rabbi who frequently thought long and hard about how Samson could have come to figure among the holy men and prophets, and how the mighty ruffian's story could have made its way into the consecrated leaves of the most sacred of books. Then something happened to show him. The prince summoned the rabbi to him – it was in the Middle Ages – and tried to extort the secret of how to prevail over the Jews. The rabbi, who was known as both the wisest and the poorest man in the community, was promised a large manorial estate if he revealed the magic charm, but the rack if he refused. Delilah's question to Samson: "Wherein lies your strength, Samson?"

The rabbi hesitated for a long while before responding. How difficult it was to find an answer that would not bring harm on his people! But then, realizing that there was nothing to lose if he told the truth, he ultimately said: "Jewry will be strong as long as it remains faithful to the vow it made in its childhood, whether its naive formulation be to eat kosher food and keep the Sabbath, or not to allow a knife to touch a hair on the head.

A Jew cannot be crushed by being robbed of his home, peace of mind, and well-being. The more he is hounded, the more tenacious he becomes. The only way to prevail over the Jews, to destroy them, is to offer them comfortable lives, to treat them like brothers. The more contented they feel, the weaker their Judaism becomes, and the easier it is for them to abandon it."

The prince thought the rabbi was ridiculing him and ordered preparations to be made for the torture. To gain his freedom the rabbi quickly had to think up a few incantations the first-born of the community had to say at a certain hour and other such things.
Oskar Baum

Left: Jewish youth from Bukovina. 1903
Opposite page: Roadmen in Wladimir Wolynsk (Russian Poland). 1914

When the rabbi of Ger visited the rabbi of Rizhyn in Sadagora, his host asked: "Are there good roads in Poland?"
"Yes," he replied.
"And who," the rabbi of Rizhyn continued, "is responsible for the work and directs it, Jews or non-Jews?"
"Jews," answered the rabbi of Ger.
"Who else," exclaimed the rabbi of Rizhyn, "could be versed in the work of making roads!"
Martin Buber

Again and again he raises his agonizingly expressive eyes from the depths of suffering, and his hope stands great and flaming among the stars in the night-black sky: the hope for permanence.
Arnold Zweig

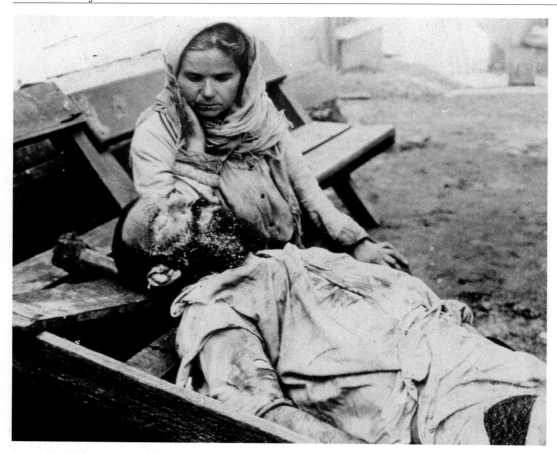

There were pogroms, and whoever could, fled the regions. That is why my father founded a refugee organization. It was thanks to his efforts that everything worked out so peacefully in our town. A house was rented to lodge the refugees. My father immediately turned to the Hilfsverein der Deutschen Juden (Aid association of German Jews) and the Alliance Israélite Universelle for subsidies for his program. The means were modest, but I am sure that he contributed money of his own.
Max Daniel

For above the lives of those whose blood flowed in him stood justice like a sun whose rays did not warm, whose light did not light their way, and beneath whose dazzling brilliance they nonetheless shaded their sorrow-laden brows in awe, with trembling hands. Forefathers who wandered – lost, the dust of all the military roads in their hair and beards, tattered, ignominiously spat upon; everyone against them, spurned by even the lowest, but never spurning themselves; not, in beggarly fashion, honoring their God according to the measure of his gifts; calling not to the Merciful God in their sufferings, but to the Just God.
Richard Beer-Hofmann

Above: After a Russian pogrom in Kischniew (Bessarabia). 1905
Right: Fleeing. Galicia. Ca. 1915

There can, you must realize, be two reasons for traveling. Either to get somewhere or to get away from somewhere.
Bruno Kisch

One of the ridiculous untruths the Jews allow to be spread about them is that they are a wandering nation. If ever they were left in peace, they would not budge from the spot. They experience their roots and feel at home where the graves of their forefathers are. And as a hopeless, defenseless minority, ideally suited as a scapegoat for mass discontent, they are driven from their homes and then called nomads.
Arnold Zweig

The Baal Shem said: "What does it mean, when people say that Truth goes over all the world? It means that Truth is driven out of one place after another, and must wander on and on."
Martin Buber

Right and below: Galician Jews fleeing from the Czarist army. 1914/15

The war swept through the Galician villages, leaving them drowned in mud or fire. I saw these Jewish and Hasidic settlements, the infinite poverty, cramped quarters, and despair of their inhabitants, who did not understand why the destruction and murders were going on and why everything was collapsing on them. Desperate, they fled on foot from the areas near the front . . .
These heart-rending images . . . did not match the naive, carefree joy in which they had lived before the catastrophe of war, the joy that was the basic spirit of all Hasidic life.
Frantisek Langer

The eastern Jew looks towards the West with a longing it in no way deserves. To him the West means freedom, the opportunity to work and make the most of his talents, it means justice and the autonomous rule of spiritual values. Western Europe sends engineers, automobiles, books, and poems to the East. It sends propaganda soap and hygiene, the useful and the uplifting; it parcels out mendacious illusions. To the eastern Jew, Germany is, for instance, still the country of Goethe and Schiller, the German poets every knowledge-hungry Jewish boy knows better than our swastika-mongering high-school students do.
Joseph Roth

Above: Refugees at a railroad station at the German-Polish border. Ca. 1918
Below: Refugees in a mass shelter set up in the synagogue of Brest-Litowsk (Lithuania). Ca. 1918
Right: Jews who wanted to emigrate, in the passenger train to Danzig (Gdansk). Ca. 1925

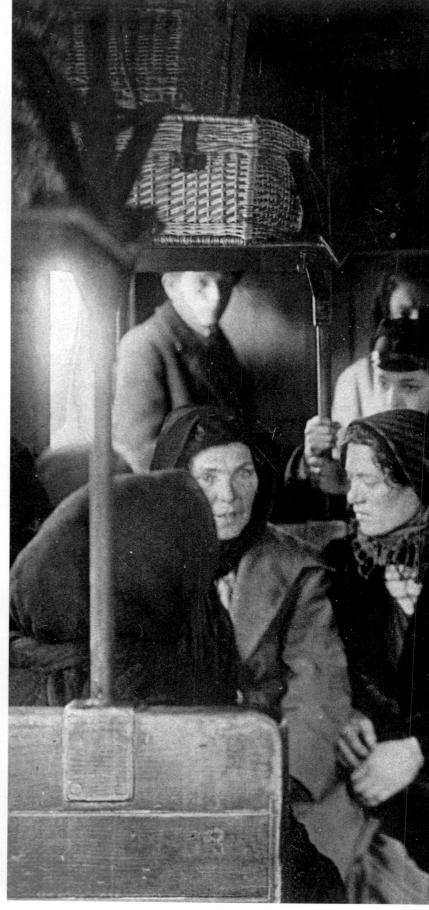

*A*nd then suddenly the news spread that
Moshe Blecher was going to the land of Israel
with his entire family. I do not recall all the
members of his family. I do remember that he
had a grown boy, or perhaps two. Moshe
Blecher's decision to go to Palestine was not
capricious, but the result of a deep-seated
urge. Everybody wondered why he had
waited so long.
The details are blurred and I recall only
isolated incidents because I was only a child at
the time. People kept going to see the tinsmith
in his cellar apartment. He was given written
messages to be placed near the Wailing Wall,
at Rachel's grave, or perhaps at the Cave of
Machpelah. Elderly people asked him to send
them bags containing holy soil. Moshe
Blecher walked around full of exhilaration,
with a look of longing and expectation in his
eyes, and a blissfulness that is not of this
world. The Holy Land seemed to be en-
graved on his face, which somehow resembled
a map.
One early evening a wagon rode up to our
house. It was so huge that it looked more like
an omnibus. I cannot to this day figure out
why Moshe Blecher hired such a wagon. Perhaps he took his furniture with him? Kroch-
malna Street was suddenly crowded with
Jews. They came to say farewell. They kissed
him, wept, and expressed the wish that the
Messiah would come and bring an end to the
Diaspora. Moshe Blecher's voyage seemed to
suggest the coming of the Redeemer, as
though he were his forerunner or minion. If
Moshe Blecher is leaving for Palestine with
his entire family, this must be a sign that the
End of Days is close.
Isaac Bashevis Singer

Below: In the Warsaw waiting-
room of HIAS, the "Hebrew Shel-
tering and Immigrant Aid Society
of America," founded in New
York in 1888. 1921

Ambition keeps most Jewish emigrants from writing as long as they are badly off; they want to be able to recommend their new home above their old one. They have the provincial's naive craving to impress the people back home. In a small town in the East, a letter from someone who has emigrated is a sensation.
Joseph Roth

I am an eastern Jew, and we are at home wherever our dead are buried . . . My son will be a complete American, for that is where I will be buried.
Joseph Roth

<u>Left</u>: Emigrants on a Hamburg-Amerika Line (HAPAG) steamer. Photograph by Joseph Byron. Ca. 1908

<u>Above</u>: Immigrant Poles on their way to the New World. 1907

Our radical impoverishment (and not only that) made me begin to see everything around me, especially the people in the street, differently from before: I saw each person in his special manner: the way he walked, the look on his face, the clothes he was wearing. And this did not change, for I am still as attentive as ever to all people who cross my path. Aside from my need to see – almost a physical need, a sort of visual hunger – that situation in Vienna is still exerting its influence. It fostered my feeling of what might be called "naked humanity," which is neither humanitarianism nor its opposite, but an incapacity to remain indifferent to anything concerning human beings – primarily their existence. In the shtetl, in any small village, no one you run into is really a stranger, aside from visitors. In a big city, the reverse is true: people who are not strangers are the exception. I walked through the streets of the metropolis, unable and unwilling to resign myself to this strangeness. Even when I accepted the fact that other people weren't interested in me, weren't concerned about me, I nevertheless felt that they all concerned me.
Manès Sperber

We knew the Talmud, we had been steeped in Khassidism. All its idealizations were for us nothing but dust thrown into our eyes. We had grown up in that Jewish past. We had the eleventh, and thirteenth and sixteenth centuries of Jewish history living next door to us and under our very roof; and we wanted to escape it and live in the twentieth century. Through all the thick gilt and varnish of romanticists like Martin Buber, we could see, and smell, the obscurantism of our archaic religion and a way if life unchanged since the middle ages. To someone of my background the fashionable longing of the Western Jew for a return to the sixteenth century, a return which is supposed to help him in recovering, or re-discovering, his Jewish cultural identity, seems unreal and Kafkaesque.
Isaac Deutscher

When we finally stepped out of the ghetto and into the world, what happened inside us was far worse than anything that had ever befallen us from outside: a deep rift appeared in our ancient foundations, that unique unity of nation and religion. Since then the chasm has become ever deeper.
Martin Buber

I did not feel very comfortable among the Jews of western Berlin and probably cut quite a pitiful figure among them, too. I was not familiar with the social graces, my clothes were shabby, my outward behavior was marked by intimidated, provincial awkwardness. Moreover I was still very "Jewish." I went to the synagogue, ate only kosher food, put on tefillin (phylacteries) in the morning, in short I was surely an "eastern Jew" in their eyes.
And yet who was considered an eastern Jew was by no means clear. Even for the proud Germanized Jews of the German west, the geographical definition of the term depended on where they lived. For Jews in Frankfurt am Main, the critical border was the Elbe, the Jews in Berlin-W pushed it to the Oder. The Warta River was not even worth discussing. While the Jews from Poland, the so-called Congress Poles, were categorized as more or less a different race; coming from the German province of Posen, we ranked as half-breeds.
Hermann Zondek

Left: Polish slum during World War I. 1914/18

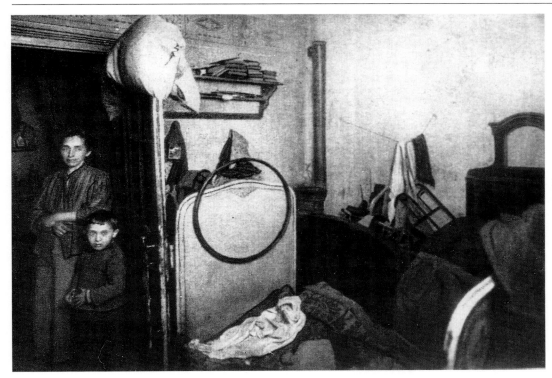

And yet most of the eastern Jews stayed in the ghetto. And stayed what they were: poor wretches. With incredibly many children. They slaved away to fill those numerous mouths somehow.

The Berlin ghetto was not surrounded by walls, and yet it was a closed-off world. It had its own laws, customs, and habits. The Orthodox Jews saw to it that they were strictly observed. The ghetto was self-sufficient, for everything had to be kosher (pure, prepared according to specific ritual laws). Narrow Grenadierstrasse was full of little shops: butchers, grocers, greengrocers, two bakeries, yes, and a fish market. That could never be missing, for what was the Sabbath without gefillte fish? They had their own artisans, shoemakers, tailors, junk dealers, and peddlers. And an excellent kosher restaurant. But everything centered around the two houses of prayer, with their two rabbis, their cantors, and their schlattenschammeses, the beadles.
Mischket Liebermann

Once, walking along the "Schüttel," we came near the railroad bridge that spanned the Danube Canal. A train was standing there, it was stuffed with people. Freight cars were joined to passenger cars; they were all jammed with people staring down at us, mutely, but questioningly. "Those are Galician – " Schiebl said, holding back the word "Jews" and replacing it with "refugees." Leopoldstadt was full of Galician Jews who had fled from the Russians. Their black kaftans, their earlocks, and their special hats made them stand out conspicuously. Now they were in Vienna, where could they go? They had to eat too, and things didn't look so good for food in Vienna.

I had never seen so many of them penned together in railroad cars. It was a dreadful sight because the train was standing. All the time we kept staring, it never moved from the spot. "Like cattle," I said, "that's how they're squeezed together, and there are also cattle cars."

"Well, they're so many of them," said Schiebl, tempering his disgust at them for my sake; he would never had uttered anything that could offend me. But I stood transfixed, and he, standing with me, felt my horror. No one waved at us, no one called, they knew how unwelcome they were and they expected no word of welcome. They were all men and a lot were old and bearded. "You know," said Schiebl, "our soldiers are sent to the war in such freight cars. War is war, my father says." Those were the only words of his father's that he ever quoted to me, and I realized he was doing it to wrench me out of my terror. But it didn't help, I stared and stared, and nothing happened. I wanted the train to start moving, the most horrible thing of all was that the train still stood on the bridge.

"Aren't you coming?" said Schiebl, tugging at my sleeve. "Don't you want to anymore?" We were en route to his home to play with soldiers again. I did leave now, but with a very queasy feeling, which increased when we entered his apartment and his mother brought us a snack. "Where were you so long?" she asked. Schiebl pointed at me, saying: "We saw a train of Galician refugees. It was standing on 'Franzensbrücke.' Oh," said his mother, pushing the snack towards us. "But you must be hungry by now." She then left, fortunately, for I didn't touch the food, and Schiebl, empathetic as he was, had no appetite either. He let the soldiers alone, we didn't play; when I left, he shook my hand warmly and said: "But tomorrow, when you come, I'll show you something. I got a new artillery."
Elias Canetti

Above left: Apartment of a Jewish working-class family in Vienna. Photograph by Anton and Hans Bock. Before 1920

Above: Overnight shelter on Dragonerstrasse in Berlin's Scheunenviertel. Ca. 1920

109

They gave up on themselves. They lost themselves. Their sad beauty fell from them, and what remained on their bent backs was a dust-grey layer of senseless grief and pathetic sorrow. Contempt clung to them – in former times only stones had been flung at them. They made compromises. They changed their way of dressing, their beards, the way they wore their hair, their religious services, their Sabbath, their household – they themselves still held fast to the traditions, it was tradition that slipped away from them. They became ordinary, commonplace citizens with ordinary, commonplace problems. They paid taxes, received registration slips, were registered and acknowledged a new "nationality," a new citizenship, that was "issued" to them after all sorts of red tape; they used streetcars and elevators, all the blessings of culture. They even had a "fatherland."
Joseph Roth

The Scheunenviertel was as exotic to long-assimilated Berlin-born Jews as to their Christian, or "Aryan," fellow citizens. There was little to connect them with the eastern Jews, disparagingly known as "planjes": of course, one's own father or grandfather may have come from the once Prussian or Russian, later Polish, east; but the link between one's own origin and those who so openly represented it was ignored, even repressed.
Günter Kunert

Many of the eastern Jews had tried, some of them repeatedly, to acquire German citizenship. They were attached to Germany not only because it was where they lived. Their children had been born there and had attended German schools, which meant that, at least by the second generation, they had become ever more German in their habits and feelings. But apart from a few isolated exceptions, they had not been granted citizenship either for themselves or their children. The blessed American law that makes any child born in that country a proper citizen of the country was unknown in Germany. A foreigner's son and grandson remained foreigners if they were not naturalized. But the authorities rejected their naturalization applications without offering a reason. There was no legal provision that would have compelled them to. The authorities were merely making negative use of their "discretionary power."
Phillipp Löwenfeld

Thanks to their conformism, the German Jews had almost achieved their goal – they were nearly taken for genuine Germans. And now these eastern Jews were standing in their way: dirty, coarse and uncivilized, they were spoiling everything.
Theodore S. Hamerow

Opposite page, above: The corner of Lazenhof and Judengasse in Vienna. Amid the company and street signs, a Hebrew signpost pointing the way to the house of prayer. Photograph by *Abraham Pisarek*. 1933

Opposite page, right: Basement shop on Grenadierstrasse in Berlin's Scheunenviertel. Photograph by Hans Thormann. Ca. 1928

Above: For new arrivals from the shtetl, life in the west must have been fraught with irritation and fear: arrival in Berlin. 1928

The author harbors the foolish hope that there are still readers before whom eastern Jews need not be defended: readers who have respect for pain, human greatness, and the dirt that accompanies suffering wherever it goes; western Europeans who are not proud of their clean mattresses, who feel that there would be much for them to gain from the East, and who perhaps know that Galicia, Russia, Lithuania, and Romania bring forth great men and great ideas; but also people who are (in their sense) useful, who uphold and help to further the established framework of western civilization – not just the pickpockets, whom that vilest product of western European society, the local news report, likes to term "guests from the East."
Joseph Roth

Sigmund Freud dreamed: "I am sitting by a well and am very sad, almost to the point of tears." His eldest son appears, but another father is already awaiting him.

"Concern about the future of the children whom one cannot give a fatherland" is what Freud later recognized in this dream. Dreaming, he watched his family leave the city and admitted to himself how much he envied the relatives whose children had already been "transplanted to different soil."

A stroll on the outskirts of the city on a hot July day. The air is filled with the fragrance of flowers, the wild roses are in full bloom. It happened suddenly, he later maintained: the key to the mystery of dreams revealed itself to Dr. Sigmund Freud. Uncharted territory. A bold concept of new contexts, unknown meanings, hidden truths. Nothing is what it seems; every image is a code – only he who can crack that code achieves clarity and control over the Self. "Dreaming replaces doing, as it does elsewhere in life too," reads a statement almost hidden away in *The Interpretation of Dreams*.

Official repudiation of the theory was radical. It was to take eight years for the 600-copy first edition of *The Interpretation of Dreams* to sell out. As the motto for his book, Freud had chosen a passage from the *Aeneid*, the epic of the traveler who has lost his home and must go out to seek a new

Two calling-card pictures of bourgeois assimilation in Vienna:
Above: Sigmund Freud at the age of sixteen, with his mother Amalie, née Nathanson. 1871

Opposite page: Arthur Schnitzler at the age of twelve, with brother Julius and sister Gisela. Their father *Johann Schnitzler* had come to Vienna penniless from Hungary and had ultimately become a university professor. Ca. 1875

land: "Flectere si nequeo superos, Acheronta movebo" ("And if Heaven be inflexible, Hell shall be unleashed!"). An arduous journey: Freud compared it to a walk through a dark wood full of misleading signposts and up a steep slope until one finally reaches the top and can enjoy the panoramic view. Knowledge to him who has penetrated the maze of human nature.

Was that the *Weg ins Freie*, the road to the open, that Heinrich Ber-

mann, hero of Arthur Schnitzler's novel, was seeking? "I do not believe that such journeys into the open can be taken with others," he says, "for the roads there run not through exterior landscapes but in ourselves. It is for each to find his own inner way."

It was a closed society one belonged to. "Because I was a Jew, I found myself free from many of the prejudices that limited others in the use of their intellect." That was how, a quarter of a century later, Freud explained the tools that had equipped him to find and go his own way. "As a Jew I was prepared to take an oppositional stand and forgo the approval of the compact majority."

He would have joined them had the "compact majority" permitted. The son of a Jewish wool merchant from Freiberg in Moravia, he had moved to Vienna as a child and experienced rejection since his early youth. A whole generation that was to grow into the cultural elite of the city was denied a place in society. Freud studied medicine, one of the few subjects to offer young Jews a future (in 1890, 48 percent of the medical students at the University of Vienna were Jews). He went to Paris, where Jean Charcot, the Napoleon of neuroses, was teaching at the Salpetrière; how gladly the eager student would have become Charcot's emissary in Vienna. But the medical establishment would not countenance it. So, barred access to common ground, the Jewish newcomer had to find his own way, which led him to his own field. He had no choice but to become the "Caesar of hysteria" (Mario Erdheim).

Assimilation had failed. Liberalism had suffered a devastating defeat. It was the anti-Semites who were at the helm now; their virulent rejection set the tone, their stale, philistine culture filled every corner of public life. There was only one way for educated Jews who had grown up in the metropolis around the turn of the century to go: they had to construct a counter-world, confront the dominant culture with a culture of their own. Where pretension and pathos reigned, they were matter-of-fact and concrete. They responded to flowery formulas with clear concepts, acknowledged hollow phrases with straightforward words. Uncharted territory indeed. That was the only place for them – a world they first had to create, first had to conquer.

They had left the past behind and were locked out of the present, only the future was open to them. Like the great Jewish department-store dynasties of Berlin, they revolutionized business life in Vienna, a metropolis that had no culture to call its own apart, perhaps, from the stubbornness of its abrasive residents; away from pettiness and the bookkeeper's mentality. Cosmopolitan, elegant, generous.

They conceived, visualized, and created their new universe. According to Schnitzler's Bermann, the Jews were a people in whose "soul the future of mankind is being prepared."

An endless list of names: Kraus, Hofmannsthal, Altenberg, Roth, Freud, Wittgenstein, Schnitzler, Eugenia Schwarzwald, . . . antithetical, contradictory, at odds with one another. In Vienna the "road to the open" led to the discovery of modernism. Though no Viennese phenomenon, nowhere else did it become as palpable as in the capital of the polyethnic Habsburg Empire. Here the Jews were one minority among many, but they were unique in being the only one to possess only a spiritual and no geographical home.

In his book *Vienna and the Jews 1867–1938: A cultural history* (Cambridge University Press, 1989), Steven Beller calls this intellectual father- and motherland the "ethics of outsiders": "Their tactic of alliance with the people and ideas of the future was, in the main, the result of trying desperately not to identify themselves as isolated outsiders. It was the image of a future in which they would cease to be regarded as different, that is, cease to be Jews, which spurred them on, just as it had spurred on their fathers . . . In attempting to escape the problem of being Jewish, Jewish individuals retreated into the same world as their ancestors had inhabited, that of the intellect. In this way the Jewish tradition was continued almost against the will of its heirs, but it was continued."

"The castration complex is the deepest unconscious root of anti-Semitism," Freud pointed out in a footnote. Was that the primeval fear responsible, as Freud saw it, for inspiring the grandiose anti-Semitism of the Jew Otto Weininger, who, in his role of victor over tradition and origin, felt a spontaneous vocation to found a religion? "The spirit of modernism is Jewish," postulated the false prophet from Vienna: "But a new Christianity is pushing its way to the light to counter the new Judaism . . . mankind once again has the choice . . . between non-value and value . . ." What was the radical anti-modernism of this desperate suicide Weininger if not another road to the open gone astray. In the irrational darkness where he died lay the heavy shadows of the modernism that shines out of the past at us with such clarity, brightness and enlightenment.

For there was no lasting place for modernism. The city was, in Broch's famous words, the European center of the value vacuum. Unlike the Jewish founding fathers of Hollywood – the Warners, Laemmles, Goldwyns, Selznicks, or Mayers, who, like their European counterparts, had had to find and create a new world because they had been refused a place in the society of their adopted home – the modern universe of the Jewish cultural elite had no foundations and no basis. It was a cloud cuckoo land, a dreamland, in which capricious flights of fancy created art, and culture became a veil that fell concealingly over reality. Only for a brief moment could modernism become a "Jewish art of survival," as I called it in a lecture several years ago (The Jewish Art of Survival. Lecture, Williams College, Williamstown, Mass., 1985): "They became what they were out of ignorance, rejection, and the refusal of the rest of the society to allow them to participate. To create a new self-understanding, be it political, economic, cultural, or scientific, to find new goals to pursue, and to scout ways out of a hopeless and desperate situation – that is what I would like to call the 'Jewish art of survival'."

The way out that they chose was to question the status quo, to break with what was accepted; it was a destructive grab for taboos: nothing is what it seems.

But they did not crack the code, did not recognize the hidden truth of their dream. The old form of assimilation – integration – was to yield to a new one: confrontation. But in all the inertia of its power, the petit bourgeoisie that had just established its rule evaded the confrontation. The blossoming of modernism – it was nothing but a delusive Indian summer. The Jews had taken their counter-world for reality – an error that was to cost millions of lives.

"I do not know whether it is a Jewish quality to find an old drunkard in a caftan more cultural than a member of the Jewish-Austrian writer's cooperative in a dinner jacket," declared Karl Kraus angrily in his 1913 essay "Er ist doch ä Jud" (But he's a Jew): "Unless it is a Jewish quality not to have any [culture]. That can happen, that is how some religions have come to be, but our time is preserved from such excrescences."

He was wrong, it was not. The home of *Luftmenschen:* the smoke that rose to heaven from the crematorium chimneys.

Leopoldstadt in Vienna (Second District), also known as the "Mazzesinsel" (matzoh island) because of its location between the Danube River and the Danube Canal, and the Scheunenviertel of Berlin were the places where Jewish immigrants from the east first settled to get their bearings.
<u>Opposite page</u>: Jewish family from Bukovina. Photograph by *Emil Mayer*. Ca. 1910
<u>Right</u>: The market in the Werd (Karmelitermarkt), Leopoldstadt. 1915
<u>Below</u>: In the Scheunenviertel of Berlin. Ca. 1930

*K*ottbuser Strasse takes us back to the canal, and we come to an agglomeration of market stalls covering the entire Maybach bank. The whole Neukölln district seems to have come here from the south to do their shopping. Everything is on offer: slippers and red cabbage, goat fat and shoelaces, ties and whitefish. Next to the old Jewess spreading out scraps of fur and unpacking bits of silk, a neighbor is eating a raw carrot from her vegetable cart. Through the penetrating stench of fish, bottles of essence of lily-of-the-valley promise a sweet fragrance at cheap prices. And again and again a "lot" of stockings made of silk gauze or so-called "Panzerseide" can be found interspersed among the other displays. Occasionally the shops along the street join the fray. The hardware store puts out its wares across the road. There are calls of "Tulip bulbs cheap before closing time" and "Bargains, madame." A man recommends his potatoes: "Winter red, nice and floury." Next to him there really are things worth seeing, things we would already con-sider museum pieces: genuine hair pins the way they had them when we were young, and the kind of round combs women used to put in their hair then.
Franz Hessel

*T*he emigrants – regrettably! – do not assimilate too slowly to our pathetic way of life, though that is what they are reproached with, but far too quickly. Yes, they even become diplomats and journalists, mayors and dignitaries, policemen and bank directors, and straight-thinking pillars of society, like anyone else.
Joseph Roth

Crossing the courtyard of the Product Exchange, which connects the busiest spot on Taborstrasse with Grosse Mohrengasse, one immediately notices, in the entrance at the right, an insubstantial, dwarf-like figure, the specter of a person, the blind beggar of the Product Exchange. On the stone floor next to him lie the earthly remains of a fiddle and the international escutcheon of the vagabonds who live on alms, the proverbial beggar's staff. To keep from losing the warmth of his own body in the February frost, he sways back and forth, and blows on his fingers, which he has covered with scraps of sacking. A son of the people of Ahasuerus, a threefold outcast of human society.

As my path often takes me through this passage, he attracted my attention. I saw how hardly any of the passers-by – the visitors to the Exchange and its coffeehouse, all the luckier members of the blind fiddler's clan – deigned to so much as glance at the man patiently waiting there, much less to give him anything. So shabby is he that one literally has to look for him in order to see him. I was curious to discover where and how this professional beggar spent the hours and nights he did not pass waiting for charity with outstretched hand. What is his lot, what are the joys and sorrows of his life? I decided to address him . . .

And he took me to where horror dwelled: filthy mass lodgings in Leopoldstadt. A dark room that soon revealed itself to be a kitchen. Between stove and cupboard, a few rags as sleeping quarters. In the room and a little pantry adjacent to the kitchen, a few unmade beds. An old Russian Jewess and her "husband" are the actual tenants of the apartment. According to the landlady's less

Where wretched poverty reigned . . .
Opposite page: Kitchen in mass lodgings in Vienna's Leopoldstadt. Photograph by *Hermann Drawe.* 1904
Left: Blind beggar in front of the Product Exchange on Taborstrasse in Vienna (Second District). Photograph by Anton and Hans Bock. Before 1920
Below: Mass lodgings in Vienna's Leopoldstadt. Photograph by *Hermann Drawe.* 1904

than credible statements, only four or five – as she puts it – "perfectly respectable people" come to her place to sleep. She pays 50 crowns a month in rent and earns 60 to 80 crowns. The men who live in the room pay her 3.50 crowns a week and those in the kitchen only 3 crowns. So much for the woman's information.

But neighbors, the caretaker, and the kitchen-sleeper Markus Seidenwurm – the beggar from the Product Exchange – have a very different story to tell. Apart from the regular boarders, a whole series of scoundrels – information as to their number varies – enjoy the landlady's nightly hospitality, too. All night there is gambling, scuffling, and screaming; and the tired beggar, blind Markus Seidenwurm, finds no rest even at night, on his paid kitchen cot. If he does not like it, he can leave; but he is not allowed to complain, and

that is only right: after all, he pays a mere 3 crowns per week, while the others pay 3.50. Distinctions even here!

And he tells me about his life: He has a wife and child, an eighteen-year-old daughter, in Lemberg. Both of them are ill, the girl is hospitalized. He shows me pitiful letters: "Father, save me!" Before he was completely blind, he went to the inns in Leopoldstadt and fiddled. He knows only two tunes, and those very badly, but he was still well off then, he "earned" up to 30 crowns a week. Now things are worse. Although he has changed locations, his cripple-like shape nonetheless attracts notice, namely from the police. When that happens he is thrown into a cell for 48 hours, where he can at least stretch out. He never goes hungry, acquaintances always help him out somehow.

Bruno Frei

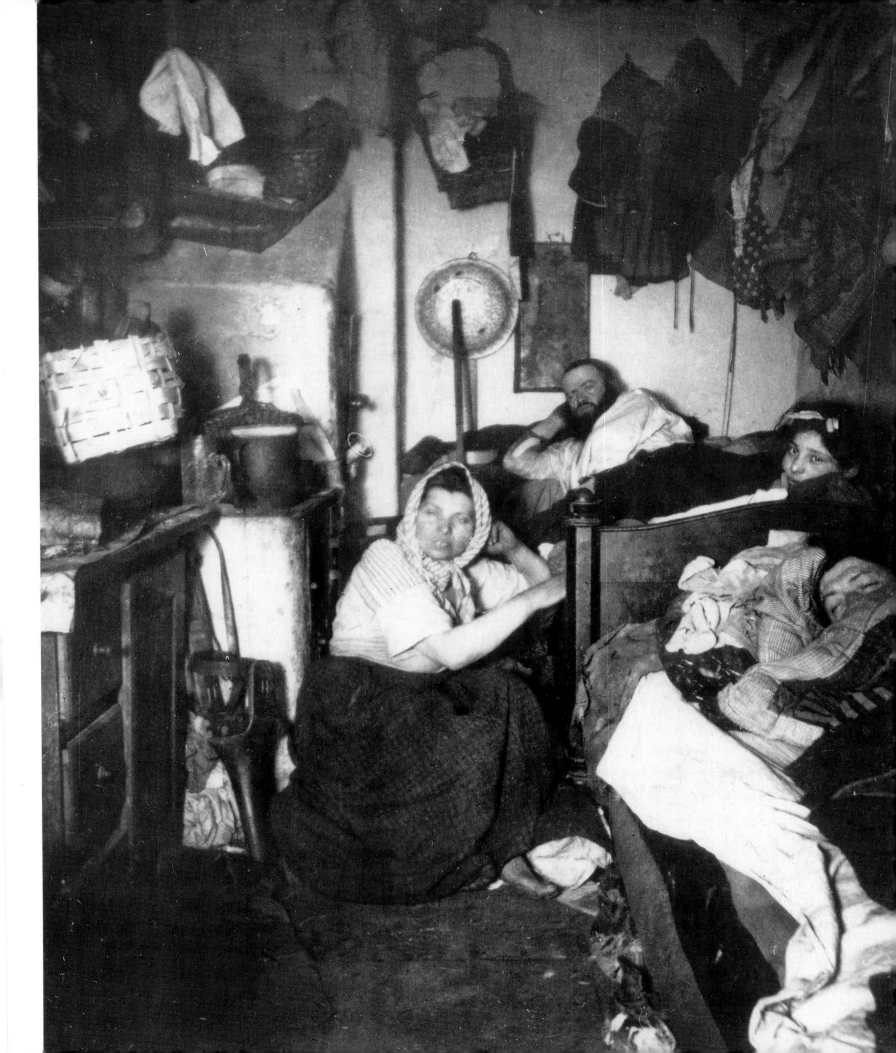

Particularly characteristic of this superior world is the immeasurable economic hardship inflicted on its inhabitants. This hopeless misery bordering on beggary has its own peculiarities and unique features, is easy to distinguish from English pauperism, and has little in common with the poverty of the Russian peasants. What distinguishes the Jewish pauper from his English colleague is his ability to pass on his penury undiminished to the next generation; and he himself could, with greater ease than many a German baron, compile an extensive genealogy of his beggary. It is to different historical causes that the Jewish pauper owes his origins: he is not an upper-class wastrel who has plunged to unfathomable depths; his native soil is as often the provincial town or village as the factory town. Economic circumstances may earn him the charming label "Lumpenproletarian," but in most cases he does not have the faintest idea of factory and industrial centers.
J. Eljashoff

The misery of the Lumpenproletariat . . .

Left: Scrap iron collectors in Berlin's Scheunenviertel. Photograph by Hans Thormann. 1930

Above: Beggars – a couple from Russian Poland in Vienna. Photograph by Anton and Hans Bock. Before 1920

Opposite page: Impoverished Jewish women on Grenadierstrasse in Berlin. Photograph by Friedrich Seidenstücker. 1930

We suffered terrible privation. There was not a kreutzer in the house, so Uncle Mareček made us a loan, but only . . . against collateral. When my blessed mother went to borrow a gulden, she took along the brass mortar and pestle and the brass candlestick; and when two gulden were needed, she supplemented the "collateral" with the last piece that remained, a wedding gift . . . the silver sugar tongs.
Alfred M. Havel-Ornstein

Between Berlin's proletarian east (Berlin O) and aristocratic west (Berlin W) lies the Bellevue district (Berlin NW, commonly known by Jews as the "Nebbich West"). Berlin O was the domain of the eastern Jews, who, strangely enough, settled on all the streets with military names, like Artilleriestrasse, Grenadierstrasse, and Dragonerstrasse, whereas the successful people lived in the west, in Charlottenburg, Wilmersdorf or the particularly fashionable Grunewald district. In Berlin, eastern Jew and western Jew were not so much geographical as chronological terms. It often happened that Jews who had emigrated from the east first settled on the above-mentioned streets. Gradually becoming prosperous, they moved to the more refined Bellevue district, home of the better variety of middle class, and then, climbing further up the social ladder, transferred their residence to Charlottenburg and became western Jews, who then looked down on the immigrant elements in eastern Berlin with great disdain.
Sammy Gronemann

Above: Grenadierstrasse in Berlin. Photograph by Walter Gircke. 1928

Right: Judengasse in Vienna, in the Inneren Stadt (inner city). 1915

The flexibility and alertness this generation needed to adapt to changing situations was astonishing. The hectic circumstances of the time demanded that the little man, particularly if he was a Jew, be adaptable if he did not want to go to wrack and ruin. That was something the previous generation had not been familiar with.
Conrad Rosenstein

*T*hen the kind of "business" one ran was important. There is the vague memory that the "Jewish district" already had currency exchange offices at that time, like the old houses of Lämel, Dormitzer, Löwenfeld, etc., which ranked highest and preceded the present-day banking houses. These were probably followed by the grocers, and the textile and dry goods dealers. Hardware stores, too, had a certain prestige as long as they sold new merchandise, whereas the genuine junk dealers, who sold scrap metal, old clothes, and all sorts of similar rubbish, were not even taken into account socially and would certainly never have been invited to any of the better bridge parties of the day.

These plebeian junk shops were usually run by women, who, dressed quite primitively, sat in front of their "vaults," gossiping and arguing noisily with their neighbors, neighbors who were just like them, for the whole lane plus the tiny, crooked, mysterious squares wedged in here and there, were actually like a single, huge room with an incredible commotion going on in it.

But the husbands of these very women, these industrious and banal women, usually represented or at least belonged to a respected, so to speak graduated class. They studied! That means they pondered and mused day after day, summer and winter, on obscure and as yet "unclarified" passages of Talmud, trying to find an ever new sense in the words and sentences whose hieroglyph-like structure allowed for many interpretations. Investigating such hidden interpretations and explanations was considered a meritorious task in life, although one knew quite well that many of the heads of families who devoted themselves to the profession of "learning" were men too incompetent or phlegmatic to display livelier activity . . .

Ottilie von Kahler

*I*n the early 1920s, Berlin became a center of the Jewish and Hebrew book trade.
<u>Right</u>: Jewish lending library on Grenadierstrasse in Berlin. Photograph by Walter Gircke. 1928
<u>Left</u>: Hebrew bookstore on Grenadierstrasse in Berlin. Ca. 1925
<u>Below</u>: Pet shop on Hirtenstrasse in Berlin. 1928

A small town is not good at expressing appreciation. It seemed enough to Hugo Frank that in all those years in Horb, neither he nor his wife or children were ever given any taste of anti-Semitism. But when, after 25 years, he moved to Stuttgart with his family in 1899, not only the Jewish congregation but Christian circles, too, had a farewell party for him to thank the man and his wife for who and what they were.

"That you are a Jew I needn't tell you," said the Mayor in his pronounced Swabian dialect, "you're proud of that, after all. But that we often said, if you want to know what a Christian is supposed to be, take a look at Hugo Frank and his wife Sophie, that I want to have told you now we're saying good-bye." It would not have occurred to a living soul to doubt that Hugo Frank was a German and a Swabian.
Fritz Frank

A s nearly all of these Jews observed the Law and lived strictly kosher, they had to deny themselves a great deal when it came to eating, for there was no kosher food to be had in the peasant villages. The spartanic way these merchants lived can hardly be imagined. They survived nearly the whole week on bread, sausage they had taken along, black coffee (they did not drink milk when they were away from home), and fruit. Naturally all of them had their tefillin with them, and the peasants were used to seeing their Jewish business associates putting on tefillin at their homes. I am sure that none of the cattle merchants of this generation ever shaved. On Friday, beards were clipped with a scissors or removed with a beastly-smelling lime preparation.
Samuel Spiro

I remember my grandfather . . . He was tall, thin, and, like all the men in the village, clean-shaven – not with a razor, which was not allowed to touch the cheeks of an honest Jew, but with a lime preparation . . . Apart from his little fields he also had a little shop and brought goods there by wheelbarrow from the nearby railroad station; sometimes when he had horses he used them and the little basket-carriage for his business. I sometimes saw him in the morning, putting on his phylacteries; he is bound to have understood the Hebrew prayers and could even write Hebrew. His German was quite respectable, and he spoke Czech with a mountain accent, like all the other people in the village.
Frantisek Langer

I t was not rare for the relationship between a farmer and the Jewish merchant of his choice to develop into a friendship that outlasted a single generation. In Hesse, business relations with the large landowners, the "tenants" as they were called there, became genuine partnerships, even if they were not so termed in the strictly legal sense. The trust these large landowners placed in their Jewish tradesmen was virtually boundless. In their eyes a Jew like that could do no wrong. He was their advisor, their confidant in all matters, from money to marriage. I would say he was – on a low social level – the direct successor of the "court Jew" of centuries past.
Henry Buxbaum

I would estimate that Bohemia had three or four hundred of these communities shortly after mid-century. Then the Jews fled the land. For economic, political, and cultural reasons they moved first to the district capital, then the provincial capital, and finally to Prague. The country communities were desolated; the rabbi was often one of the last Jews in every community; and as long as he lived, there was a community; when he died no new rabbi was hired; the birth and death registers, Torah scrolls, and liturgical objects were given to the nearest Jewish community (today even many of these are already depopulated).
Hugo Herrmann

A typical case was what happened shortly before the death of Sally Löwenstein, my sister's brother-in-law and a cattle merchant in Echzell. He was already on his deathbed and no longer able to get up when a farmer, one of his old customers, came to his house to ask his advice. Sally's competitor, a gentile cattle merchant, wanted to sell the farmer a milk cow and had assured him that the cow was a first-class milk producer. But the farmer felt lost without Sally's opinion. Sally was really too weak to get out of bed, but the farmer simply would not leave. If Sally could not take a look at the cow, he did not want to buy anything at all. Finally a way was found. Family and neighbors dragged Sally's heavy bed into the living room to the window that opened onto the street. The farmer brought the cow under the window and tied it up there. Then everyone helped to heave the bed with the sick man in it to the level of the window sill so he could study the animal thoroughly and make a decision. Only then did the farmer buy the cow.
Henry Buxbaum

The rural Jewish petit bourgeois . . .
Above: The Meyer family in front of their house in Bardewisch (Oldenburg). Ca. 1900

Opposite page, above: Butcher Elias Laupheim and his wife Klara, from Buchau (Württemberg). Ca. 1890
Opposite page, below: Wolf and Lina Hofheimer from Buchau (Württemberg). Ca. 1890

Jewish life in small Jewish communities [in the west], which I got to know both through my father's stories and personally, when I accompanied him on his inspection trips, was curious enough. It was totally different from life in the small communities in the east, where traces of traditional Jewish life had survived . . . In the west, there was no question of any kind of traditional Jewish life, if only because these communities were often diminutive . . . Some consisted of two or three Jewish families, and in one case a single family formed the community, which did not prevent them from having a mayor and a town council complete with statutes and minutes, etc. Usually there was a big Jewish cemetery bearing witness to the fact that a larger community had existed there once upon a time, and just maintaining it caused problems enough for the living.
Sammy Gronemann

From the family album of the assimilated bourgeoisie . . .

Left: Susanne Hahn, née Lazarus, from Hamburg, with seven of her eleven children. Daguerreotype by *Herman Biow*, a pioneer of early portrait photography. 1843

By that time the German Jews had already been emancipated for decades. But neither then nor later, when they had gained total legal equality, were they universally accepted as complete members of society; and that should actually have made every Jew think. However, very few took this inconspicuous fact seriously and arrived at the appropriate conclusion. Most of them persisted in their rapturous state, dazzled by the brilliance of European Christian culture. So luminous was it that minds liberated from oppression and narrowness had fallen ever more deeply under its spell since the days of the ghetto. In the intoxication of newly-acquired freedom – as if escaped from prison – they thought only of shedding the loosening fetters of Jewishness as completely as possible and adjusting utterly to their Christian surroundings in the belief that this way, whether converted or not, they would be able to elude their Jewish fate once and for all.
Paul Mühsam

Only complete, unconditional equality, which has by no means been bestowed on us as a gift or favor, as you seem to believe, but to which we have both a moral and a legal right, can compensate for the damage wrought on a noble race by thousands of years of oppression and humiliation. By working towards the goal of significantly widening the gap that is still by no means closed, by impeding the practical implementation of equality though never challenging its legal status, and thus preventing social assimilation, you are, in my opinion, laying yourself open to severe reproach. You are preventing the very thing you want: the development of a hard-working, patriotic bourgeoisie.
Levin Goldschmidt to Heinrich von Treitschke

The Jews struggled for emancipation – and this is the tragedy that moves us so much today – not for the sake of their rights as a people, but for the sake of assimilating themselves to the peoples among whom they lived. By their readiness to give up their peoplehood, by their act of disavowal, they did not put an end to their misery; they merely opened up a new source of agony. Assimilation did not, as its advocates had hoped, dispose of the Jewish question in Germany; rather it shifted the locus of the question and rendered it all the more acute. As the area of contact between the two groups widened, the possibilities of friction widened as well. The "adventure" of assimilation, into which the Jews threw themselves so passionately (it is easy to see why) necessarily increased the dangers that grew out of the heightened tension.
Gershom Scholem

In the period that concerns us, the proportion of observant Jews, i.e., those whose way of life more or less conformed to Jewish tradition, was roughly 20 percent of the total number of Jews in Germany. The remaining Jews had either totally or at least largely eliminated these traditions in their private lives. Certain residues of the tradition survived in varying degrees, particularly when it came to family life . . .

But only a very small, though conspicuous, minority lived by the principles that genuinely govern an observant life, such as strictly keeping the Sabbath, obeying the dietary laws inside and outside the house, and adhering to the sexual restrictions resulting from the laws pertaining to the women's ritual bath.

Gershom Scholem

<u>Above left and right</u>: Clementine Feldmann, née Wiener (1824–1860), and Dr. Siegmund Feldmann (1814–1864) from Prague. Daguerreotypes by Wilhelm Horn. Ca. 1845
<u>Right</u>: The family of Anselm Heinrich Dülken from Deutz. Ca. 1860

Left: The Rothschilds' original establishment ("Zum grünen Schild") on Frankfurt's Judengasse. Mayer Amschel Rothschild (1744–1812) founded the banking house that was to acquire international stature in the nineteenth century. The Frankfurt house ceased to exist in 1901. Ca. 1860
Opposite page, left: The F.V. Grünfeld Linens building on Leipziger Strasse in Berlin opened in 1889. Ca. 1900
Opposite page, right: A. Liebmann, luxury stationery store in Berlin, purveyor to the Prussian court; Crown Prince Wilhelm was among its customers. Ca. 1910

*I*n the pre-1914 era there were approximately 620,000 Jews in Germany who declared themselves as such. The number of Jews among the dissidents (those who declared themselves as having no religion) cannot be established; but one would hardly go wrong to assume that they accounted for a very small number – it grew larger in the twenties. The number of converts was significantly higher, and if the children or even grandchildren of these converted families are counted, the category would, according to Nazi statistics, which are fairly accurate in this respect, come to over 100,000. Though they had broken with Judaism both officially and in their own lives, the world around them still largely regarded them as Jews, usually to their considerable annoyance. During this period approximately a quarter of the children born into mixed marriages were preserved for Judaism; in the preceding two generations they had been as good as lost to it. Renunciation of Judaism and conversion are relevant to our subject in so far as they symbolized the conscious attempt at total assimilation, with the resulting sacrifice of everything Jewish, an attempt all of these people made but by no means all achieved. A further important factor is that over half of the Jews were concentrated in the ten cities of the Empire numbering more than half a million inhabitants, though apart from Berlin, with its approximately 200,000 Jews, the figures still remained astonishingly small. Frankfurt am Main, which probably possessed the most famous Jewish community in Germany, never had more than 30,000 Jews – and that in the year 1925, when they accounted for 7 percent of the population, whereas in 1875, their 12,000 still represented 11 percent. Most of the other Jews lived in the middle-sized towns, and only a minority of them were in small towns and villages, where the majority of Jews had originally lived. But it is interesting to note that around 1930, some 30 percent of the Jews in Württemberg and Bavaria could still be found in small towns and villages.

Gershom Scholem

Many Jewish students came from the eastern provinces of Germany, and not a few of them were from pious families; but very few were to remain faithful to the Law. Most of them came from liberal, assimilatory backgrounds and had grown up without any, or any profound, Jewish knowledge. What most of them had in common was their total lack of interest in the Jewish-national question.
Aron Sandler

Most of the Jewish boys attended the Friedrichs-Werdersche Gymnasium [academically oriented high school], whereas the 13th Realschule, which ended in the Obersekundareife [non-academically oriented diploma] had comparatively few Jewish students. The Kirschner School was a special case and will be discussed in greater detail here because it can be described from personal experience. It was located not in the Hansa district but in Moabit. Despite the greater distance, many Jewish parents decided for this school because they preferred the curriculum, with its emphasis on modern languages and natural science, to a classical [Greek and Latin] syllabus; that this was to be an advantage in later emigration could naturally not be foreseen at the time. The proportion of Jewish students, particularly in the Realgymnasium [modern subjects] division, was about one third or one quarter up to the end of the Obersekunda [seventh year], in the three higher classes it was smaller. Relationships between Jewish and non-Jewish students were generally not close, the reason being that

the two groups differed not only with respect to religion and background but also to economic status. Most of the Jewish students lived in the Hansa district and were middle-class, while most of the non-Jewish students lived in petit bourgeois Moabit, though there was, of course, overlapping in both directions. It was therefore understandable that many non-Jews envied their Jewish classmates' better living conditions; for the Jews, large apartments (with servants) and annual summer vacations were often matters of course, whereas their own families lived in modest circumstances (frequently their fathers were minor civil servants). This difference, in conjunction with the anti-Semitism that tended to exist in any case, had an effect on the atmosphere, and many of the non-Jewish students later joined the National Socialist Party. Most of the teachers were politically right-wing. For example, when a Jewish student made reference to the anniversary of the March Revolution of 1848 in his speech at a graduation ceremony, several teachers left the auditorium in protest and the speech was terminated. But it is interesting that after 1933, some of these teachers steadfastly refused to make a pact with the Nazis. Conversely some of the teachers who had been considered comparatively progressive later threw themselves enthusiastically into the arms of the new regime.
Werner Rosenstock

Human progress and the consolidation of the emancipatory idea, whether through political liberalism or the Social Democratic Party program, were expected to bring salvation for the Jews, in particular the total disappearance of anti-Semitism. That was a conviction shared by young and old, east and west, in academic and non-academic circles. This optimism paired with German patriotism made them all, whether pious or freethinking, into anti-Zionists as a matter of principle.
Aron Sandler

The special feature of this kind of central European culture does indeed lie in a unique synthesis of relentlessly critical intellect and faultless bourgeois propriety. Traditional taboos and conventional lies are demystified with melancholy perspicacity, while the very integrity of this analytical, scholarly seriousness causes any gesture of bohemian revolt or blatant avant-gardism to be rejected. People like Freud and Schnitzler hurl social fetishes from their pedestals, but write bashful letters to a bride (Freud) and wear the sad face of the nineteenth century (Schnitzler).
Claudio Magris

<u>Below left and right</u>: Alexandra Adler, sister of Alfred Adler, the founder of individual psychology, in Vienna. Ca. 1870

Gustav Mahler at the age of six in Iglau (Moravia). Ca. 1865

Above: The first grade of the municipal Jewish elementary school in Essen. 1922

Below: The "Octava" of the Akademisches Gymnasium (Academic High School) in Vienna; one of the elite schools of the Monarchy, its students included such future luminaries as Peter Altenberg and Arthur Schnitzler. 1891/92. In the second row from the top, second from the left: Hugo von Hofmannsthal. A fellow student's handwritten note on the cardboard backing of the photo indicates that the class had 14 Catholics, 3 Protestants, 20 Jews, and "3 or 4 with some Jewish blood."

I would distinguish between approximately the following strata:

1. Those whose self-awareness told them they were totally "Germanized," who lived at or beyond the boundaries of Jewishness, were half-Jews or converted, favored mixed marriages, were completely alienated from everything Jewish, and play a disproportionate role in the literature on the subject. These include, at the inner periphery, the totally assimilated Jews who, out of some feeling of honor, shrank back from conversion and remained Jews. That was a small marginal group, who might assemble in the organization of so-called "German-national Jews." Judaism no longer represented a problem to these groups. They considered themselves altogether German, and felt neither a need for nor an obligation towards the Jewish heritage. From their standpoint, all problems between Jews and Germans had been solved. They were inclined to associate almost exclusively with people of like character or with Germans who were ready to accept them in the same spirit. Their ignorance of everything Jewish was total. In certain striking cases they adopted anti-Semitic attitudes and arguments . . .

2. The transition to the main stratum, whom I consider of the greatest interest to our observations, is formed by the rich Jews: this group overlaps with the one mentioned above in so far as its members were, with very few exceptions, totally assimilated, and a substantial proportion were on the road to conversion and had largely reduced Jewish ties to a minimum. Because this group had so much security, it was easier to commit the fundamental error of regarding them as typical of German Jewry. Their wealth was usually of relatively or very recent origin, for the overwhelming proportion of prosperous or very rich families from the first half of the nineteenth century had long moved into the stratum of totally assimilated Jews. That made this group particularly vulnerable, as so many of them displayed the features of the nouveaux riches . . .

They tended to have political affiliations with the moderate Liberals and gave them financial support, but believed in providing their children with a rigorously patriotic upbringing . . .

3. By far the largest group numerically was the liberal Jewish middle class, the middle and petit bourgeoisie . . . Here, with respect to the individual's self-awareness, Judaism – its religious concepts, traditional practices, and customs – had largely been lost without having been totally abandoned . . . Fragments of the ritual were widely practiced: for example, the high Jewish holidays were observed, or Friday night and the Seder celebrated, or women attended synagogue on holidays when there were services commemorating deceased parents or children. The Bar Mitzvah celebration, when a son enters his fourteenth year, was also retained by the large majority of this group . . . Education and reading were limited exclusively to the German cultural sphere . . .

Above: Dr. Werner and his family with other physician friends on an outing in the vicinity of Vienna. Ca. 1910

Below: The Fischer family from Vienna on a Sunday excursion. Before 1914

Assimilation went very far.

All of us shared the fundamental conviction that the overwhelming majority of Jews around us lived in a vacuum and – more problematic and more exasperating to us – in a world of self-deception, where they took their wishes for reality and consciously feasted their eyes on a phantasm of German-Jewish harmony that corresponded to nothing in life. Retrospectively, I am more convinced than I could have been in the passion of my protest-filled youth that in many of these people, illusion and utopia ran together and perhaps awakened anticipatory feelings of happiness at being "at home." There was something really authentic in that, namely the authentic quality that we must grant utopia. I harbor some doubts as to the extent of the authenticity of this feeling; that it existed, I do not wish to deny. The more enchanting the dream, the more terrible the awakening. There is no way to do justice to German Jewry of that time without acknowledging that mixture of self-deception and a genuine wish for happiness.
Gershom Scholem

Above: A large bourgeois family in eastern Galicia. Ca. 1910
Right: Young members of the bourgeoisie in Warsaw. 1938

"*Spinoza, Heine, Lassalle . . . these are your three heroes,*" *Isaac used to tell his father,* "*you are pushing their works into my hands, you read them with me and you are passing on to me your enthusiasm for their philosophy and their ideas. All three of them left Judaism and religion or transcended it. And you want me to remain true and faithful to what already for Spinoza in the seventeenth century was an anachronism and for Heine and Lassalle nearly a hundred years ago was ridiculous. You want me to accept meekly the life you mapped out for me and yet all your heroes were rebels, apostates, subverters.*"
Isaac Deutscher

I was hardly three feet tall when my father began telling me: "*By nationality you are not a Pole, not a Ruthenian, not a Jew – you are a German.*" *But even then he as often told me:* "*By faith you are a Jew.*"
Karl Emil Franzos

The reasons – political, sociological, and technical in nature – are obvious. The regular clientele of these coffeehouses, like the intellectually and artistically interested public altogether, was largely Jewish. Prior to 1938, there were almost a quarter of a million Jews living in Vienna. Today they number barely ten thousand. That is the one thing, and there is no questioning it. Certainly it applies in other areas of public life as well, but not with such lasting and profound effects as here. This is not to say that there are no literary people, no intellectuals, no artistically interested people left in Vienna. Of course they exist. But not only have they been perceptibly reduced in number, their opportunities to visit coffeehouses have been reduced as well. They are – and this is where sociology comes in – busy. They have things to do. They are only potential, no longer actual coffeehouse regulars now. They bring with them all the requirements of a habitué except themselves. They have no time. And having time is the most important, the one indispensable prerequisite for coffeehouse culture (and probably for any kind of culture at all). The habitués of the earlier literary cafés were busy too: their busyness consisting partly in sitting in the coffeehouse, partly in doing things they could and wanted to get done at the coffeehouse. They wrote novels and poetry there, received and answered their mail there, were telephoned there, and if they happened not to be in, the waiter would take a message for them. They met their friends and enemies there, were sought out there by anyone who wanted to talk to them. They read their papers there, debated the topics of the day there, lived there. (For many years, Kürschner's literary calendar gave "Café Central, Wien I" as Peter Altenberg's address.) The only thing they did at home was sleep. Their real home was the coffeehouse.
Friedrich Torberg

*A "Stammtisch" [habitués' table] is a table at which the incivilities, impertinences, and vanities of fellow human beings grow to gigantic proportions in the evening! A swill-bucket for everything that has annoyed and upset the busy living-machine during the day! To try and ease the burden on myself, I have therefore decided to charge some modest fees. Nursery anecdotes and wondrous experiences with the little ones: 70 hellers!
A man's attempts to embarrass or denigrate his wife or mistress or to make her look a fool: 1 crown 20! Revenge taken by either sex for something that angered them during the day: 80 hellers! A gentleman's conspicuous attempt to agree with any foolishness a lady may express: 1 crown 40! Conversations about hygiene that do not correspond to the teachings of my "prodromos": 90 hellers!*

Attempts to conquer a soul that, like all souls, belongs to me: 3 crowns 80! Sitting too close to a woman that appeals to me: 5 crowns! On the evening I introduced my charges, Mr. T. paid me:

		70 hellers
1 crown	20	hellers
		80 hellers
1 crown	40	hellers
		90 hellers
3 crowns	80	hellers
5 crowns	–	hellers

| 13 crowns 80 hellers |

Peter Altenberg

A definition of the coffeehouse literati? People who have time to sit in a coffeehouse pondering what other people outside are not experiencing.
Anton Kuh

I divide literature into a head table and an adjacent table.
Anton Kuh

*T*he coffeehouse is a "world view . . . whose innermost objective is not to view the world," wrote Alfred Polgar.
Below: The Grabencafé in Vienna. Photograph by *Emil Mayer.* 1908

Opposite page: The large reading room at the Café Griensteidl in Vienna, famous as the meeting-place of the "Jung-Wien" (Young Vienna) literary group. 1897

*He considered whether he should go into the café. He did not really feel keen on it. . . . George was not much attracted by the other young people, most of them Jewish writers, with whom he had recently struck up a casual acquaintance, even though he had thought many of them not at all uninteresting. Speaking broadly, he found their tone to each other now too familiar, now too formal, now too facetious, now too sentimental: not one of them seemed really free and unembarrassed with the others, scarcely indeed with himself. . . .
He for his part knew that it was not so much friendship that attracted him to the young author, as the curiosity to get to know a strange man more intimately. Perhaps also the interest of looking into a world which up to the present had been more or less foreign to him.*
Arthur Schnitzler

*At a café there is no intellect, no mood, no knowledge. The only thing that reigns there is His Majesty's Whim.
Cafés kill friendships and enmities: a demoralizing sitting-around-next-to-one-another, a sad cameraderie in feeble-mindedness.
At a café no one acts but everyone talks.*
Berthold Viertel

The air is alive with figures and miasmas. Upon entering, one is greeted by tumultuous shouting, perceived at first as inarticulate sounds. Gradually, noisy cries in all inflections – barked, bellowed, chirped, croaked – can be made out, most of them intended to emphasize a point. Only when one listens more closely can one begin to distinguish: . . . says he! – Say that to him! – What shall I say! – That's what you say! – And if I say so! – Well, I say so! – Listen, just let me say something! – So, what shall I say? – What do you say to that! – HE says! – About him I should say something! – I mean what I say!
Karl Kraus

*The two big streets in Leopoldstadt are Taborstrasse and Praterstrasse. Praterstrasse is almost manorial. It is the direct way to entertainment. Jews and Christians populate it. It is smooth, broad, and bright. It has many cafés.
There are many cafés in Taborstrasse, too. Jewish cafés. Their owners are usually Jewish, their patrons almost always are. The Jews like to go to the coffeehouse to read the paper, play tarok and chess, and do business. Jews are good chess players. They may have*

Christian partners. A good Christian chess player cannot be an anti-Semite. The Jewish cafés have standing patrons, who form a "running clientele" in the literal sense. They are habitués, though they do not partake of food or drink. They come to the restaurant eighteen times in the run of a morning. On business. They make a great deal of noise. They speak urgently, loudly, uninhibitedly. Because all of the customers are well-bred men of the world, no one attracts notice, however noticeable he may be.
At a genuine Jewish coffeehouse, you can carry your head under your arm. No one will bother about it.
Joseph Roth

Coffeehouses are the Viennese vice. There are few alcoholics in Vienna and even fewer morphinists, but there are many thousands of coffeehouse addicts. Time flies at the coffeehouse. It is a place to play cards and billiards, to read the paper, smoke a cigarette, talk, write letters, and meet people who are so interesting that one could never invite them home. In Vienna, a disdainful way of describing an acquaintance is to call him: a coffeehouse acquaintance. The coffeehouse is where one runs from the family, from wives – after women . . .
Otto Friedländer

I found many acquaintances from Vienna at that coffeehouse. Many gifted people had been born in Vienna, but they later went to Berlin. Only when they had become successful there would they achieve recognition at home. So the artists' haunts of Berlin were swarming with young Austrians. Nonetheless I soon discovered that there was an enormous difference between bohemian life in the two cities. Here in Berlin everything was fiercer and flashier, whether Weltanschauungen, artistic fads, or vices. The militarism of the reign of Wilhelm II and the patriarchal regime of Franz Joseph aroused completely different kinds of opposition in rebellious young people. In Austria scions of the bourgeoisie thought themselves heaven knows how radical if they sympathized with Victor Adler and the Social Democrats. In Berlin they were anarchists and talked about throwing bombs. In Vienna an affair with a "sweet girl" from the suburbs was the epitome of libertinism. In Berlin there were male prostitutes, and nightclubs where men in make-up and women's clothes danced with each other. In Vienna they drank wine, in Berlin they sniffed cocaine.
Arnold Höllriegel

One very important thing was to keep being seen, for days, weeks, and months. The visits to the Romanisches Café (and, on a lofty

level, to Schlichter and Schwanecke), which were certainly pleasurable, were not meant for pleasure alone. They were also impelled by the need for self-manifestations, a need that no one eluded. If you didn't want to be forgotten, you had to be seen. This obtained for every rank and every stratum, even for any moocher who went from table to table in the Romanisches Café, always getting something, so long as he maintained the character he performed and did not tolerate any distortion of it.
Elias Canetti

The Café Leu, frequented by presidents, representatives, and staff of the congregations, was, so to speak, at the pulse of Berlin Jewry. The distinguished preacher from the Grosse Synagoge, Dr. Weisse, a sort of bishop of Mosaic origin, went there from time to time. It was there that the Talmudist Albert Katz philosophized and was teased by Fabius Schach. It was there that the Zionists fought their battles against the "Centralvereinler," that the Orthodox conspired against the Liberals and the Liberals fought it out with the Orthodox. It was there that western Jews refused to deal with eastern Jews, and eastern Jews provoked their western brethren from across the table. It was there that charity drives were begun and news of anti-Semitic outrages came over the telegraph. It was there that, with caustic derision and loving heart, Sammy Gronemann caricatured the whole "tempest in a teacup."
Conrad Rosenstein

In the Germany of Wilhelm II the younger generation grew up without the slightest grasp of the realities of political and social life. The Café Grössenwahn (Megalomania) in Berlin and its counterpart in Munich, the Café Stefanie, were like islands in a vast, inimical ocean, and to the rest of the population their inhabitants seemed like neurotic savages. When Wilhelm's Germany collapsed one day and the young opposition came to power, they were a total failure. During that moment in the year 1919 when the Café Stefanie ruled Munich, the artists from the café covered the walls of the city with futuristic posters that no ordinary citizen understood; and the literati, some of whom were high-minded, kind-hearted idealists, could not find the language of the masses they were supposed to rouse and lead. But there was one man in Munich who already knew how to speak the language of the mob even then: Hitler.
Arnold Höllriegel

This convergence of various intellectual force fields – modern post-war theatrical culture, Toller, Brecht, caustic satirical cabaret, politics at the "Zwiebelfisch" (Onion fish), the increasingly crooked goings-on at the Kurfürstendamm cafés, and . . . Russian emigré life – created a heady atmosphere with an intoxicating, bewildering and occasionally personality-threatening effect on the sensitive individual. At least that is how I felt.
Bruno Ostrovsky

Right: Sigmund Freud and his daughter Anna on summer vacation in the Dolomites. 1913
Left: Abraham Sonne (fourth from the left) and Richard Beer-Hofmann (fourth from the right) with their families and friends on summer vacation in Mayrhofen in the Zillertal (Tyrol). 1922

The institution of summer vacation involved certain customs like the arrival telegram or the family whistle. The latter, usually a theme from an opera by Wagner, served to inform parties that belonged together of everyone's location if they threatened to lose each other in the hubbub of a railroad station or when an excursion steamer landed. The telegram was to notify the father, who was still at home, that everyone had arrived at their destination and inevitably began with the words "arrived safely." Telegrams, not to mention inter-city telephone calls, still had an air of excitement, whether festive or ominous, about them; they were kept very terse and, if necessary, held out the prospect of more detailed information with the phrase "letter follows." (A now famous example of such a case: "Be worried, letter follows.") Telegrams were never sent on ordinary occasions. It had to be an extraordinary event. And arrival at one's summer holiday destination was one.
Friedrich Torberg

Left: Theodor Herzl with family and friends on summer vacation in Altaussee in the Salzkammergut (Styria). Ca. 1900

Right: Hasidic Jews in Krynica-Zdroj, the most famous spa in Poland. Ca. 1930

The Spring Season of 1894 was shaping up so well that we decided to go to the seaside. "Being seen" was important; after all, a girl with money might fall in love with us. Joseph went to Westerland-Sylt and I to Helgoland for a week. At the time, people who indulged in seaside vacations were regarded as rich. There was little traveling done as a rule, ordinary employees never went on vacation.
Isidor Hirschfeld

"Now look, children. It's not that Marienbad is so beautiful – lots of places are beautiful. But it has very good coffeehouses, where you get all the newspapers – you can get a decent meal at a few of the restaurants – the theater isn't bad at all, especially with the guest performances in summer – you meet people there – and that little bit of fresh air, well, you just have to live with it."
Friedrich Torberg

Right: Rabbis in Karlsbad (Bohemia), the most elegant spa in the Austro-Hungarian Monarchy. Ca. 1900

139

Apart from Jewish history, Zionism, and Palestinology, other topics were also discussed at our "at home evenings": contemporary literature, theater, and art. Our intensive track and field training took place at the university sports field in Grunewald on Thursday afternoons and Sunday mornings. Members of the Bar Kochba and active members of the sports fraternity of Jewish students (Sport V. J. St.) also trained there on Sunday mornings. Sport V. J. St.'s most prominent representative was Ernst Simon, later 800-meter champion of Brandenburg. Very impressed by Simon's victory, we did everything we could to emulate his athletic skills. Herbert Treumann, the tallest in our group, distinguished himself particularly. Son of the screen star Wanda Treumann, he soon became an outstanding junior athlete, especially in the 400-meter competition.
Felix Simmenauer

Left: Members of the Bar Kochba (Jewish athletics club) in Berlin. 1902
Opposite page and below: Athletes from Vienna's Hakoah sports club. Two of the most successful male long-distance runners were Arpad Blödy (left) and Walter Frankl; Frankl won the Austrian championship several times in the late 1920s. Photographs by Lothar Rübelt. Ca. 1928

Berlin, the capital of the Empire, turned into a center for Jewish sports . . . Apart from the Jewish athletics and sports club "Bar Kochba-Hakoah," there were four other associations that belonged to the German "Maccabee" circle: the "Hagibor" Jewish sports club (Hebrew for "the strong Jew"), the "Maccabee" Jewish boxing club, the "Bar Kochba" tennis club, and the "Iwria" Jewish rowing club. In addition to these increasingly Zionist oriented organizations, there were the many groups belonging to the "Schild" (Shield) athletics union of the Reichsbund jüdischer Frontsoldaten (Imperial league of front-line soldiers) and those of the Verband jüdisch-neutraler Turn- und Sport-Vereine (VINTUS – Federation of neutral Jewish athletics and sports associations). These organizations were joined after 1933 by a number of further ones, founded by ejected former members of now "Aryanized" organizations.
Kurt Schilde

In his youth, my father was very active in the Berliner Turnerschaft (gymnastics team), in other words, in an organization clearly representative of the petite bourgeoisie of the liberal period. Several brothers and other relatives belonged to it as well. When anti-Semitic tendencies appeared and swept through the team in the 1890s, he withdrew to passive membership, while one of his brothers helped to found the first Jewish gym club in Berlin in the early years of the twentieth century.
Gershom Scholem

Left: Favoritner A.C. against Hakoah on the FAC field in Vienna. Photograph by Lothar Rübelt. 1928

The Hakoah football team won the Austrian championship in 1925.

Right: Swimmers in the starting area of the Dianabad in Vienna. Photograph by Lothar Rübelt. 1926

Below: The water polo team of Hakoah Vienna, founded in 1922, won the Austrian title for three consecutive years, from 1926 to 1928. Photograph by Lothar Rübelt. Ca. 1925

Friedrich Torberg, who made his debut with Hakoah Vienna, was a member of Hagibor Prague when that team won the Czechoslovakian championship in 1928. His novel *Die Mannschaft* (The Team) was a memorial to Jewish water polo.

For the spring championship game at the Brigittenauer AC field, Hakoah had to compete against the home team, who were in second-to-last position in the rankings, only one point ahead of Vorwärts 06. If the Brigittenauer team lost against Hakoah, Vorwärts 06 would still have a chance of saving itself from relegation to the third division. Consequently all the Vorwärts supporters appeared at the Brigittenau to "root" for Hakoah. For the longest time the score was 0:0. Despite their superiority in the field, the Hakoah forwards had no opportunities to score against the solid Brigittenauer defense. Then, finally, that nimble outside left Norbert Katz received a long pass and started

running towards the Brigittenauer goal. The cheers of the crowd rose to a roar, with the Vorwärts supporters naturally joining in. One Vorwärts supporter in particular was leaning against the barrier and screaming himself hoarse. It is customary in these situations to cheer the player on by name – but the enthusiastic spectator didn't know Katz's name. And the term he would ordinarily have applied to a Jew, namely "Saujud" (Jewish pig), did not really seem appropriate under the circumstances. So he screamed "Come on!" and again, "Come on!" Then suddenly he had a flash of inspiration. His next shout went: "Come on, Mr. Jew!"
Friedrich Torberg

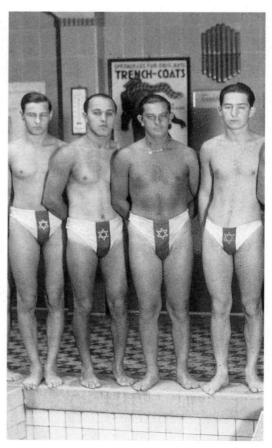

Left: Maccabee Championships in Berlin. Photograph by *Abraham Pisarek*. 1935
The winners of the women's competitions from left to right: Martel Jacob, Berlin; Ruth Reich, Berlin; Lore Meyer, Frankfurt; Lotte Eichhorn, Berlin; Ilse Borchardt, Berlin.
Below: Athletic meet in Zilina (Slovakia); the banner reads: "Support the young Maccabees!" 1932
Opposite page: Helene Mayer, German champion in women's foil fencing for many years. 1930 Although she had already emigrated, she competed for Germany once more at the 1936 Berlin Olympics, winning a silver medal; the following year – already competing for the United States – she became world champion.

*Y*es, *that is how it was. Jews were not admitted to German rowing associations. The same applied to German university fraternities. Discrimination had its place in the Weimar Republic as it had in the German empire before it. Long before the nationalist tyranny. My father thought about informing the Centralverein about the matter, and suggested at the same time that I should join the Kameraden. I was not unfamiliar with the Jüdische Sport- und Wanderverein Kameraden ("Comrades" Jewish sports and hiking club). It was a youth group affiliated with the Centralverein deutscher Staatsbürger jüdischen Glaubens (Central association of German citizens of Jewish faith). My father had been one of the first members of the Centralverein (founded in 1893). Like the Verein zur Abwehr des Antisemitismus (Association for the prevention of anti-Semitism) founded in 1890, which also had non-Jewish members, such as Hermann Sudermann, Gustav Freytag and Theodor Mommsen, the organization fought the spread of anti-Semitism. An undertaking doomed to failure, considering that anti-Semitism is a more than one-thousand-year-old evil.*
The idea behind the C.V. was: "to assemble German citizens of Jewish faith, regardless of their religious and political orientation, in order to reinforce them in their exercise of equal rights as citizens and members of society and to support them in their unerring cultivation of the German mentality." The ideology of the Centralverein (assimilation to the greatest possible extent) stood in marked contrast to another movement, whose maxim was: self-emancipation.
Felix Simmenauer

But as the Jews' physical accomplishments are continually – and irresponsibly – being disputed, it needs to be pointed out from time to time that in fencing and tennis Helene Mayer and Daniel Prenn won world titles for Germany (1928 Olympics and 1932 Davis Cup), as Dr. Fuchs had been saber champion for Hungary some years earlier. Among the athletes who acquitted themselves honorably for their countries in other fields, the Hakoah soccer team and the glider pilot Kronfeld distinguished themselves for Austria; France had the tennis players Suzanne Lenglen and René Lacoste; Finland had the runner Katz; France also had the aviatrix Lena Bernstein. That Jews had always been strongly involved in helping boxing to achieve its present-day gladiatorial pre-eminence is confirmed by the history of the sport, from Daniel Mendoza, who was responsible for the acceptance, in London in 1790, of fixed rules and the use of gloves, to the American boxer Max Baer, who defeated Max Schmeling. If we had to prove Jewish courage by listing Jewish boxing champions, we could quickly come up with a dozen famous names.
Arnold Zweig

Elsa Galafres (born Berlin 1879, died in exile) originally wanted to be a pianist and gave a concert at Philharmonic Hall in Berlin as early as 1893. But she soon decided to become an actress and received her first major engagement at the Hoftheater (Court Theater) in Berlin in 1895. She moved to Vienna with her second husband, the composer and pianist Ernst von Dohnányi, in 1904 (she had divorced her first husband, the famous violinist *Bronislaw Huberman*, after a brief marriage). Elsa collaborated with von Dohnányi on musical "pantomimes in scenes," for example *Schleier der Pierrette* (Pierrette's veil), after a story by *Arthur Schnitzler*. Elsa and Ernst von Dohnányi spent the period from the twenties until their emigration to the United States in Budapest, where the pantomime *Die heilige Fackel* (The Sacred Torch) received its premiere.
<u>Left</u>: Elsa Galafres. Photograph by *d'Ora*. 1910

*V*eza's mystery was in her smile. She was conscious of it and could evoke it. But once it had appeared, she was unable to revoke it. It persisted, and then it seemed to be her actual face whose beauty deceived so long as it didn't smile. Sometimes, she closed her eyes when smiling, her black lashes plunged deep, grazing her cheeks. At such times, she seemed to be contemplating herself from the inside, with her smile as a light. The way she appeared to herself was her mystery; yet, despite her silence, you didn't feel excluded. Her smile, a shimmering rainbow, reached from her to the observer. Nothing is more irresistible than the temptation to enter another person's inner space. If he is someone who knows how to place his words, his silence intensifies the temptation to the utmost. You set out to obtain his words and you hope you will find them in back of his smile, where they await the visitor.
Veza's restraint could not be overcome, for it was permeated with grief. She fed her grief incessantly; she was sensitive to every pain if it was someone else's pain. She suffered from another person's humiliation, as though experiencing it herself. She didn't stop at mere

sympathy: she showered the humiliated with praise and gifts.
She bore such pains long after they had been alleviated. Her grief was abysmal: it contained and preserved everything that was unjust. Her pride was very great and could easily be wounded. But she granted the same vulnerability to anyone else and imagined herself surrounded by sensitive people who needed her protection and whom she never forgot.
Elias Canetti

*I*n this one movement, when she raised her arms, lay all her beauty. Her movement simultaneously evoked every aspect of beauty, supplication, disrobing, denial and submission. She lowered her arms. The right hand began to stretch a glove over the left with scrupulous care.
Joseph Roth

*T*he long-established fashion house of Ludwig Zwieback & Bruder opened its elegant new headquarters in a spacious building at the corner of Weihburggase and Kärntner Strasse in Vienna (First District) in 1895. It also had branches in Graz, Budapest, and Karlsbad. The premises on Kärntner Strasse offered a broad range of services for the sophisticated woman. There were hundreds of saleswomen to help them and models to show the clothes, some of which were made in the company's own ateliers. The company's exquisite apparel was delivered by messenger if the customer so desired. There was also a restaurant, a tea room, and an American Bar in the building to supply refreshment.
<u>Above</u>: Salon of Ludwig Zwieback & Bruder. Photograph by *d'Ora*. 1913

Above: Edith Wohlgemuth from Agram (Croatia). Ca. 1925
Below: "Aunt Toni" from Breslau. Ca. 1910

Right: Ida Coblenz. Ca. 1900. The only woman in the life of poet Stefan George (1868–1933), she later married the poet Richard Dehmel (1863–1920).

He said to her: "I know the ten thousand variations of your beloved face. I know the slackness of boredom and the tension of stimulating hours! I know the death mask of disappointment and the artist's transfiguration of reverie. I can never be sure of you and you spare me the terrible, barbaric belief that I ever could! Worlds eternally ebb and flow on that most beloved of faces, and I stand before that surging ocean, helpless and yet awash with adoration!"
Peter Altenberg

<u>Right</u>: Unemployed seamstress in Bialystok (Poland). 1921

Oppenheim, Gabriele, and Paul: known for their "Déjeuner" on Saturdays from 12:30 to 4:00 p.m. at the house at Schaumainkai 55, where two dozen intellectuals were generally invited for an excellent meal. Invitations were extended informally, i.e., by telephone, and went to "people who fit together, but not too well" (Gabriele Oppenheim-Errera). Though care was taken to ensure a variety of participants, there was an established group of regular guests, including Paul Tillich, Theodor Wiesengrund-Adorno, and the neurologist Kurt Goldstein. Conversation, though not restricted to specific questions, often circled around a single topic, perhaps a participant's account of a conference or trip, or the discussion of a new book, etc. Gabriele Oppenheim née Errera (from the Brussels family) "was a very pretty, provocative blond, who flirted with every male creature within reach of her flashing eyes" (Max Born). Paul Oppenheim, the son of the jewel merchant Moritz Oppenheim, was a mathematician and for a time an employee of the I.G.-Farben Concern.
Wolfgang Schivelbusch

Berta Zuckerkandl (Vienna 1867 – Paris 1945) was a daughter of the newspaper publisher and journalist Moriz Szeps, one of the founders of modern Austrian journalism. Her sister Sophie married René Clemenceau, a cousin of the French statesman Georges Clemenceau. Bertha's husband Emil Zuckerkandl was one of the most distinguished anatomists at the Zweite Wiener Medizinische Schule (Second Viennese medical school). The Zuckerkandls had one of Vienna's most illustrious literary and cultural salons, frequented by such luminaries as *Gustav Mahler*, *Arthur Schnitzler*, and *Hugo von Hofmannsthal*. Berta herself had a literary bent and began writing articles (for instance, theater and art reviews for the *Allgemeine Wiener Zeitung*) early on, championing, among other things, the modern arts and crafts movement of the "Wiener Werkstätte." She published a collection of essays in 1907 (*Zeitkunst* [Contemporary Art]); her memoirs, *Österreich intim* (Austria, An Intimate View), appeared posthumously. She emigrated to France in 1938.

What the salon of Franziska von Arnstein was to Vienna's social life at the beginning of the century, the hospitable, generous home of Josefine von Wertheimstein née Gomperz represented in the period of maturing emancipation. "Une reine poétique de la societé viennoise," Taillendier called her. That this was no exaggeration is proven by the many letters from poets and artists who saw the Wertheimsteins' as their spiritual home.
Franz Kobler

Your last letter is terribly sad. It shows that the poor woman (Josefine von Wertheimstein) is exhausted from her long physical suffering and has no strength left . . . She must be so ill that her spirit can no longer prevail over her physical afflictions, otherwise she would certainly forget her own distress, if only out of kindness to those around her. I do not delude myself: we must fear the worst; and I spend despondent hours thinking how dreary it will be to go about in Vienna and to work without ever seeing our dear friend again.
There is no denying it, the happy hours we were assured of are over now; but that would not matter. We want to share her grief and spend hours in vain attempts to comfort her – if she is still with us at all. It would be the end of all my joy, that I know . . .
Moritz von Schwind to Eduard von Bauernfeld

I want . . . to thank you in the name of art, which you . . . loved, valued – understood as did few others . . . How deep was your perception, how refined your taste . . . how finely you knew how to distinguish genuine from sham. You were able to do it . . . because you yourself had the spark that kindled a flame in others. And that was the spell you cast on all artists. They were happy in your presence . . .
Times have changed. It is not for us to complain . . . But I can only hope that in this and later eras there will be women who, like you, though in their own way, spread their blessings wherever they go – women as esteemed, admired, and loved as you were . . .
Ferdinand von Saar at the grave of Josefine von Wertheimstein

The muses were also at home with Frau Josefine von Wertheimstein's family: with the kind-hearted Baroness Sophie Todesco, who received almost all of the Villa Wertheimstein's friends in her own art-filled rooms; with Professor Theodor Gomperz, the stimulating historian of Greek philosophy; with the Brünn [Brno] industrialist Julius Gomperz, whose wife, the singer Karoline Bettelheim, made their pied-à-terre in Vienna into a genuine Vienna music salon for months at a time.
Adolf Wilbrandt

Above: Drawing room of the Villa Wertheimstein in Vienna's select residential district of Döbling, where Josefine von Wertheimstein received the intellectual elite of Vienna. Ca. 1900

Below: At Vienna's Cercle-Club; seated at the left, Baron Alfons Rothschild, head of the Vienna branch of the banking house. Photograph by Lothar Rübelt. 1924

I felt that what existed in Frankfurt were on the one hand "Jewish people" (eastern Jews) and on the other "Jewish cosmopolitans," who oriented themselves by Frankfurt's southwest German character, but with an additional touch of Jewish family tradition. Frankfurt has something like a genuine Jewish aristocracy, old established Jewish families who, as a result of centuries-old ties with Frankfurt and its history, have acquired a tradition of their own, which these families are extremely proud of and take great pains to pass on under all circumstances.
Bruno Ostrovsky

Right: The Kulps, a wealthy Frankfurt family. Photomontage. 1891

Left: The Warburgs, a wealthy Hamburg banking family, also produced distinguished scientists and philanthropists. 1884

That Germany has experienced unparalleled economic growth over the last seventy years is something of which the whole world is aware. And that Jews make outstanding contributions to a country's economic growth, as well. In the opinion of many nations, being Jewish is altogether tantamount to being rich; that the large majority of Jews belongs to the lowest of the middle classes and lives in grinding poverty will only be discovered by someone who wanders amazed through areas of Jewish mass settlement. The German Jews never constituted a mass, their number always remained somewhere around one percent of the German population; and of these six hundred thousand, at most 15 percent participated in the economic ascent . . .

The German banking world had, since emancipation, had a Jewish sector, the breadth of which, however, tended to be overestimated: there had always been non-Jewish bankers in all of Germany's major commercial centers. Nonetheless the house of Rothschild became

an exceedingly important artery in Germany's international commercial relations, particularly after it branched out from its original establishment in Frankfurt to the major European capitals. The Mendelssohn banking house, brought forth by the family of Moses Mendelssohn, was, next to the later Bleichröder, one of the most distinguished, respected firms in Berlin . . .

Relations with America were entertained by Frankfurt banks like Kahn, Speyer-Ellissen, or the Warburgs of Hamburg. At the Versailles Peace Conference in 1919, Max Warburg rendered the Germans similar services to the ones Gerson Bleichröder had for Count von Bismarck in 1871. While the banks in the large state and provincial capitals remained in Jewish hands, and were often clearly family enterprises (like the Aufhäusers or Feuchtwangers in Munich), the large banks were already subject to a de-Jewification trend before the war . . .
Arnold Zweig

Above: Baron Alfons Rothschild (in the gray top hat) with the winner of the 1932 Derby in the Vienna Freudenau. Photograph by Lothar Rübelt. 1932
The Austrian Derby, usually organized by the fashionable Jockey Club established in 1867, was one of Vienna's major social events.

Below: Otto Pollack von Parnegg at the Vienna Freudenau. Ca. 1900. Originally from Bohemia, the textile magnate was the son of a "well-known Viennese wit, Frau von Pollack," whose attributed comments have gone down in the history of anti-Semitically tinged jokes ridiculing parvenu-like behavior.

Right: The well-known banker Eduard Baron von Oppenheim on his way to the August races at the Cologne race track. Ca. 1910

*T*his sort of nobility, which many Jewish families arrogated to themselves, sometimes amused and sometimes annoyed my brother and me, even when we were children. We were always being told that these were "fine" people, that others were "not fine." Every friend's pedigree was examined back to the earliest generation, to see whether or not he came from a "good" family, and all his relatives, as well as his wealth, were checked. This constant categorization, which actually was the main topic of every familar and social conversation, at that time seemed to be most ridiculous and snobbish, because for all Jewish families it was merely a matter of fifty or a hundred years earlier or later that they had come from the same ghetto. It was not until much later that I realized that this conception of "good" family, which appeared to us boys to be a parody of an artificial pseudo-aristocracy, was one of the most profound and secret tendencies of Jewish life. It is generally accepted that getting rich is the only and typical goal of the Jew. Nothing could be further from the truth. Riches are to him merely a stepping stone, a means to the true end, and in no sense the real goal. The real determination of the Jew is to rise to a higher cultural plane in the intellectual world . . . And that is why among Jews the impulse to wealth is exhausted in two, or at most three, generations within one family, and the mightiest dynasties find their sons unwilling to take over the banks, the factories, the established and secure businesses of their fathers. It is not chance that a Lord Rothschild became an ornithologist, a Warburg an art historian, a Cassirer a philosopher, a Sassoon a poet. They all obey the same subconscious impulse, to free themselves of cold money making, that thing that confines Jewry.
Stefan Zweig

*T*o the generation of Isaak Hofmann, an assimilation that did not hold fast to Judaism was absolutely unthinkable. The fact that the Rothschilds, Wertheimsteins, Sinas, Eskeles, Arnheims, with whom now the Hofmannsthals were also to associate, were socially, or at least halfway socially, accepted by the old aristocracy was based not so much on economic motives as on their Judaism, that is, on their membership in an exotic lineage which in them had dispatched its princes to the capital with the claim to equal status with the nobility. This is how they felt themselves, and this was the ambition of these banker barons, an ambition dedicated to the creation of a Jewish feudalistic noble class, insane as such, even more insane in its fulfillment, nevertheless one of the few social realities grounded purely in romanticism and in this case supported above all by the penchant for the international, for the foreign, for the exceptional, to which the Viennese nobility of the time fell prey. No wonder the end of romanticism signified the end of this too, all the more because the migration of Jews to Vienna and their constantly increasing naturalization – the very foundation of the "Religious Community" indicated the decisive turning point – had turned the Jews from an exotic into an economically as well as a socially undesirable foreign body. To be sure, the Rothschilds had guarded their special position, but that they owed exclusively to their uniquely international family and business structure. For the others, all their wealth notwithstanding, the dream of a subfeudal pseudoassimilation was fundamentally exhausted.
Hermann Broch

Opposite page and below right: Mansion of Albert Ballin (1857–1918) on Feldbrunnenstrasse in Hamburg. 1916.
Ballin, thanks to whom the German merchant marine acquired its international reputation, became director-general of the Hamburg-Amerika-Line (HAPAG) in 1899 and was also an advisor to Kaiser Wilhelm II, who relied on him in matters of offensive naval policy.

Above right: The Palais Itzig on Neue Friedrichstrasse in Berlin. Photograph by F. Albert Schwartz. 1857
Center: The Palais Todesco across from the Hofoper (Court Theater) on Kärntner Strasse in Vienna. Ca. 1870
The Palais, built 1861–1864 by Ludwig Förster and Theophil Hansen, was the residence of the Todescos, an originally Milanese family of industrialists and bankers of Sephardic descent. The Palais Todesco was one of the centers of Viennese social life during the so-called "Gründerzeit," the period of industrial expansion.

Immeasurable is the part in Viennese culture the Jewish bourgeoisie took, by their co-operation and promotion. . . .
It became apparent for the first time that nine-tenths of what the world celebrated as Viennese culture in the nineteenth century was promoted, nourished, or even created by Viennese Jewry. . . .
Nowhere was it easier to be a European . . .
Stefan Zweig

Above: The Palais Ephrussi by the Schottentor in Vienna. 1870
The Ephrussis, a Sephardic family of bankers, were major financiers during Vienna's "Gründerzeit."
Left: The Palais Rothschild on Prinz-Eugen-Strasse in Vienna. Ca. 1920

Right: Baron Franz Wertheim (Krems 1814 – Vienna 1883). Photograph by Ludwig Angerer. Ca. 1865
After spending several formative years in France and England, Wertheim established a tool manufacturing company; in 1853 his company began producing fire-proof safes, which were to become famous the world over. His residence, the Palais Wertheim on Vienna's Kärntner Ring, even had its own theater.

Above: Emma von Ephrussi, née Baroness Schey von Koromla. Ca. 1910

Below: Eduard Baron von Todesco (1814–1887), textile manufacturer and railroad magnate. Ca. 1875

Left: Joseph Baron von Hirsch (Würzburg 1805 – Munich 1885), whose father had already been banker to the court of King Maximilian I of Bavaria, himself became a financial advisor to the Bavarian court. He also financed the construction of numerous stretches of railroad in Bavaria. Photograph by Franz Hanfstaengl. Ca. 1860

Above right: Alexander Mendelssohn (1798–1871) led the banking house founded in Berlin by his father Joseph to international renow his grandfather was the distinguished philosopher Moses Mendelssohn. Ca. 1860

Below right: Carl Fürstenberg (Danzig 1850 – Berlin 1933) spent his apprenticeship period with the R. Damme banking house in Danzig and later with *Gerson von Bleichröder* (1822–1893) in Berlin, banker to the court of Kaiser Wilhelm I and advisor to Bismarck, whose favorite business associate he became. Invited to join the Berliner Handels-Gesellschaft in 1883, Fürstenberg rapidly restored that bank's financial soundness by encouraging cooperation with industry. As a result, he became one of the foremost financiers of German heavy industry. Ca. 1910

Opposite page: Karl Mayer Baron von Rothschild (Naples 1820 – Frankfurt am Main 1886) was the first "Mosaic" member appointed to the Upper Chamber of the Prussian Parliament by Kaiser Wilhelm I. As the eldest son of Carl Mayer Rothschild, one of the "five Frank- furtians," he had headed the Frankfurt branch of the banking house since 1855. He was, among other things, founder of the Stiftung Carolinum, a foundation administered by the University of Frankfurt. Ca. 1880

The modern financial history of the German Jews can probably be said to have begun with Mayer Amschel Rothschild (b. 1743 in Frankfurt a.M.) and his sons, the "five Frankfurtians." How important they were in their time is shown by a remark attributed to Frau Gudula, Mayer Amschel Rothschild's mother; she is said to have comforted a woman worried that war would break out with the words: "I'll tell my son not to give the Prince any money, then they can't go to war." The history of the Rothschilds does indeed extend from the era of the enterprising court Jews of lesser and greater potentates directly into the efflorescence of capitalism, from Mayer Amschel through Baron Anselm Mayer to Baron Mayer Carl, member of the Upper Chamber of the Prussian Parliament, and on to all the ramifications of European influence. And theirs was an influence without which, in the economic and social circumstances, the continent could hardly have been imagined, although towards the end of the nineteenth century the prestige of the house appeared to be waning everywhere.

But more important than the rise of individual Jewish families is the development of German Jewry as a collective force in the modern German economy. It began with the dawn of the machine age and culminated in the era of Wilhelm II, when Germany was preparing to find its place in the sun. The importance of the German banking industry and stock exchange grew in parallel with Germany's transformation from a purely agrarian country into a central European industrial center. And it was the German private banker that stood at the head of this development. Only rarely were the early private banks in Germany established as pure financing institutions or banks in the present sense. They usually developed organically, when circumstances demanded the foundation of such enterprises.

Thus the first private banks, some of which survived until the Nazi era, were established during the three wars waged by Frederick the Great. Most of them began as procurers of war supplies, mainly cloth, and – where they were not requisitioned – provisions for the troops. Of necessity, financial transactions ensued, and even into the modern era certain grain businesses, particularly in the German provinces, were also active in the banking trade. Some of these firms had been founded by Jews and had already been in the possession of the family for many decades. There were also a number of more or less important banking businesses that had originally begun in the cloth trade and only gradually changed

over exclusively to banking. Most of these firms fell victim to either unfavorable circumstances or the expansionist activities of the large banking houses.
Daniel Bernstein

And, may God withdraw his favors if it is not true, Herr Doktor, I sat next to Salomon Rothschild and he treated me as an equal, as if I were famillionaire.
Heinrich Heine

161

*T*he significance of all the companies that have been built up by Jews over the last thirty years – by the Wertheims, Tietzes, Jandorfs, Karstadts, Schockens: To demonstrate the goods a single one of these companies purchases and turns over in a single one of its divisions, let us use the figures that the Tietz concern published about its food business, which, after all, served as a market for German farmers. In 1932, surely already a bad year, it sold its customers the meat and fat of 15,000 cows; 32,000 calves; 101,000 pigs; 13,000 sheep; plus 9 million eggs; 3.8 million kilos of cheese; 16.3 million kilos of vegetables; and 11.6 million kilos of fruit – food and other agricultural produce totaling some 60 million marks. To complete the picture these figures give, let us add that in the same year it bought goods for 30 million marks from the textile industry, for 25 million marks from the clothing industry, and spent a total of 131.82 million marks for goods that created work for almost all German manufacturers, from optical equipment and rubber balloon factories to publishing houses, for its new and used bookstores were among the best in Berlin.

To take only one Jewish occupation, the tailor's trade (over 14,000 Jewish tailors in Germany alone), Jews turned the production of ready-made suits, dresses, and coats into an important branch of the economy, a garment industry that covered a whole district of Berlin and guaranteed numerous home-workers a meager existence. Jews also organized large-scale catering of food and drink in Berlin; the names Aschinger and Kempinski became world famous. The coal business made two companies big, Hultschinsky and Caesar Wollheim – the latter, later taken over by the Arnholds, enabled Geheimer Kommerzienrat (Privy commercial counselor) Eduard Arnhold to become the philanthropist he was.

Arnold Zweig

Left: Tietz Department Store on Alexanderplatz in Berlin. 1908
The Tietz brothers, Hermann and Oskar, opened their first department store in Munich in 1895, and then further stores in Cologne and Berlin. Other German department stores and department store chains founded by Jews were Wertheim, Gerson and Schocken.

Above: The Jacob Rothberger Department Store on Stephansplatz in Vienna. 1899
On special occasions like the annual Corpus Christi procession, the windows across from the Cathedral were rented out to spectators. Several highly reputed Vienna department stores – Gerngross, Herzmansky, and Zwieback – were also owned by Jews.

163

The engineer Emil Rathenau and the manufacturer Felix Deutsch found a business producing and selling electric light-bulbs and appliances. Under their highly intelligent management, it develops into an international company: AEG. After the death of his son Walter Rathenau, Jewish influence at AEG virtually disappears, and in 1933 the company proclaims itself to be Aryan. The OSRAM light-bulb factory goes a similar way. These are only two examples of industries that owe their success to Jewish initiative, and Jewish capital and boldness. There would be a great deal to do if one wanted to accumulate all the other examples from Berlin, Frankfurt, Nuremberg, or the Rhineland.
Arnold Zweig

Thus dealing in metals leads the antecedents of the Hirsch-Kupfer- und Messingwerke (Hirsch copper and brass works), for example, to the metal industry. The metal dealer Aron Hirsch established a copper works in the southern Harz Mountains as early as 1820, only 8 years after emancipation, and participated in founding the Kupferhammer-Betriebs-Gesellschaft (Copper works operating company) in Ilsenburg in 1823. It was his grandson who brought the company to world renown around the turn of the century by turning the Hirsch-Kupfer- und Messingwerke into a corporation, buying into mining companies in Australia, Central and South America, Siberia, France, and Belgium, and at the same time establishing his own sales offices in almost all the European capitals. Though the Jews had almost no share in developing heavy industry in Rhenish Westphalia – Paul Silberberg, who gained distinction only as the organizer of the Rheinische Braunkohlenwirtschaft (Rhenish brown coal industry), and Ottmar Strauss of the Wolff company being the exceptions made possible by the post-war period – they were virtually the sole creators of Upper Silesian heavy industry. Moritz Friedländer already co-founded the Minervahütte (smelting works) at the beginning of the last century. In the 1860s, his son built the Heinrichgrube (pit) and the Moritzhütte, which, under the name of Julienhütte, is the largest plant in Upper Silesia today. The Pringsheims made enormous contributions to railroad construction. None of these companies belong to Jews any longer, they have been merged into the Oberschlesische Hüttenwerke-Aktien-Gesellschaft (Upper Silesian smelting works corporation).
Arnold Zweig

Above: Emil Rathenau with Thomas Alva Edison during one of the American inventor's numerous visits, in front of an AEG turbine in Berlin-Moabit. 1911

Emil Rathenau (Berlin 1838 – Berlin 1915) installed the first telephone in Berlin in 1880. Very quick to recognize the importance of electrical engineering, he acquired Edison's patents in 1881 and founded the Allgemeine Elektrizitäts-Gesellschaft (AEG), which subsequently grew into one of the largest concerns in Germany.

Opposite page: Funeral procession for Emil Rathenau through the AEG plant in Berlin. 1915

Marcel Reich-Ranicki
OUTSIDERS AND PROVOCATEURS

On September 1, 1772, the *Frankfurter gelehrte Anzeigen* (Frankfurt scholarly notices) published the review of a book entitled *Gedichte von einem polnischen Juden* (Poems by a Polish Jew). The reviewer – a twenty-three-year-old lawyer attached to the imperial law courts at Wetzlar, a certain Johann Wolfgang Goethe – assured his readers that the title had made "a very favorable impression."

The verses of that Polish Jew who wrote in the German language – his name was Isachar Bär Falkensohn and he lived from 1746 to 1817 – turned out to be a deep disappointment to the young Goethe: he reproached them with "the mediocrity hated by gods and men." What he particularly disliked was the author's allusion to his "Jewishhood," though he "accomplishes no more than a Christian *étudiant en belles lettres* would."

Goethe's disparaging criticism was undoubtedly justified. Yet more remarkable than the rigor of his judgment, in my opinion, is his belief that he was permitted to expect the extraordinary from the Jewish poet. Goethe regarded him above all – and once again rightly so – as a representative of a minority group; from this insight he then assumes that the special position in which the author finds himself grants him a special perspective. Further, in fact, it even commits him to a perspective of this kind.

Goethe understandably saw in that Polish Jew, whose poems he criticizes mercilessly and not without irony, a newcomer, a stranger, an alien nature.

That belonging to a hard-pressed, persecuted minority group reinforces and potentiates certain human qualities, that membership in such a group might even be capable of substantially determining an individual's psychological structure is indisputable and does not apply only to Jews. But when it comes to the Jews, with their age-old intellectual and ethical tradition, centuries of living in circumscribed and isolated conditions – a sort of insular existence on various parts of the European continent – produced extraordinary results.

Consider the *bon mot* by Heine: "When good, the Jews are better than the Christians; when bad, they are worse." Though this may be a highly questionable generalization, its ultimate point is not really inapposite. For Heine will have been addressing nothing more than the Jews' famous, or infamous, intensity, their astonishing, sometimes alarming radicalness, their tendency to be uncompromising, and their occasionally admired, often maligned inclination to extremism.

These and similar attributes made many Jews attractive but somehow disturbing to the world around them. The source of numerous achievements and deeds, they were also the cause of infinite suffering and sacrifice. That mankind owes much to this extraordinary intensity – frequently a well-camouflaged, pent-up yearning for boundaries – is well known. But for the Jews themselves, who tried often enough to battle their own nature, its consequences generally contributed to their hardships – even when they were not being driven from their homes, crucified or exterminated in gas chambers. All this is especially true of the Jews in German literature: the writers, critics, and major publishers. Some of them genuinely succeeded in accomplishing what Goethe had already demanded in 1772.

These outsiders and newcomers were often capable of seeing the common and familiar in a new and different way. Standing inside and yet somehow outside the world they were trying to come to terms with, they succeeded in combining familiarity and intimacy with skeptical distance: the periphery was an especially good position from which to perceive and portray centrality with particular clarity.

Admittedly the whole of world literature lives to a considerable extent from the tension between proximity and distance. It is only that, to their regret, Jewish writers were continually given ample opportunity to test the artistic productiveness of this tension: whoever believes he has found a home and is then cast out, or at least undeceived, necessarily views that "home" with ambivalent feelings and from a different perspective.

But above all Goethe had hoped that Polish Jew would "tear [the German readers] out of their customary indifference . . . a hundred things that you can *overlook* [would have to be] intolerable [to him]." It was a troublemaker, possibly a *provocateur,* that he wanted to welcome onto the literary scene. With this attitude, the young Goethe anticipated the task and role the Jews were to have in German literature and literary life in the German-speaking world: their influence was to be largely a challenging, irritating, and above all provocative one and that is precisely what won them a great many admirers – and even more opponents and enemies.

With "his experience of suffering, his tested spirituality and ironic reason," wrote Thomas Mann in 1937, the Jew constitutes "a hidden corrective to our passions." And in fact it was in this function – as an element of irritation and provocation, as perpetual leaven and "hidden corrective" – that the Jews were needed most and presumably loved least.

Individual Jews were already exercising this sort of function – *nolens volens* – even during Goethe's lifetime; I am, of course, referring to Ludwig Börne and Heinrich Heine.

Both of them came from the ghetto, both of them hoped to acquire "the admission ticket to European culture" by means of a baptismal certificate, and Heine's pronouncement applies to both: "I make no secret of my Judaism, to which I did not return because I never left it." Both rose to extraordinary fame in the German intellectual world, both were hated, vilified, and driven out of their country. Both ultimately died in exile.

Börne and Heine were able to give the German literature of their epoch what it had never had much of but needed desperately: sophistication and urbanity, wit and *esprit,* charm and lightness of touch.

At the same time the works of Börne and Heine prefigure some of the most important themes German writers of Jewish origin would be dealing with in later years. We can already find the characteristic combination of lucid skepticism and faith in reason. The peculiarly ambivalent relationship to Germany is already perceptible, as is the perspective that implies maximum intimacy while at the same time profiting from the distance that widens horizons and makes a broad general view possible.

Unmistakable in the works of both, as much as they try to camouflage them with mockery and irony, wrath and even arrogance, is the disappointment of the rejected and the pain of the outcast, the yearning of the exile and the grief of the homeless.

Both had a need to belong, both yearned for a feeling of security, both wanted a home – and both of them had to recognize unequivocally that they would not be able to find all this in the largely backward Jewish milieu they came from. It was with good reason that they had dissociated themselves from the Jewish world, which, despite the efforts of a few

distinguished men, was still trapped in medieval thinking; this was a world they had totally outgrown.

And could they, Börne and Heine, be considered German patriots? They certainly wanted to be, at almost any price. They had achieved a great deal; those who considered them compatriots unquestionably respected them. But were they also accepted? Germany was more prepared to admire the two Jews than to integrate them. Heine and Börne had no cause for complaint: they were abundantly acclaimed – and at the same time unmistakably rejected. And so Heine and Börne suffered from unrequited love of country.

Both of them also typify many of their successors in German literature because, though outsiders and exiles, they believed they had found a home of sorts in the radical political movements of their era. But precisely because Börne and Heine wanted no part of convenient illusions, they suffered increasingly under their solitude and isolation, their lack of a home, in other words, their not-belonging.

Thus Börne and Heine were exceptional and yet typical figures; they stood at the periphery and yet in the center. They were forced to remain outsiders in the German literature of their time, and could nonetheless become its typical representatives. But does this apply only to Börne and Heine? Of course, they were born in the eighteenth century and lived in an era when the emancipation of the German Jews was only beginning. But are there no other important Jews in German literature who were outsiders and marginal figures while at the same time being central and representative?

To begin with, those writers of Jewish descent who had hoped to gain total political and social equality through the rapid recognition of their achievements must have been particularly vulnerable to the reaction of the non-Jewish world around them, though this influence is not consistently in evidence.

There are essentially two discernible tendencies here. On the one hand, a Jew who wanted a literary career in Germany was long under pressure, direct or at least indirect, to convert; it is well known that not only Börne and Heine but a goodly number of their successors in the nineteenth and twentieth centuries came to this decision. The surrounding populace, on the other hand, viewed these writers, whether converted or not, as representatives of the Jewish minority, and almost automatically searched for Jewish qualities and traits of character, genuine or presumed, good and bad, in their works.

That this aroused piqued, perhaps exaggerated, reactions and even occasional acts of defiance is only too easy to understand. Though some of these Jewish writers attempted to ignore this not necessarily malicious attitude in others, none succeeded, since, as members of a minority that had experienced centuries of discrimination, they were subject to numerous and diverse traumas and complexes.

"It was impossible for a Jew, particularly for one who was in the public eye, to disregard the fact that he was a Jew, as others did not do so, not the Christians and even less the Jews. One had the choice of being considered insensitive, obtrusive, and impertinent or then sensitive, shy, and paranoiac. And even if one maintained sufficient inward and outward bearing to display neither the one nor the other, it was as impossible to remain indifferent as it would be for a person who had, for example, had his skin anesthetized and was forced to watch, with wakeful, wide-open eyes, as a dirty knife scratched and then cut into it until the blood flowed." Thus Arthur Schnitzler in his autobiography *Jugend in Wien* (A Viennese Youth), which was not published until 1968.

In the first third of our century, Judaism became such a burden to nearly all the German writers of Jewish descent that they wanted to throw it off, or dragged it along resignedly, or tried to flaunt it like a banner. Almost all of them suffered under their Judaism, almost all of them wrestled with it for decades, a fact that can more often be inferred – as in Schnitzler's case – from letters and diaries, memoirs and autobiographical sketches not intended for publication than from their novels, plays, or poems.

A not insignificant number of these writers sooner or later parted ways with or dissociated themselves from Judaism – and ultimately realized that this was basically impossible to accomplish as it was not up to the individual to decide.

In a letter that Kurt Tucholsky wrote to Arnold Zweig from his Swedish exile in December 1935 – only a few days before he committed suicide – he admitted: "I resigned from Judaism in the year 1911, and I know that cannot be done."

But whether these writers wanted to abandon Judaism or not, their origin, position, and role in non-Jewish society helped shape their characters, complexes, and ambitions, and thus their work as well. Judaism, or, to be more exact, the isolation and defensiveness generated by Jewish origins, drove Franz Kafka into solitude and sorrow, Joseph Roth and Ernst Toller into melancholy and political quixotism, Carl Sternheim, Alfred Kerr, and Kurt Tucholsky into aggressiveness and provocation, Else Lasker-Schüler and – appearances to the contrary – even Anna Seghers into mysticism and ecstasy. Judaism – admittedly in the broadest sense of the word – influenced the mentality of the great Viennese feuilletonists, from Peter Altenberg to Egon Friedell and Alfred Polgar, and such diverse Austrian writers as Richard Beer-Hofmann, Arthur Schnitzler, and Joseph Roth.

The proportion of Jews in Austrian literary life was enormous: "Nine tenths of what the world celebrated as nineteenth-century Viennese culture was a culture promoted, nurtured and even created by Viennese Jewry," wrote Stefan Zweig in his illuminating autobiography. In her discussion of the "Jung-Wien" (Young Vienna) group of poets, who were responsible for the European status of late nineteenth-century Austrian literature, Hilde Spiel understandably refrained from continually referring to the Jewish origins of its members. Hers is the opposite approach: she says that the group included only a single non-Jewish author, namely Hermann Bahr. At the same time she recalls the Jewish ancestry of great Austrians of earlier generations, such as Grillparzer and Johann Strauss.

If we talk about a fortunate, unique, and unrepeatable symbiosis in this connection, there is one point that should not be forgotten, a point Stefan Zweig put very appositely: Viennese Jewry was by no means productive "in a specifically Jewish way . . . but, by a miracle of empathy, found an exceedingly intense means of expressing what was Austrian, what was Viennese." And it is, of course, no coincidence that what typified Berlin, too, was reflected most clearly and forcefully in the prose of Jews – the novels of Georg Hermann, the feuilletons of Kurt Tucholsky and, above all, Alfred Döblin's masterpiece *Berlin Alexanderplatz*.

As the attitude of Jews in the non-Jewish world included, and had to include, a defensive element, the position of the Jews in German literature seems to me to have always been largely a counter-position. This is certainly true of Stefan Zweig, who for many years claimed to be totally unacquainted with the issue, as well as of Max Brod, the consistent Zionist; the esoteric elitist poetry of an Alfred Mombert and a Karl Wolfskehl testify to it as much as does the arch-conservative German traditionalism of Rudolf Borchardt and the almost touching love of Prussia shown by Bruno Frank and Arnold Zweig.

A counter-position and the occasional act of defiance can likewise be recognized in certain writers' ostentatious devotion to Jewish themes and figures – Else Lasker-Schüler, Lion Feuchtwanger, Max Brod and, once again, Arnold Zweig being cases in point. Finally, the only way to understand why Catholic ideas and themes were capable of exercising decades of extraordinary and particular fascination on such writers as Alfred Döblin, who converted towards the end of his life, and Franz Werfel, who did not, is in light of their Jewish origin and Jewish fate.

That factors such as these must also become apparent in the work of literary scholars and essayists – from Moritz Heimann and Friedrich Gundolf to Walter Benjamin – is selfevident. Benjamin's case is particularly illuminating. Not until his letters were published in 1966 did a factor often expressed only between the lines of his professional writings become a distinct reality, namely his relationship to Judaism and the exceeding importance of certain Jewish principles in determining his thinking.

In a letter to Max Brod written in 1921, Kafka speaks of "the relationship of the young Jews to their Judaism" and of "the terrible inner circumstances of this generation." In his opinion: "To get away from Judaism is what most of those who began to write in German wanted, usually with the vague approval of their fathers (this vagueness was the infuriating thing); that is what they wanted, but with their little back legs they were glued to the Judaism of their fathers, and their little front legs could find no new footing. Their despair over this was their inspiration."

He is describing a situation that enabled more than a few Jewish writers – them in particular! – to sense and anticipate, even before World War I in many cases, the coming isolation and alienation of the intellectual in bourgeois German and Austrian society, and to articulate it so trenchantly. Schnitzler and Karl Kraus, Döblin, Broch, and Werfel, Albert Ehrenstein, Alfred Lichtenstein, and Ernst Toller, Tucholsky and Benjamin – all of them suffered under "the terrible inner circumstances of this generation" and allowed themselves to be – more or less consciously – inspired by them. Certainly some of these authors only touch briefly on themes such as these – the rootlessness and alienation of the individual, his loneliness and isolation as a product of concrete social reality. But these are precisely the themes that dominate the prose of Franz Kafka, to restrict myself to the most outstanding example.

Max Brod already pointed out during Kafka's lifetime that the word "Jew" never occurred in any of his novels and stories, but that the suffering of the Jews was continually being depicted. K.'s "feeling of alienation" in *Das Schloss* (The Castle) was, according to Brod, "the special feeling of a Jew who would like to put down roots in alien surroundings, who strives with all the strength of his soul to draw closer to the strangers around him, to become completely like them – and who cannot achieve this union."

Thus one might say: if Heine was a central and representative figure although he was an outsider, Kafka became a central and representative figure of German and European literature because he was an outsider.

In no other language have the European Jews put down such deep roots as in German; and to say language is to say spirit . . .
Ludwig Bamberger

The language of my intellect will remain the German language for the very reason that I am a Jew. As a Jew, I want to preserve in myself what remains of that thoroughly ravaged country. The fate of its language is my fate too, although I also carry a universal human heritage in myself. I want to give back to German what I owe it.
Elias Canetti

Since the beginning of the twentieth century the following writers – Jewish, half-Jewish and quarter-Jewish (of "Semitic origin," to use the language of the Third Reich) – have made their contribution to German literature!
The Viennese Peter Altenberg, a twentieth-century troubadour, who writes so sensitively about the most inconspicuous and discreet sort of female beauty, and whom those barbarians of the theory of race have long vilified as a "decadent pornographer"; Oscar Blumenthal, an author of subtle comedies that, though lacking ultimate greatness, are in the best of taste; Richard Beer-Hofmann, noble wordsmith of the German language, heir to and interpreter of Biblical tradition; Max Brod, selfless friend of Franz Kafka, storyteller in a great tradition, keen and erudite, he has brought the brilliant figure of Tycho Brahe back to life; Alfred Döblin, the first in German literature to discover and embody the common Berliner as a type, one of the most original creations the intellectual world possesses; Bruno Frank, conscientious craftsman of the word, experienced playwright, pacifist, and singer of Prussia's past; Ludwig Fulda, author of charming, wittily perceptive comedies; Maximilian Harden, the indefatigable and perhaps only genuine German political commentator; Walter Hasenclever, one of the most incandescent of dramatists; Georg Hermann, a simple, sincere storyteller of the petit bourgeoisie; Paul Heyse (half-Jewish), the first German Nobel Prize winner; Hugo von Hofmannsthal, a patrician among writers of poetry and prose, classic heir to the Catholic treasures of old Austria; Alfred Kerr, a drama critic brimming with imagination; Karl Kraus, the great polemicist, a master of German literature, a fanatic in matters of linguistic purity, a virtually unassailable apostle of style; Else Lasker-Schüler, a poet – any other epithet would be gratuitous, the one suffices; Klaus Mann (half-Jewish, son of Thomas Mann), a promising young writer with a considerable stylistic gift; Alfred and Robert Neumann, notable epic writers; Rainer Maria Rilke (quarter-Jewish), one of Europe's greatest poets; Peter Panter

Writers of Jewish descent had a major share in shaping the literature of Germany and Austria from the turn of the century until the 1930s . . .

Above: A meeting of the literary section of the Prussian Academy of Arts in Berlin. Seated from left to right: *Alfred Mombert*, Eduard Stucken, Wilhelm von Scholz, Oskar Loerke, Walter von Molo, *Ludwig Fulda*, Heinrich Mann. Standing from left to right: *Bernhard Kellermann, Alfred Döblin*, Thomas Mann, Max Halbe. Photograph by *Erich Salomon*. 1929

[ed. note: pseudonym of Kurt Tucholsky], a polemicist of sparkling intellect; Carl Sternheim, one of the most perceptive storytellers and dramatists; Ernst Toller, the poet of the Schwalbenbuch, a revolutionary dramatist who spent seven years in a Bavarian prison because he loved the freedom of the German people; Jakob Wassermann, one of Europe's foremost novelists; Franz Werfel, a lyrical dramatist, novelist, and marvelous poet; Karl Wolfskehl, the great and noble interpreter of the myths; Carl Zuckmayer, a forceful playwright; Arnold Zweig, author of the wonderful Sergeant Grischa and De Vriendt kehrt heim, God's gift of a novelist and essayist. A very incomplete list of the soldiers of the intellect who have been defeated by the Third Reich! Readers need not note each name. Let it be enough for them as it is for us to salute them as well as other Jewish writers, who number among my dearest friends and whom my friendship fears to deck with an epithet: Stephan Zweig, Hermann Kesten, Egon Erwin Kisch, Ernst Weiss, Alfred Polgar, Walter Mehring, Siegfried Kracauer, Valeriu Marcu, Lion Feuchtwanger, the late Hermann Ungar and the revered prophet and seer Max Picard. May those German-Jewish writers whose names do not appear in this list forgive me for having forgotten them. May those who have been introduced here not object to their juxtaposition with this or that personal enemy. All of them have fallen on the honorable battleground of the spirit. All of them have a common flaw in the eyes of the German murderers and arsonists: their Jewish blood and European spirit.
Joseph Roth

As if an age-old dam had burst, Jews suddenly appeared in virtually all spheres of literature – poetry, novellas, novels, essays, plays – with achievements that at least a certain stratum of intellectually-minded people considered epoch-making.
Hans Tramer

Vse poéty židy.
All poets are Jews (Marina Zwetajewa).
Paul Celan

Berthold Auerbach (Nordstetten 1812 – Cannes 1882), originally Moyses Baruch, should have become a rabbi but studied law and philosophy instead. He acquired his reputation as a regional writer through his *Schwarzwälder Dorfgeschichten* (Black Forest Village Stories [1843– 1854]). Jewish subjects interested him only in his youth. In *Das Judentum und die neueste Literatur* (Judaism and Recent Literature [1836]) he defended the writers of the "Young Germany" movement, like *Heine* and *Börne*, and championed liberal ideas, intellectual emancipation, and Jewish cultural consciousness. Auerbach ultimately acknowledged the failure of Jewish integration into German society. Opposite page, left: Berthold Auerbach. Photograph by F. Brandseph. Ca. 1875

But it is absolutely certain that I felt an ardent desire to say farewell to the German fatherland. It is not so much wanderlust as the torment of personal circumstances (e.g. one can never wash off the Jew) that drives me away.
Heinrich Heine

The undeserved good fortune . . . to be at the same time a German and a Jew, to be able to strive for all the virtues of the Germans and yet not to share any of their flaws. Yes, because I was born a slave, I love freedom more than you. Yes, because I was raised in bondage, I understand freedom better than you. Yes, because I was born without a fatherland, I wish for a fatherland more passionately than you, and because my birthplace was no larger than Judengasse (Jews' Lane), and foreign parts began beyond the locked gates, the city is no longer enough as a fatherland for me, nor is a region or a province; only the truly vast fatherland is enough, as far as its language reaches.
Ludwig Börne

our fervent, urgent desire should thus have become a self-evident axiom of mankind – who would still dare to say that there is ever a right to despair of the victory of pure thought? And now the additional news that Winterstein is to become Minister of Commerce. I do not actually want the Jews to assume such high positions, they must prove themselves in small, inconspicuous posts, not always trying to be Kapellmeister, but becoming members of the orchestra, keeping time with the others, merging into the whole . . .
Berthold Auerbach

When I was still a peasant boy in Upper Styria, I already had an opportunity to read the "Schwarzwälder Dorfgeschichten" (Black Forest Village Stories); I developed profound admiration for their author, who knew peasant life so well and whose descriptions of it were so wonderfully appealing.
Peter Rosegger

The vinegary essence of the nation's humor lies in its highly tragic fate. The age of its pain has left sarcastic wine sediment on its cerebral membrane . . . Plaints and words can be stifled, but laughter, terrible laughter, horrible laughter, is possible even when gagged. The Jews resorted to humor because it is the one branch of service where they can in time become officers before an army order takes account of baptismal certificates rather than merit . . .
Moritz Gottlieb Saphir

How I wish I could be with you today, dear Jakob [Auerbach], and share with you the happiness of being allowed to experience this: the way the Hungarian Reichstag (Diet) accepted the emancipation of the Jews unanimously, without a debate. That is something we did not think we would live to see. That

Above: A German men's choir singing "Ich weiss nicht, was soll es bedeuten . . ." at Heinrich Heine's grave in the Montmartre Cemetery in Paris. 1901

Moritz Gottlieb Saphir (Lovas-Benény/Pest 1795 – Baden/Vienna 1858), originally Moses Saphir, studied theology and classical philology before becoming a critic for Adolf Bäuerle's *Allgemeine Theaterzeitung* (General Theater Paper) in Vienna. After his expulsion in 1825, he went to Berlin, where he worked as a drama critic and founded several short-lived newspapers (among them the *Berliner Schnellpost*). Feared for his malicious wit – the reason he had to leave Berlin in 1827 and Munich in 1834 – he published a satirical magazine, *Der Humorist*, in Vienna (to which he had returned in 1834) between 1837 and 1855.
Right: Moritz Gottlieb Saphir. Daguerreotype by *Hermann Biow*. 1843

The Café Griensteidl was located in the Herbersteinschen Palais at the corner of Herrengasse and Schauflergasse in Vienna (First District). Soon after it opened it became the meeting place for young writers, actors, and other "aesthetes." In the 1890s the Café acquired literary significance because it was frequented by a circle of older writers, the "Iduna," but especially because the representatives of "Jung Wien" (Young Vienna) met there. With its artists' and reading rooms, the Griensteidl became a forum for fresh artistic ideas. The "coffeehouse literati" inaugurated one of the most creative eras of Viennese literature. When the Café closed its doors on January 21, 1897, there was only one regular patron who ironically welcomed the fact that Vienna would "now be demolished into a big city": it was *Karl Kraus*, getting back at what he considered "coffeehouse-decadence-modernism."
Left: Café Griensteidl; photograph from a New Year's card. Ca. 1895

The meeting place for the whole Jung Wien (Young Vienna) literary circle was the Café Griensteidl on Michaelerplatz . . .
One day Richard Beer-Hofmann joined us. His clothing was of an excessive noblesse, a select elegance born of the subtlest of taste, and always with something gently challenging about it. Each day he wore a different boutonniere, carefully chosen to express his mood. He was (and has remained) so captivatingly eloquent, so thoroughly permeated by luminous intellect, that I awarded him the title "Patron of Comprehension" at the time. He did not even seem to want to write at first; it was almost as if he found himself too valuable for that . . .
But it was Loris, the not yet sixteen-year-old schoolboy Hugo v. Hofmannsthal, author of the one-act verse play "Gestern" (Yesterday), that roused everyone's enthusiasm. Both the formal, musical beauty of Hofmannsthal's lines and the profound thoughts they contained affected us like a sort of high-minded intoxicant.
Felix Salten

Total intimacy impossible; – with Loris because of intolerance, with Richard because of affectation, with Salten because of unreliability.
Arthur Schnitzler

I was repulsed by all dogma, from whichever pulpit it was preached or at whatever school it was taught. I found the subject in the true sense of the word, undiscussable. I had as little relationship to the so-called beliefs of my fathers – to that which was truly belief and not merely memory, tradition and atmosphere – as to any other religion.
Arthur Schnitzler

The following pages will have a great deal to say about Judaism and anti-Semitism, more than some may find necessary, just or in good taste. But if these pages are read in the future, it will be very difficult – at least I hope it will – truly to grasp the significance (a significance nearly more spiritual than political and social) of the Jewish question as I write these lines. It was impossible for a Jew, particularly one who was in the public eye, to disregard the fact that he was a Jew since no one else did, not the Christians and certainly not the Jews.
Arthur Schnitzler

You ask me in which of my works apart from "Weg ins Freie" I have dealt with Jewish problems, characters, and circumstances. My response must be that allusions to the position of the Jews in modern culture and society can be found in some of my other books, that the occasional figure expressly described as a Jew appears episodically, but that there is nothing that might be termed a thorough treatment of the problem or problems, either socially or psychologically.
Arthur Schnitzler

In regard to Arthur Schnitzler in particular, this does not seem the occasion for a literary evaluation, but it should nonetheless be pointed out that he did and does represent an epoch, a country, a monarchy; that his dramatic and epic achievements cannot be compared to the ridiculous private confessions and reports of the "young generation"; that his language is marked by the poetic appeal of melancholy and not the smooth, naked glitter of an accumulation of facts or the exclamatory pathos of political accusations.
Joseph Roth

The world of his plays is the world of a certain educated, or, to be more accurate, intellectual bourgeoisie: . . . there is a very specific social and mental nuance at work here – which will remain highly characteristic of the period between 1890 and the Great War, and may one day be known simply as the Schnitzler world, the way a certain stratum of society in the Louis-Philippe era, which in reality never existed in quite that form, must be called the Balzac world.
Hugo von Hofmannsthal

Schnitzler's famous line, "We are all playing a game, he who realizes that is wise," summarizes the way he understood the world. He viewed what is commonly known as truth as no more than a questionable meaning – dictated by the need for reason – read into this kind of a game without changing the game's essential character: a game where masks are more than faces, passionate miens more than passions, and the players pretend to more blood and spirit than they have.
He looked upon life serenely because it continually springs from death, and with resignation because it continually ends in death. He observed the world lovingly, and lovingly gave shape to everything he saw. But when the world began to reel, bad times befell pensive, sensitive observers, and the words of

the poet were drowned in the frightened, angry screams of a world gripped by panic; and he did not want to cease being a poet, no matter how urgently the situation advised it.
Alfred Polgar

The only thing which gives me a certain amount of confidence is simply the consciousness of being able to see right into people's souls . . . right deep down, every one, rogues and honest people, men, women and children, heathens, Jews and Protestants, yes, even Catholics, aristocrats and Germans, although I have heard that that is supposed to be infinitely difficult, not to say impossible, for people like myself.
Arthur Schnitzler

I have often asked myself in amazement where you might have acquired this or that piece of recondite knowledge that I had to gain by arduous research of subjects, and have finally come to the point where I envy the poet I otherwise admired.
Sigmund Freud

He was already dramatizing psychoanalysis when these theories were still evolving. And in his novels and plays he captured fin-de-siècle Vienna and preserved it for later generations: a whole city with its unique culture, the special breed of people it nurtured and developed, and the way they lived to the full at a certain moment of maturity and decadence, came resoundingly, luminously to life in them.
Egon Friedell

We must admit it to ourselves, Poldy, we have a home but no fatherland – and in its place only a specter. That one might some day have to sacrifice one's children's blood for this phantom is a bitter thought.
Hugo von Hoffmannsthal

Though outwardly he appeared a rare embodiment of German-Jewish harmony, inwardly he suffered under his component natures . . . He tore at his roots, but would not tolerate anyone else touching them. And even if no one wounded him in his dual descent, both his Judaism and his Germanhood remained a now denounced, now carefully nurtured, but always sacrosanct unease.
Heinz Politzer

Arthur Schnitzler (Vienna 1862 – Vienna 1931), like his father Johann, studied medicine. A doctor at the Wiener Allgemeines Krankenhaus (Vienna General Hospital) between 1885 and 1888, he worked at the outpatient clinic from 1888 to 1893, but gradually began devoting more and more of his time to literary pursuits. He belonged to the "Jung Wien" literary circle, which met at the Café Griensteidl and included *Richard Beer-Hofmann*, Hermann Bahr, *Felix Salten*, and *Hugo von Hofmannsthal*.
A typical representative of Viennese impressionism, he was an excellent observer with extraordinary psychological insight. The early twentieth-century Viennese characters he created convey an artistic message of universal validity. He was among the first to apply the technique of interior monologue, using it in *Leutnant Gustl* and *Fräulein Else*. The *Reigen* (La Ronde) caused a scandal because it described playful, erotic situations, a world that was taboo – and consequently fascinating – at the time.
Professor Bernhardi is an almost clinical examination of anti-Semitism in its Austrian guise. In his novel *Der Weg ins Freie*, Schnitzler probes Jewish society in Vienna in its search for identity between assimilation and Zionism. His autobiography *Jugend in Wien* (Youth in Vienna) offers his views on the topics of the time, including anti-Semitism.

Hugo von Hofmannsthal (Vienna 1874–Rodaun 1929) came from a Jewish-Bohemian silk manufacturing family. When he was only seventeen, he published his first poems in the *Neue Freie Presse* under the pseudonym of Loris. Later he became part of the literary circle at the Café Griensteidl on Michaelerplatz in Vienna. As a dramatist, Hugo von Hofmannsthal was interested primarily in material from classical antiquity. It was through his adaptation of *Electra* that he came to the attention of composer Richard Strauss, and this led to long and fruitful years of collaboration (*Der Rosenkavalier, Ariadne auf Naxos*, etc.). Together with *Max Reinhardt*, he founded the Salzburg Festival, creating *Das Salzburger grosse Welttheater* (after Calderon) and *Jedermann* (Everyman) for it. His plays *Der Schwierige* (The Problematic One) and *Der Unbestechliche* (The Unbribable One) reveal him as the most Austrian of Austria's fin-de-siècle writers.
Above: Otto Brahm (1856–1912), the influential Berlin theatrical producer, on a visit to Semmering with (from the right) *Arthur Schnitzler, Hugo von Hofmannsthal*, and *Felix Salten*. 1905

173

Richard Beer-Hofmann (Vienna 1866 – New York 1945) completed his law degree in Vienna in 1890, the same year he first visited the Café Griensteidl. He was soon able to number *Arthur Schnitzler, Hugo von Hofmannsthal,* and *Felix Salten* among his close friends. His well-known poem "Schlaflied für Mirjam" (Lullaby for Mirjam), composed for his daughter in 1897, already characterizes the basic orientation of his scant literary output: how to shape the Jew's destiny and task, the religious event of being "chosen." A Biblical subject inspired the cycle *Die Historie von König David* (The History of King David), which Beer-Hofmann began working on shortly after the turn of the century; only the prologue, "Jakobs Traum" (Jacob's Dream), and the seven scenes for "Der junge David" (Young David) were completed.

Above: Richard Beer-Hofmann. Photograph by *d'Ora.* 1909

When we were young, we were fascinated by the idea of confronting the shallow, banal world of outward appearance with the "inner" world – the world rooted in the depths of the soul, in the "unexplorably profound depths" (we were Tristan enthusiasts, too) with the "mothers," in the mystery of the past – and overwhelmed by Buber's first talk in 1909, where it was called "the blood." We were under the spell of Richard Beer-Hofmann's "Schlaflied für Mirjam" (Lullaby for Mirjam): "Blood of what has been – to what is coming it rolls, blood of our fathers, full of restlessness and pride" . . . this mystical concept was as powerful in us as that of the dream, both of which were reflected in pre-1914 Viennese literature. Many passages in Hofmannsthal (". . . and my ancestors, who in their shrouds are as much a part of me as my own hair . . ."), Schnitzler (". . . he who understands the connections, lives forever"), and others appeared to us as a confirmation of the way we experienced life.
Robert Weltsch

Felix Salten (Budapest 1869 – Zurich 1945), whose real name was Siegmund Salzmann, came to Vienna as a child and began his literary activities as early as 1887. In 1891 he joined the staff of the *Allgemeine Kunst-Chronik* (General Art Chronicle) and soon became the Burgtheater and art critic for the *Wiener Allgemeine Zeitung*. Like *Arthur Schnitzler, Richard Beer-Hofmann, Hugo von Hofmannsthal,* and Hermann Bahr, he belonged to the literary circle known as "Jung Wien," which met at the Café Griensteidl. He founded one of the first "cabarets" (satirical revue theaters) in Vienna in 1901, the "Jungwiener Theater Zum lieben Augustin," modeling it on the "Überbrettl" in Berlin and the "Elf Scharfrichter" in Munich. In 1906 he became arts and literature editor of the *Neue Freie Presse*, and spent approximately three decades with the paper. Salten's oeuvre is so diverse that it is difficult to categorize. His reviews, essays, and feuilletons, the best of which were already anthologized early in his career, deserve particular mention. However, Salten's novels, novellas, and short stories brought him his greatest literary success. The anonymous novel *Josephine Mutzenbacher*, one of the finest specimens of erotic literature in the German language, is attributed to him. Salten gained great popularity and international renown for his animal novels, especially *Bambi* (1923), which was made into a full-length cartoon by Walt Disney.

His book about Palestine, *Neue Menschen auf alter Erde* (New People on Old Soil [1925]), is his affirmation of Zionism.

Left: Felix Salten with his children. Photograph by d'Ora. 1911

175

Peter Altenberg im Café Central 1907

Peter Altenberg (Vienna 1859 – Vienna 1919), born Richard Engländer, created a genre and a language to capture the atmosphere of fin-de-siècle Vienna. A poet, bohemian, and eccentric, he wrote descriptive sketches of day-to-day life and its peculiarities, becoming one of Vienna's principal representatives of literary impressionism.

Left: Peter Altenberg at the Café Central in Vienna. 1907

Alfred Polgar (Vienna 1873 – Zurich 1955) began writing theater reviews for the *Weltbühne* (World Stage) and the *Tagebuch* (Diary) in Berlin in 1925. He retired to Vienna in 1933 and emigrated in 1938, arriving in the United States by way of Paris in 1940. A distinguished satirical feuilletonist, he is regarded as a master of the small form thanks to his cultural and critico-literary sketches, and his witty commentaries and musings (e.g. *An den Rand geschrieben* [Marginalia]).

Opposite page, below: Alfred Polgar. Ca. 1950

Anton Kuh (Vienna 1891
– New York 1941) was one of the
brightest minds on Vienna's coffeehouse literary scene. Though he
wrote for newspapers in Vienna
and Berlin, he became famous for
his unique extemporaneous
speeches – his friend *Egon Friedell*
called him "the speechwright."
Kuh's best-known works are *Von
Goethe abwärts* (Downwards from
Goethe [1922]), *Der unsterbliche
Österreicher* (The Immortal Austrian [1931]) and *Der Affe Zarathustra* (Zarathustra the Ape),
based on an improvised diatribe
against *Karl Kraus*.
Left: Anton Kuh. Photograph by
Albert Hilscher. 1931

It is in connection with minor occurrences that he [Alfred Polgar] demonstrates his mastery. He polishes the ordinary until it becomes extraordinary. What does he need the extraordinary for? It is no match for him. What does he need thrilling "events" for? Each of his sentences contains sensational linguistic events. His form is so subtle that coarse material or violent action dare not enter there. Sensations treat the poet with care and shun his company. They fear him. He might mock them, and then – oh, woe is them – they would no longer be sensations! Even truth is powerless against his style. When he allows grave tragedy to end in a joke, the reader does not even notice that the latter was arbitrary and the former serious. When he writes about something, he has genuinely created that "thing." Nowhere is there another (German-speaking) observer so like a creator to surpass a hundred creators.
Joseph Roth

Polgar Alfred, a classic today – so provocative in his introverted gentleness that the pianissimo of his nature makes the cups rattle – played tarok; but it was not the tarok of the ordinary citizen, it was Buddha's escape into tarok. Seeing him sitting like that for hours, one could hardly suppress the thought: "My God, what that man could achieve if he did not sit there for hours playing tarok." Which is precisely why he sat and played.
Anton Kuh

A particular characteristic of Vienna feuilletons is the jocose mixture of the essentially Jewish and the essentially Aryan nature. Of synagogal plaintiveness and Grinzing inebriation. Is the sorrow of more than a thousand years of diaspora best drowned in Viennese heurigen [young wine]? It seems to be. Carousing, that's my life as surely as I am standing here! The mixture certainly shows itself in the structure and style of the Viennese feuilleton. It has an emotional intellect and a remarkably intelligent emotional life. It plays elaborate mental games of logic with feelings and, on the other hand, always has a modicum of pathos lodged comfortably in its brain. The Viennese feuilleton has a resigned view of the world where it lacks thoughts, and a cerebral busyness where emotions cannot follow.
Alfred Polgar

Altenberg was a genuine Viennese and yet he had no home; the ground under his feet did not welcome him. He was a Jew. His life moved, Ahasuerus-like, from hotel room to hotel room, café to café. His humor was Jewish, antithetical, mercurial, self-ironic – but his wrath was prophetic, his rage Biblical. Peter Altenberg was strong evidence of the consistency of the Jewish race. His words are as immortal as those of any biblical poet.
Albert Ehrenstein

The way Peter Altenberg perennially sees women is the way every man has seen a woman at least once in his life: when he was in love.
Egon Friedell

Kurfürstendamm Theater crowded to the rafters . . . One and a half hours he walks around, speaking, struggling. From the table to the footlights, and back to the bottle. Now digressing, now hesitating, now with a new idea. Does not kowtow to the audience, becomes unpleasant instead. Unafraid of embarrassment. Immediately seizing himself by the collar, tearing away defenses wherever he scents only the suspicion of concealment on his own part.
Alfred Kerr on Anton Kuh

He [Egon Friedell] was – it must be recalled again and again – almost unbelievably versatile. A distinguished cultural philosopher and brilliant essayist, he also knew and loved the theater, and not only wrote for it but appeared in it as an actor. His satirical cabaret improvisations, in no way inferior to Anton Kuh's, made even the greatest sourpuss laugh, but he could . . . also laugh himself, heartily and uncontrollably.
Friedrich Torberg

Maximilian Harden (Berlin 1861 – Montana, Switzerland 1927), born Maximilian Felix Ernst Witkowski, was a left-wing social critic and satirist who always opposed the established order in the period of Kaiser Wilhelm II.

After surviving an assassination attempt, he retreated to Switzerland in 1923.
Below: Maximilian Harden. Photograph by Rudolf Dührkoop. Ca. 1905

In the hell of German-Jewish writers, Karl Kraus is the great watchdog and disciplinarian . . . The only thing he forgets is that he himself belongs in this hell, among the ones to be disciplined.
Franz Kafka

Alfred Kerr was witty, keenly appreciative, subjective, a man who judged from case to case; he was an impressionist, for whom a review was the recreation of an evening in the theater: he loved illusion, the beautiful façade, feasting the eye and the intellect.
Hans Sahl

The man who spoke was our last European of distinction [Maximilian Harden]. The man who spoke was a man with whom a vanished world emerged once more, the representative of an era almost gone, a man who still believed in justice, fair play, ethical behavior, and decency, even in the battle of opinions. "I always opposed the Emperor, from the very first day – but in his reign there was no killing." He rose far above himself. High above the heads of the petits bourgeois surrounding him spoke a man who used the language of the world, not the language of this Germany. He spoke of a nation that responded to his life's work by joining in the idiotic refrain of "Isidor." (And his name was not even Isidor, though he had once been called Felix.) He spoke of his enduring crime, Judaism, and the enduring stupidity of a régime.
Kurt Tucholsky

Maximilian Harden and Karl Kraus, Siegfried Jacobsohn, Stefan Grossmann, and Leopold Schwarzschild: all of them could have chosen for their periodicals and pamphlets the same subtitle that Erich Mühsam, the unluckiest of them all, tortured at Sonnenburg prison, did for his "Kain" – "Zeitschrift für Menschlichkeit" (Journal for humaneness). The volumes of "Zukunft" (Future), "Fackel" (Torch), "Weltbühne" (World stage), "Pan" (Kerr), or "Tagebuch" (Diary) contain, immortalized for all posterity, everything in the way of intellectual life that has flowed between Berlin and Vienna since 1890. Including the ephemeral, and particularly that. Captured and expressed in a language that some writers were capable of formulating abstrusely, others classically and with striking effect, those forty years that have filled our lives so far pass through our minds as we leaf through them.
Arnold Zweig

I learned from Karl Kraus that anything can be done with other people's words. He had a breathtaking way of dealing with what he read. He was masterful at denouncing people in their own words, which did not mean that he failed to indict them in his own blunt language. He supplied both and crushed everyone. One enjoyed the drama because one recognized the law that had dictated the words . . . One would not have wanted to miss any of these experiences, one did not miss any of them. One even attended those lectures sick and with a high temperature. It was also a way of gratifying one's inclination to be intolerant, which was innately strong and now, so to speak legitimately, grew to virtually inconceivable proportions.
Élias Canetti

Alfred Kerr (Breslau 1867 – Hamburg 1948), whose real name was Alfred Kempner, studied philosophy and German in Breslau and then in Berlin, where he settled. Berlin's most important, influential drama critic between 1895 and 1920, he wrote reviews for the *Tag* (Day) from 1900 to 1919, and from 1920 on for the liberal *Berliner Tageblatt* (Berlin Daily), the newspaper favored by the Jewish bourgeoisie. Writing in a brilliant, mannered style sparkling with wit, he commented on Berlin's illustrious rise to eminence as a theater city and on the "stylistic duel" between Erwin Piscator and *Max Reinhardt*, whom he criticized sharply. His pieces were informed by extraordinary intuition and an analytical intellect; his spiritual roots could be traced to Lessing's "Hamburger Dramaturgie" and the Romantic movement. *Die Welt im Drama* (The World in Drama [1917]), his most important work, is a significant document of the theatrical and cultural history of his time. In *Die Diktatur des Hausknechts und Melodien* (The Dictatorship of the Errand Boy and Melodies), he describes his life as a Jewish emigré writer.
Right: Alfred Kerr. Photograph by *Lotte Jacobi.* Ca. 1930

Karl Kraus (Vienna 1879 – Vienna 1936) renounced Judaism in 1898 and converted to Catholicism in 1911. In his mercilessly caustic essays, satirical commentars, and poems – particularly in the *Fackel* (Torch), the periodical he founded in 1899 – he denounced the excesses of the literary cliques and newspaper journalism of his time, viewing the degeneration of language as a sign of the distorted *Zeitgeist*. He attacked Judaism in his anti-Zionist polemic *Eine Krone für Zion* (A Crown for Zion [1898]) and in various essays in the *Fackel.*
Opposite page, left: Karl Kraus. Photograph by *d'Ora.* 1908

I am a German and I am a Jew, one as much and as completely as the other, the one inseparable from the other.
Jakob Wassermann

How tormented the man was! Tormented by himself, by his surroundings, by fate, hunger, cold, and unemployment, by the inability to find his way in the crude, pedestrian world of moneymaking, and the hypocritical world of unprincipled citizens in their velvet jackets or horn-rimmed glasses – torment and indecisiveness, despair and self-hatred; desolation inside, mockery outside . . . He was accused – he, the Jew – of being more German than the Germans; what is certain is that he helped the German soul to express itself, and that he is far removed from the Germanness of today. How the dark landscape begins to sing under his hands! How music, forests, machines, farms, and stony streets proclaim what they are, what they are to him and what they are to us! He expressed the inexpressible; he is what the French call "bourdon," the big, sonorous church bell.
Kurt Tucholsky

There are two strands of thought and experience that, inextricably woven together, sometimes separately, sometimes parallel, sometimes entwined, run through all of Wassermann's life and endeavors: his exploration of the fate of the Jews in the German world and his battle for justice in human society. Justice and Judaism – for Wassermann they are indissolubly linked.
Peter de Mendelssohn

The last time I saw Jakob Wassermann – it was in Zurich – death had not yet placed its sign upon him. He spoke enthusiastically, even passionately. He spoke of Germany, his father- and motherland, the land of his heart. For he was, as one knows, a Jew, and a German Jew has a twofold bond to Germany: he is linked with it by both selfless and truly tragic love. He also spoke with bitterness, yes bitterness. Not death, but bitterness, the precursor of death, had placed its sign upon him. He had not traveled to the end of his road as a German and Jew. That road led nowhere. Only to a wall that suddenly loomed before him, a wall of hatred and brutality. Before that wall Jakob Wassermann had to turn back and, the ancient Jewish pikestaff in hand, go into exile.
Joseph Roth

Jakob Wassermann (Fürth 1873 – Altaussee, Styria 1934), being an S. Fischer Verlag author and having lived in Vienna since 1898, moved in the *Arthur Schnitzler-Hugo von Hofmannsthal* circle. His psychoanalytical, sometimes sensationalistic novels chronicled the search for justice and the struggle against the "inertia of the heart." In *Die Juden von Zirndorf* (The Jews of Zirndorf [1897]) he described Jewish life in the city of his birth. His autobiography in 1921, *Mein Weg als Deutscher und Jude* (My Life as a German and a Jew) was a reaction to growing anti-Semitism. He advocated Zionism in *Selbstbetrachtungen* (Reflections on Myself [1933]), written after Hitler came to power. Above: Jakob Wassermann. Photograph, Atelier Kolliner. Before 1933

Stefan Zweig (Vienna 1881 – suicide in Petropolis, Brazil 1942) began his career as a poet of the Viennese impressionist school and, through his friendship with Emile Verhaeren and Romain Rolland, developed into a pacifist-humanist writer. Like *Hugo von Hofmannsthal*, he regarded himself as one of the last representatives of European bourgeois culture, which he described in numerous novellas, novels, and his autobiography, *Die Welt von Gestern* (The World of Yesterday [1942]). Judaism was treated in greater depth in the collection *Kaleidoskop* (1924) and the short novel *Der begrabene Leuchter* (The Buried Chandelier [1937]), written after he had fled from Salzburg in the wake of rising nationalism (1934). Opposite page: Stefan Zweig. Ca. 1925

I do not think that we are called upon to establish a "Jewish," a national literature; we need merely write what we are impelled to. And as we are Jews, and do not deny it, our works will automatically take on a Jewish character. All attitudinizing and conscious accentuation, on the other hand, seem superfluous to me.
Stefan Zweig

W hat I had remotely sensed and then seen confirmed by ten years of wandering – the absolute freedom to choose between nations, to feel a welcome guest wherever I went, as a participant and a mediator, this international feeling of freedom from the insanity of a fanatic world – has saved me in these times; and I am grateful that it is Judaism that has made this supranational freedom possible.
Stefan Zweig

B ut of all their lies, perhaps none is more false, cruel and further from the truth than the claim that the Jews in Germany ever expressed hatred or hostility toward German culture. On the contrary, Austria provided indisputable evidence that in all those peripheral areas where the survival of the German language was at risk, the Jews were the only ones who upheld German culture. The names of Goethe, Hölderlin, and Schiller, Schubert, Mozart, and Bach were no less sacred to these Jews of the east than those of their own patriarchs. It may have been an unrequited love and today is certainly an unappreciated one, but all the lies in the world cannot obliterate the existence of this love, for there are a thousand works and deeds to attest to it.
Stefan Zweig

N ever before have I felt so liberated by Judaism as I do now, in this time of nationalist madness; and all that separates me from you and yours is that I have never wanted the Jews to become a nation again and humiliate themselves by entering the contest of rival realities. That I love the diaspora and affirm it as the sense of Judaism's idealism, as the principle behind its vocation for world citizenship and universal humanity.
And I would wish for no other union than in the spirit, our only real element, never in a language, in a people, in traditions and customs, syntheses as attractive as they are dangerous.
Stefan Zweig

181

And there is a brod-eling and a werfel-ing, a kafka-ing and a kisch-ing.
Anton Kuh

Most of Prague's German authors were Jews, but they were pervaded by a feeling of Jewishness only in isolated cases. Their German linguistic consciousness was more crucial to their sense of history than their tribal sense could ever have been . . . The German-speaking poets and writers had access to at least four ethnic sources at once: the Teutonic, of course, to which they belonged culturally and linguistically; the Czech, which, as their habitat, surrounded them everywhere; the Jewish, even if they were not themselves Jews, for it constituted a widely perceptible, principal historical factor in the city; and the Austrian, in which they were all born and raised, and which played a fateful role in shaping them, whether they accepted it . . . or found this or that to criticize.
Johannes Urzidil

"Prague is traversed by the Nebbich, which ultimately flows into the Elbe," writes Gustav Meyrink, who, as we know, was only a Praguer by choice and consequently, or nonetheless, was the only one far and wide on the Prague literary scene to preserve a certain critical attitude toward the golden Moldau granny. No Praguer, whether a literary man or not – but then, everyone essentially was or considered himself to be a literary man; even if he had never published a line in his life, he considered himself better than the acclaimed writers – I beg your pardon, but who is this Werfel supposed to be, his father has a glove store on Mariengasse – no Praguer, I say, has ever found the least thing about Prague to find fault with (meanwhile the most malicious self-criticism is at home in supposedly cozy Vienna, from Nestroy through Karl Kraus to Qualtinger), no Praguer has ever hesitated to consider Prague the navel of the world and himself the navel of Prague.
Friedrich Torberg

What do I have in common with the Jews? I hardly have anything in common with myself and ought to go and stand quietly in a corner, grateful that I can breathe.
Franz Kafka

For as K. lives in the village near the Schlossberg, so the human being of today lives in his body; he eludes it, he is hostile to it. A human being may wake up one morning and find himself transformed into vermin. Alienation – his own alienation – has become his master.
Walter Benjamin

To get away from Judaism is what most of those who began to write in German wanted, usually with the vague approval of their fathers (this vagueness was the infuriating thing); that is what they wanted, but with their little back legs they were glued to the Judaism of their fathers, and their little front legs could find no new footing. Their despair over this was their inspiration.
Franz Kafka

But what sort of Judaism was it that I got from you? . . . Later, as a young man, I could not understand how, with the insignificant scrap of Judaism you yourself possessed, you could reproach me for not making an effort to cling to a similar, insignificant scrap . . . Four days a year you went to the synagogue, where you were, to say the least, closer to the indifferent than to those who took it seriously, patiently went through the prayers as a formality. . . . That's how it was in the synagogue; at home it was, if possible, even poorer,

182

Egon Erwin Kisch (Prague 1885 – Prague 1948) took up journalism in 1904, at the early age of 19. On the staff of the *Berliner Tageblatt* in 1913/14, his contact with revolutionary groups antithetical to his firmly bourgeois origins dates from around this period. He was with the Red Guards in 1918 when they stormed the offices of the *Neue Freie Presse* in Vienna. Beginning as a local reporter, he went on to write crime reports and extensive accounts of his travels. As a writer of Jewish-Bohemian descent, German was the language in which he wrote. The title of his book *Der rasende Reporter* (The Racing Reporter) became his nickname.
His *Geschichten aus sieben Ghettos* (Stories from Seven Ghettos) is a lovingly ironic description of Jewish life in Europe around 1930.
Right: Egon Erwin Kisch. Photograph by *Lotte Jacobi*.
Ca. 1930

Franz Kafka (Prague 1883 – Kierling/Vienna 1924) came from a family with a commercial background. His development was shaped by the "magic reality" of Prague. His novels and stories ("The Trial" 1923, "The Castle" 1926) portray modern man despairing of his existence.
Opposite page: Franz Kafka as a student. Ca. 1905

being confined to the first Seder, which more and more developed into a farce, with fits of hysterical laughter. . . . This was the religious material that was handed on to me. . . . How one could do anything better with that material than get rid of it as fast as possible, I could not understand; precisely the getting rid of it seemed to me to be the devoutest action. . . .
Franz Kafka to his father

Human truth never resides in the exception, not even in the exception of the persecuted but only in what is, or should be, the rule. It was out of this insight that Kafka's Zionist tendencies sprang. He affiliated himself with the movement that wanted to liquidate the exceptional position of the Jews, to make them into a "people like all other peoples." He, possibly the last of the great European writers, could certainly not have desired to become a nationalist.
Hannah Arendt

So I was a Jew! I was different! I was not a human being like all the rest! . . . Alien here and alien there! Alien beyond all imagination! Alienation, the arch-feeling of my life.
Franz Werfel

Musil wanted to know whether Kisch was still such a militant communist. "Of course," said Roth, "and he'll always stay one." – "Strange that he should be a good reporter," observed Musil. "Is he a good reporter?" asked Roth. "I can't judge. I like him too much."
Soma Morgenstern

My experience of Judaism was "pleasant." I was not ashamed of my origin; it would never have occurred to me that there might be anything disgraceful in it. Nor was I particularly proud of my people. The atmosphere that surrounded me was one of absolute normalcy. For a long while things Jewish did not concern me at all, but I had not forgotten them. The sensitivity that seizes many a western Jew if even the slightest allusion is made to his association with his people – this over-sensitivity, which is a particularly distasteful sign of weakness and insecurity, was totally alien to me.
Max Brod

Alfred Wolfenstein (Halle 1888 – Paris 1945) wrote expressionist poetry, plays, and novellas, as well as theoretical essays such as "Jüdisches Wesen und neue Dichtung" (The Jewish Nature and New Poetry [1922]). After years of flight from National Socialism, he committed suicide in 1945.
Above: Alfred Wolfenstein. Photograph by *Lotte Jacobi*. Ca. 1930

Franz Werfel (Prague 1890 – Beverly Hills 1945) was a writer equally at home in Prague and Vienna. He began his career as a poet and developed into a novelist and dramatist whose works rely on the effects of baroque prolixity, operatic pathos and religious profundity. Above all his later books are informed by the appeal for "religious renewal in a materialistic world."
Below: Franz Werfel. Photograph by *d'Ora*. Ca. 1922

The secret of Jewish energy is the knowledge of impending doom. For two thousand years the Jews have continually been on the brink of annihilation. Since the tin can, as a wit once called the ghetto, burst, they have been exposed, open to all dangers, which is why their energy has, ever since, been marked by such explosive activity in all spheres. Now virtually inescapable, the danger of eradication each carries far within his unconscious, is a powerful stimulus.
Oskar Baum

I am a German-Jewish writer, i. e., a Jew writing in the German language. I have known from the beginning that I am one, and since then this knowledge has been augmented at most by the likelihood that I will be the last one . . . If I have any Jewish function left at all, then it is solely to shape my public activities in such a way that as many non-Jews as possible will experience the death of the last German-Jewish writer as a loss.
Friedrich Torberg

The social position of Jewish Expressionists seems to exemplify the isolation and marginalization typical of all modern artists.
Thomas Anz/Michael Stark

The summum bonum, "Paradise on Earth," will not be created by any social system; the only point is to fight for the comparative best that mankind can find and implement.
Ernst Toller

"Do you really believe that the Jews killed a Christian baby in Konitz?" I ask Stanislaus. "I'll never eat Passion-cake again." "Idiot! You can give it to me then." "Why do they shout, 'Yah, yah, dirty Jew'?" "Don't you shout 'Polack' after us?" "That's different."

*"Different, hell! If you want to know,
Grandmother says it was the Jews killed our
Savior on the cross."
I run into the barn and crawl into the straw,
feeling miserable. I know the Savior. He
hangs in Stanislaus' room; red tears run down
his cheeks, and he carries his heart open in his
breast and it is all bleeding. Underneath it
says: "Suffer little children to come unto me."
When I am there and nobody can see me I
pray to the Savior.
"Please, dear Savior, forgive me for letting
the Jews killed you dead."
When I am in bed I ask Mother: "Why are
we Jews?"
"Go to sleep, you naughty boy, and don't ask
silly questions."
But I can't go to sleep. I don't want to be a
Jew. I don't want the other children to run
after me shouting "Dirty Jew!"*
Ernst Toller

*Shall I capitulate to the insanity of the
persecutors and replace my German airs with
Jewish ones? . . . if someone asked me where I
belonged, I would answer: a Jewish mother
bore me, Germany nourished me, Europe
educated me, my home is the earth, the world
my fatherland.*
Ernst Toller

*He is handsome and wise
And good.
And still prays like a child:
Now I lay me down to sleep,
Pray the Lord my soul to keep.*

*He is a magnolia tree
Filled with white flames.
The sun shines -
Children always play catch
Around him.*
Else Lasker-Schüler. "Ernst Toller"

*As if an allegory of late union, the Jewish
temperament and the German language meet
in this new poem.
Among the western European languages,
German seems to have a different relationship to the Jewish temperament than others:
in German it preserves itself, it remains alive;
in the romance languages it tends to vanish
without a trace. Here the Jewish nature
moves confidently, as close to the language as
a swimmer to his element. This is not because
the German language is freer and more
yielding and flows more gently over fixed
things. What we see beyond all the differences
is a strange kinship. Sometimes, when the
contradictions and love between them come
to the fore, the Jew appears to be a Doppel-
gänger of the German.*
Alfred Wolfenstein

Walter Hasenclever (Aachen 1890 – Les Milles camp, France 1940) was a poet and dramatist. His rebellious *Sohn* (Son [1914]) was the first expressionist play performed on the German stage (1916). Revolutionary ideas and the desire to politicize the spirit and convert others to pacifism are the factors that shaped his works. In later years he also wrote witty, entertaining comedies.

Like Walter Hasenclever, *Ernst Toller* (Samotschin, Posen 1893 – New York 1939) became a convinced pacifist as a result of the horrors of World War I. His friendship with *Kurt Eisner* and *Gustav Landauer* led him to the "ethical socialism" he espoused during the November Revolution and the *Räterepublik* (worker's republic). In 1919 he was sentenced to five years at Niederschönenfeld prison. Toller achieved literary success above all as a dramatist and political essayist. His plays (*Hoppla, wir leben noch!* [Whoops, We're Still Alive] in 1927 and *Hinkemann* [Limping Man] in 1923) advocate social revolution as the solution to the dilemma of society. *Above:* Walter Hasenclever (left) and Ernst Toller. 1928

Else Lasker-Schüler (Elberfeld 1869 – Jerusalem 1945) came from a religious family. Briefly married to *Herwarth Walden*, she spent most of her life in Berlin, where she soon became the hub of bohemian circles. When her works were banned from publication in 1933, she fled to Zurich, going on to Jerusalem in 1937. Her *Hebräischen Ballade* (Hebrew Ballads [1913]) and prose piece *Hebräerland* (Land of the Hebrews [1937]) evidence how firmly rooted she was in Jewish tradition.
Left: Else Lasker-Schüler. 1912

Mascha Kaléko (Schydlow, Poland 1912 – Zurich 1974) grew up in Berlin and emigrated to the United States in 1938, also living in Jerusalem for some time. She wrote wittily melancholy poems ("Stenogrammheft" [Shorthand Pad] 1933, *Verse für Zeitgenossen* [Verses for Contemporaries] 1945).
Below: Mascha Kaléko. 1932

The Kleist prize so often desecrated by both the bestower and the recipient has been ennobled again by being awarded to you. Congratulations to german poetry.
Gottfried Benn

Suddenly it was dark and Frau Lasker-Schüler stepped onto the stage. She was robed in blue silk. Wide trousers, silver shoes, a sort of wide jacket, her hair like silk, jet black, part wild, then again sensuously soft . . . Jussuf was so very much a woman, she was so beautiful, so full of sensuality, I would never have thought she was already 38 years old.
Wieland Herzfelde

When I was a child and starry-eyed, I so loved to study the artistic, awe-inspired, priestly countenance of my great-grandfather, the Chief Rabbuni of Rhineland and Westphalia, supreme head of his congregation to their religious and political benefit, bringing such sacred years of peace.
Else Lasker-Schüler

Whoever does not carry the promised land in his heart will never reach it.
Else Lasker-Schüler

The rock decays,
From which I spring,
And which I sing my songs of God . . .
Abruptly I fall from the path
And trickle all in myself
Far away, alone over lamenting stones
Towards the sea.

Have flowed so far away
From my blood
Cider-fermented.
And still, still the echo
In me.
When horribly towards the East
The decayed skeleton of rock,
My people,
Cry out to God.
Else Lasker-Schüler. "My People"

This deaf and dumb time, which has only sneers for the truly original, cannot be provoked often enough by references to Else Lasker-Schüler, the strongest, most recondite lyricist of modern Germany . . .
Karl Kraus

Else Lasker-Schüler is the Jewish poetess. Speaking of Deborah! She has wings and chains, the exultation of a child, the chaste ardor of a blissful bride, the weary blood of thousands of years of exile and age-old wounds . . . Her poetic spirit is black diamond, cutting and painful in her head. Very painful. The black swan of Israel, a Sappho whose world has been torn asunder. Childlike radiance, depths of gloom. Through the night of her hair wanders the winter snow. Her cheeks delicate fruits, consumed by the spirit. She romps with her overserious Jahve, and the mother in her chats away about her boy, as is right and proper, not philosophically . . . no . . . right out of a fairy tale.
Peter Hille

Abandoned
In a barque of night
I drifted
And drifted to the shore.
I leaned on clouds against the rain.
On sand-dunes against the raging wind.
There was nothing to rely on.
Only miracles.
I ate the greening fruit of longing,
Drank of the waters that create thirst.
An alien, silent before unexplored zones,
I froze my way through the dark years.
The home I chose was love.
Mascha Kaléko. "The Early Years"

Have never really been a poet as the word is probably understood. Have never up to this very moment possessed a desk – my manuscripts are stored here in the kitchen cupboard. In Germany, before Hitler came, I lived at home with my parents. Had much to endure, and took care of the household, did the nursing when there was illness and, when it became difficult to breath, began scribbling on scraps of paper now and then . . .
But that life – in the nights of many sleepless years and continually hurled into "otherness," confronted with death each night anew, when I saw the last remaining creature beloved to me ensnared so far away – always imposed on me, face to face with the sufferers, the words that were later called my poems and dramatic attempts.
Nelly Sachs

What you ask is right and proper, for it goes directly to the heart of the matter. A person, himself an inextricable universe of blood-suffused galaxies, will always become guilty on earth, that is his tragedy. Why? Because! The extent of his share of guilt varies – the more sensitive the disposition, the more lacerating his own feeling of guilt.
Nelly Sachs

Can we hold our own before these poems or not? No honors, no standing in society will help us if we fail before these verses.
Walter Jens

Walter Mehring (Berlin 1896 – Zurich 1981) founded the radical leftist "Politisches Cabaret" in Berlin in 1920 and was one of the co-founders of the Berlin Dada group. Whether in caustically satirical songs or his play about an inflation profiteer (*Der Kaufmann von Berlin* [The Merchant of Ber-lin] 1929), he leveled his criticism at the middle classes. In *Die verlo-rene Bibliothek* (The Lost Library [1952]) he offered a skeptical anal-ysis of twentieth-century political-intellectual development.
<u>Above:</u> Walter Mehring. Photo-graph by *Lotte Jacobi.* Ca. 1929

With his verse Mehring introduced a completely new tone into literature; that there is a French influence here and there does not explain that tone. These poems are strangely unreal, brittle; sometimes we are strangled by a deliberately stilted phrase; sometimes the rhythm suddenly stands still – this poet can even influence his readers' heartbeat if he wants to.
Kurt Tucholsky

You have confirmed it for me again and again: that the new, false pathos disgusts you as much as the old. It is enough even to spoil emigration for a person! You have it behind you!
And we don't know what we have ahead of us! But there is one thing I do know, namely that some time – in ten or twenty years – the same people who today want to criticize you for the consistency of your unerring intellect will discover how prophetically right Peter Panter was when he wrote: "And then every-thing will be as if nothing had happened? and: 'Oh, you know, in my heart I was always against Hitler – but look, under the circumstances - - -'."
Walter Mehring

I remain particularly silent during anti-Semitic attacks – and there is a particular reason for that. The question of Judaism has never affected me much. You can see from my writings that I rarely even touch upon the whole complex; my knowledge in the field is not very extensive, I do not know if the Zionists are right or wrong, and so I remain silent. The people who want to hit the Jew in me shoot wide of the mark. My heartbeat does not accelerate when someone shouts "dirty Jew" after me; it is as alien to me as if he said "You weed whose name starts with a T – what possible good can there be in you." I do not say that I am right; I am simply stating my feelings, and not even publicly. The question does not affect me.
Kurt Tucholsky

I "resigned from Judaism" in the year 1911, and I know that cannot be done.
Kurt Tucholsky

And then came your [Tucholsky's] letter, and it talked about nothing but Jews or mainly about them. I wrote that we had lost a battle. I meant that "We" as a far more comprehensive collective than the sector of German Jewry. We, that was the political Left of this world, the civilization of this world, the democracy of this world, the freedom, decency, breathability of this world.
Arnold Zweig

Nor is it any coincidence that I was taken with one of Peter Panter's most dubious creations: Herr Wendriner. The "model" of a bourgeois Berlin Jew, he was probably in the garment business somewhere in the Spittel-markt area, but resided in the Bayerische Viertel, of course. Probably moved to Berlin from Posen, which was still the Prussian provincial capital at the time, or from Breslau a few decades ago . . . Here in Berlin I had them before my eyes all the time: their arrogant insecurity; the eternal know-it-all manner of the ignorant; the way they quoted Theodor Wolff's editorials from the "Berliner Tageblatt"; the way they worshipped success, regardless of what kind. Jewish self-hatred had helped Tucholsky to create the figure; he had even made Herr Wendriner to a small extent according to his own image. And, naturally, the perceptive man had known that.
Hans Mayer

I had already heard at home in Stettin that my parents were of Jewish descent and that we were a Jewish family. I did not notice much more of that Judaism within the family. Outside, I was confronted by anti-Semitism, as if it were perfectly natural.
Alfred Döblin

This Left Poot [Alfred Döblin] tickles with his sword where Heinrich Mann lunges – and he is wittier than Prussia is brutal, which is surely saying something. He deals gently, incisively, wittily, unabashedly, and passionately with the new Germany. It is a totally novel kind of humor, unlike anything I have ever read in the German language.
Kurt Tucholsky

In the first half of the twenties, pogrom-like events took place in Berlin, in the eastern part of the city, on Gollnowstrasse and vicinity. This happened against the background of the insensate brutality of those years; it was Nazism uttering its first cries. At that time representatives of Berlin Zionism invited a number of men of Jewish descent to meetings where these events, their background, and the aims of Zionism were discussed. After a discussion of this kind, one of them came to my apartment to urge me to take a trip to Palestine, an idea alien to me. His suggestion affected me in a different way. Though I did not agree to go to Palestine, I decided I had better find out something about the Jews. I realized that I did not actually know any Jews. I could not call those of my friends who called themselves Jews, Jews.
They were not, either by faith or language; perhaps they were the remnants of a people that had disappeared, that had long merged with its new surroundings. So I began to ask myself and others: where are there Jews? In Poland, I was told. Upon which I went to Poland.
Alfred Döblin

Kurt Tucholsky (Berlin 1890 – Hindas, Sweden 1935) studied law in Berlin, Jena, and Geneva. He began his career as a journalist in 1911, writing cultural and socio-critical columns for the social democratic *Vorwärts* (Forward). In 1913 *Siegfried Jacobsohn* offered him a post with the political-cultural magazine *Schaubühne* (Theater; from 1918, *Weltbühne* [World Theater]), which he also edited for a year following Jacobsohn's death. Carl von Ossietzky succeeded him as editor-in-chief of *Weltbühne* from 1926 to 1933. Disappointed with the politics of the Weimar Republic, Tucholsky moved to Paris in 1924. In 1929 he

moved on to Sweden, where he wrote his only novel (*Schloss Gripsholm* [Castle Gripsholm] 1931). In 1933 he was stripped of his citizenship in absentia and his books were burned. His suicide was an act of despair.
As several of Tucholsky's articles might appear in a single magazine issue, he invented four pseudonyms (Kaspar Hauser, Peter Panter, Theobald Tiger, Ignaz Wrobel). Split up into four egos, he fought an embittered battle against narrow-mindedness, reactionism, nationalism, and National Socialism, making his points with biting irony and penetrating wit.
Above: Kurt Tucholsky. Ca. 1930

Inside Jewish and a genius,
Outside just that bit unvirtuous,
never alone, always à deux: -
the neveu!-
K.-
Kurt Tucholsky

Self-hatred is the first step to improvement.
Kurt Tucholsky

A plump little Berliner wanted to use his typewriter to keep a catastrophe at bay.
Erich Kästner

Döblin saw the Jews with the incorruptibility that is a virtue of love . . . He should have called his book "Journey to the Jews." He understood them better than did his western European "co-religionists" of French, German, and British "nationality," who out of pity for their distant cousins bestow charity on them and distribute clean collars and enlightenment to the "oppressed masses."
Joseph Roth

Alfred Döblin (Stettin 1878 – Emmendingen/Freiburg i.B. 1957) came from a Jewish family with a commercial background. In 1888 he and his mother moved to Berlin, where he studied medicine and later practiced as a nerve specialist. He began pursuing his literary inclinations early, founding the expressionist periodical *Der Sturm* (The Storm) with *Herwarth Walden* in 1910. His first major success as an author was the novel *Die drei Sprünge des Wang-lun* (The Three Leaps of Wang-lun [1915]). In 1918 he declared his advocacy of revolution and, as a journalist, subsequently directed sharp criticism at the reactionary forces at work in the Weimar Republic, using the pseudonym "Linker Poot." One day after the Reichstag fire he left Germany, fleeing to New York by way of Zurich and Paris. His most famous work, *Berlin Alexanderplatz* (1929), is the most important German novel of the big city ever written. His later propensity towards a Catholic world view was preceded by the discovery of Judaism. Against the background of pogrom-like conditions in the eastern part of Berlin, Döblin took a trip to Poland in 1924 and recounted it in book form (*Reise in Polen* [Journey through Poland]).
Right: Alfred Döblin. Photograph by *Lotte Jacobi*. Ca. 1930

*H*ermann Broch was a poet in spite of himself. That he was born a poet and did not want to be one was the fundamental trait of his nature, inspired the dramatic action of his greatest book, and became the basic conflict of his life. Of his life, not his psyche; for this was not a psychological conflict that could have been expressed in psychic struggles, with no other consequences than what Broch himself half ironically, half disgustedly called "soul clamor."
Hannah Arendt

*T*he aristocraty has a family history, the Jewish bourgeoisie a history of neuroses . . .
Hermann Broch

*T*he Germans are the most curious people in Europe – this hysterical mixture of violence and sentimentality which breaks through again and again and which will affect the fate of all Europe disturbs me deeply. One cannot remain simply an aesthetic onlooker! People like you and like me must after all make quite clear where we stand.
Hermann Broch

*A*nd now let me tell you a story from the "Ethics of the Fathers" (from the year 100 A. D.) . . . A stranger comes to Rabbi X and asks: "Rabbi, what is higher, knowledge or kindness?" Rabbi X answers: "Knowledge, of course, for it is the center of life. Naturally, if someone has only knowledge without kindness, it is as if he possessed the key to the innermost chamber but had lost the one to the antechamber."
Hermann Broch

*E*lias Canetti (Rustchuk 1905) comes from a Sephardic family. Since emigrating from Austria (1938) he has lived in London and Zurich. His first book, *Die Blendung* (The Blinding [1936]), has remained his sole work of fiction and already introduces the leitmotif of his whole oeuvre, the phenomenon of power. *Masse und Macht* (Crowds and Power [1960]) is a study of societal behavior. His three-volume autobiography describes his childhood and youth, ending with Nazi Germany's *Anschluss* of Austria. Canetti was awarded the Nobel Prize for Literature in 1981.
<u>Above</u>: Elias Canetti. Can. 1935

*H*ermann Broch (Vienna 1886 – New York 1956) gave up the management of his father's textile business in 1927 to study mathematics, philosophy, and psychology at the University of Vienna (until 1931). Arrested by the National Socialists (1938), he was freed thanks to the intervention of foreign friends (among them James Joyce) and emigrated to New York.
A fiction writer, cultural philosopher, and essayist, he depicted the fin-de-siècle disintegration of values in his trilogy *Die Schlafwandler* (The Sleepwalkers). In *Hofmannsthal und seine Zeit* (Hofmannsthal and His Time) he examined the rapidity of the assimilation process, using the Hofmann family as an example, and offered an analysis of Viennese bourgeois culture in the nineteenth century.
<u>Left</u>: Hermann Broch. 1937

*A*ll this is only another way of saying that the humanitarianism of brotherhood scarcely befits those who do not belong among the insulted and the injured and can share in it only through their compassion. The warmth of pariah peoples cannot rightfully extend to those whose different position in the world imposes on them a responsibility for the world and does not allow them to share the cheerful unconcern of the pariah.
Hannah Arendt

*J*udaism does not exist outside Orthodoxy, on the one hand, and Yiddish-speaking, folklore-producing Jewry, on the other. What also exist are people of Jewish descent, for whom Jewish concepts in the sense of a tradition do not exist and who, for certain social reasons and because they belonged to a circumscribed clique in society, constituted something like a "Jewish type."
Hannah Arendt

I was a friend of hers [Hannah Arendt] for more than fifty years, ever since she turned up at the age of eighteen as a first-semester philosophy student among the many young people who flocked to Marburg from all over Germany . . . Shy and introverted, with strikingly beautiful features and lonely eyes, she immediately stood out as "extraordinary," as "unique" in an as yet indefinable way. Intellectual brilliance was not a rare commodity at the time. But with her it was an intensity, an inner direction, an instinct for quality, a search for what was essential, a penetration to the depths that cast a magic spell around her. One sensed her absolute resolve to be herself, the doggedness to achieve this goal despite her own vulnerability . . .

She was passionately moral, but not at all moralistic. Whatever she had to say was important, often provocative, sometimes incorrect, but never trivial, never indifferent, and always unforgettable. Even her errors were worth more than the truths of many less significant minds. Naturally she liked to be right and could occasionally become terribly belligerent; but she did not believe, as she once confessed to me, that we could nowadays possess the "truth." She believed in the constant and always preliminary attempt to apprehend the facet that happens to show itself in present circumstances. Thinking that idea to the end – that in itself is reward enough, for if we do, we will understand more than we did before. We will have more light, though still not the "truth."

Hans Jonas

W alter Benjamin (Berlin 1892 – suicide in Port Bou, Spain 1940) lived in Berlin as a freelance writer and translator after receiving his Ph.D. Going out from an anti-bourgeois stance, he made a case for Marxism in his essays and literary and social criticism. Whereas his closest friend, the Zionist *Gershom Scholem*, had already emigrated to Palestine in 1923, Benjamin emigrated to France in 1933 and in 1935 joined the Institut für Sozialforschung (Frankfurt School), which had moved to Geneva and was later transferred to New York. He devoted himself largely to establishing a new aesthetic philosophy, which was to be integrated into a philosophy of history.

Right: Walter Benjamin. Photograph by *Gisèle Freund*. Ca. 1930

H annah Arendt (Hannover 1906 – New York 1975) first studied philosophy with Martin Heidegger and theology with Rudolf Bultmann in Marburg, then went on to study philosophy with *Edmund Husserl* in Freiburg and Karl Jaspers in Heidelberg. In 1933 she fled to France and in 1941 to the United States, where she taught political philosophy. Her most important works are: *Origins of Totalitarianism* (1965) and *The Life of the Mind* (1960). The concept of the "banality of evil," which she used in her book *Eichmann in Jerusalem* (1964), led to heated controversy, particularly in Israel and New York. In *Rahel Varnhagen* (1959) she described the life of a German Jewess whose salon was attended by the brightest minds of the time.

Below: Hannah Arendt in Paris. After 1933

G ermans and Jews have the affinity of related extremes.
Walter Benjamin

T he only way I have ever been able to study and reflect is, if I may put it that way, in a theological sense – namely in accordance with the Talmudic teaching of the forty-nine levels of meaning in every passage of the Torah. In my experience, even the tritest Communist platitude has more hierarchies of meaning than today's bourgeois profundity, which deals only in apologetics.
Walter Benjamin

M y experience has led me to the following insight: the Jews constitute an elite among intellectuals . . . For to me Judaism is by no means an end in itself, it is one of the distinguished vehicles and representatives of the intellect.
Walter Benjamin

A mong the Jewish categories he [Walter Benjamin] introduced as such and upheld to the last, there is, apart from the Messianic idea – nothing is more inaccurate than the notion that he derived it from the works of Ernst Bloch, even if it was what they shared on Jewish ground – above all the concept of remembrance.
Gershom Scholem

For two thousand years the Jews had only one thing in common: their Book. This book was their state, nation, and history; it gave meaning to their suffering and was the only thing that held them together. This book, and only this book, made them into a people. Is it any wonder that they commented on it, turned every letter this way and that, based their life on it? That a people whose sense, essence, and life was a book should become "literary"? On his highest holiday, the Jew calls out to his God: "Nothing has remained for us, only this Book." His ritual law demands that he know how to read and write. Even in the darkest times, there were only very few illiterates among the Jews . . . The life and lot of the Jews could not but cultivate in them all the skills that make a writer.
Lion Feuchtwanger

I have often pored over the works of German authors of Jewish descent, looking for some linguistic trait that unequivocally indicates their Jewish origin. No matter how diligently I study, I can find no such trait in any of the works of the great German writers of Jewish descent, from Mendelssohn to Schnitzler and Wassermann, from Heine to Arnold and Stefan Zweig.
Lion Feuchtwanger

Striving for knowledge for its own sake, love of justice bordering on fanaticism, and striving for personal autonomy – these are the traditional themes of the Jewish people that allow me to experience my kinship with them as destiny's gift.
Arnold Zweig

You know how passionately, indeed how joyfully I am a Jew.
Arnold Zweig

Lion Feuchtwanger (Munich 1884 – Los Angeles 1958) began his career as a theater critic. In 1908 he helped to found the cultural periodical *Der Spiegel* (The Mirror). In 1918 he took part in the November Revolution in Berlin. He fled to Sanary-sur-Mer in the south of France in 1933 and was interned at Les Milles camp in 1939. In 1940 he succeeded in escaping to the United States by way of Spain and Portugal. With Bertolt Brecht and Willi Bredel he edited the literary magazine *Das Wort* (The Word), published in Moscow from 1936 to 1939. A critical political playwright and novelist, he devised a new approach to the historical and historical-cultural novel (*Jud Süss*, *Erfolg* [Success], *Josephus-Trilogie*), which brought him considerable success.
Above: Lion Feuchtwanger. Photograph by *Lotte Jacobi*. Ca. 1930

My brain thinks like a cosmopolitan, my heart beats like a Jew . . . Judaism is a shared mentality, a shared intellectual attitude. It is the agreement of all who belong to this group, the "consensus omnium" on all crucial problems. It is the concord and agreement of a three-thousand-year-old tradition on what is good and bad, fortune and misfortune, desirable or hateful, agreement on the fundamental views concerning God and man.
Lion Feuchtwanger

Arnold Zweig (Gross Glogau, Silesia 1887 – Berlin 1968) studied philosophy, German literature, and languages. He became a freelance writer, living first at the Starnbergersee in Bavaria and from 1923 on in Berlin. He emigrated to Palestine by way of Czechoslovakia, Switzerland, and France in 1933, returning to (East) Berlin, where he became a member of the SED Cultural Council, in 1948. From 1950 to 1953 he was president of the Deutsche Akademie der Künste (German Academy of Arts) and succeeded Bertolt Brecht as president of the German PEN-Zentrum Ost und West in 1957. Zweig's plays, stories, and essays deal consciously with Judaism; *Caliban oder Politik der Leidenschaft* (Caliban or the Politics of Passion [1927]) is an attack on anti-Semitism. It was followed by *Bilanz des deutschen Judentums 1933* (A Balance-sheet of German Judaism 1933), published in 1934 and (with Lion Feuchtwanger) *Die Aufgabe des Judentums* (The Task of Judaism [1933]).
Opposite page: Arnold Zweig. Photograph by *Lotte Jacobi*. Ca. 1930

I have had to travel many miles. My life is more easily measured in space than in time. It lies between the place I was born and the cities, countries, villages I have passed through in the last ten years to stay, staying only to leave again. The streets I have traveled are the years I have traveled.
Joseph Roth

He [Joseph Roth] was one of the first to despair in those times. His characters were always in flight, and he predicted that everyone would have to flee. His books are no more than pale reflections of what he produced during those conversations in the dark hours of the night. In visionary images he depicted what we all dreaded and then fell into self-absorption again. When he looked up, he might casually remark: "It's all nonsense, folks. Don't take my agonies so seriously, I simply don't know how to live."
Max Tau

In his memoirs, Bertaux recalls a Sunday in the Grunewald with us in February 1928, when he met many of our friends: Jakob Wassermann, Alfred Döblin, Ernst Toller, Alfred Kerr, George Grosz, and Joseph Roth, who said: "In ten years a) Germany will be at war with France, b) if we are lucky, we will be able to live in Switzerland as emigrés, c) Jews will be beaten up on Kurfürstendamm." No one was ready to believe the despairingly smiling Roth. But very soon his prophetic words were to come true.
Brigitte B. Fischer

Joseph Roth (Schwabendorf/Brody, Galicia 1894 – Paris 1939) enlisted in the Austro-Hungarian army in World War I. His career as a journalist began in Vienna in 1918. He moved on to Berlin in 1921 and spent the period between 1923 and 1932 as a correspondent for the *Frankfurter Zeitung*. After Hitler's seizure of power he emigrated to Vienna, Marseille, Nice, and Paris. Although originally revolutionary in spirit, once he had become stateless and "homeless," he mourned the passing of the Austro-Hungarian Monarchy – if only in the abstract – in his works. He described Austria's old supranational society and the lives of military officers and public officials in a polyethnic nation with delicate irony, skepticism, and melancholy. He showed particular interest in eastern Jews, characters who shared his own Galician background, a subject movingly portrayed in his novel *Hiob* (Job), for example. His essay "Juden auf Wanderschaft" (Journeying Jews [1926]) was a defense of the religiously rooted but disintegrating world of eastern Jewry against the arrogance of assimilation.
Above: Joseph Roth. Ca. 1925

Observing and writing, he [Joseph Roth] traveled throughout Europe, from Moscow to Marseille, even to the remotest corners of Albania and Germania. He quickly became Germany's best-known feuilletonist, a first-rate prose writer, a master of short prose and the German language. The best of the articles and feuilletons he wrote over more than twenty years deserve a privileged place in every anthology of "classic" German prose. He saw with new eyes and wrote with the forcefulness of the poet and the courage of the moralist, with the mordant, sometimes profound wit of the pessimistic skeptic and with the gentle bitterness of the melancholy romantic.
Hermann Kesten

To me personally . . . my Judaism is approximately what it is to a Hasidic master: a metaphysical matter, far beyond, high above anything related to the "Jews" on this earth.
Joseph Roth

Eight books to date, more than 1,000 articles, ten-hour working-days for the last ten years, and today, with my hair forsaking me, as well as my teeth, my potency, and the most primitive capacity for joy, there is no possibility of living a single month without financial worries. The canaille that calls itself literature!
Joseph Roth

I have had many friends in my life, but only Joseph Roth called me a friend of his soul.
Józef Wittlin

careers of so many, among them David Pinski (1872–1959), Hirsch David Nomberg (1874–1927), Abraham Reisen (1876–1953), Schalom Asch (1880–1957), I. M. Weissenberg (1881–1938), Peretz Hirschbein (1880–1948), Solomon Bloomgarden (1870–1927), who wrote under the pseudonym of Jehoasch, and Menachem Boraischa (1888–1949).
Helmut Dinse/Sol Liptzin

The powerlessness of the Jews, the way they endure afflictions with Hasidic "bitochn," a mixture of resignation and hope, lend Scholem Aleichem's works their specific atmosphere. His laughter is the laughter of the hero of the passive resistance that gave the people in the Pale of Settlement the strength to hold their own despite their unparalleled misery.
Jacob Allerhand

Our program is called education. We want to educate the people: make wise men out of fools, intelligent human beings out of fanatics; transform idlers and Luftmenschen into workers, useful honest people who work for themselves and are thus a benefit to society . . . We simply say: we Jews are as human as all human creatures! We are neither demigods nor demons, no, merely human. And human creatures should educate themselves to become wiser, better, freer every day.
Jizchak Leib Peretz

To find the essence of Jewishness in all places, at all times, in all parts of a people scattered throughout the world . . . and to see it illuminated by the prophetic dream of man's future – that is the task of every Jewish artist.
Jizchak Leib Peretz

Scholem Aleichem (Perejaslav 1859 – New York 1916), his real name Schalom Rabinowitsch, was the best-loved of the three classic Yiddish writers (Mendele Mojcher Sforim, Jizchak Leib Peretz). He emigrated to the United States by way of Switzerland in 1905, after the Kiev pogrom. Scholem Aleichem's world is the world of the poor eastern European shtetl. The most outstanding figure he created was "Tevje, the Milkman," a man who endures many hardships and trials, vacillates between resignation and optimism, but never loses his trust in God.
Above: Scholem Aleichem. Ca. 1900

The Jews were always in difficulties and exposed to a hostile environment. Scholem Aleichem taught them how to laugh at their tribulations. He addressed them as members of a big family, who, though they might gossip and quarrel, nonetheless lived together without malice, imbued with a profound sense of responsibility for their fellow man and always ready to help each other in an emergency. They feel the pain of all humanity though humanity takes no notice of them; their clothes are drab and shabby, but their souls are aglow with color and life. – Scholem Aleichem loved them with all their follies and foibles.
Helmut Dinse/Sol Liptzin

He taught them how to escape pain through laughter – and how to acquire joy of life by observing the traditional and timeless customs of Judaism. His humor lights up the grey, dull day, his laughter echoes wherever Yiddish is read and understood. With him – and Peretz – Yiddish literature reached its peak; the only regrettable part is that, unlike Peretz, he did not inspire a successor. Peretz advanced the

Schalom Asch (Kutno, Poland 1880 – London 1957) lived in Palestine from 1906 to 1910; then he moved to the United States and in 1923 to England. In 1955 he settled in Israel. His novels, plays, and stories offer a true-to-life, though sometimes romanticized, picture of Jewish small-town life and the religious world of eastern Europe (*A Shtetl*, *Mottke der Dieb* [Mottke the Thief], *Petersburg - Moskau - Warschau*). His plays are among the highlights of Yiddish drama. He gained international renown when Max Reinhardt put on his *Gott der Rache* (God of Vengeance) in Berlin in 1910. His novels about major Christian figures were violently rejected by Jewish readers.

Jizchak Leib Peretz (Zamosc 1851 – Warsaw 1915) originally wrote in Hebrew, under the influence of the Haskala (Enlightenment). A lawyer, he found his way to the Yiddish language through his involvement in political-cultural affairs. His stories are descriptions, often ironic, of Jewish life in the small towns of eastern Europe. But his name remains linked with the introduction of Hasidism into Yiddish literature.
Right: Shalom Asch (left), Jizchak Leib Peretz (center), Hirsch David Nomberg (lying) and Peretz's son (right). Ca. 1900

Samuel Fischer (Liptó Szt. Miklós, Slovakia 1859 – Berlin 1934) founded the S. Fischer Verlag (Publications) in Berlin in 1886 and took a great personal interest in promoting post-naturalist German literature. The political-cultural periodical *Die Neue Rundschau* (The New Review), which appeared under various names from 1890 on, exercised a major influence on German intellectual life. Its editors included *Otto Brahm*, *Oscar Bie*, and *Samuel Sänger*. In the autumn of 1935 the company split up into the S. Fischer KG, Berlin, and the "Exil"-Verlag (Vienna, Stockholm, New York, Amsterdam), headed by Gottfried Bermann-Fischer. The two publishing houses were reunited in 1950.
Left: Samuel Fischer. Photograph by Rudolf Dührkoop. 1911

Moritz Heimann (Werder 1868 – Berlin 1925) discovered and encouraged modern German literature as a publisher's reader with the S. Fischer Verlag (from 1906). He also wrote poems, essays, comedies, dramas, and masterly aphorisms himself.
Opposite page, above left: Moritz Heimann. Before 1933

Salmann Schocken (Margonin, Posen 1877 – Jerusalem 1959) was one of the co-founders of the Schocken concern, which owned over thirty department stores. He and his brother Simon founded the Schocken-Verlag in Berlin in 1931. Salmann Schocken emigrated to Palestine in 1933.
Opposite page, above right: Salmann Schocken. Photograph by *Lotte Jacobi*. Ca. 1950

The Jüdische Verlag was founded by Martin Buber, Ephraim Moses Lilien, Berthold Feiwel, Chaim Weizmann, and David Trietsch in Berlin in October 1902. The works it published were primarily cultural Zionist in orientation. There were, for example, books by Achad Haam, Simon Dubnow, Chajim Nachman Bialik, Theodor Herzl, Max Nordau and Arthur Ruppin.
Opposite page, below: The founders of the Jüdischer Verlag in Berlin. Seated from left: Berthold Feiwel, Martin Buber. Standing from left: Ephraim Moses Lilien, Chaim Weizmann, Leo Motzkin. 1902

And so let us take a look at an example of something rounded off and complete, the life's work of the important Jewish publishers, of an Albert Langen, Paul Cassirer, G. H. Meyer (at the Kurt Wolff-Verlag), and Jacob Hegner, a group epitomized by a figure who has already achieved classic stature – the old man, Samuel Fischer. For almost forty years the S. Fischer-Verlag stood for a specific kind of quality, good taste, artistic refinement, and a new spirit. Samuel Fischer did not publish the trailblazers like Heinrich Mann, Wedekind, Strindberg, Hamsun, Alfred Mombert, Peter Hille, or Detlev von Lilien-cron, who were first published by Schuster & Löffler in Berlin or Albert Langen in Munich. But with his magazine "Die Neue Rundschau" (The new review), with his excellent readers and reviewers, staff and editors – Moritz Heimann, Alfred Kerr, Oskar Bie, Samuel Saenger – he remained loyal to a whole new literary epoch and helped it to achieve public recognition, investing the profits of his successes in the constant search for new, unassuming, in the main non-Jewish talents. The general public knows him best as the publisher of Henrik Ibsen, Gerhart Hauptmann, Bernhard Shaw, Hermann Bang, Thomas Mann, Arthur Schnitzler . . . He published the most distinguished storyteller of the pre-war era, Count Eduard Keyserling, master of the small form; and he acquired the existing oeuvres of Hugo von Hofmannsthal, Jakob Wassermann, and Joseph Conrad – who, like René Schikele, Annette Kolb, or Alfred Döblin, had all begun with smaller, bolder publishers – and went on to publish their new works. Of the talented Swiss, he took on above all Hermann Hesse and Jacob Schaffner; of the modern French, the more refined, gentler authors. And we must be grateful to him for a host of cultural documents that accompanied us along our road to education: the letters of Browning or Hans von Bülow, the collected writings of Alfred Kerr, and essayists from Meier-Graefe to Lytton Strachey. And in this rich and diversified catalogue, Jewish writers play an extremely minor role. They were more likely to be welcomed by Rütten & Loening in Frankfurt, or Bruno and Paul Cassirer, and were championed by non-Jews; Kurt Wolff and Ernst Rowohlt, Gustav Kiepenheuer and Georg Müller in Munich, or the Insel Verlag in Leipzig – many of them advised by Jewish publishers' readers or Jewish writer friends, all of them less hesitant about rebellious, leftist intellectual ideas than S. Fischer himself. Further examples to stand for many others would be Erich Reiss, who represented Georg Brandes in Germany, or Georg Bondi, who slowly and insistently advanced the standing of the problematic, haughty Stefan George and his circle – a circle of predominantly Jewish minds assembled to worship the great Stefan when the nationalist

 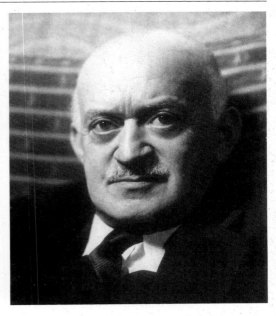

literary historian Adolf Bartels was still obstinately maintaining that this George was actually a Jew by the name of Abeles. But Rudolf Borchardt, a Jewish German-nationalist warrior, descended from this circle, as did other faithful followers – Friedrich Gundolf, Friedrich Wolters (his father still called Wolfsohn) or Karl Wolfskehl, whose passion was the revival of Old and Middle High German poetry and who had collaborated with George in editing the finest selection of early German poetry for Georg Bondi.
Arnold Zweig

I believe that the only books worth reading are the ones that bite and sting. If the book we are reading does not wake us up with a blow to the head, what are we reading it for? That the way you write should make us happy? For heaven's sake, we would be happy as well if we had no books at all, and in an emergency we could write the kinds of books that make us happy ourselves. But we need the books that affect us like a disaster that causes us great pain, like the death of someone we loved more than ourselves, like being cast out in the woods, away from all human life, like a suicide. A book must be the axe for the frozen sea in us.
Franz Kafka

197

Leopold Ullstein (Fürth 1826 – Berlin 1899) founded the Ullstein-Verlag in Berlin in 1877. His five sons – Hans, Louis, Franz, Rudolf, and Hermann – transformed the publishing house into one of Germany's largest, most modern newspaper and book publishers. The circulation of the *Berliner Morgenpost* (Berlin Morning Post), which they started in 1898, was as high as that of the *Berliner Zeitung* (acquired in 1878, called *B.Z. am Mittag* from 1904) and Berlin's oldest newspaper, the *Vossische Zeitung* (acquired in 1914). 1907 also saw the establishment of a book-publishing house, which began issuing the Propyläen-Verlag editions of the classics in 1919. In 1934 the Ullsteins were forced to sell their publishing company to the Nazis – posing as "an unknown person" – for a ridiculously small sum.
Left: Leopold Ullstein. Ca. 1860

Dr. Ullstein, who was also general manager of the publishing house, did not attend editorial meetings regularly. When he did appear in the conference room, he counted for no more than any other participant. In no case known to me would Dr. Ullstein – the other publishers hardly came into direct contact with their editorial staff – have tried to impose his authority on the editors. He was too impassioned a journalist for that, though he rarely wrote a line himself; moreover, he valued freedom of opinion and expression too highly. I once happened into his office when he was being quite ungracious with one of his executives: "You were not hired as your master's voice. I know my own views, I want to hear yours!"
Max Rainer

Journalism is not a Jewish invention, but it received its essential complexion, its natural laws, its blood, and its soul from Jews – at least in Germany. For the others, writing was one possible occupation among many; for the talented Jew, it was the only profession that guaranteed him a tiny particle of power, imaginary or real.
Paul Mayer

We are talking about the foundation of newspapers that had originally specialized in advertising and in fact usually developed out of printing houses. That is how Rudolf Mosse, Ullstein publications, and Leopold Sonnemann's "Frankfurter Zeitung" were established . . . Thus the "Frankfurter Zeitung" (as a whole), the "Berliner Tageblatt," and the "Vossische Zeitung" (through their leading Jewish journalists Theodor Wolff, Georg Bernhard, and a host of internationally respected staff members and special features) represented European culture in Germany.
Arnold Zweig

I do not consider the "Frankfurter Zeitung" a springboard, at best it is a trampoline, like the ones we have seen in variety theaters,

with zebra-striped acrobats bouncing on it. It is my only home soil and something of a replacement for a fatherland and a revenue office.
Joseph Roth

But there was another, deeper affinity that tied him to Frankfurt: the "Frankfurter Zeitung." He began subscribing to it the year it was founded. Not only did he read it, he believed it, trusted it and loved it. Reading it through from beginning to end was a daily obligation, and a Sabbath-like, holiday-like joy. As the years passed, the "Frankfurter" so thoroughly shaped his political views that he was overjoyed to find it confirming his opinions again and again.
Fritz Frank

The editor of the "Presse," Karl Etienne, made the paper into the mouthpiece of Liberalism in the broadest sense of the word and, in particular, into the paper favored by educated Jewish circles. His successor Moriz Benedikt, Theodor Herzl's "slave driver," though far better known in our time, was only a poor imitation . . . My father repeatedly pointed out with a certain pride that our family had

Jews also played a decisive role as newspaper publishers. The *Frankfurter Zeitung* (founded in 1856 by Leopold Sonnemann and published under that name from 1866) and the Viennese *Neue Freie Presse* ([New Free Press] founded in 1864, published by Moritz Benedikt from 1881) were considered "quality" papers.
Above: Newspaper stand in Berlin. Photograph by Friedrich Seidenstücker. 1928

Arthur Koestler (Budapest 1906 – London 1983) broke off his engineering studies and went to a kibbutz in Palestine in 1926. Through a happy coincidence he became a foreign correspondent for the Ullstein-Verlag and spent 1926 to 1931 in the Near East, Paris, and Berlin. In the summer of 1931 he was the only journalist to accompany the Graf Zeppelin during its flight over the North Pole. A member of the Communist Party from 1931 to 1937, he participated in the Spanish Civil War as an observer in 1936 and was taken prisoner. He was released thanks to the intervention of the foreign press. From 1942 on he lived in London. His reports and novels deal with ethical and political problems and conflicts, such as his personal struggle with communism and totalitarian societies. His late works focus primarily on psychological questions. In accordance with his belief in suicide, he and his wife chose this form of dying together.
Left: Arthur Koestler as a journalist on the spectacular flight of the airship "Graf Zeppelin." 1931

been readers and subscribers of the "Presse" since the day it was founded. Before the world war and even after it had broken out, I often quarreled with my father because of it. I was certainly influenced by Herzl's desperate (at the time only very sketchily publicized) battle with Benedikt and by the raging polemic Karl Kraus (a Bohemian Jew fom Jičin) aimed at the "Neue Freie Presse" in his own "Fackel" (Torch). I accused the "Presse" of being bribable and war-mongering, whereas my father warmly defended it. When I returned home on leave in about 1916, I found that the "Presse" had been replaced by the "Prager Tagblatt" (Prague Daily News), and my father offered me an almost solemn declaration that he had now recognized the justice of my reproaches against the paper. In any case, it had had a not insignificant influence on the political and general views of all the members of our family for almost fifty years.
Hugo Hermann

There are two beautiful things in the world: being on the staff of the "Neue Freie Presse" or despising it. I never hesitated for a moment as to what my choice would have to be.
Karl Kraus

This is a an illustration of the peculiar fact that the German Jews appeared to confirm the prejudice that said the Jews had only a rudimentary gift for the fine arts. And in fact, compared with the abundance of major literary and musical talents, their role in painting and sculpture in Germany and Europe was secondary. They had indeed produced a master like Joseph Israels in Holland, the wonderful impressionist Pissaro (and family) in France, and the classic old master Max Liebermann in Germany; Liebermann, long-lived as so many great painters from Titian to Renoir have been, still creates his beautiful, mature portraits and landscapes with undiminished freshness and power today, at the age of 86. But even such decent, serious artists as Hermann Struck, Eugen Spiro, Philip Franck, or such younger men as Ludwig Meidner, Jakob Steinhardt, or Joseph Budko did not embody the mighty breakthrough from perception to created and animated substance . . .

And then, at the beginning of the twentieth century, the liberation known as Expressionism burst in on the rigidity of European artistic life . . . And suddenly Jews, too, stood in the front ranks of modern art. Not German Jews, but the sons and daughters of the great Russian Jewry that had so long been culturally smothered . . .

It is not the task of this book to characterize all the artists who acquired stature, above all in Paris, and proved themselves deserving of it, such artists as Modigliani and Chagall, Soutine and Channa Orlowa, Altmann and Menkes, Ryback and Gottlieb, Kisling and Zach, and cultivated Viennese like Josef Floch, Georg Ehrlich, Eisenschitz, or the Ukrainian Reder . . .

Let us point out only one more thing here, namely that in the sequence "public, connoisseurs, creators," the German Jews had reached the second step by the time Hitler's art dictatorship rendered Jewish artistic life in Germany a thing of the past . . . We can, for example, name Adolf Goldschmidt, the distinguished professor of art history at the University of Berlin, a typical indomitable scholar, exemplary in his meticulousness, to whom Germany owes an infinite debt in the field of medieval art, whether he was working on ivory carvings, miniatures, or sculptures. We can mention Max J. Friedländer, who headed the Kupferstichkabinett (Department of prints and drawings) in Berlin for many years before being invited to take over the Kaiser-Friedrich-Museum; Friedländer was incontestably the greatest authority on Dutch fifteenth-century painting. Kurt Glaser stands out among the modern minds in the field. Former director of the state art library in Berlin, he ensured that it would retain and even increase its stature. His exhibitions in the air well of the old Kunstgewerbe-Museum (Museum of applied art)

provided Berlin's intellectual life with the new impulses that can be generated by boldly, intelligently chosen displays of unfamiliar designs – be they the cave drawings discovered by Leo Frobenius or Russian icons. Owing to his Jewish descent, Erwin Panofsky, the most distinguished representative of the younger generation, was never even given an opportunity to work in Berlin. He stayed in Hamburg, where the world famous Aby Warburg library and its librarian Saxl provided him with the best possible conditions to make his very special discoveries . . .

. . . let us conclude with a look at the critics and lecturers who helped the people to understand art – who made art into public property . . . Fritz Stahl had the talent to rejuvenate himself again and again, and was an important advisor to the older generation. The new generation was served by Paul Westheim, who, first in the "Frankfurter Zeitung" and then in his own "Kunstblatt" (Art paper), offered such sensitive appreciations of precisely those painters and sculptors who, because of their new way of seeing and designing, would still be unknown to the Germans had he not been so bold. And if we also mention . . . Dr. Max Deri and the writer Carl Einstein, who indisputably deserves the credit for discovering and describing the importance and beauty of exotic sculpture, our list seems long enough.
Arnold Zweig

There is, of course, simply art as such: it knows neither religious nor political boundaries. But the artists who are linked by both their fatherland and their religion are something else again. And if throughout my life I have felt a German, my vivid sense of belonging to the Jewish people has been no less strong.
Max Liebermann

Throughout my long life I have tried with all my might to serve German art. As it is my conviction that art has nothing to do with either politics or descent, I can no longer remain a member of the Prussian Academy of Arts, of which I have been a full member for over thirty years and whose president I was for twelve years, as my standpoint is no longer considered valid. I have also resigned the honorary presidency awarded to me by the Academy.
Max Liebermann

Emil Orlik (Prague 1870 – Berlin 1932) belonged to the Berlin Secessionists around *Max Liebermann*, Max Slevogt, and Lovis Corinth. He gained his reputation in the graphic arts: etchings and lithographs were a perfect medium for his improvisational drawing talent. Orlik's extensive oeuvre includes portraits, illustrations, and travel sketches. From 1905 on, he was given the opportunity to pass on his technical know-how to students as a professor at the Berlin Academy. Numerous portraits of Jewish friends and prominent figures have been preserved.
Above: Emil Orlik. Photograph by Nicola Perscheid. Before 1905

Despite these obstacles, several very well-known painters emerged from the Jewish-bourgeois circles of Prague. For example Emil Orlik. He was the son of a well-known Prague tailor. The other Prague tailor whose work was of equally high quality had strong artistic proclivities himself. He was Herr Klimpel, an active member and one of the mainstays of Prague's German amateur theater.
Bruno Kisch

Max Liebermann (Berlin 1847 – Berlin 1935) studied painting and graphics in Paris, Holland, and Munich, and moved back to Berlin in 1884. Under the influence of *Josef Israëls*, one of the leading nineteenth-century Dutch realists, he became a naturalist, but went on to become the "master" of German impressionism. In 1894 he founded the Berlin Secession. As president of the Prussian Academy of Fine Arts (1920–1933), he received the "Pour le merite" medal. In 1927 the President of Germany, von Hindenburg, awarded him the "Eagle-shield of the German Reich."

His early pictures depict Biblical subjects and genre scenes. When the painting "Jesus in the Temple" caused a scandal in 1878 and anti-Semitic protests were heard, he abandoned Biblical motifs; Jewish themes occurred only rarely in his pictures. In 1933 he resigned as president of the Academy.
Opposite page: Max Liebermann in his studio in Berlin. Ca. 1900

201

The walls of the Synagogue were bare and grim, even though sublime liturgical poetry and song resounded under its roof. The little town within the Jewish pale of Eastern Europe, the "Shtetl," had its superb cantors and musicians, its bards, poets, and composers of folk tales; but it had no painters or sculptors. Even the Khassidic revolt against Talmudic scholasticism did not weaken the millennia-old abhorrence of the "graven image"; and the Khassidic revivalism too quickly ossified into yet another rabbinical orthodoxy.
It was in defiance of tradition, outside the Synagogue, in opposition to it, that the Russian or Polish Jew began to paint; and it was only just before the close of the nineteenth century that he did so.
Isaac Deutscher

For a Jew to paint was to rise in revolt, to achieve an act of emancipation.
Isaac Deutscher

Are my zealous efforts really leading me in the right direction, are they taking me closer to my goal? If only I could eradicate the prejudice against my co-religionists! If only I could wipe out the hatred welling up against my suffering people! If only I could reconcile the Poles and the Jews, for the history of both is a history of suffering!
Not really a modest claim I am making, is it, to feel a calling to be an apostle? But if I do not possess the strength to achieve my goal, at least the sympathies my compatriots demonstrate and the way my character is described in Polish newspapers prove that I am going in the right direction.
Moritz Gottlieb

In the artist E. M. Lilien, the son of a poor orthodox Jewish wood turner from Drohobycz, I encountered for the first time an Eastern Jew, and a Judaism which in its strength and stubborn fanaticism had hitherto been unknown to me.
Stefan Zweig

Jankel Adler (Tuszyn/ Lodz 1895 – Aldbourne/London 1949) apprenticed as an engraver from 1906 to 1912 and then worked for the royal postal engraving office in Belgrade. After studying with Gustav Wiethüchter at the Kunstgewerbeschule (School of Applied Arts) in Barmen-Wuppertal (1913/14), he settled in Poland briefly, moving on to Berlin in 1920, where he met *Marc Chagall* and *Else Lasker-Schüler*. He was a member of the Novembergruppe, a progressive artists' association founded in Berlin in 1918. From 1922 to 1933 Adler lived and worked in Düsseldorf, remaining very much an individualist, this time in the circle around Otto Dix. Despite his love for Germany, he never lost contact with his eastern Jewish roots. As a Jew and so-called "degenerate" artist, Adler was forced to leave Germany in 1933, emigrating to England by way of Paris. Left: Jankel Adler. Photograph by August Sander. 1928

Moritz Gottlieb (Cracow 1856–1879) studied painting in Munich. Despite his youth he was considered by far the most important of the eastern Jewish artists (along with Johann Goldstein and Emil Löwenthal). He painted outstanding portraits; his "Praying Jews" hangs in the Tel Aviv museum today.
Below: Moritz Gottlieb. Ca. 1875

The link between Cologne and Düsseldorf was Jankel Adler, who lived in Düsseldorf but was also a Progressive. This young Pole with burning black eyes was an untiring talker and had an animating, sometimes even disturbing effect on Düsseldorf's by now sedate circle of painters. His art combined the strict pictorial order of the Cologne school with the poetic, atmospheric world of his compatriot Chagall. His fresco-like treatment of picture surfaces was absolutely novel, quite a few colleagues succumbed to his influence. After emigrating, Adler lived in London; when he died in 1950, he was at the threshold of fame.
Anna Klapheck

Everywhere they call him dearest Jankel.
We come from the same town and went to the same school
And loved to slide around on frozen streets.

Dearest Jankel already had two buds on his face then,
They're burgeoning now, transfigured he tells us biblically of the Baal Shem.

Solemnly they carry him in nightly dreams
As once they did his fore-rabuni-father on twig and leaf
from the still forest into the hallelujah town.

Every picture that he paints, he dedicates
With great, poetic harp-script
To his young God Zebaoth.

. . .

In this loftiness of timeless treasures Jankel Adler becomes the Hebrew Rembrandt.
Else Lasker-Schüler: Jankel Adler

Mela Koehler-Bormann (Vienna 1885 – Stockholm 1960) attended the Kunstgewerbeschule in Vienna from 1905 to 1910, where she studied with Kolo Moser. Her works were frequently published even while she was still at school. She illustrated children's books for the Konegen Verlag and worked for the magazine *Wiener Mode*. As a member of the Austrian Werkbund (League for Crea- tivity in the Applied Arts) and Wiener Frauenkunst (Vienna Women's Art), she participated in numerous exhibitions, for instance the Kunstschau Wien in 1909. For the Wiener Werkstätte she designed postcards, pictorial broadsheets, textiles, and utilitarian graphic designs. Mela Koehler emigrated to Sweden in 1934.
<u>Right</u>: Mela Koehler-Bormann. Photograph by *d'Ora*. 1912

Alfred Flechtheim (Münster 1878 – London 1937) was considered one of the most important modern-art dealers in Germany, with galleries in Düsseldorf and Berlin. He was, for example, the man who introduced Germany to Picasso. Flechtheim was responsible for making Max Beckmann, Carl Hofer, and Paul Klee famous, and championed African art as well. He also founded the legendary periodical *Der Querschnitt* (Cross-section), published by Ullstein as *Magazin der aktuellen Ewigkeitswerte* (Magazine of Current Eternal Values) from 1924. Left: Alfred Flechtheim. Ca. 1928

Herwarth Walden (Berlin 1878 – Saratow, USSR 1941), whose real name was Georg Levin (he changed it on the advice of his first wife, *Else Lasker-Schüler*), studied musicology in Italy and Berlin. He also wrote expressionist plays and edited literary magazines. In 1910 he founded the magazine *Der Sturm* (The Storm) and opened the "Sturm"-Galerie in 1912 with the exhibition "Der Blaue Reiter." In 1913 he organized the "Herbstsalon"(Autumn Salon) exhibition with European avant-garde artists, whom he enthusiastically supported. His art salon and "Der Sturm" publications became the hub of expressionism, and he himself developed into a major promoter of modern art. Works by *Marc Chagall*, Paul Klee, Oskar Kokoschka, Lyonel Feininger, Wassily Kandinsky, *Franz Marc*, and August Macke could be seen at his gallery. In the twenties he became a follower of bolshevism and went to Moscow as a language teacher in 1931. Opposite page, below: Herwarth Walden with his wife Nelly in their Berlin house. 1920

*T*hese art dealers and their colleagues in the antiquarian book trade (Goldschmidt in Frankfurt, Rosenberg and Bernheimer in Munich, Martin Breslauer and Paul Graupe in Berlin, and many of their colleagues in the whole Reich) were often scholars in their field and more erudite than famed art historians. And they supplied Germany's taste in luxury with the confident high standards it had lacked in the era of Bismarck and the young Kaiser Wilhelm. Through them and the branches they established in the large cities of the world, art collecting in Germany was spurred on and promoted until it achieved the quality that distinguished the von der Heydt collection in Berlin, the galleries of Markus Kappel, Harry Fuld, and James Simon, and the numerous collections of pictures, large and small, that so worthily represented the intellect and taste of German affluence. The picture dealers of the Paul Cassirer or Alfred Flechtheim type did the same for modern art, from the birth of Impressionism to the works of the great wood sculptor Ernst Barlach, who would have starved in the little town of Güstrow in Mecklenburg had it not been for Paul Cassirer. Everyone who struggled boldly for new forms of expression, all the artists of the "Brücke" (Nolde, Kirchner, Schmidt-Rotluff), the Rohlfs and Beckmanns, the Kokoschkas, Hofers, Klees, Lehmbrucks, and Kandinskys, Franz Marc (killed in action in 1915) and Kubin – all non-Jewish pioneers of a modern concept of form and a renewal of painting and sculpture: if they are honest, they will have to admit that of the dealers

who exhibited them, writers who understood them, and buyers who bought them, non-Jews accounted for a very small proportion. The same strata – most of them Jews or of Jewish origin – who had learned to understand the French Impressionists and then Cézanne and van Gogh also enabled these later artists not only to live and travel but to forge further ahead into the Unformed, and to refine their personal rhythm to an ever purer state. As picture buyers the Jews have been as much the backbone of painting in Germany over the past thirty years as they have filled the theaters and bought up editions of German books of all kinds.
Arnold Zweig

*T*he Galerie Thannhauser in Munich, formerly Thannhauser & Brakl, opened a new art salon in 1909. That year it held the first exhibition of the "Neue Künstlervereinigung München" (New Artists' Association Munich), founded by Wassily Kandinsky, Alexej Jawlensky, and Alfred Kubin, among others; in December 1911, the gallery mounted the first exhibition of the "Blaue Reiter" group started by Kandinsky and *Franz Marc*.
<u>Above</u>: Galerie Thannhauser in Munich during the first exhibition of the "Blaue Reiter." 1911

With the expansion of trade, industry, and banking after the victorious war of 1870/71, the general standard of living in Germany rose. These improved circumstances, shared in by broad Jewish circles, enabled German Jews to assemble major art collections in the years of peace preceding World War I. Interest in art generally grew, which meant that living artists, too, received greater encouragement. Thus there were, in particular, many Jewish collectors who, through donations and endowments, contributed to the proliferation of museums and the support of scholarly institutes. Even if many of the collections later came under the hammer again and valuable works ended up abroad, chiefly in America, their presence, if only temporary, undeniably gave rise to a rich flowering of art. The catastrophe that began in 1933 and brought Jewish collecting to an end in the German-speaking world also put an end to artistic culture in Germany as a whole.

If only the larger private collections can be mentioned here, they are already proof enough of the important role Jewish collectors and collections played in Germany and the German-speaking world. Collecting is not merely a matter of finances, it is a passion that, properly nurtured and guided, leads to connoisseurship. A serious collector tends to limit himself to one specialized area; he studies it carefully and becomes ever more discriminating with regard to potential acquisitions. He does not collect for the sake of

possession alone but out of love for art, one manifestation of which is his desire to let the general public share in it. In this way he becomes a vehicle of civilization and a patron of the arts. And he will normally part with his treasures only if there are very compelling reasons to do so. Often he donates them to the public during his lifetime or makes provisions for this to be done after his death.
Karl Schwarz

It was only in regard to art that all felt an equal right, because love of art was a communal duty in Vienna.
They were the real audience, they filled the theaters and the concerts, they bought the books and the pictures, they visited the exhibitions, and with their more mobile under-standing, little hampered by tradition, they were the exponents and champions of all that was new. Practically all the great art collections of the nineteenth century were formed by them, nearly all the artistic attempts were made possible only by them; without the ceaseless stimulating interest of the Jewish bourgeoisie, Vienna, thanks to the indolence of the court, the aristocracy, and the Christian millionaires, who preferred to maintain racing stables and hunts to fostering art, would have remained behind Berlin in the realm of art as Austria remained behind the German Reich in political matters. Whoever wished to put through something in Vienna, or came to Vienna as a guest from abroad and sought appreciation as well as an audience, was dependent on the Jewish bourgeoisie.
Stefan Zweig

One of the signs of these changing times is that the death knell has sounded for home living in the old sense, where a feeling of protectedness was the first criterion. Giedion, Mendelssohn, Corbusier make human dwellings largely into transit areas for all conceivable forces and waves of light and air. What lies ahead is marked by flexible transparency: not only of space but, if we can believe the Russians, who are now intending to abolish Sundays in favor of movable holiday-shifts, even of weeks.
Walter Benjamin

Erich Mendelssohn (Allenstein, East Prussia 1887 – San Francisco 1953) studied architecture in Berlin and Munich from 1907 to 1911. He worked as a freelance architect and designer in Munich until 1914 and opened an office in Berlin in 1919. A founding member of the Novembergruppe, his idea of clarity in the "uncompromising use" of reinforced concrete, steel, and glass were expressed in such buildings as the Einstein Tower in Potsdam (1920/21) and the Schocken department stores in Stuttgart (1927) and Chemnitz (1928). He also designed a cemetery for the Jewish congregation in Königsberg.
He left Germany in 1933 and worked in England for some time. He also saw the implementation of some of his designs in Palestine, for example the Hadassa University Medical Center in Jerusalem (1938).
Left: Erich Mendelssohn. Photograph by *Tim Gidal*. Ca. 1927

Albert Figdor (Baden/Vienna 1843 – Vienna 1927) was a banker. He was also an art collector for sixty years of his life. His special field was applied art, an interest stimulated by the art historian Alois Riegl and the collection of the Österreichisches Museum für Kunst und Industrie (Austrian Museum of Art and Industry). Figdor's collection, completely characterized by nineteenth-century historicism included paintings, sculptures, wall hangings, and small objects spanning the centuries, from antiquity to the nineteenth century. It was considered the most important and multifaceted collection in Austria before World War II.
Opposite page, above: Albert Figdor. Ca. 1920

Geheimrat (privy councilor) Eduard Arnhold (Dessau 1849 – Neuhaus 1925), a banker, shipping magnate, and proprietor of the Cäsar Wollheim Coal Company, was an eminently knowledgeable collector of modern French and German painting. It was through him and other Jewish collectors that the French impressionists became known in Germany. Thanks to his position and expertise, he was made an honorary member of the Academy of Fine Arts in Berlin. In 1910 he bought the Villa Massimo in Rome and left it to the Academy. In his generosity, he also endowed a fellowship for artists to spend time there.
Opposite page, below: Eduard Arnhold in his house in Berlin. Ca. 1920

Oskar Strnad (Vienna 1879 – Bad Aussee 1935) was one of the representatives of modern architecture in Vienna. He was responsible, along with *Josef Frank* and *Oskar Wlach*, for much of the modern residential housing built in Vienna between the wars, e.g. the Werkbund settlement. In 1914 he took part in designing the Österreich-Haus at the Cologne Werkbund exhibition. The same year he built a mansion in Vienna for the writer *Jakob Wassermann*. In 1918 Strnad began designing stage sets for theatrical productions, above all by *Max Reinhardt*, and was so successful that a "school" formed around him. In the last years of his life he even found his way into the motion picture studio, designing sets for *Maskerade* and *Episode*.
Left: Oskar Strnad. Ca. 1930

207

Erich Salomon (Berlin 1886 – Auschwitz death camp 1944) was a photographer who had the ability to capture the atmosphere of diplomatic conferences and artistic and social events with occasionally "Daumier-like expressive power" (*Nachum T. Gidal*). His photos date from a period when picture-taking was still discountenanced in many areas of public life. Consequently he specialized in "unobserved moments," as a book of photographs first published in 1931 was called. Erich Salomon is regarded as a pioneer of modern photographic journalism. The groundbreaking form of modern picture journalism that developed in Germany beginning in 1928/29 is connected above all with two newspapers, the *Berliner Illustrierte Zeitung* (B.I.Z.) and the *Münchner Illustrierten Presse*; their editors, who included *Kurt Korff* in Berlin and Stefan Lorant in Munich; and their photographers, most of whom acquired an international reputation only once they had emigrated: *Alfred Eisenstaedt, Martin Munkacsi, Felix H. Man, Umbo*, and the *Gidal* brothers, *Georg* and *Ignaz (Tim)*.
Among the forerunners of live photography and pioneers of social documentary photography were the lawyers and amateur photographers *Dr. Emil Mayer* (Neu Bytschow, Bohemia 1871 – suicide in Vienna 1938) and *Dr. Hermann Drawe* (Vienna 1867 – Vienna 1925). In the period between the wars, three photographers rendered invaluable services by documenting the Jewish world in Poland and Berlin before the Holocaust, namely *Roman Vishniac, Alter Kacyzne*, and *Abraham Pisarek*.
Right: Erich Salomon. Photograph by Lore Feininger. 1928

Lotte Jacobi (Thorn, West Prussia 1896) studied art history and literature in Posen and, from 1925 to 1927, in Munich. After training at the Bayerische Staatslehranstalt für Lichtbildwesen (Bavarian State Institute of Photography), Jacobi began working at her father's photographic studio in 1927, and developed into a major portrait photographer in the thirties. In 1935 she emigrated to the United States, where she married *Erich Reiss*, a publisher from Berlin, in 1940. Two Viennese women, *Madame d'Ora* (Vienna 1881 – Frohnleiten, Styria 1963), actually *Dora Kallmus*, and *Trude Fleischmann* (Vienna 1895), also number among the twentieth-century masters of portrait photography.
Opposite page: Lotte Jacobi. Self-portrait. Ca. 1930

Fritz Lang (Vienna 1890 – Los Angeles 1976) achieved his first major success as a film director with *Der müde Tod* (Tired Death [1921]), produced by the UFA (*Paul Davidson*), which had merged with Decla-Bioskop (*Erich Pommer*). His monumental films – *Dr. Mabuse, der Spieler* (Dr. Mabuse, The Gambler [1922]), *Die Nibelungen* (1923/24), *Metropolis* (1926), etc. – provided the German silent-film industry with decisive impulses. *Peter Lorre* first appeared in Lang's talking picture *M* (1931). *Das Testament des Dr. Mabuse* (The Last Will of Dr. Mabuse [1932]) was no longer able to be shown in Germany. Lang emigrated to the United States in 1933. Opposite page: Fritz Lang on the set of *Metropolis*. 1926

Erich Pommer (Hildesheim 1889 – United States 1966) founded Decla-Bioskop in 1919, producing such famous motion pictures as *Das Kabinett des Dr. Caligari* (Dr. Caligari's Little Room [1920]) and Fritz Lang's *Der müde Tod* (1921). In 1921 his company merged with the UFA (Universal-Film AG), which belonged to *Paul Davidson* and *Hermann Fellner*. Fritz Lang's *Metropolis* (1926) was a Pommer production. After a brief stay in Hollywood, Pommer produced *Der Kongress tanzt* (The Congress Dances), with Lilian Harvey, and *Der blaue Engel* (The Blue Angel), with Marlene Dietrich, who achieved international stardom in the role of Lola.
Right: Erich Pommer (left) with Joe May. Ca. 1925

Ernst Lubitsch (Berlin 1892 – Hollywood 1947) studied with *Max Reinhardt* in Berlin and soon began directing motion pictures. He made his name with monumental costume films like *Madame Dubarry* (1919). But it was in operettas and comedies like *Lady Windemere's Fan* (1925), *Trouble in Paradise* (1932), and *Ninotchka* (1939) that he developed the unique style known as the "Lubitsch touch." He went to Hollywood early, in 1922. Above: Ernst Lubitsch with Pola Negri. After 1922

J osef von Sternberg (Vienna 1894 – Hollywood 1969) went to live in the United States in 1901. His early film *Salvation Hunters* was acquired for United Artists by *Charles Chaplin*, Mary Pickford, and Douglas Fairbanks. But his greatest success was a talking picture he made in Germany: *The Blue Angel*, with Marlene Dietrich. He considered her his "personal discovery."
Above: Josef von Sternberg. Ca. 1925

P eter Lorre (Rosenberg, Hungary 1904 – Hollywood 1964); his real name Laszlo Löwenstein, arrived in Berlin via Vienna and Breslau. He achieved international fame in the role of the pathological criminal in *Fritz Lang's M* (1931). He emigrated first to England in 1933 and then to the United States in 1935, where he was able to continue his career.
Below: Peter Lorre in Fritz Lang's *M*. 1931

And Pallenberg?
With him, method becomes madness. He
fractures, tears, shreds language with the
bone-dry malice of a child with its doll. He
rips out its arms and legs, breaks off its head,
shakes the sawdust out of its glue-scented
body. He has devised the most malicious
technique: chattering. He chatters away hap-
pily, innocently, naively, uninhibitedly, with
no guarantee of an end; a water tap with
subjects, predicates, attributives trickling in-
discriminately from it; a phonetic express
train that nothing can stop. The charming
little man: he plays the game of speech. Will
not allow his toy to be taken away. He enjoys
it too much! Pallenberg demolishes language
using not a dialect but his own sense of sound.
Others pay language their sanctimonious re-
spects, which has a comic effect. But he
confronts it with the greatest possible lack of
understanding. He reproduces sounds as they
rain down on him. This unsystematic quality
is the apex of malice.
Anton Kuh

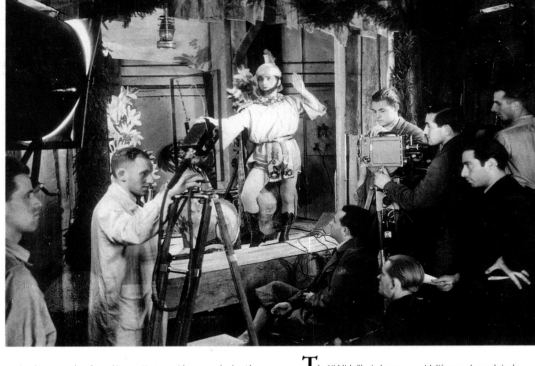

Max Pallenberg (Vienna 1877 – Karlsbad 1934) began his career as a character comedian in 1904, appearing in Vienna, Munich, and Berlin. His performances under the direction of *Max Reinhardt*, often with his wife *Fritzi Massary*, were major artistic achievements. "Pallenberg could do everything, and that is no exaggeration," wrote *Fritz Engel* in *Juden im deutschen Kulturbereich* (Jews in the German Cultural Context). He played comic and tragic roles, sang and performed in satirical "cabaret" revues and was famous for his extemporary criticisms of contemporary conditions. His first motion picture role was in *Der brave Sünder* (The Worthy Sinner [1931]), directed by *Fritz Kortner*, with a screenplay by *Alfred Polgar*.
Opposite page, right: Max Pallenberg. Ca. 1925

The Yiddish film industry grew out of the Yiddish theater, with famous stage actors playing a crucial role in its development. The repertoire – folk drama and sentimental stories – remained the same. Newsreels about events in Jewish life were also made in the thirties.
Between 1923/24 and 1938, *Zygmont Turkow* and his wife *Ida Kaminska* produced classics in Yiddish and original Yiddish plays, which they also filmed. Their ensemble, the WJKT (Warschawer jiddischer kunstteater" – Warsaw Yiddish Art Theater) also performed in Polish films.
Lodz-born *Joseph Green* achieved his greatest success with *Jidl mit dem Fidl* (Yidl with the Fiddle [1936]), made in Warsaw and starring Molly Picon. He shot all his other films – *Der Purimschpiler* (The Purim Gambler [1937]), *Mamele* (1938), and *A Brivele der Mamen* (A Letter from Mamma [1938]) at Warsaw studios and in the country.
Further films made before Poland fell to the Nazis include *Der Dibbuk* (1938) and *On a Heim* (1938). Of course, Yiddish films were also produced in America, but the Polish ones have the advantage of cultural and geographical authenticity.
Above: During the shooting of *Freileche kabzonim* (Happy Paupers), after a story by Mosche Broderson. Ca. 1924
Left: Scene from *Auf dem jüdischen Ball* (At the Jewish Ball). Ca. 1924

Moses Mendelssohn's grandson, having already composed immortal music himself, was the first German to rediscover the St. Matthew Passion in 1829, a hundred years after its first performance; like him, many other Jewish composers and conductors have gratefully, and more than amply, repaid their debt to German music. How European and Jewish joy and melancholy dance in the music of Jacques Offenbach, the immortal master of "Tales of Hofmann"! How Gustav Mahler's music, with its purity of form, soars into the spiritual and religious world: Mahler, a composer whose genius reached untrodden heights in "Lied von der Erde" and whose path led through the desert and dirt of enmity, an example to us all! How strict and bold that controversial pathfinder Arnold Schoenberg, in whom contemporary music, seeking a new, abstract tonal language, found its pioneer! How striking the impact of Kurt Weill and half-Jew Hanns Eisler's marvelous compositions when they turn infectious and popular, singable and speakable as settings for the great songs and chorales by the poet Brecht. These innovators can be set against the serious cultivators of tradition, all the conductors who have helped to keep the great music of Germany and Europe alive so that it might overcome death and survive to procreate, rejoicing the ear and heart. Joseph Joachim and Siegfried Ochs, Hermann Levy, Arthur Nikisch, and Bruno Walter, Leo Blech, Oskar Fried, Heinz Unger, and Otto Klemperer – to suggest only the generations – pledged themselves with unreserved devotion to the perfection of Beethoven, Brahms, Bruckner, Mozart, Schubert, and Bach . . . The great Jewish violinists and pianists, the quartet players and opera singers, all of them should be named here, and still some man or woman who in the distant or more recent past delighted and affected us would be forgotten . . . How many good violinists alone! How many outstanding pianists!

Arnold Zweig

Giacomo Meyerbeer (Berlin 1791 – Paris 1864), originally Jakob Liebmann Meyer Beer, began receiving piano lessons at an early age and took up opera composing during a stay in Italy. He moved to Paris in 1826, where he wrote his first French opera, *Robert le diable*, a work that brought him great success. He retained the style of French grand opera, helping to shape the operatic theater of his time with his combination of German, Italian, and French elements. After a production of *Les Huguenots* in Berlin, Meyerbeer was appointed Generalmusikdirektor of the Berliner Oper by King Friedrich Wilhelm IV in 1842. Left: Giacomo Meyerbeer. Photograph by L. Haase. Ca. 1860

Pauline Lucca (Vienna 1841 – Vienna 1908) was engaged by the Berliner Oper as early as 1861 and gave brilliant performances there in the Mozart operas as well as Georges Bizet's *Carmen*. The soprano, celebrated as "the Viennese Nightingale," was a protegée of Kaiser Wilhelm I and Otto von Bismarck, among others. In 1874 she joined the k.k. Hofoper (Royal and Imperial Court Opera) in Vienna. Pauline Lucca was one of the leading singers of her time. Right: Pauline Lucca. Photograph by H. Lehmann. Ca. 1865

Giacomo Meyerbeer, a composer already "much admired and much faulted" in his lifetime, died in 1864. His work survived the battle over the authenticity and value of his music, which became even fiercer after his death – particularly as a result of Richard Wagner's essay "Das Judentum in der Musik" (Judaism in music), published in 1869. And yet even today, in the eighth decade after the death of the creator of "Les Huguenots," a final judgment about his work is not permissible. In accordance with Meyerbeer's will, the extensive collection of autographs of unpublished works still remains under lock and key in the archives of the Berliner Staatsbibliothek (Berlin state library). Only when these manuscripts are published will he be able to be appreciated as a composer of sacred works, for the unexplored treasure contains, among other things, twelve psalms for double choir.

Meyerbeer's strong personal affinity for the emotional sensibilities of Jewish religiosity was documented orally in the last year of his life. In conversation with Heine's friend Alexander Weill, Meyerbeer remarked that neither the French "Dieu" nor the German "Herr" or "Ewiger" corresponded to his religious needs as well as the series of four Hebrew letters that subsume past, present, and future.

Franz Kobler

Alexander Zemlinsky (Vienna 1871 – Larchmont, N.Y. 1942) studied at the conservatory of the Gesellschaft der Musikfreunde in Vienna from 1884 to 1892. He was soon a recognized composer of orchestral, piano, and chamber works, and was awarded various prizes. His friendships with *Gustav Mahler* and *Arnold Schoenberg*, who became his student in 1895 and brother-in-law in 1901, provided him with crucial artistic impulses. As Kapellmeister at the Volksoper and Hofoper in Vienna (1907/8), he offered authoritative interpretations of the works of the Second Viennese School. He was opera director at the German Landestheater (National Theater) in Prague between 1911 and 1927, and was subsequently invited to the Krolloper in Berlin by *Otto Klemperer*. Zemlinsky returned to Vienna in 1933 and emigrated to the United States in 1938.

<u>Above</u>: Alexander von Zemlinsky. Ca. 1905

At Kaasgraben, the first stop, Zemlinsky got on; I knew him as a conductor, not as a composer; black birdlike head, jutting triangular nose, no chin. I saw him often, he paid no attention to me, he was really deep in thought, musical thought no doubt, while I was only pretending to read. Every time I saw him I looked for his chin. When he appeared in the doorway, I gave a little start and began to search. Will he have one this time? He never did, but even without a chin he led a full life. To me he was a substitute for Schönberg, who in my time was not in Vienna. Only two years younger than Zemlinsky, Schönberg had been his pupil and had shown him the reverence which was an essential part of his nature, and which Schönberg's own pupils Berg and Webern were to show him. Schönberg, who was poor, had led a hard life in Vienna. For years he had orchestrated operetta music; gnashing his teeth, he had contributed to the tawdry glitter of Vienna, he who was restoring Vienna's fame as the birthplace of great music. In Berlin he obtained regular employment as a teacher of music. When discharged for being Jewish, he emigrated to America. I never saw Zemlinsky without thinking of Schönberg; his sister had been Schönberg's wife for twenty-three years. The sight of him always intimidated me, I sensed his extreme concentration; his small, severe, almost emaciated face was marked by thought and showed no sign of the self-importance one would expect in a conductor. It may have been because of Schönberg's enormous reputation among serious-minded young music lovers that no one ever spoke of Zemlinsky's music; when I saw him on the streetcar, I didn't even suspect that he had composed anything. But I did know that Alban Berg had dedicated his "Lyrical Suite" to him. Berg was dead and Schönberg was not in Vienna; I was always moved when his vicar Zemlinsky entered the car at Kaasgraben.

Elias Canetti

It is not difficult to sense Mahler's Jewish nerves; but there is no place for the term Jewish in a judgment of his music – that can only be a question of achievement.
Otto Flake

Of all the musicians composing today – and I value some of them very highly – none has given me more than Gustav Mahler: joy and deeply felt emotion such as only the very greatest have offered me. Rarely have I felt the need to demand a critico-aesthetic justification from myself concerning the ultimate causes of intense artistic experiences; and to begin doing so in connection with a tonal structure, whose basic laws derive from the rigid roots and depths of mathematical formulae and whose ultimate effects are decided at the most distant, metaphysically blurred frontiers, strikes me as even more hopeless. Thus all that is left to me – and is often the last resort of more pedantic connoisseurs as well – is to trust my innate instincts and to offer thanks where I have received.
Arthur Schnitzler

That is how it was from the very first day. From the start his [Gustav Mahler's] effect was incendiary, provocative, alarming – equally: he is simply one of those electric and electrifying natures who produce or ignite sparks at the slightest touch. Admittedly only his frenetic unpopularity made him popular at the start. Borne by the good grace of hatred, meticulously illuminated by envy – that eternally sleepless and mighty protector of all that is real – by ridicule, resentment, and slander, in other words proclaimed by the noisiest voices at every street corner, he became famous.
Felix Salten

Gustav Mahler (Kalischt, Bohemia 1860 – Vienna 1911), a tradesman's son, attended the conservatory of the Gesellschaft der Musikfreunde in Vienna from 1875 to 1878. After Kapellmeister posts in Olmütz, Kassel, Prague, and Leipzig, he became director of the Royal Hungarian Opera House in Budapest from 1888 to 1891. In 1897 Mahler, who had in the meantime converted to Catholicism, was appointed director of the Hofoper in Vienna. During his ten years there (until 1907) he revitalized the Viennese opera scene, hiring young talents (e.g. the singer Anna Bahr-Mildenburg, the set designer Alfred Roller), meticulously training the opera chorus and mounting new productions. His conducting was marked by fanatic faithfulness to the score. Mahler's compositions include ten symphonies, and song cycles such as *Lieder eines fahrenden Gesellen* and *Kindertotenlieder*. With works like *Das Lied von der Erde* he created a bridge to modern music.
Opposite page: Gustav Mahler. 1907

I have now finally grasped what I have been forced to learn during the past year and will never forget it again. Namely that I am not a German, not a European, perhaps hardly even a human being (at least, the Europeans prefer the worst of their race to me), but that I am a Jew.
And I am content with that! Today I no longer even wish to be an exception; I have nothing against being thrown into the same pot as all the rest.
Arnold Schoenberg

Arnold Schoenberg (Vienna 1874 – Los Angeles 1951) and his students Alban Berg and Anton Webern founded the so-called Second Viennese School, and were thus seminal influences in the development of modern music. All three composers began by writing "conservative" works. Schoenberg's *Harmonielehre* (1911) challenged all the existing rules of composition. His early atonal works (George-Lieder, Klavierstücke op. 11) are considered counterparts to expressionist painting. In the early 1920s he developed the twelve-tone technique. He also painted numerous expressionist pictures and deserves to be regarded as a universal artist.
Above: Arnold Schoenberg. Ca. 1920

Dear Kandinsky, I am writing to you because you write that my letter disturbed you deeply. That is what I hoped of Kandinsky, although I did not say a fraction of what the imagination of a Kandinsky must show him if he is to be my Kandinsky! Because I have not yet said that when I walk down the street, for example, and everyone looks at me to see if I am a Jew or a Christian, that I cannot tell them all that I am the one whom Kandinsky and various others consider an exception, whereas Hitler admittedly is not of that opinion . . .

My question: Why are the Jews equated with their swindlers? Are Aryans also said to be like their worst elements? Why is an Aryan measured by Goethe, Schopenhauer, and the like? Why don't they say the Jews are like Mahler, Altenberg, Schoenberg, and so many others? . . .

With his crooked nose, every Jew reveals not only his own guilt but the guilt of all absent crooked noses. But if one hundred Aryan criminals are assembled, the only thing that will be read from their noses is a fondness for alcohol, otherwise they will be taken for honorable men . . .

Arnold Schoenberg

Where should anti-Semitism lead if not to acts of violence? Is that so difficult to imagine? It may be enough for them to strip the Jews of their rights. That will, however, mean disposing of Einstein, Mahler, myself, and many others. But one thing is certain: there are far tougher elements, thanks to whose resilience Judaism has survived unprotected against the whole of mankind for twenty centuries, and they cannot be wiped out. For they are evidently so organized that they can fulfill the task God has assigned to them: to preserve themselves in exile, uncorrupted and unbroken, until the hour of deliverance comes! . . .

Arnold Schoenberg

Arnold Rosé (Jassy, Romania 1863 – London 1946), born Arnold Rosenbaum, received his first violin lessons when he was seven and studied at the conservatory of the Gesellschaft für Musikfreunde in Vienna from 1874 to 1877. Between 1881 and 1938 he was concertmaster of the orchestra of the Hofoper in Vienna, a member of the Vienna Philharmonic, and later concertmaster of the Bayreuth Festival Orchestra. He had already founded the Rosé Quartet in 1882 with his brother Eduard (Jassy, Romania 1859 – Theresienstadt 1943). The quartet gave its first performance in Vienna in 1883, made numerous international concert tours, and achieved world renown. Arnold Rosé, who married *Gustav Mahler*'s sister Justine in 1902, emigrated to London in 1938.

<u>Right</u>: The Rosé Quartet. Photograph by *d'Ora*. 1915

Joseph Joachim (Kittsee/ Pressburg 1831 – Berlin 1907), a student of Joseph Böhm in Vienna, was introduced to Leipzig audiences as a child prodigy in 1845 by *Felix Mendelssohn Bartholdy*. His violin playing left its mark on a whole generation of musicians, including *Bronislaw Hubermann*. Joachim was appointed director of the Hochschule für Musik (Conservatory) in Berlin in 1868 and founded a string quartet, which specialized in Beethoven's late quartets. Joachim's compositions include *Hebräische Melodien* (Hebrew Melodies).
Above: Joseph Joachim (standing) and Johannes Brahms. Ca. 1865

*E*ven at the risk of being a nuisance, I cannot refrain from letting you [Joseph Joachim] know how grateful I am to you for the pleasure you brought me and so many others this evening. As much as I admire your incredible, unflagging technical virtuosity, it is the loftiness of pure art, the beauty of the music, that has the magical power to draw me to you again and again. What can I say about the perfection of your performance and stylistic artistry that you have not already heard a thousand times! But there are moments of musical transfiguration in the sounds of your violin that send your listeners into almost abstract, transcendental states. "The tears well up," but it is not the earth that has us again; instead "we see the heavens open." The eternal youth of beauty as we dream it seems to be our own at moments like these – we are overcome by happiness of the purest, most beautiful, most sublime sort! Freedom! Light! Bliss!
Theodor Billroth

219

Leo Fall (Olmütz 1873 – Vienna 1925) was the son of Moritz Fall a military bandmaster. He studied at the conservatory in Vienna and began his career directing a theater orchestra. He lived in Vienna as a composer after 1906.

His operetta *Die Dollarprinzessin* (1907) took audiences by storm. He ranks with Franz Lehár, *Oscar Straus* and *Emmerich Kálmán* as one of the finest operetta composers of the twentieth century.
Above left: Leo Fall. Ca. 1913

Oscar Straus (Vienna 1870 – Bad Ischl 1954) studied in Vienna and Berlin and began his career conducting theater orchestras in Pressburg, Bürnn, Teplitz, Mainz, and Hamburg. Engaged by Ernst von Wolzogen as a pianist at the "Überbrettl" in Darmstadt in 1900, he achieved success with such songs as "Der Ehemann kommt" (Husband's Coming). His operetta *Ein Walzertraum* (A

Waltz Dream) was produced in Vienna in 1907. Straus is one of the most important representatives of the "silver" Viennese operetta. He emigrated to New York and Hollywood in 1939 . After his return to Europe (1945) he lived mainly in Bad Ischl and wrote film scores, for example for *Max Ophüls' La Ronde* (1950).
Above center: Oscar Straus. Ca. 1910

Emmerich Kálmán (Siófok, Hungary 1882 – Paris 1953) began his career as a piano *Wunderkind*. After an illness he started studying composition. 1906 saw the premiere of his first comedy, *Das Erbe von Pereszlény* (The Inheritance of Pereszlény); two years later he moved to Vienna. *Herbstmanöver* (The Gay Hus-

sars) brought his great breakthrough; *Die Czsárdásfürstin* (The Gypsy Princess [1915]) and *Gräfin Mariza* (Countess Maritza [1924]) reinforced his reputation. Kálmán emigrated to Paris and New York via Zurich in 1938 and returned to Europe in 1948.
Above right: Emmerich Kálmán. Ca. 1916

Bruno Walter (Berlin 1876 – Beverly Hills 1962), actually Bruno Walter Schlesinger, was appointed Kapellmeister at the k.k. Hofoper in Vienna in 1902 by *Gustav Mahler*. He remained there until 1912, collaborating with Mahler and the set designer Alfred Roller in introducing groundbreaking reforms on the opera stage. He was Generalmusikdirektor of the Opera in Munich from 1913 to 1922 and headed the Vienna State Opera from 1934 to 1936. Walter settled in the United States in 1940 and began conducting in Europe again in 1948. An exponent of the works of such major composers as Anton Bruckner, *Gustav Mahler*, and Hans Pfitzner, he was famous the world over for his Mozart and Mahler interpretations.

Otto Klemperer (Breslau 1885 – Zurich 1973) ranks alongside such great conductors as *Gustav Mahler*, Arturo Toscanini, and *Bruno Walter* in musical achievement. He conducted at the Krolloper in Berlin from 1927 to 1931 and at the Deutsche Staatsoper (State Opera) in Berlin until 1933, the year he was invited to take over the Los Angeles Philharmonic and reinvigorate musical life there. After an engagement at the Budapest Opera from 1947 to 1950, he spent most of his remaining years in London, where he became principal conductor and honorary president of the New Philharmonia in 1959. He acquired Israeli citizenship in 1970. A distinguished interpreter of classical music, Klemperer also championed so-called modern composers, e.g. Ernst Krenek, Paul Hindemith, and Igor Stravinsky.
Right: (from left to right) Bruno Walter, Arturo Toscanini, Erich Kleiber, and Otto Klemperer in Berlin. 1930

Leo Blech (Aachen 1871 – Berlin 1958) studied with Engelbert Humperdinck and, with a few intermittent intervals, conducted at the Staatsoper in Berlin from 1906 to 1937. Like *Bruno Walter*, he was strongly influenced by *Gustav Mahler*. He emigrated to Riga in 1937, to Stockholm in 1941, and then returned to Berlin from 1949 to 1953.
Above: Leo Blech. Ca. 1930

Erich Kleiber (Vienna 1890 – Zurich 1956) studied music, philosophy, and history in Prague, and began his career at the Landestheater in Prague in 1911. In 1912 he went to Darmstadt as Kapellmeister and in 1922 was appointed director of the opera in Düsseldorf. The following year he became Generalmusikdirektor of the Deutsche Staatsoper and principal conductor of the Staatskapelle in Berlin, remaining in these posts until 1935. Sensational premieres, such as Alban Berg's opera *Wozzeck* in 1925, and unconventional programming policies were at the source of his international reputation. Kleiber left Germany in 1935, subsequently conducting in North and South America, and contributing to the golden age of the Teatro Colon in Buenos Aires, Argentina.

Bernhard Paumgartner (Vienna 1887 – Salzburg 1971) was the son of *Rosa Papier*, one of the great singers at the k.k. Hofoper in Vienna. He first studied law and then conducting with *Bruno Walter*, plus piano, horn, and musicology. Director of the Mozarteum in Salzburg for many years (1917 to 1938, 1945 to 1953) and its president until 1959, he took over the presidency of the Salzburg Festival in 1960. Paumgartner was an early exponent of an emphatically Salzburgian style of Mozart performance and was also known as a writer, e.g. for his Mozart biography (1927).
Right: Bernhard Paumgartner. Photograph by *d'Ora*. 1911

Actually there is a special sound characteristic of every woman, one that is hers and hers alone: some have to squeal to be completely themselves, some warble, and some sigh softly. If one thinks of Massary, one immediately hears a low, guttural sound that can mean so many things: above all abundant irony. It would be great fun some time to hear how this bundle of superior nerves reacts to eight different declarations of love . . .
Yes, Massary knows all, can do all – and with what ease! She lifts and drops her shoulders once, and sways along with the song a little – a delightful parody on all the operetta dancing in the world. What one must be grateful for again and again is her discretion – she never goes overboard.
Kurt Tucholsky

Richard Tauber (Linz 1891 – London 1948) made his début as Tamino in Chemnitz, Bohemia, and rapidly established a reputation as an outstanding Mozart tenor, appearing in Dresden, Vienna, Berlin, and at the Salzburg Festival. From the twenties on, he sang in almost all of Franz Lehár's operettas; written for him, they made both the singer and the composer popular. Tauber was one of the first to venture into the world of talking pictures. He emigrated to London in 1938 and subsequently sang primarily at the Covent Garden Opera House.
<u>Below</u>: Richard Tauber. Photograph by *d'Ora*. Ca. 1920

Fritzi Massary (Vienna 1882 – Hollywood 1969), originally Friederike Masarek, was the most celebrated operetta diva of the twenties. From 1904 to 1933 she acted and sang in Berlin, where she married *Max Pallenberg* in 1918. "Suddenly, there stood this messenger from the operetta center, Vienna, in the very midst of the hurly-burly of Berlin's theater scene and . . . the jubilant crowds at the Metropol-Theater cheered and were completely carried away . . . She also possessed the secret of animating spoken or sung dialogue with an astonishing variety of mimetic-gestural details, often with a virtually imperceptible undertone of sarcasm, irony, or satire." (Rudolf Kastner, "Nachschaffende Musiker" [Performing Musicians] in *Juden im deutschen Kulturbereich* [Jews in the German Cultural Context]).
<u>Left</u>: Fritzi Massary. Photograph by *d'Ora.* 1923

Kurt Weill (Dessau 1900 – New York 1950) studied with Engelbert Humperdinck and Ferruccio Busoni in Berlin and took up composing for the satirical, topical musical theater in 1926. His aggressive songs for Bertolt Brecht's *Dreigroschenoper* (1928) and *Aufstieg und Fall der Stadt Mahagonny* (Rise and Fall of the City of Mahagonny [1927, 1930]) combined contemporary dance and popular music, jazz for example, with the street-ballad, chanson, and chorale form. After leaving Germany in 1933, he collaborated with Bertolt Brecht in Paris on *Die sieben Todsünden der Kleinbürger* (The Seven Deadly Sins), a ballet with singing. He emigrated to the U.S. in 1935. His wife *Lotte Lenya* was the ideal interpreter of his works.
<u>Left</u>: Kurt Weill. Photograph by *Lotte Jacobi.* Ca. 1920

Lotte Lenya (Vienna 1900 – New York 1981), originally Karoline Blamauer, became famous as the interpreter of her husband *Kurt Weill*'s songs. She experienced her first major success in the role of Pirate Jenny in the *Dreigroschenoper* (Threepenny Opera) by Bertolt Brecht and Kurt Weill. She emigrated to the U.S. with her husband in 1935 and began performing in Europe again in 1955.
<u>Above</u>: Lotte Lenya. Photograph by *Lotte Jacobi.* 1930

Rarely has the theater played as important a role in people's consciousness as in the era of the Weimar Republic.
Hans Sahl

Theatrically speaking, the Viennese temperament revolted against Berlin. But the social and economic circumstances in Vienna no longer allowed the rise of a distinguished new theater, so the Austrian Reinhardt led his thorough southern-German style theater, his actors' theater, to triumph in Berlin.
Julius Bab

Amid the eclectic conglomeration of styles which made up the non-style of the nineteenth century, the theater, or more precisely, the art of the actor, was the sole domain in which a true stylistic tradition continued to flourish, and because it was a tradition, it was not eclectic. It was Baroque art; during the classical period it had acquired a certain simplicity and breadth, and it was this that was practiced with an almost noble rigor at the Comédie Française and the Vienna Burgtheater.
Hermann Broch

Max Reinhardt (Baden/Vienna 1873 – New York 1943), originally Max Goldmann, was engaged as an actor at the Deutsches Theater in Berlin under *Otto Brahm* in 1894. In 1901 he and some fellow-actors and members of the "Brille" (Glasses) circle started a literary "cabaret," or satirical revue, "Schall und Rauch," which he reopened under the same name in 1919. As director of the Deutsches Theater (1905 to 1920, 1924 to 1933) and the Kammerspiele (Chamber Theater) in Berlin, he reformed the stage. His sensuous, "magical" productions contrasted sharply with those of Erwin Piscator, with whom he fought an artistic "duel." In 1920 Reinhardt and *Hugo von Hofmannsthal* founded the Salzburg Festival. In 1924 he began directing plays at the Theater in der Josefstadt in Vienna, his Shakespeare productions bringing him particular success. Reinhardt left Berlin for Austria in 1933 and emigrated to the U.S. in 1937.
Opposite page, below: Max Reinhardt at a rehearsal in Salzburg. Ca. 1922

The theaters of the Austro-Hungarian Monarchy and the German Reich were similar in their late nineteenth-century architectural pomp; their "archetypes" could be found in large cities like Berlin, Vienna, Budapest, or Prague they were perpetuated everywhere, down to the smallest provincial towns.

Above: The Königliches Schauspielhaus (Royal Theater) on Gendarmenmarkt in Berlin; at the left, the Deutscher Dom (German Cathedral). Photograph by Hermann Rückwardt. 1879
Below: The theater in Lemberg (Galicia). Ca. 1895

No European country possessed so many good theaters so filled with life as the German Reich. There were good theaters in Königsberg and Hamburg, Hannover and Bochum, Leipzig, Dresden, and Frankfurt, Mannheim, Darmstadt, Nuremberg, even Munich, and four or five in Berlin. In all of these cities, Jewish theater directors exercised an influence on audiences strongly permeated by Jews, audiences saturated with the local cultural climate.
Arnold Zweig

Looking back we can be happy to have lived in a city where theatrical eras were shaped by Otto Brahm, Max Reinhardt, and Leopold Jessner, and where the non-Jew Erwin Piscator and the Russian Jew Alexej Granowsky broke new ground. And what a plethora of directors, of acting talent both strong and subtle! What unforgettable evenings, even in recent years, when the star system and huge motion picture salaries had already done severe damage to the literary stage! Even such people as the unfortunate Rotter brothers, denounced by Jewish and non-Jewish critics alike, were capable of putting on splendid theatrical evenings. From the Wall-
ner Theater in the east of Berlin to the Städtische Oper in Charlottenburg, what lively stage activity! What effort invested in mounting new, attractive, riveting productions! And motion pictures, never allowed to develop without censorship in Germany, also benefited: they got the talented actors and the directors the theater had discovered and trained. Max Pallenberg and Ernst Deutsch, the late Rudolf Schildkraut and, very much alive, Fritz Kortner, the very old Max Pohl and the young Peter Lorre, all shades of masculinity trod across those stages that are no longer the world. It was a time when Alexander Moissi could be seen as Faust and Alexander Granach as Mephisto, and in comic roles there might be three or four artists at one time, gloriously displaying the Jewish gift for mimic, wit, and humor. Women, Jewesses of all types and styles, offered their art and charms to the German stage: Ilka Grüning and Frida Richard as much as Elisabeth Bergner and Sybille Binder, the Mosheim sisters, Helene Weigel, or Lucie Mannheim. And then, unforgettable in their affinity with Ibsen, Wedekind, and modern operetta, Irene Triesch, Maria Orska, and the great Fritzi Massary, who all gave us so much.
Arnold Zweig

Reinhardt was a magician who worked with illusions and made an actors' festival out of every performance; Piscator was an engineer of the stage, who incorporated the principle of movement and change into his productions and worked with cranes, moving belts, spotlights, and projections. Reinhardt and Piscator, those were the two trends in the German theater of the twenties, and they appeared to preclude each other. The one was bourgeois, liberal, aesthetic, apolitical, the other revolutionary, anti-bourgeois, politically committed. Nonetheless the two complemented each other wonderfully.
Hans Sahl

The Deutsches Theater (German theater) has come to the decision, after discussions with Hinkel, Commissar for Special Duty of the Prussian Ministry of Culture, that Max Reinhardt no longer has any connection with the artistic management of the Deutsches Theater and that the management of the Deutsches Theater will in future take account of the requirements of German culture . . . There is no doubt that the formulation chosen in the communiqué is meant to indicate that, as a Jew, Max Reinhardt is unable to fulfill the requirements of German culture. It is so to speak the condemnation of his life's work.
Jüdische Rundschau (Jewish Review)

The idea of a Salzburg Festival had already existed for some time before its foundation in 1920. Hermann Bahr and *Max Reinhardt* had seriously discussed the subject as early as 1905. 1917 saw the birth of the "Salzburger Festspielhausgemeinde" (Salzburg Festival Playhouse Association) in Vienna, its members including not only Max Reinhardt and *Hugo von Hofmannsthal*, but Franz Schalk and Richard Strauss as well. Hofmannsthal provided an idealistic framework for the project that transcended its artistic significance.

I have always considered it a great mistake . . . to offer the masses nothing but one-dimensional kitsch. Only the best is good enough for them. They must be introduced to spiritual and intellectual values as well, and then the echo will be stronger among them than among the jaded people in the expensive seats.
Max Reinhardt

Max Reinhardt: a prodigal genius of the theater. A man who enjoys his own effects, who savors the aftertaste of his own appeal. Max Reinhardt, the most colorful theatrical talent of all times, intuitive, casually improvisatory. Taking up impulses, dispensing impulses. Max Reinhardt played for people who considered the theater a luxury, a treasure, the greatest ornament of existence. Max Reinhardt, the genius who perfected the upper middle class theater, incomparable in his achievements, inexhaustible in his artistic versatility – Max Reinhardt and the Volksbühne (popular theater)?
Erwin Piscator

But Sonnenthal is the absolute master of heartfelt acting. For him the phrase "to be whole-heartedly involved" has a genuine meaning. The great, gentle dedication one senses in him casts a spell on the whole audience, particularly its kinder members. One constantly feels a spectator at an event that is not only artistic but truly human. The almost maternal warmth of his feelings overcomes the theatrical illusion that divides; one is directly confronted with a natural sensitivity that can liberate, plunge into melancholy, or move to tears. No one plays loyalty, pity, warmth, resignation – in short, all the noble qualities of the heart – better than Sonnenthal. He is never greater than in roles that experience pain. He redeems the souls of such roles by taking all their pain upon himself, not acting but suffering them. His most wonderful technique is his nature; his greatest art, his kindness.
Alfred Polgar

Adolf von Sonnenthal (Pest 1834 – Prague 1909) began his acting career at the Burgtheater in Vienna in 1856. In 1884 he took on the additional post of chief stage-director and was also director of the theater from 1887 to 1890. His most famous roles were Wallenstein and, late in his career, the title role in *Nathan der Weise*.
Right: Adolf von Sonnenthal as *Nathan der Weise* at the Burgtheater in Vienna. Ca. 1900.
Below: Max Reinhardt as *Roter Itzig* in *Richard Beer-Hofmann*'s *Der Graf von Charolais* (The Count of Charolais). 1904.

Fritz Kortner (Vienna 1892 – Munich 1970) joined the ensemble of *Max Reinhardt*'s Deutsches Theater in Berlin in 1911. In 1919, *Leopold Jessner* offered him an engagement at the Staatliches Schauspielhaus in Berlin, the city that was to be the principal site of Kortner's activities until 1933. He celebrated his greatest triumphs in plays by Shakespeare and Wedekind; his Shylock is legendary.
Opposite page: Fritz Kortner as Shylock in *The Merchant of Venice*. Ca. 1924

Alexander Granach
(Wierzbowce, Galicia 1890 – New
York 1945) first appeared in the
Yiddish theater. After a year at the
Reinhardt-Seminar in Berlin he re-
ceived an engagement at the Deut-
sches Theater in Berlin. He spent
1919/20 at the Schauspielhaus in
Munich and performed at various
theaters in Berlin from 1921 on
(Lessing-Theater, Piscator-Bühne,
Deutsches Theater, Volksbühne,
Junge Bühne). In 1933 he emigrated to Poland, where he appeared
with the Jiddisches Theater in
Warsaw and later in Kiev. In 1938
he went to the U.S., where he
acted in such motion pictures as
Joan of Paris (1942) with Paul
Henreid. He was one of the
youngest actors to play Shylock on
the stage.
Above: Alexander Granach as Shylock in *The Merchant of Venice*.
1936

*No, the roles were listed in chronological
order, as in a book, but with the name of the
actor added. My tiny role was listed in the
same small print as the lead's. There it was in
black and white: A waiter: Jessaja Granach. –
Oh, I was so happy. I could hardly believe it.
Then, after a few days, my name was
changed: Hermann Granach. That I did not
appreciate. I went to the theater secretary to
protest – I did not want to be called Hermann. "All right," said the secretary, "but
Jessaja is no good either. It sounds too Jewish
for the German Theater." "That's true," I
mumbled, " but I don't like Hermann. I
don't want to be called Hermann. It doesn't
suit me." "But my dear boy," the secretary
tried to soothe me diplomatically, "you take
everything far too seriously. Believe me, a
name doesn't mean anything. Names signify
nothing." "Not to me," I replied. "Well, what
do you want to be called then?" "Stefan," I
said. He thought it over and answered, "No,
that's no good. Stefan is too Hungarian. What
do you think of Alexander? Alexander
Granach, that gives you four A's in your
name, and Moissi has only two! All right?"
"All right."*
Alexander Granach

The part I was playing at the time [in Ernst Toller's "Wandlung" (Transformation)] is what I was myself: a young German Jew and rebel in conflict with the world around him. Like a startled Jewish deer, Ernst Toller had already scented the still distant hunters.
Fritz Kortner

The famous tragedian from the east of the former Monarchy, Rudolf Schildkraut (whose son Joseph later became a Hollywood star), was giving guest performances in Vienna as King Lear, Nathan der Weise, and in several other starring roles. His fondness for playing tarok was coupled with a keen sense of humor, and when he was told about Dr. Sperber, he could hardly wait to meet the eccentric fellow. The problem was that, like many real characters, Sperber was very shy and withdrawn with strangers, and he could hardly get out a word, let alone a witty one, in the presence of famous people. And that is what happened when he and the great actor finally met. To Schildkraut's disappointment, Sperber limited himself to trivial, embarrassed remarks: "Where do you usually play, sir? . . . At the Café Reichsrat, well, well . . . In the afternoon, I take it . . . And how are you enjoying your stay otherwise?" Schildkraut answered along the same lines, and the pover-

Therese Giehse (Munich 1898 – Munich 1975), originally Therese Gift, performed with the Munich Kammerspiele from 1925 to 1933 and after 1950. With Erika and Klaus Mann, she started "Die Pfeffermühle" (The Peppermill), a political-satirical "cabaret," in 1932, emigrating to Zurich with the group the same year. In 1937 Giehse joined the ensemble of the Schauspielhaus in Zurich, where she appeared in the premiere of Bertolt Brecht's *Mutter Courage* (Mother Courage). In 1949/50 she belonged to the Berliner Ensemble formed by Bertolt Brecht and run by his wife Helene Weigel. Giehse became famous for her one-woman shows, evenings of Brecht recitations.
Below: Therese Giehse as Mutter Wolffen in Gerhart Hauptmann's *Der Biberpelz* (The Beaver Coat) at the Munich Kammerspiele. 1928
Right: Paul Baratoff (left) as the eastern Jewish merchant Kaftan and Reinhold Schünzel as the German nationalist lawyer Müller in the premiere of *Walter Mehring*'s *Der Kaufmann von Berlin* (The Merchant of Berlin) at the Piscator-Bühne in Berlin. 1929

ty of the conversation began to take on paralyzing proportions.
To put an end to it, the game was begun. The cards were dealt. Dr. Zeisel, who had arranged the meeting, started, which meant that Schildkraut and Sperber had to play together against him. As he was sitting ahead of Sperber, Schildkraut had to lead. Naturally there was no way for him to know the first time round which suit his partner would welcome and which he would not. As luck would have it, he decided for the suit not represented in Sperber's hand and struck his partner right in the tarok guts. At that, Sperber's inhibitions were radically cast off: "Oh, you eastern Jewish abomination!" he roared. "What ghetto spat you out?"
The spell was broken, and Schildkraut was given plenty to laugh at after that.
Friedrich Torberg

We saw the Wilnaer Jiddische Theater two years ago. Genuine, sirs! Absolutely genuine, one hundred percent. "Ghetto art," you laugh. Maybe so, but one hundred percent genuine.
Alfred Döblin

*A poor troupe of touring eastern Jewish players, thrust into the west, were just appearing at a little café in Prague; and they touched off my transformation, as I have already mentioned. Everything they did was wrong and wretched, but everywhere the authenticity shone through: things traditional, honorable, gentle, and intense; Shakespearean uncouthness; fresh impulses that affected me (and soon afterwards Kafka, as well) . . .
I learned to distinguish genuine lore from eastern operetta, already a product of decline, if not as low as the "entertainments" shown in Vienna and Budapest; but its pleasant superficiality was well suited to blur the boundaries that had just been discovered . . .*
Max Brod

*Moscow's Hebrew theater offers samples of overwhelmingly intense scenic art. The new Russian spirit has penetrated the age-old Jewish life-form. Ritual and theater meet in a passionate embrace. The mysterious, uncanny quality of a special emotional and conceptual world, the comedy, soulfulness, grotesquery and pathos of this world – all of these are invoked and transfixed in strong scenic symbols. The Habima Theater provides a marvelous substitute for the art of acting.
This is already expressed symbolically in the masks. Faces of unequivocally sharp physiognomy, unmasking masks of the Ego they cover. Wonderful masks – but, rigid with paint and make-up, they allow no facial mimicry.
No individual countenance in this remarkable troupe has any claim to that.
Each face is accorded the role of one feature of the collective face.*
Alfred Polgar

The poet *Abraham Goldfaden* (1840–1908) provided the impulses for a modern Yiddish theater – which grew out of the Purim plays that had existed since the sixteenth century – when he founded the first Yiddish theater ensemble in Jassy (Romania) in 1877. In 1883 a czarist ukase banned all the groups that had been created and numerous actors emigrated to western Europe and the U.S. *Jakob Beer Gimpel* founded an ensemble in Lemberg, Austria, that existed until 1938.

The "Wilnaer Truppe" was founded in 1916 against the background of an array of independent Yiddish plays written around 1900. In 1921 the ensemble split up into the "Jüdisches Künstlertheater" (U.S.) and the Wilnaer Theater (Poland, Romania). There was also a "Jüdisch-akademisches Theater" in Moscow, which had evolved from the "Yiddische Kammerspiele" founded in Leningrad in 1918. Poland alone had as many as fifteen Yiddish theater groups in 1934. One of the most popular plays in the repertoire was *Der Dibbuk* by *Salomon Anski*.

Above: The Vilna operetta ensemble in the musical comedy *Kawkaser liebe* (Caucasian Love). 1927

The Hebrew "Habima" ensemble was founded by *Naum Zemach* in Moscow in 1916. The performances were impressive for their uniquely haunting style of acting, developed through years of rehearsal under a Stanislavsky student, *Wachtangow*. The troupe toured Europe and the U.S. with its most successful plays: *Chajim Nachman Bialik*'s Hebrew translation of *Salomon Anski*'s *Dibbuk* and *Die Nacht auf dem alten Markt* (The Night at the Old Market) by *Jizchak Leib Peretz*. Some members of the ensemble stayed in the U.S. in 1927, the rest went to Palestine (the "National Theater" since 1956).

Above: Scene from *Der Dibbuk*. Guest performance of the Habima at the Carltheater in Vienna. 1926

Fritz Grünbaum (Brünn [Brno] 1880 – Dachau concentration camp 1941) acquired a law degree before becoming master of ceremonies at the "Hölle" (Hell), a Viennese theater-cabaret. In 1907 he joined "Chat noir," a satirical cabaret in Berlin, returning to Vienna in 1914. After World War I he appeared at the "Simplicissimus" in Vienna and developed the double-moderator technique with *Karl Farkas* in 1922. The author of numerous satirical routines and, with Farkas, the revue *Wien lacht wieder* (Vienna laughs again), he also wrote successful popular songs ("Ich hab' das Fräulein Helen baden sehn," etc.).

Egon Friedell (Vienna 1878 – suicide in Vienna 1938) was awarded his Ph. D. in 1904 and worked as artistic director of the Cabaret Fledermaus, a satirical revue theater in Vienna, from 1908 to 1910. Apart from works in the field of literary history (*Kulturgeschichte der Neuzeit* [A Cultural History of the Modern Era], etc.), he collaborated with *Alfred Polgar* on one-act parodies for the revue and liked to perform in them himself. His friend *Peter Altenberg*'s skits and anecdotes became famous through Friedell's interpretations on the small stage. As an actor he began appearing at *Max Reinhardt*'s theaters in Vienna and Berlin in 1924.
Left: Fritz Grünbaum (left) and Egon Friedell (right) with their busts on the cabaret stage in Vienna. Photograph by Lothar Rübelt. Ca. 1925

The satirical cabaret differs from all of humanity's other public conveniences: one does not allow oneself to be lied to there. People who go to cabarets do not pretend to want moral purification for their money. There are orchestra seats at the Burgtheater for that. But what one does not have the courage to admit at the Burgtheater is demanded from the "cabaret" artist: that he throw out the muse and give the audience, whose spirits are already low enough these days, a few enjoyable hours . . .
Fritz Grünbaum

And so if we take a look at the world,
The whole creation: the woods and the field,
The oxen on land, in the water the fishl,
The Christians in Linz and the Jews in Ischl,

The sun shines by day, and the moon at night –
In short, when we think it's all quite all right,
And know that the whole thing, right through and through,
Was actually only a deadline job too,
Because all of it, body, spirit and soul,
The dog and the horse and the pig and the mole,
The anti-Semite and the Israelite,
The roses, the lilies, the crimes of the night,
The solemn bank manager, shoemaker, primate,
They all took a mere seven days to create –
Then all we can say to the range on the shelf
Is "I couldn't have done any better myself!"
Fritz Grünbaum

Fritz Grünbaum – a unique figure in a unique period of cabaret: the little man who made very big points that always hit the mark without wounding – because their caustic effect was always mitigated by kindness. He thought with his heart, a sensitive philosopher as drastic comedian.
For fifteen years we worked together at home and abroad, on large stages and small ones. During that time I learned to love and admire him. The duel of wits we pretended to fight in front of the audience every night developed into a new style of the by now already monotonous number cabaret. We devised a kind of repartee that has been part of the heritage of the cabaret stage ever since: the double-moderator technique . . .
Karl Farkas about Fritz Grünbaum

Let us just stay on the subject of Egon Friedell in Berlin. It must have been in the late twenties that he appeared in the opening program of a new literary cabaret there. I had already heard him tell his famous Altenberg anecdotes at Fritz Grünbaum's "Simplicissimus" in Vienna, so I can vouch first-hand for his ability to display the originality of his wit and personality to its best advantage on the cabaret stage, too. But the Berlin critics thought differently and tore him apart with a ruthlessness he had never experienced before. Friedell reacted to one of these scathing reviews, which referred to him as, among other things, "a drunken Munich dilettante," with an open letter that went something like this: "It does not disturb me to be termed a dilettante. Dilettantism and serious artistic endeavors do not preclude one another. Nor do I deny that I am not averse to the occasional drink, and if someone wants to use that against me, I will have to accept it. But to call me a native of Munich – for that someone is going to be taken to court!" That letter shows the whole Friedell, his sarcasm, his readiness to be self-ironic, with all the superiority that implies, and his enjoyment of caustic arguments, his joy of life altogether.
Friedrich Torberg

Heinrich Eisenbach (Cracow 1870 – Vienna 1923) began his career as an artist at the age of 16. After a stay in Budapest, he advanced to the post of director of the "Budapester Orpheum" in Vienna. Around the turn of the century he appeared with *Fritz Grünbaum* at the "Hölle" theater-cabaret in Vienna.
Below: Heinrich Eisenbach. Ca. 1910

We shall never hear that "ne-bisch!" again. Not even in perfect imitation. For the difference between Eisenbach and his distinguished equals among the ranks of popular artists is that he was inimitable. His effect more than theirs – all the more because apart from his cheekiness and the mournful quality round his protrusive mouth, there was nothing conspicuously unique about him – consisted in the particular intensity of his type: let us say of the Leopoldstadt Viennese. Or to use Zionist terminology, the assimilatory Jew of the lower variety. He portrayed this character with such purity that – unlike certain artificial, "national" sensitivities – it had the effect of virtual purification. He normally portrayed him as the conned conman. Namely: his parodistic brain conned, and his (vain, fearful, hateful, and gentle) nature was conned. He had the whole world in his pocket – and yet it took him in.
Anton Kuh

So the parodist Eisenbach, that brilliant representative of the slippery breed, was truly an element of national reconciliation in the old Monarchy: he held the Jews up to the ridicule of the Viennese, the Viennese to the ridicule of the Jews, and the Hungarians, Czechs and Poles to the ridicule of both (as an intermezzo). But because he really knew their hand, he played his own part honestly. This honesty was characterized by an uninhibited vehemence directed both upwards and downwards, whether at piteous humility or superior audacity.
Anton Kuh

How urgently mankind needs the mixture embodied in this little Mosaic clerk of an Eisenbach: unimpressed by factitiousness – reverent before the miracle of life!
Anton Kuh

Like many of the stars in Vienna's theatrical and satirical cabaret heaven, he [Armin Berg] came from Brünn [Brno] (from near-Brünn, as his colleague Fritz Grünbaum loved to insist in his genuine central-Brünn arrogance), and he enjoyed enormous popularity in those parts of the former Habsburg domain that understood the aberrant variety of German he cultivated.
Friedrich Torberg

In his last revue on March 10, 1938, Grünbaum still joked on the darkened stage: "I see nothing, absolutely nothing. I must have lost my way and landed in National Socialist culture."
Pierre Genée/Hans Veigl

Valeska Gert (Berlin 1892 – Kampen, Sylt 1978), originally Gertrud Valesca Samosch, was the "inventor of modern dance-pantomime." After acting lessons with Maria Moissi, she made her debut as a dancer in Berlin in 1916 and was soon giving solo performances ("Tanz in Orange," etc.). After engagements at the Kammerspiele in Munich and the Deutsches Theater in Berlin, she also appeared in the "Schall und Rauch II" satirical cabaret (1920) and in the Fritz Hollaender revue "Laterna magica" (1926). Apart from her solo dance performances, she also appeared in films (*Die freudlose Gasse* [The Joyless Lane], 1925, among others). She emigrated to New York in 1938 and returned to Europe in 1947.
Above: Valeska Gert in her pantomime *Boxen*. Ca. 1925

If someone here makes a good political joke, half of Germany sits on the sofa and takes offense.
Satire seems a thoroughly negative business. It says, "No!" A satire that inspires people to buy war bonds is no satire. Satire stings, laughs, whistles, and beats the big colorful landsknecht's drum against everything slack and sluggish.
Satire is a thoroughly positive business. Nowhere do the spineless betray themselves more quickly than here, nothing more rapidly exposes a nonentity without a conscience for what he is, someone who attacks one person today and someone else tomorrow.
The satirist is a wounded idealist: he wants a good world, it is evil, and he launches out against that evil. So the satire of a strong-willed artist who champions the good does not deserve the bourgeois disregard and indignant snarl with which the art is dismissed in this country.
Kurt Tucholsky

to get myself invited to the Passover Eve dinner by an old relative, a brother-in-law of my mother's; that is how I got to know one of the nicest, oldest Jewish customs, and with as much curiosity as an outsider. My uncle later said I had sat there like a "goy."
Fritz Mauthner

I feel totally German; but I know that I have some sort of a cast of mind that is known as Jewish; all the worse or all the better, I cannot and do not wish to change it. Your conclusion is different, and that is the only point where we differ.
Fritz Mauthner

The task of philosophy is to show the fly the way out of the glass.
Ludwig Wittgenstein

Thus the legend replaced the life even during his lifetime, a legend of self-denial, of the attempt at a saintly life, of the attempt to obey the sentence with which the "Tractatus" concludes: "Whereof one cannot speak, one must be silent." And it was . . . the attempt to realize philosophy silently, an absurd attempt it seems, but the only legitimate one for him once everything expressible had been clearly put forth (as he demanded from philosophy), everything conceivable, which limits the inconceivable from inside and thus points to the inexpressible.
Ingeborg Bachmann

That which is inexpressible perhaps provides the background against which that which I can express acquires meaning.
Ludwig Wittgenstein

All philosophy is linguistic criticism.
Ludwig Wittgenstein

Fritz Mauthner (Horitz, Bohemia 1849 – Meersburg 1923) attended lectures in philosophy, archaeology, art history, theology, and medicine while studying law from 1869 to 1873. He soon turned to writing and journalism, especially theatrical journalism, and was a co-founder of Berlin's "Freie Bühne" (Free Heater [1889]). An autodidact, he devoted himself to problems of linguistic philosophy and criticism throughout his life; his *Beiträge zu einer Kritik der Sprache* (Contributions to a Critique of Language [1901/1902]) and *Wörterbuch der Philosophie* (Dictionary of Philosophy [1910]) are works of fundamental importance. Above: Fritz Mauthner. Ca. 1909

I cannot understand how a Jew born in a Slavic region of Austria could feel no urge to undertake linguistic research. He used to learn to understand three languages at once, to be exact; German as the language of officialdom, education, poetry, and everyday life; Czech as the language of the peasants and servant girls . . . a little Hebrew as the sacred language of the Old Testament and the basis for the "Mauscheldeutsch" he heard from Jewish junk dealers, but occasionally also from reasonably well-dressed Jewish tradesmen of his acquaintance or even from his relatives.
Fritz Mauthner

However much I think back, I cannot remember ever catching my uncle or my father in the act of observing a Jewish custom. In the Jewish view, being a Jew without knowing the Hebrew language is inconceivable; but my father did not know a single letter of the Hebrew alphabet. On Jewish high holidays he used to say with a certain self-reproach: "Why, you are growing up like heathens," that was the sum total of the religious education he lavished on us. When I wanted to acquaint myself with the old ceremonies of the Jewish Easter festival, I had

Ludwig Wittgenstein (Vienna 1889 – Cambridge 1951) originally studied engineering and then went on to study mathematics and logic with Bertrand Russell. His most important work, *Tractatus logico-philosophicus*, appeared in English and German in 1922. From 1920 to 1926 he taught school in Austria, returning to Cambridge in 1929, where he held a professorship between 1939 and 1947. His philosophical theories about the nature and possibilities of language and thought influenced the "Vienna Circle," which included *Otto Neurath*, among others. His theories took a new turn around 1933. Initial interest in his critical linguistic philosophy came from the English-speaking world. Right: Ludwig Wittgenstein. Ca. 1920

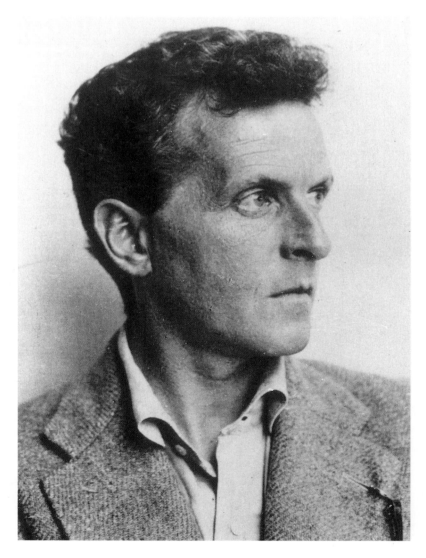

Merely to be gentle is not yet to be good. And the many weaklings we have are not yet peaceful. If purely as that frequent blend of lemonade and empty rhetoric, pacifism would not be what many democrats feel it must: the resistance of socially humane reason, active and without excuses. To prevent being emasculated in the process, it is imperative to distinguish between struggle and war.
Ernst Bloch

For the Jews are not yet weary. They will not fail, they are like heart cells and do not allow themselves to slacken.
Ernst Bloch

For it is as the Baal Shem says, and his words indicate the a priori of the intrinsically social nature of man: the Messiah can come only when all the guests have sat down at the table; but it is first a table for work and only then, but then immediately, the table of the Lord.
Ernst Bloch

*I would like to express my veneration for Ernst Bloch, an old – now wise – man with a restless mind, although I am likely to figure among those whose approval does not matter much to him and whose censure would hardly give him grounds for critical reflection. The waters that separated us were far too shallow to provide the depths necessary for a true encounter.
And yet our first meeting in Interlaken in 1919, when I had already decided to dedicate my scholarly life to the study of Judaism – a nocturnal, sometimes heated conversation many hours long – numbers among the most unforgettable events of my youth. Its prelude deserves to be described here because during the first minutes of my meeting with Bloch an unexpected outlook on my own spiritual world was revealed to me.
The young Bloch, an overwhelming physical and intellectual presence, threw himself unflinchingly into apocalyptic visions that caused the mystical images he luxuriated in to perish. The ninety-year-old has become a blind seer, a master who has survived the dragon he battled for forty years to become a wise man according to the old Jewish definition of the "Old Man" as he who "has acquired wisdom," a commodity whose inexplicability Job already lamented.*
Gershom Scholem

Ernst Bloch (Ludwigshafen 1885 – Tübingen 1977) gained his reputation as a philosopher through his books *Geist der Utopie* (Spirit of Utopia [1918]), *Thomas Münzer* (1922), and above all his main work, *Das Prinzip Hoffnung* (The Principle of Hope [1954–1959]). A Marxist, he developed a highly individual philosophy of history, to which theology is indispensable. He became one of the major inspirations of the leftist student movement in the 1960s.
<u>Right</u>: Ernst Bloch. Photograph by *Lotte Jacobi.* Ca. 1937

In 1923, F. Weil established the Institut für Sozialforschung (Institute for Social Research) in Frankfurt am Main, giving the so-called Frankfurt School a geographical focus. This circle of social scientists and cultural philosophers, who based their critical-social analyses on the theories of *Karl Marx* and *Sigmund Freud,* included, among others, *Karl Mannheim, Siegfried Kracauer, Theodor W. Adorno,* and *Max Horkheimer.* The Frankfurt School also influenced such thinkers as *Ludwig Marcuse, Walter Benjamin,* and *Erich Fromm.*

I understood Judaism as my religious affiliation and the German Reich as my homeland.
Max Horkheimer

That throughout the long centuries of persecution the Jews preserved their teachings, though these emphasize neither the reward of individual salvation nor eternal punishment; that they remained loyal to a law after the state which could have enforced it had disappeared, only because of the hope placed in the just of all peoples in the future – that is the contradiction that links them with the great German philosophy, in fact with everything popularly and ironically known as Idealism.
Max Horkheimer

It cannot be helped, justice and freedom are dialectical concepts. The more justice, the less freedom; the more freedom, the less justice. Freedom, equality, brotherhood, that is a fine phrase. But if you want to obtain equality, *you must restrict freedom, and if you want to leave human beings their freedom, then there can be no equality.*
Max Horkheimer

In the twentieth century it is not the conformist mass that is the object of ridicule, but the outsider who still dares to think for himself.
Max Horkheimer

If there was anything to the famous twenties, it could be experienced in that circle. We often fell upon each other like wild animals; our outspokenness, which did not stop short of the sharpest attack on others, can hardly be imagined today: we called each other ideologues or the reverse, accused each other of untenable thinking or whatever – but all without even the slightest harm . . . to friendships.
Theodor W. Adorno

T heodor Lessing (Hannover 1872 – murdered in Marienbad 1933) was a distinguished philosopher of history and culture, and a controversial professor at the Technische Hochschule in Hannover. His works took a critical view of civilization; equal rights for women was among the causes to which he was committed. He was one of the first to analyze teh phenomenon of Jewish self-hatred.
Below: Theodor Lessing. 1932

E dmund Husserl (Prossnitz, Moravia 1859 – Freiburg i. Br. 1938) became a lecturer at the University of Halle in 1887, an associate professor at the University of Freiburg in 1901 and a full professor there in 1906. He is the father of phenomenology.
Above: Edmund Husserl. Ca. 1930

M artin Buber (Vienna 1878 – Jerusalem 1965) studied in Vienna, Berlin, Leipzig, and Zurich and was one of the co-founders, with *Berthold Feiwel*, *Ephraim Moses Lilien*, and *Chaim Weizmann*, among others, of the Jüdischer Verlag in Berlin in 1901. An early exponent of cultural Zionism, he built on *Achad Haam's* idea of Palestine as a spiritual-cultural center for the Jewish people. His own spiritual roots were in Hasidism, which he revealed to the west in his anthologies and other writings (e.g., *Die Geschichten des Rabbi Nachman* [The Stories of Rabbi Nachman], 1906; *Mein Weg zum Chassidismus* [My Path to Hasidism], 1918). The starting point of his pedagogic, religious, and political views (*Ich und Du* [I and Thou], 1922) was the way human beings relate to one another. Buber copublished various periodicals, among them *Der Jude* (1916 to 1924). Between 1924 and 1933, he taught religion at the University of Frankfurt, made a new German translation of the Bible in collaboration with *Franz Rosenzweig*, and headed the Jüdisches Lehrhaus (Jewish Institute) and the institute for adult education in Frankfurt. From 1938 to 1951 he held a professorship in social philosophy in Jerusalem.
Right: Martin Buber. Photograph by *Lotte Jacobi*. 1928

T his Jewish thinker (Edmund Husserl, born in Moravia, converted to Christianity), who, along with Dilthey and Nietzsche, was responsible for the rise of modern philosophy, made first Göttingen and then Freiburg into the liveliest philosophical centers in Germany and, next to Paris, where Henri Bergson was teaching, on earth. His followers Moritz Geiger and Alexander Pfänder, Max Scheler (half-Jewish) and Adolf Reinach (converted to Christianity in 1915, killed in action in 1916) devoted themselves to phenomenological problems of existence, a priori foundations of the doctrine of the will, aesthetics, and logic; the realm of ethical values was Max Scheler's main field . . . At the time Hermann Cohen, the spirited head of the neo-Kantian school, a mighty intellectual and Jewish factor, was teaching in Marburg; next to him, Ernst Cassirer, who was later to distinguish himself in Berlin and Hamburg. Georg Simmel (1858–1918), prematurely and unjustly forgotten, presented his distinguished, keen-witted philosophy first in Berlin and then in Strassburg . . .
The promising younger generation included Adolf Lask (killed in action in 1915) and Otto Weininger, who, out of wild, unresolved

emotions, distilled an intellectual system intended to devalue Jewishness and women . . . From Frankfurt thrust the spirit and social will of Franz Oppenheimer, whose sociology, elaborated and supplemented by many of his students, always strove to move beyond the theoretical stratum of scholarship into the practical sphere of social experiment. His successor Karl Mannheim went a different direction with a new generation. The spirit that underlies all of these disciplines is the intrepid, confident spirit of our century.
Arnold Zweig

I am a German! And when I say I am a German, that is no mere lip service and does not come from fear nor is it a concession to the nationalist madness of our times. It is the drop acknowledging its source. The tree its roots. An affirmation of the language that flows from me. The spiritual bread on which I live. The earth in which all who loved me rest, from which all of those I love grew.
Theodor Lessing

Genuine religious movements do not seek to offer man the solution to the mystery of the world, they seek to equip him to live through the power of that mystery; they do not seek to teach him about the nature of God but to show him the path where he can encounter God.
Martin Buber

The spirit is not in the I, but between I and Thou. It is not like the blood that courses in you, but like the air in which you breathe. Man lives in the spirit if he is capable of responding to his Thou. He is capable of it if he enters into the relationship with his whole nature. It is solely his capacity for relationships that enables man to live in the spirit.
Martin Buber

Judaism is a spiritual process that has been documented in the inner history of the Jewish people and the works of the great Jews . . . The spiritual process of Judaism manifests itself in history in the form of striving for an ever more perfect realization of three interlinked ideas: the idea of unity, the idea of the deed and the idea of the future.
Martin Buber

Of all the connections Jewry has established with other peoples . . . none has, despite everything, been so profoundly fruitful as the German-Jewish.
Martin Buber

The strongest influence on us was Martin Buber. The Judaism he opened up to us with his stories of the Hasidic masters was totally different from that of impatiently tolerated religious instruction and alien-seeming, traditional High Holiday services: a Judaism filled with joy and Messianic hope. If I remember correctly, I owe my first acquaintance with the writings of Meister Eckhart to a collection of sayings and writings of "ecstatic thinkers" edited by Buber: a communicator of Jewish tradition had led me to a profoundly German mystic for whom he, and soon I, felt an affinity.
At the time – as today – Jewish thinking was predominantly understood as rational thinking, representing the holiness of reason in an era when dark dreams and emotional deeds threaten the painstakingly erected edifice of intellect and law. But the other, the visionary tendency, at the same time hopeful and fraught with danger, also exists in and through Judaism with a force seldom acknowledged and often even denied. But it was what led me – through Buber at first – back to Judaism, which I, like generations of parents and grandparents, had hitherto experienced only as a burden, but now learned to appreciate as an opportunity, an undeserved privilege.
Robert Jungk

Moritz Lazarus (Filehne, Posen 1824 – Merano 1903) began lecturing at the University of Bern in 1860 and moved on to Berlin in 1873. He and the philosopher Heymann Steinthal founded the discipline of scientific ethnic psychology and published a periodical on the subject in 1859/60. Lazarus also wrote a book on the *Ethik des Judentums* (Ethics of Judaism).
Above: Moritz Lazarus. 1898

The term "Wissenschaft des Judentums" (science of Judaism), was coined by *Leopold Zunz*, who, with *Eduard Gans*, *Moses Moser*, and others, founded the "Verein für Cultur und Wissenschaft des Judentums" (Association for the Culture and Science of Judaism) in Berlin in 1819. He began publishing a periodical on the subject in 1823. The idea of "modern" research into all trends of Judaism appeared in three countries at approximately the same time: in Germany with Zunz and *Abraham Geiger*, in Galicia with *Nachman Krochmal* and *Salomo Juda Rapoport*, and in Italy with *Salomon David Luzzatto*. Zacharias Frankel and *Heinrich Graetz* were among the principal nineteenth-century representatives of the movement. A proper institute for the discipline was not established until 1872 in Berlin. *Ismar Elbogen* (Schildberg, Posen 1874 –New York 1943) taught at this Hochschule für die Wissenschaft des Judentums in Berlin (Academy for Jewish Scholarship), from 1902 to 1933.
Left: Seminar with Ismar Elbogen at the Hochschule für die Wissenschaft des Judentums in Berlin. Photograph by *Abraham Pisarek*. 1935

Although my German fatherland currently makes it impossible for me to do at home what I can manage here in a strange land. I am at home in the German spirit, to it I owe the strength of my thoughts and words; its flag is the one I raise and carry, even if governments and university professors force me to carry it to a foreign country.
Moritz Lazarus

Even if the German Reich ceased to exist, my German identity would remain exactly what it is. Language is, after all, more than blood.
Franz Rosenzweig

The program of the Culturverein (Association for culture) was to familiarize broad circles of the Jewish population with knowledge of Jewish history and culture again, and to teach them to understand their Judaism as part of, and not a contradiction to, culture at large.
Heinz Mosche Graupe

Albert Einstein (Ulm 1879 – Princeton 1953) moved to Switzerland with his parents in 1894. During his time as a "technical expert 3rd class" at the Patent Office in Bern (from 1902), he began publishing treatises in 1905 offering proof for the atomic structure of matter. 1905 was also the year he developed the Special Theory of Relativity, which, expanded into the General Theory of Relativity (1914/15), was the source of his international fame. He became an associate professor at the University of Zurich in 1909, spent 1911/12 as a full professor at the Deutsche Universität in Prague, and then returned to Zurich to teach at the Institute of Technology. From 1913 to 1933 he taught in Berlin as a member of the Prussian Academy of Sciences and director of the Kaiser-Wilhelm-Forschungs-institut. He was awarded the Nobel Prize for his contribution to quantum theory in 1921. In 1933 Albert Einstein resigned his academic posts in Germany and emigrated to the U.S.

Above left: Albert Einstein. Ca. 1925

Above: Albert Einstein at the Einstein Tower in Berlin-Babelsberg. 1921. The building was constructed with funds from the Einstein Foundation, supported by American philanthropists.

Max Born (Breslau 1882 – Göttingen 1970) began teaching physics at the University of Göttingen in 1921. He emigrated to England in 1933, receiving a chair in physical chemistry at the University of Edinburgh in 1936. Born did work on *Albert Einstein*'s Theory of Relativity and, with his students Werner Heisenberg and Ernst Pascual Jordan, began developing wave mechanics in 1925. He received the Nobel Prize (1954) for his statistical interpretation of quantum mechanics and the theory of crystal grating.

The unfathomable is the most marvelous thing we can experience. It is the original feeling that stands at the cradle of true art and science. Whoever does not know it, whoever has lost his sense of wonder and amazement, is so to speak dead, his eye extinguished.
Albert Einstein

If someone can enjoy marching to music in rank and file, I can feel only contempt for him; he has received his large brain by mistake, a spinal cord would have been enough. This disgrace to civilization should be made to disappear as quickly as possible. Heroism on command, senseless violence, and that tiresome fatherland rubbish, how passionately I hate them, how cruel and contemptuous the war seems. I would rather let myself be hacked into pieces than have any part of such vile doings! I do think well enough of mankind that I believe the nightmare would long have been over had the healthy common sense of nations not been systematically corrupted by the schools and press acting in the service of business and political interests.
Albert Einstein

The Germano-Christian Weltanschauung, which tests truths by their Aryan heritage, was irritated by the reek of Jewry emanating from the Theory of Relativity, published by Ullstein and Mosse, and pricked up its ears. Thrust between reporters and reportaryans, scientific findings were transformed into a political football. In the Hall of Discord, German scientists assembled for learned debates with an anti-Semitic point of departure. Suddenly the Theory of Relativity was a racial theory.
Joseph Roth

Producing an atom bomb. I was certainly aware of the terrible menace to mankind should the enterprise succeed. But the likelihood that the Germans were working on the same problem with good prospects of success forced me to undertake this step. I had no other choice, although I have always been a convinced pacifist.
Albert Einstein

Striving for knowledge for its own sake, love of justice bordering on fanaticism, and striving for personal autonomy – these are the traditional themes of the Jewish people that allow me to experience my kinship with it as a gift of fate.

Looking at the Jews as such, I can't say I enjoy it much. Looking at the rest I'd say I'll be Jewish any day.
Albert Einstein

Those who rage today against the ideals of reason and individual freedom and want to enforce mindless public slavery by means of brutal violence, rightly see us as their implacable opponents. History has confronted us with a harrowing battle; but as long as we remain the obedient servants of truth, justice, and freedom, we shall not only survive as the oldest of the living peoples, we shall also continue to work productively towards creating values that contribute to the ennoblement of mankind.
Albert Einstein

I am convincend that this is not due to any special wealth of endowment, but to the fact that the esteem in which intellectual accomplishment is held among the Jews creates an atmosphere particularly favorable to the development of any talents that may exist.
Albert Einstein

Do not complain about your fate, see in these events a reason to remain faithful to the cause of the Jewish community . . . Consider, too, that difficulties and obstacles are a valuable source of health and strength for every community. We would not have survived the millennia as a community had life been a bed of roses . . . But let me tell you, the existence and destiny of our people depend less on external factors than on our faithful adherence to the moral traditions that helped us endure the millennia despite the heavy storms that befell us.
Albert Einstein

Einstein was the born non-conformist. For him what existed were the laws of nature as he saw and knew them. Everything in him rebelled against the arbitrary laws of man.
Kurt Blumenfeld

As regards my wife and children, they have only become conscious of being Jews or 'non-Aryans' (to use the delightful technical term) during the last few months, and I myself have never felt particularly Jewish. Now, of course, I am extremely conscious of it, not only because we are considered to be so, but because oppression and injustice provoke me to anger and resistance.
Max Born

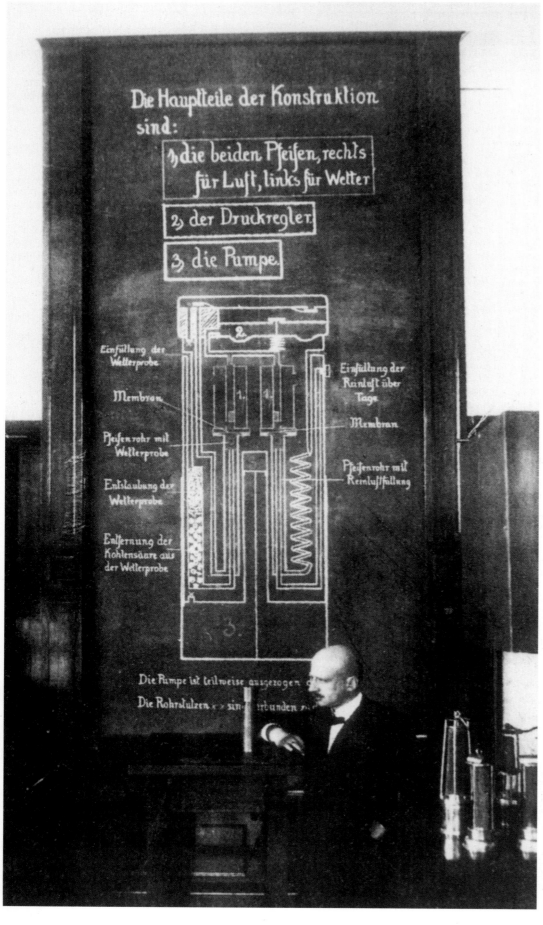

It would take a scientist, which the author is not, to pay proper tribute to the valuable work and the men who can be mentioned here. Consequently there is no way to spare the reader a rather dry list of men whose discoveries are still regarded as part of German science. V. K. Goldschmidt shed light on the crystalline structure of minerals; Eugen Goldstein discovered canal rays; Gabriel Lippmann accomplished direct photography of colors via interference. Hermann Aron recognized that electricity was measurable and created a means of relaying electrical signals without a wire connection; his famous factory in Berlin manufactured the best electric current meters available. The chemistry of tar derivatives owes important stages of its development to Victor Meyer (benzine nucleus, tolnole, etc.), Karl Theodor Liebermann (alizarin, with Grähbe), Heinrich Caro (aniline brown, etc.), Nathansohn, Warschau (fuchsine) – discoveries indispensable to the production of modern drugs . . .

A Jewish chemist named Lunge developed the soda industry on the basis of hard-coal distillation, while Ludwig Mond emigrated to England, where he later established the Imperial Chemical Trust and devised a different soda process (going out from ammonium sulfhydrate), thus making a contribution to the English chemical industry. Richard Willstädter, a chemist at the University of Munich, became famous for breaking down chlorophyll, the green pigment in plants; two sons of Jewish mothers, L. Bayer and Alfred Nobel, are generally known as inventors of explosives . . .

It is with some reluctance that we Jews adopt what appears to be an air of boastfulness when we establish our share of prize-winners; but we cannot be over-exacting in times of such grave danger. Of one hundred and forty men and women up to the year 1928, there were twelve Jews and four half-Jews, the latter being attributed to us by the racial insanity of the new savior: the medical scientists Paul Ehrlich, Elias Metschnikow (half-Jewish), Robert Baranyi, and Otto Meyerhof; the chemists Richard Willstädter, Fritz Haber, A. von Baeyer (half-Jewish); the physicists Albert A. Michelson, Gabriel Lippmann, Albert Einstein, James Franck, and Nils Bohr (half-Jewish); in the field of literature, the great French philosopher Henri Bergson and the German poet Paul Heyse (half-Jewish); while Carl Asser and Alfred H. Fried figure among the exponents of peace. Considering how difficult access to an academic career has always been for the Jews of central and eastern Europe, we can be justifiably proud to point out that although we represent only one percent of the earth's population, we have had nine to twelve percent of the Nobel prizewinners . . .

German mathematics in particular witnessed a whole series of eminent mathematicians in

the nineteenth century: in the theory of sets, Georg Cantor and Adolf Fränkel; in the theory of functions, C. G. I. Jacoby and L. Königsberger; while E. Landau, M. Minkowsky (Kowno), M. Pasch, and L. Kronecker distinguished themselves in other areas. Inventions always evolve from needs – frequently they are widespread needs, and sometimes they go back to age-old human dreams. Being able to fly, being able to speak to loved ones across vast distances, being able to destroy one's enemy by pushing a button or to extract magic sounds from the air by pulling a lever: all these are fairy-tale visions of all peoples and, in the form of myths, manifest desires from the spiritual depths that only dreams can reach nowadays. The fulfillment of our fantasies, however, lies at the end of a chain of unceasing experiments and new concatenations of materials, equipment, and forces . . .
And yet we have only recently begun encountering Jewish names, for the social conditions requisite for work with machines or machine parts are seldom found in Jewish history . . . Thus Moritz H. Jacobi (Dorpat, Petersburg), the (converted to Christianity) discoverer and applier of electroforming and the electrically fired mine, is rarely taken for a Jew; and that is why far more important Jewish inventors are still unknown to the public. And yet they

were pioneers in the fields of automobile construction, radio technology, and airship design . . .
When it comes to wireless telegraphy and radio, we find them based theoretically and practically on the great discoveries of the half-Jew Heinrich Hertz, who established the electromagnetic wave characteristics of light and produced very long waves in the ether under experimental conditions. Emil Berliner (born in Hannover, died in Washington in 1924), the inventor of the gramophone and one of the three inventors of the telephone, introduces the microphone and thus creates the practical conditions necessary to listen to these broadcasts. Robert von Lieben, from a family of Moravian Jews – his father was a titled banker in Vienna – laboriously constructs the radio tube, the instrument that enables us to receive wireless waves and transform them into sound again, and so the circle closes . . .
That the Jewish wood merchant David Schwarz, from Agram, Croatia, had all the crucial insights necessary to build a gas-filled dirigible airship with rigid system, equipped with engine and aluminum hull, and then patented it . . . That Jewish engineers also made valuable contributions in airplane design, namely Wiener (Albatros) and Rumpler, are mentioned only in passing; likewise that

Emil Berliner (Hannover 1851 – Washington 1929) came to America in 1870, where he invented a microphone for the telephone in 1877 and significantly improved the Edison phonograph.
Above: Emil Berliner. Ca. 1910

the first electrically driven motorboat was built by the above-mentioned M. H. Jacobi. But as decisive, and equally tragic, are the figure and achievements of Siegfried Marcus (born in Malchin, Mecklenburg in 1831), a Jew whose monument, a white herm, stands before the Technische Hochschule (Institute of technology) in Vienna. That is where, in 1875, he built his gasoline-driven automobile, today a valuable possession of the Gewerbemuseum (Museum of industry) of that city.
Arnold Zweig

Edmund Rumpler (b. 1872) was a brilliant engineer. In 1911 he constructed the "Rumpler-Taube," a German airplane feared on all fronts in World War I. And it was in this craft that the first major overland flight in Germany was accomplished. Rumpler was also very important to the Daimler and Adler works for his contribution to the development of the German automobile industry. In 1919 he built the "Tropfen-Auto," and at the 1926 Berlin Automobile Exhibition he showed another of his constructions, the first car with front-wheel drive.
Daniel Bernstein

Fritz Haber (Breslau 1868 – Basel 1934) converted to Protestantism in his youth, under the influence of Theodor Mommsen. It was under Haber's direction (1911–1933) that the Kaiser-Wilhelm-Forschungsinstitut of physical chemistry in Berlin-Dahlem rose to prominence as a research institute. He received the Nobel Prize in chemistry in 1918 for his synthesis of ammonia (developed with Robert Bosch).
Opposite page: Fritz Haber in front of a sketch for the construction of a firedamp pipe. Ca. 1923

Adolf von Baeyer (Berlin 1835 – Starnberg 1917) was of Jewish descent on his mother's side. After studying with Robert Bunsen and August Kekulé, he published fundamental works on the production of synthetic indigo. He received the Nobel Prize in chemistry in 1905.
Right: Adolf von Baeyer. Ca. 1914

239

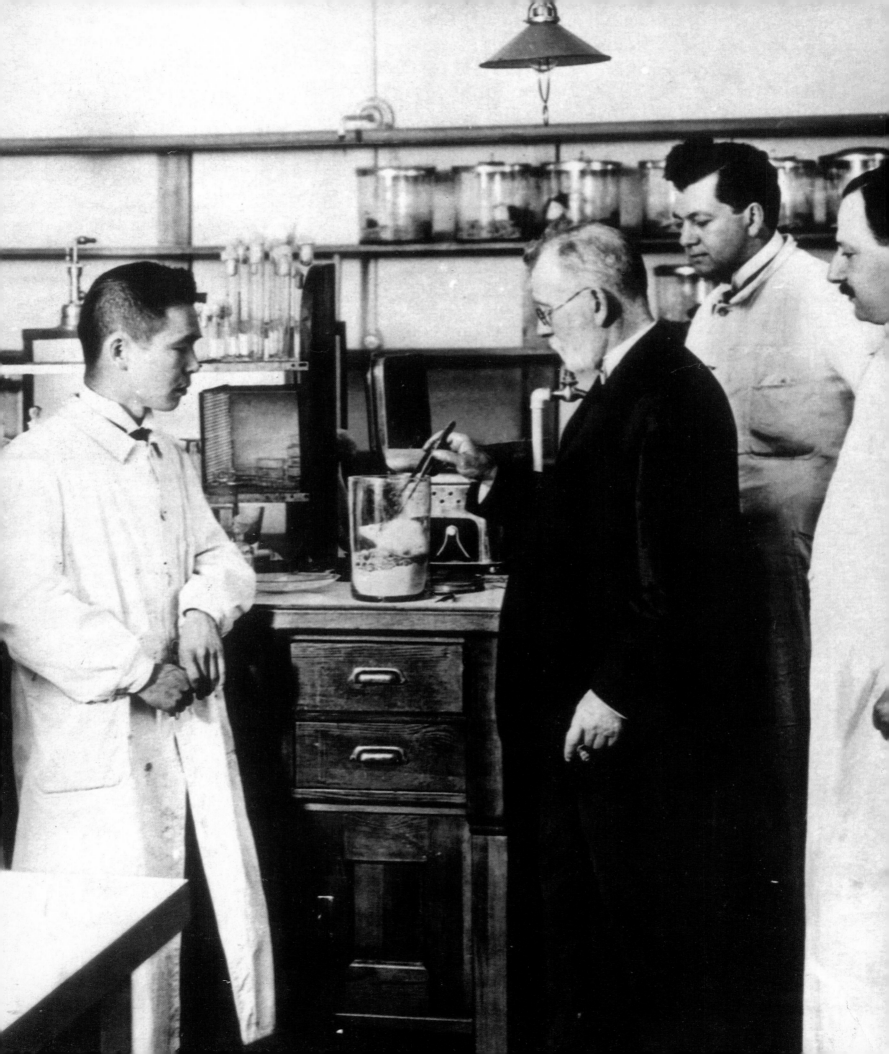

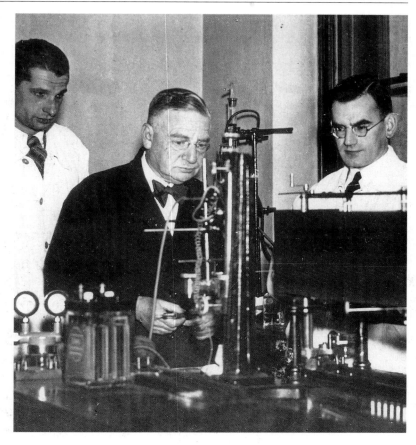

Paul Ehrlich (Strehlen 1854 – Bad Homburg 1915) worked with Robert Koch in Berlin and headed the Institut für Experimentelle Therapie in Frankfurt am Main, receiving the Nobel Prize in 1908 for his work in this field. He discovered salvarsan in 1909 and is consequently considered the father of modern chemotherapy.
Left: Paul Ehrlich in his laboratory in Frankfurt am Main. Ca. 1914

Otto Loewi (Frankfurt am Main 1873 – New York 1961) began teaching at the University of Graz in 1909. In 1921 he offered exact proof of the chemical transmission of nerve impulses, for which he received the Nobel Prize in 1936. He emigrated to New York in 1938.
Right: Otto Loewi with students in Graz. Ca. 1928

The Jewish world view emphasizes the value of human life. It does not negate its significance by promising a better life in the next world. In Judaism, physical welfare is a significant possession, it demands care and is of vital interest. The Jewish physician is an instrument of this will, and his existence and work are a necessity to Jewish society. The Jewish world needs physicians. Thus in the circumscribed Jewish cultural world of the Middle Ages, the medical profession developed and went on to become an overwhelming intellectual force as doctors collected the writings of the classical Roman and Greek masters, the works of Arab doctors, and the works of contemporaries in Hebrew, and learned from them. Bishops and popes, kings and sultans, princes of every kind summoned Jewish physicians to their courts and allowed them to live in countries usually prohibited to Jews as if they were lepers. Despite the persecutions, there were always those princes who, while entrusting their souls to the clergy, preferred to entrust their bodies to Jewish doctors.
At the beginning of the modern era, the central European universities that were gradually flourishing started educating a well-trained body of medical practitioners.

From then on, systematic teaching provided the basis for all further research and well-founded medical knowledge. Excluded from studying at most universities, Jewish doctors, with their autodidactic education, generally fell behind in comparison. Germany and Poland, where Jewish doctors had for centuries enjoyed an excellent reputation, did not tolerate Jewish students where medicine was taught. Few Jews were in a position to study in distant Louvain or Padua at the time, and it was not until the eighteenth century, when German universities started accepting Jews, that Jewish doctors began taking an active part in medical research again. For a long while they were still prohibited from working at public institutes, as professors, or in leading hospital positions if they had not converted. It is nonetheless striking that in the nineteenth century the Jews eminent in the medical field were predominantly pure scientists and not practitioners. Empiricists and eclectics, who made their reputations as famed diagnosticians, clinicians and skilled surgeons, take second place to the pioneers of scientific knowledge, who achieved distinction in the service of research . . .
Felix A. Theilhaber

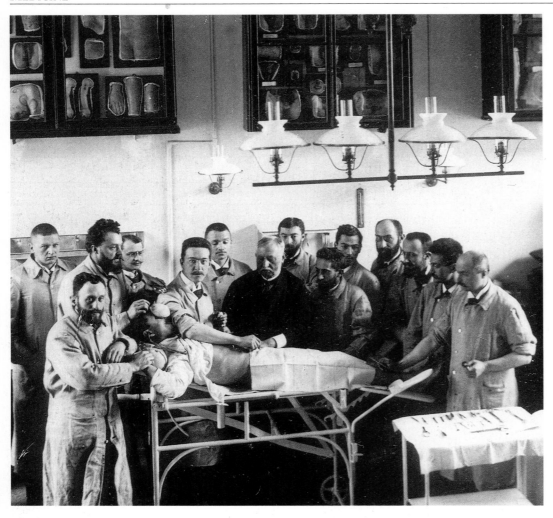

In connection with the history of medicine, let us mention only a few more [names]: the biologist Jacques Loeb, who did research on artificial insemination; Karl Morgenroth and August von Wassermann, whose Wassermann reaction made it possible to determine pregnancy from urine only ten days after fertilization – true benefactors of women; Hermann Senator, a specialist in internal medicine; the gastrologist I. Boas; pediatricians Henoch, Finkelstein, and Baginsky; orthopedist Joachimsthal; dermatologists Lassar, Lesser (Berlin), and Unna (Hamburg); sexologists Iwan Bloch, Blaschko, and above all Magnus Hirschfeld, who rendered pioneering services for a more just assessment and more reasonable method of treating early proclivities and unusual sexual behavior, especially in homosexuals; the eye-specialists Jakobsohn, who successfully tackled glaucoma, and Robert Liebreich and Hermann Cohn (Breslau), benefactors of countless near-sighted school children; the renal surgeon James Israel; toxicologists Louis Lewin (author of a basic book on poisons), Otto Liebreich, and Max Jaffe (Königsberg); and, among the many gynecologists, the discoverer of the heart hormone, Hermann Löwy, the cancer researcher F. Blumenthal, and the two creators of a new method of pregnancy testing, Bernhard Zondek and I. Aschheim . . . We have not yet mentioned two men whose name the whole world knows: Paul Ehrlich, the discoverer of salvarsan, and Sigmund Freud.
Arnold Zweig

The doctor, who had been asked to look after the Baroness at her confinement, pronounced that the moment had not come, and suggested to the Baron that in the meantime they should have a game of cards in the next room. After a while a cry of pain from the Baroness struck the ears of the two men: "Ah, mon Dieu, que je souffre!" Her husband sprang up, but the doctor signed to him to sit down: "It's nothing. Let's go on with the game!" A little later there were again sounds from the pregnant woman: "Mein Gott, mein Gott, what terrible pains!" – "Aren't you going in, Professor?" asked the Baron. – "No, no. It's not time yet." – At last there came from next door an unmistakable [Yiddish] cry of "Aa-ee, aa-ee, aa-ee!" The doctor threw down his cards and exclaimed: "Now it's time."
Sigmund Freud

They often spoke of relatives who went to Vienna to consult famous physicians. The names of the great specialists of those days were the very first celebrities that I heard about as a child. When I came to Vienna subsequently, I was amazed that all these names – Lorenz, Schlesinger, Schnitzler, Neumann, Hajek, Halban – really existed as people. I had never tried to picture them physically; what they consisted of was their pronouncements, and these pronouncements had such a weight, the journey to them was so long, the changes their pronouncements effected in the people around me were so cataclysmic, that the names took on something of spirits that one fears and appeals to for help. When someone came back from them, he could eat only certain things, while other things were prohibited for him. I imagined the physicians speaking in a language of their own, which nobody else understood and which one had to guess. It never crossed my mind that this was the same language that I heard from my parents and practiced for myself, secretly, without understanding it.
Elias Canetti

The title: "Doctor." Way of referring to people who suffer from an eye disorder and consequently wear pince-nez or spectacles. Favored by barbers in addressing their customers. (According to a different version: Jewish first name.)
Anton Kuh

The physician interested in medical history is familiar with many Jewish doctors to whom we owe highly original findings in these peripheral areas, among them: the comparative anatomist Gustav Born; Ludwig Lewin Jacobson (after whom Jacobson's organ was named); the Breslauer Leopold Auerbach (plexus Auerbach), who established the modern theory of fertilization and cell division; his compatriot, the biogeneticist S. M. Pappenheim; the morphologist David Gruby, who also discovered the thrush fungus; and Gottlieb Gluge, who found his way from Brakel in Westphalia to a professorship in Brussels. Ludwig Budge was the first to undertake research on the vagus nerve, which innervates the heart; he also determined the functions of the various centers of the spinal cord, going on to develop the theory of the autonomy of the spinal cord.

Romberg recognized the early symptoms of tabes and described how the sufferer staggers and begins to teeter when his eyes are shut. Valentin discovered the ciliated epithelium of the eye, Cohnheim identified white blood cells as being identical with pus cells . . . In the nineteenth century, a large number of histologists and physiologists of Jewish descent helped to develop special disciplines. Among them: intestinal histologist S. K. von Basch, cardiac pathologist Karl Bettelheim, and muscle physiologist Julius Bernstein. Robert Re-

Robert Barany (Vienna 1876 – Upsala 1936) received the Nobel Prize in 1914 for his *Physiologie des Bogengang-Apparates beim Menschen* (Physiology of the Semi-Circular Canal in the Human Inner Ear [1907]). He took up a university post in Upsala, Sweden, in 1917. He was the inventor of "Barany's noisebox," a device for examining the hearing of each ear individually.
Opposite page: Isidor Neumann, a prominent dermatologist of the Zweite Wiener Medizinische Schule (Second Viennese Medical School) during an operation at the university clinic in Vienna. Ca. 1900
Below: Robert Barany. Ca. 1910

mak made the important discovery that the three principal systems of the body evolve out of the three germ layers. Munk became the father of brain physiology, Zuntz of nutritional physiology, A. Axenfeld the nerve king. To name a few more of the fortunate medical discoverers: Rosenbach found the tetanus bacillus, Fränkel the pneumonia bacillus, and Neisser the pathogenic organism of gonorrhea.
Felix A. Theilhaber

Karl Landsteiner (Vienna 1868 – New York 1943) discovered the classic blood groups in 1901 and was awarded the Nobel Prize for this discovery in 1930. He also recognized polio to be a viral disease. Head of the pathology department of the Wilhelminenspital (Wilhelmine Hospital) from 1908, he was invited to the Rockefeller Institute for Medical Research in New York in 1922. In 1940 he and his student *Alexander S. Wiener* discovered the rhesus factor.
Above: Karl Landsteiner. Ca. 1935

243

*N*o reader of this book will find it very easy to enter into the author's emotional situation, an author who does not understand the holy language, is totally alienated from the religion of his fathers – as from every other religion – cannot share in nationalistic ideals and yet has never denied his kinship with his people, experiences his nature to be Jewish and does not wish it to be otherwise. If he were asked: what is Jewish about you if you have given up so much of what you have in common with your people? he would answer: "A great deal still, probably the essential part." But he could not at present find the words to define the quality of this essence.
Sigmund Freud

*S*oon there was the additional insight that I had only my Jewish nature to thank for two of the qualities that had become indispensable on my difficult path through life. Because I was a Jew, I found myself free from many prejudices that limit others in the use of their intellect; as a Jew I was prepared to go into the opposition and forgo the acceptance of the "compact majority."
Sigmund Freud

*P*urely external difficulties also contributed to the intensification of resistance against psychoanalysis . . .
Finally the author can, with due moderation, raise the question of whether his own personality as a Jew who never tried to conceal his Judaism did not play a part in the antipathy his milieu felt toward psychoanalysis. Only rarely has an argument of this kind been mentioned aloud; we have, sadly, become so distrustful that we cannot help suspecting that this circumstance has not remained totally without effect. It is perhaps no mere coincidence that the first representative of psychoanlysis was a Jew. Advocating it demanded a substantial degree of readiness to accept the fate of being isolated in the opposition, a fate more familiar to the Jew than to anyone else.
Sigmund Freud

*W*e were both Jews and knew that we bore in ourselves the same mysterious something that has thus far been inaccessible to any analysis – the thing that makes us Jews!
Sigmund Freud

A particularly favourable occasion for tendentious jokes is presented when the intended rebellious criticism is directed against the subject himself, or, to put it more cautiously, against someone in whom the subject has a share – a collective person, that is (the sub-

Sigmund Freud (Freiberg, Moravia 1856 – London 1939) studied hysteria and hypnosis with Jean-Martin Charcot at the Salpê-trire in Paris in 1885/86 and subsequently devoted himself to the field of psychopathology. Following his *Studien zur Hysterie* (Studies in Hysteria), he progressed through *Kathartische Verfahren* (Cathartic Processes) – by means of which repressed experiences are brought to consciousness – and ultimately arrived at psychoanalysis. His successful collaboration with *Josef Breuer* ceased when Freud began seeking the cause for psychoneurotic disturbances in the realm of sexuality. Freud also studied problems of anthropology, religion, and mythology, as well as sociological and aesthetic questions. He was and remains a seminal influence on modern thought.
Opposite page: Sigmund Freud. Photograph by Hermann Clemens Kosel. 1912
Left: Sigmund Freud posing for a sculpture by Oscar Némon. Ca. 1932

It is very obvious why Freud belongs to the same intellectual line. In his teachings, whatever their merits and demerits, he transcends the limitations of earlier psychological schools. The man whom he analyses is not a German, or an Englishman, a Russian, or a Jew – he is the universal man in whom the subconscious and the conscious struggle, the man who is part of nature and part of society, the man whose desires and cravings, scruples and inhibitions, anxieties and predicaments are essentially the same no matter to what race, religion, or nation he belongs. From their viewpoint the Nazis were right when they coupled Freud's name with that of Marx and burned the books of both.
Isaac Deutscher

He deserves the credit for introducing a constitution into the anarchy of dreams. But it works as in Austria.
Karl Kraus

Ah, Freud. What fascinates me again and again is his relentless decency, it sets him off to such advantage against his students. Modest, untainted, and honest in the extreme. If there is something he does not know, he says: I don't know. How far removed from the Strassers it all is! Strange, this matter-of-factness. "He is religiously unmusical," one of them once said. He says so himself. Touching when he, the typical man of intuition, wants to convince us that he discovered everything by "purely scientific deduction." But otherwise: someone who has opened a door.
Kurt Tucholsky

It is a country with which one can be deathly angry and where nonetheless one wants to die.
Sigmund Freud

ject's own nation, for instance). The occurrence of self-criticism as a determinant may explain how it is that a number of the most apt jokes of which we have given plenty of instances have grown up on the soil of Jewish popular life. They are stories created by Jews and directed against Jewish characteristics. The jokes made about Jews by foreigners are for the most part brutal comic stories in which a joke is made unneccessary by the fact that Jews are regarded by foreigners as comic figures. The Jewish jokes which originate from Jews admit this too; but they know their real faults as well as the connection between them and their good qualities, and the share which the subject has in the person found fault with creates the subjective determinant (usually so hard to arrive at) of the joke-work. Incidentally, I do not know whether there are many other instances of a people making fun to such a degree of its own character.
Sigmund Freud

The Freud family, alienated from Jewish religion and Jewish rites, was not an exception among the Jewish population of Vienna. Rich and poor, but more so the rich, had all followed the same path. But in one way we all remained Jewish: we moved in Jewish circles, our friends were Jews, our doctor, our lawyer were Jews.
Martin Freud

All these great revolutionaries were extremely vulnerable. They were, as Jews, rootless, in a sense; but they were so only in some respects, for they had the deepest roots in intellectual tradition and in the noblest aspirations of their times. . . .
Isaac Deutscher

*A*nd the majority of followers were, characteristically enough, Jews like him, above all Austrians – not Karl Abraham, Ernst Simmel, or A. Eitingon, but Alfred Adler and Wilhelm Stekel, S. Ferenczy and Theodor Reik, Otto Rank and Siegfried Bernfeld, and dozens of older and younger specialists whose work fills the eminently worthwhile journals of the psychoanalytic movement and helps to cure the nervous and hysterical in many cities of Europe and America . . . When they burned the books of Sigmund Freud with ours in Berlin and elsewhere, they did us the greatest honor barbarians can bestow today. For one day the Jew Sigmund Freud will be recognized as a figure that shaped a century, like Plato. He made a breach in the stone wall of our repressions that can never be sealed again. He taught us that there was a new way to understand and evaluate human drives. Arnold Zweig

The center of psychoanalytic research in Germany was the Psychoanalytisches Institut in Berlin, founded by *Karl Abraham*. Freud's students included *Otto Rank* (Vienna 1884 – New York 1939), who was preeminent in the field of myth research and literary psychology, and parted ways with Freud in 1924 because he considered the birth trauma the source of neuroses; *Hanns Sachs* (Vienna 1881 – Boston 1947), co-editor with Rank of the periodical *Imago*; *Karl Abraham* (Bremen 1877 – Berlin 1925), who investigated myths and the symbolism of dreams as well as the development of sexuality in the child; *Ernest Jones* (Rhosfelyn 1879 – London 1958), who, as one of Freud's first students, played a decisive part in constructing the theory of psychoanalysis and wrote an essential biography of Freud; *Max Eitingon* (1881–1943), who, with Karl Abraham, opened a psychoanalytic polyclinic in Berlin in 1920, plus a training and research institute; *Sándor Ferenczi* (Miskolc, Hungary 1873 – Budapest 1933), founder of the Hungarian Psychoanalytic Association; and *Wilhelm Reich* (Dobrzcynica, Galicia 1897 – Lewisburg 1957), who estranged himself from Freud by adopting Marxist ideas, criticizing the repressive society, which, he claimed, maintained its authoritarian order primarily through sexual repression, and by propounding his spectacular "orgone theory," which reached a wide general public in the sixties.

Above: The Berlin circle around Sigmund Freud. Standing from left: Otto Rank, Karl Abraham, Max Eitingon, Ernest Jones. Seated from left: Sigmund Freud, Sándor Ferenczi, Hanns Sachs. 1922

Anna Freud (Vienna 1895 – London 1982), Sigmund Freud's daughter, received her psychoanalytic training in Vienna. She was very close to her father and assisted him in his work. She is considered one of the co-founders of child psychoanalysis.
Below: Anna Freud. Ca. 1935

Alfred Adler (Vienna 1870 – Aberdeen 1937) was a member of the Wiener Psychoanalytische Gesellschaft (Vienna Psychoanalytic Society) and Sigmund Freud's student until their conflicting views led to a breach in 1911. He was the founder of individual psychology, which considered the need to compensate for feelings of inferiority and the desire for power to be the principal mechanisms behind human behavior. He settled in the U.S. before 1933.
Right: Alfred Adler. Ca. 1910

Julius Schoeps
ONE HAND FOR EMANCIPATION

Delighted by the possibility of identifying with Germany and its culture, a great many Jews shed their last inhibitions. They wanted to be German, that was all . . .

<u>Above:</u> The "Verein Jüdischer Studierender" (Association of Jewish Students) in Breslau. Ca. 1900

Jewish participation in political life coincided with the emancipation process initiated in the late eighteenth century and lasting until 1867 in the Austro-Hungarian Dual Monarchy and in Germany until after the era of the foundation of the empire. Step by step, the Jews were granted civil and political rights, rights finally allowing them to activate abilities that had been stifled for centuries by the world around them – in the spheres of politics, commerce, and burgeoning industry, and in a wide variety of scientific, scholarly, and cultural fields.

The emancipation process also had consequences for the Jews' view of themselves because they now began to define themselves not only as Jews but also as citizens of the country in which they lived. In Germany the designation that ultimately found favor was "deutscher Staatsbürger jüdischen Glaubens" – German citizen of Jewish faith. The notion that the Jewish cause was identical "with the cause of the fatherland, with which it will stand or fall," as the Frankfurt rabbi Leopold Stein formulated it, began making inroads.

The more resolutely Jewish intellectuals broke away from the premises of their collective consciousness as Jews, the more sharply they rejected the existing power structure and the more consistently they fought for a democratic political and human order that would eradicate all forms of discrimination. It was clear to the Jews in Germany, as well as to those in the Austro-Hungarian Monarchy, that their political, legal, social, and cultural integration in society was elementally linked with the foundation of a democratic order. Despite the broad spectrum of political thought and action represented in the Jewish community, the Jews were vehemently involved in all the democratic trends of their time. There was never any doubt that they considered their destiny to be dependent on the strength of democracy: the stronger the democratic principle, the more secure the equality of the Jews.

In 1848, the year of revolution, some 750 German Jews were active in political organizations – as members of national and regional parliaments, town councils, electoral bodies, associations, and clubs. But they did not constitute a monolithic group steering a clear political course; they acted as much out of personal, social interest as did the rest of the population. All possible political hues were represented among them. Oriented towards upward mobility, the preponderant majority sought to categorize themselves as bourgeois and tended to favor moderate constitutional liberalism, in which they placed great hope – not only with respect to the attainment of democratic freedoms but also to the solution of the so-called "Jewish question." "Being at the same time Jew and German," commented Johann Jacoby, a physician and writer from Königsberg, "the Jew in me cannot become free without the German, nor the German without the Jew. Being unable to divide myself in two, I cannot divide the freedom of the one from that of the other . . ."

Of the 586 delegates in the Paulskirche in Frankfurt, Germany's first democratically elected parliament, sixteen men were of Jewish origin. Probably the most representative of them was Gabriel Riesser, who was elected chairman of the standing-orders committee and secretary of the constitutional committee, and held the post of second vice president of the national parliament between October and December 1848. Riesser had already belonged to the preliminary parliament and succeeded in pushing through active and passive suffrage for all Germans who were of age, regardless of their rank, fortune, or religion. He described his political program and his ties to German culture in *Der Jude* (The Jew), a periodical he had formerly published, as follows: "If one hand offers me emancipation, the object of all my deepest wishes, and the other offers the fulfillment of the beautiful dream of a politically unified Germany accompanied by political freedom, I would unhesitatingly choose the latter; for I am most firmly and deeply convinced that it would also include the former."

The Bismarck era saw impressive Jewish participation in parliamentary life and the building of an imperial Reich. In contrast to Austria, where Jews rarely obtained seats and a voice in public representative bodies, the newly founded German Reich gave them an opportunity to gain a foothold. For example, Eduard Lasker and Ludwig Bamberger were members of parliament who enjoyed extraordinary popularity among liberal bourgeois circles. Both of them were regarded as convinced democrats, as Jewish Germans known to identify with Germany and the German cause. Committed to preserving the principles of law and justice, Lasker had a major part in working out the imperial constitution and legal code. Bamberger was one of the founders of the Reichsbank and was operative in introducing the gold standard. Each in his own way contributed to encouraging democratic awareness in Germany.

The German social democratic movement included four Jewish figures of historical significance: Paul Singer, Eduard Bernstein, Hugo Haase, and Ludwig Frank. Singer became party chairman in 1890 and founded the Social Democratic Presse-verlag, which published the party paper *Vorwärts* (Forward). Bernstein, a member of the Reichstag since 1902, became the theoretician of social democratic revisionism. Hugo Haase was the leader of the secessionist wing, which constituted itself as the USPD, and became spokesman for the small minority that fearlessly and uncompromisingly condemned German imperialism and annexations – without denying the obligation for national defense – undaunted by short-lived military successes.

Delighted by the possibility of identifying with Germany and its culture, a great many Jews shed their last inhibitions. They wanted to be German, that was all. Gabriel Riesser expressed this attitude as follows: "There is only one baptism that initiates into nationality, and that is the baptism of blood in the common struggle for freedom and fatherland." Demonstrative love of country and patriotism (Walther Rathenau: "Whoever loves his fatherland can and should be a slight chauvinist.") brought a whole series of Jews to the point where they believed in a profound similarity between the basic natures of German and Jew, an inner identity of German and Jewish characteristics.

In that "fateful hour," August 1, 1914, the Centralverein deutscher Staatsbürger jüdischen Glaubens (Central Association of German Citizens of Jewish Faith), the organization of assimilated Jewry, made an appeal to the Jewish public: "That every German Jew should be prepared for the sacrifices of property and blood that obligation demands is self-evident . . . We summon you to dedicate more of your strength to the fatherland than obligation demands!

Hasten voluntarily to the colors! All of you – men and women – place yourselves at the service of your fatherland by offering personal assistance of every kind and by donating money and property!" (*Israelitisches Gemeindeblatt* [Cologne], August 7, 1914). Many Jewish congregations in Germany invested all their capital in war bonds at the time, with the result that everything was lost in the inflation.

Ludwig Frank might be regarded as symbolic of the attitude of the German Jews in World War I. Although a European pacifist and socialist patriot who had always opposed war with all his heart, Frank enlisted in the army and was one of the two members of the German Reichstag killed in action. He died on a battlefield in Lorraine on September 3, 1914, believing that the war would lead to democracy and social liberation for the people of Germany. In his last letter, he wrote: "I have the fervent wish to survive the war and then to cooperate in building up the Reich from within. But at present the only possible place for me is among the ranks . . ."

Jewish hopes that emphatically patriotic behavior would consolidate their social position were severely disappointed in World War I. The so-called "Judenzählung" (Jewish census) at the end of 1916, by means of which the War Ministry wanted to verify the percentage of Jews among the fighting troops, was motivated by anti-Semitic pressure. The results of the survey were never published because they would have proven the untruth of accusations that the Jews were unreliable and evaded their patriotic duty. Protests were of little help. Even repeated evidence that there were 100,000 Jews fighting and some 12,000 of them had died in action (corresponding to the percentage of non-Jews among the war dead) was of little avail. Public opinion had made its judgment. The malicious way anti-Semites commented on the news that the Social Democratic member of the Reichstag, Ludwig Frank, had been killed was typical: It's always the same with the Jews. They have to put themselves into the limelight, even when it comes to dying.

The more sensitive individuals were tormented by the rejection and thinly veiled hatred they encountered. In their despair, some Jews unintentionally adopted the prejudices of the world around them. A well-known case is that of the young philosopher Otto Weininger, who committed suicide because he could not bear the contempt and prejudice he had to face. Another was that of writer Arthur Trebitsch, who, himself of Jewish descent, developed into the crudest kind of anti-Semite. Others made efforts to adapt, never realizing that their desire for acceptance was causing them to behave in an undignified manner. A case in point would be the writhings of the conductor Hermann Levi, who, though a great admirer of Richard Wagner, suffered intolerably under Wagner's anti-Semitism and underwent an unparalleled "spiritual odyssey."

There were already those in the 1880s who considered it warranted to ask whether, with anti-Semitism growing more and more fanatic, attempts to acculturate and assimilate were not futile. Jewish nationalist slogans began finding an increasingly receptive ear, particularly among students. Was not declaring one's Judaism, though it be scorned, and returning to the traditions of one's fathers the best means of asserting oneself? In various cities of the German Reich, but especially in Vienna, a center of Jewish agitation before the turn of the century, organizations demanding "opposition to assimilation," "the raising of Jewish consciousness," and "the settlement of Palestine" were founded. An editorial on May 1, 1885, *Selbst-Emancipation* (Self-emancipation), a paper published in Vienna by Nathan Birnbaum, included the words: "Jewish efforts at de-Jewification number among the ugliest chapters of world history." It goes on: "Of course, anti-Semitism, with the elements of self-interest, prejudice, envy, pleasure in inflicting pain, intolerance, and conceit that accompany it, is no less repugnant a chapter in the history of the universe; but – we do not hesitate to say it – in view of the assimilation mania, it is justified; the Jewish people as it has portrayed itself until now deserves anti-Semitism."

A common view was that Jewish life could be normalized only by way of occupational realignment. In his opening speech at the Kattowice Conference (1884), where supporters of Palestine had gathered to negotiate a supranational organizational structure, Leon Pinsker, a doctor from Odessa, pointed out that because the Jews were prohibited from farming, they were concentrated in the cities and a very few professions, pre-eminently in commerce. To Gentiles their occupations appeared unproductive. The coming battle between capital and labor would be carried out at the cost of the Jews. The Jews had hitherto rendered only "messenger and mediator services." The only way to accomplish a change for the better would be by re-organizing professional activities, in other words by colonizing Palestine. That would create a basis for developing a normal economic life. "Let us reach for plough and spade," Pinsker shouted to the conference delegates, "instead of the yardstick and scales we have used up to now, and let us once again be what we once were, before we became the object of other peoples' derision."

There are those who maintain that the Jews' westward emigration from Eastern Europe since 1880 had reinforced certain efforts at re-nationalization. This view is correct insofar as this emigration was accompanied by the Jews' movement from the country to the cities, from the cities to the metropolises. The resulting Jewish centers experienced the development of a kind of Jewish national consciousness that was articulated in a multiplicity of ways – in the flowering of Jewish literature, the foundation of more and more publishing houses, newspapers, and magazines, and the establishment of theaters, institutes of popular education, welfare facilities, and social institutions. Probably a more important factor, however, was that the beginnings of the Jewish nationalist movement coincided with the national awakening of other groups, the Czechs, Slovaks, Magyars, and Balkan peoples.

The Jewish nationalist idea and the vision of an autonomous national existence in Palestine attracted few followers at first. It was Theodor Herzl's *Der Judenstaat: Versuch einer modernen Lösung der Judenfrage* (The Jewish State: Attempt at a Modern Solution to the Jewish Question), published in 1896, that provided the actual impulse for an organizational merger of existing Jewish nationalist associations and created what we understand today as political Zionism. Herzl took the standpoint that the Jewish problem could be solved only if the Jews and Judaism regained their inner and outer freedom. The only solution to the "Jewish question" would be concentrating as large a proportion of Jews as possible in a country of their own. "I consider the Jewish question," he wrote in his brochure, "neither a social nor a religious one, even if it is tinged with both. It is a national question . . . We are one people, *one* people."

Herzl's "Judenstaat" encountered as much spontaneous approval as violent rejection. Groups sprang up everywhere, lively political agitation ensued. A number of respected rabbis expressed their support for Herzl's Zionism by referring expressly to the Messianic promise. The National-jüdische Vereinigung für Deutschland (Jewish National Association for Germany) made a public declaration countering the claim that Zionist efforts contradicted Messianic hopes. This had become necessary because many Orthodox Jews opposed Herzl, regarding him as a heretic. In their view Herzl was rebelling against "the divine destiny of exile" and "usurping the role of the Messiah" instead of waiting humbly and obediently for the coming of the Messiah, who, according to tradition, would redeem the Jewish people and establish the New Kingdom.

Despite these attacks, Herzl possessed the diplomatic and propagandistic skill to unite the Zionists of all countries in a well-structured, international organization within an astonishingly short time. That he succeeded in winning over such a diversity of political, social, and religious factions can surely be attributed in part to the fact that he reduced the Jewish question to a national one, excluding all religious and spiritual-cultural components. Otherwise the first Zionist Congress, convened by Herzl in Basel (Switzerland) in 1897 would never have been able to adopt a program pointing the way to the future. The declaration ultimately approved by the elected delegates – "Zionism strives to create for the Jewish people a home in Palestine secured by public law" – was in line with Herzl's vision. He had opened the congress with the words: "We want to lay the cornerstone for the house that will one day shelter the Jewish nation." Under the influence of his success, he noted in his diary several days later: "If I summarize the Basel Congress in a phrase – that I will take care not to utter in public – it is this: I saw the Jewish state founded in Basel. If I said that aloud today, the response would be universal laughter. Perhaps in five years, but certainly in fifty, everyone will recognize it to be true."

This much we have learned here, too: that the Jews gain their freedom through the victory of democracy and not from princes. Three decades ago there were still restrictions on marriage; no Jew was permitted to own more than one house; they were excluded from both active and passive suffrage, and now they can hold even the very highest government positions. In 1800 a certain medical doctor still announced that two rooms in his bathhouse were reserved for the local Jewry, and that no Christian would be admitted to a Jewish bath and no Jew to a Christian bath; the linens for the two sections were also specially marked. And now there is no place of entertainment, no public or private association where religion throws up a barrier, no academic or social institution and no mercantile administration where the Jews do not actively invest their mental and material powers for the public good. A commercial resurgence and widespread affluence in our city have given the lie to all those who once opposed our emancipation; they are now forced to confess that the city itself paid the penalty for the injustice done to the Jews. These few words describe the present position of the Jews in the public and social life of our free city, and you will find it perfectly natural that for us the Messiah question has been decided, and that sooner or later all civilized countries will arrive at the same solution to this problem.
Rafael Kirchheim to Leopold Löw

We were so happy finally to be allowed, as free citizens, to work for the welfare of the country whose language we spoke, whose glory we shared, and in whose armies and administration our fellow believers had distinguished themselves.
Israelitische Wochenschrift (Jewish Weekly), 1887

For once they did speak a true honest word, they, who cannot otherwise take and do not much like the truth: they said that Judaism and Liberalism were firmly, organically linked, and that is really the case, for Jewish and liberal are largely identical. When the Israelites began recording time, as prescribed by the Bible, they counted the month that brought them that precious commodity freedom as the first; Pessach, the Jewish festival celebrated with the largest number of observances, is a celebration of freedom, and the restrictions this holiday places on all food consumption are already evidence enough that an Israelite

The Paulskirche in Frankfurt; in the foreground, the Salzhaus am Römerberg. 1860 Of the 586 representatives who convened in 1848 as the first democratically elected German parliament, sixteen were of Jewish descent. One of them, Gabriel Riesser, held the post of Second Vice President from October to December 1848.

must never confuse the concept of freedom with the concept of intemperance. According to the Talmud, "freedom" came with the tablets of the Law, which the people of Israel considered their most sacred possession. Order as prescribed by laws is the natural element of Judaism; and what keeps arbitrariness, oppression, and the unjust limitation of man by man at bay is – Jewish-liberal. Thousands of years ago the Jews spurned and would no longer tolerate slavery of the kind the pious ancestors of our present opponents imposed on their serfs and slaves in the Middle Ages.
Die Wahrheit (The Truth), 1871

It was thus only too understandable that the Jews considered the struggle against princely absolutism, and the development and implementation of a liberal form of government to be in their interest. As there were rights for them to fight for that other citizens had already been granted, at least in part, their will to fight was clearer and stronger. They stood up for the recognition of human and civil rights. They expected an extended sphere of personal freedom and guaranteed freedom of the press and assembly to have a politico-educational effect. Defending equality before the law was vital to them. They sought to augment the power of parliamentary institutions at the expense of the executive, seeing the former as a bulwark, or potential bulwark, against governmental arbitrariness.
Ernest Hamburger

Shortly before I went to university, racial and religious prejudices began to poison student life. The fraternities, once a vanguard of liberal, democratic, youthful idealism, had just introduced the notorious Aryan clause and thus succeeded in having their most respected alumni – not only members of Jewish descent but also men like the famous Mayor Kirschner, a Teuton from Breslau – return their ribbons.
Isidor Hirschfeld

The purpose of the Central-Verein is to assemble German citizens of Jewish faith, without regard for their religious or political affiliation, in order to support them in their active endeavors to safeguard their civil and social equality and in their unswerving cultivation of the German outlook.
Bylaw of the Central-Verein, 1893

So let us be Germans then. And Jews. Both, without concerning ourselves with the "and," indeed without talking much about it – but truly both. How, that is essentially – a question of the cadence.
Franz Rosenzweig

Jews and Germans: the Creation's two tragic groups of literal-minded people.
Anton Kuh

Who created the Liberal movement in Austria? . . . the Jews. By whom have the Jews been betrayed and deserted? By the Liberals. Who created the National-German movement in Austria? the Jews. By whom were the Jews left in the lurch? . . . what – left in the lurch! . . . Spat upon like dogs! . . . By the National-Germans, and precisely the same thing will happen in the case of Socialism and Communism. As soon as you've drawn the chestnuts out of the fire they'll start driving you away from the table. It always has been so and always will be so.
Arthur Schnitzler

The gentle, great-hearted, and introverted reader of Lessing and Schiller takes to the young people's heated "modern" discussions at the Warsaw cafés the evidence of respect for the individual and a religion of humanity. Thus does Judaism prove itself to be the essence of central European, and of German, culture and the only genuine, unspoilt mediator of its ideals.
Claudio Magris

Below: For a long while it was impossible for unconverted Jews to join elite regiments: banker Otto H. Kahn (1867–1934) as a Mainzer Hussar. Ca. 1888

Right: They fought for their fatherland in the Franco-Prussian War in 1870/71: Meyer Dinkel (center) from Mannheim and his fellow soldiers Albert Gautier and Peter Metz. 1871

Only Jews who had converted were admitted to the officers' corps. They were treated with reserve and their origins never forgotten, but they were more or less accepted. The enormous significance of this discrimination was unmistakable. Anyone who could not become an officer was barred from the upper class. Thus total equality could not be achieved as long as this key position remained inaccessible . . . Had this barrier been eliminated, a solid basis for the realization of total emancipation would have been gained.
Ernst Herzfeld

Assimilation. . . . A phrase. . . . Yes, that'll come all right some time or other . . . in a very very long time. It won't come at all in the way many want it to – it won't come either in the way many are afraid it will. . . . Further, it won't be exactly assimilation . . . but perhaps something that beats in the heart of that particular word so to speak. Do you know what it will probably look like in the end? That we, we Jews I mean, have been a kind of ferment in the brewing of humanity – yes, perhaps that'll come out in anything from one to two thousand years from now. It is a consolation, too. Don't you think so?
Arthur Schnitzler

253

Left: Jewish fraternity in Berlin. 1912
Right: Jewish fraternity in Munich. Ca. 1913/14

I ask you [Thomas Mann], what has possessed German students in the last 6–8 decades to declare their Jewish fellow students inferior and incapable of satisfaction [in duels]. A mere trifle, you will respond lightly. Yes, it is, for someone who does not have to experience it, but there are thousands who do.
Jakob Wassermann

*A*t that time it was a very pressing issue for us young people, meaning especially for us Jews, as anti-Semitism was growing with mounting force in university circles. The German-nationalist fraternities had begun removing Jews and anyone of Jewish descent from their midst. On Saturday morning 'strolls' or evenings of ceremonial drinking sessions street brawls between anti-Semitic fraternity factions and parties of liberal, regional associations and corps, some of which were largely composed of Jews (there were no purely Jewish dueling fraternities yet) were not rare. Whether in the lecture hall, corridor, or laboratory, demands for satisfaction were the order of the day. It was not only the pressure of these circumstances that turned many of the Jewish students into extremely formidable, dangerous fencers; tired of waiting for their opponents' effrontery and insults, they not infrequently provided the provocation themselves. And the ever more embarrassing superiority they exhibited in ceremonial duels was certainly the main reason for the famous Waidhofen decision, with which the German-Austrian student association declared Jews incapable of satisfaction once and for all. The exact wording of the decree should not be neglected here. It read as follows: "Every son of a Jewish mother, every person in whose veins Jewish blood flows, is by birth dishonorable and devoid of all nobler feelings. He cannot distinguish between depraved and pure. He is morally degenerate. Any intercourse with a Jew therefore constitutes a loss of honor; all association with Jews must be avoided. As a Jew cannot be insulted, no Jew can demand satisfaction for insults suffered."
Arthur Schnitzler

*I*t is with great regret that I learn from the daily papers that the "Richard-Wagner-Kommers" [ceremonial drinking session], one of whose sponsors was the fraternity I have the honor of belonging to as an inactive member, that this session ultimately turned into an anti-Semitic demonstration. I would not think of launching a polemic here against this regressive fashion of the day. I merely wish to mention in passing that even if I were not a Jew, from the standpoint of my love of liberty I would have to condemn this movement, which, as it appears, my fraternity has also joined.
It should be evident that today, flawed as I am by Semitism (a word still unknown when I was initiated), I would not seek admission to the B[urschenschaft] A[lbia], which, for the reasons given, would be denied to me. That I do not wish to remain where I must assume this to be the case will be clear to any decent person.
. . . as an inactive member I hereby request termination of my affiliation with the fraternity.
Theodor Herzl

Albert Ballin (Hamburg 1857 – Hamburg 1918) was responsible for making the HAPAG Line (Hamburg-Amerika-Linie) into a major shipping company and, as a result, turning Hamburg into an international port. Not only was he a businessman, he was also an economic advisor to the imperial court and became a personal friend of Kaiser Wilhelm II. Although he supported the German fleet during World War I, he continued to hope that Germany would be able to achieve a balance of power with Great Britain by peaceful means. He committed suicide in November 1918, in despair over the collapse of the German empire.
Left: Kaiser Wilhelm II with Albert Ballin on the way to the launching of the "Fürst Bismarck" in Stettin. 1890

Walter Rathenau (Berlin 1867 – Berlin 1922) succeeded his father Emil as president of AEG in 1915. From 1914 to 1915 he organized Germany's supply of raw materials for the war. In 1919 he took part in the preparations for the Peace Conference of Versailles. Minister for Reconstruction and Foreign Minister in 1921/22, he was assassinated by nationalist anti-Semites in 1922. His analyses of social and political problems were always founded on philosophical and critical-cultural reflections (*Zur Mechanik des Geistes* [On the Mechanics of the Spirit], 1913; *Von kommenden Dingen* [Of Things to Come], 1917).
Right: Walter Rathenau. Photograph by *Moriz Nähr*. Ca. 1917

Should history ever be just, it will rank the Jews highly because, not possessing a "fatherland," they were permitted to preserve common sense when the whole world abandoned itself to patriotic madness.
They have no "fatherland," the Jews, but every country in which they live and pay taxes demands patriotism and a hero's death from them, and reproaches them with having no predilection for dying. In this situation, Zionism really is the only way out: if patriotism, then at least for one's own country.
Joseph Roth

The Jews have frequently given themselves over to an intransigently Teutonic attitude that earns them no gratitude and little recognition from their taskmasters. Is there a solidarity of the pathetic to equal that of the German-nationalist Jews, who are bearers of a mission that in peace time was already an oxymoron, like the eclipse when the moon shone so brightly and a speeding car drove slowly through the streets? . . . Jews who feel the urge to be nationalistic represent a combination of two inferiority complexes both of which should be repressed.
Karl Kraus

In the youth of every German Jew there is a painful moment he will remember throughout his life: the moment he first becomes fully aware that he has entered the world as a second-class citizen, and that no amount of hard work and nothing he achieves can ever rescue him from this situation.
Walter Rathenau

*T*hough Rathenau professed a Christian attitude and repeatedly declared that he stood "on the foundations of the Gospels," he nonetheless persevered in refusing to convert to Christianity. He also stated that the overwhelming majority of German Jews "had only one feeling of nationality: the German one." It was "clear and self-evident" to him that "for an educated and respectable Jew there can be no feeling of nationality but German nationality." There was no longer any such thing as a Jewish people or a Jewish nation: "To me, as to any other German, eastern Jews are Russians, Poles, or Galicians; western Jews are Spanish or French." "My people is the German people, my home the country of Germany." He defined peoples and nations solely according to "shared soil, experience and spirit" and to "heart, spirit, attitude, and soul." He did term himself "a German of Jewish descent." But, like Riesser and Fuchs, he considered German Jews "a German tribe, like the Saxons, Bavarians, or Wends." He located them "somewhere between inhabitants of the Mark and of Holstein, they are perhaps a little closer to me than the Silesians or the Lorrainers" . . .
Egmont Zechlin

*N*o people should regard itself as the Chosen People. Every group has its saints, its incurious, its weaklings, and its criminals; the mixture is similar everywhere, and I do not see that the war has brought any improvement on this account. Every tribe, every people has its shortcomings; I believe these failings should be understood and perhaps cured, not used as reason for blame.
The war is not over yet. It will leave behind a human race in need of cure; and we must offer each other mutual support if we are to fulfil our mission.
My task is not a Jewish one. I feel German and will never cut myself off from my German people.
Walter Rathenau

I remained part of the Jewish religious community because I wanted to avoid neither reproach nor complaint, and have by now experienced an abundance of both.
Walter Rathenau

*H*e was not the last Jew to defy the rabble. He had the Jew's courage to die a lonely death and to pay no heed to the bestial brutality of the eternal "boche" . . . A fairly ordinary Jew. And far, far too good for this nation . . .
Arnold Zweig

Enthusiasm swept through Germany during the 1914 mobilization: Unter den Linden in Berlin. One of the most frequently published photographs of the time shows the cavalry officer *Ludwig Börnstein* bidding his friends *Fritz* and *Emma Schlesinger* farewell. All three of them succeeded in escaping from Germany to Israel after 1933.

I went to war as a German, to defend my sorely pressed fatherland. But also as a Jew, to fight for the full equality of my fellow-believers.
Josef Zürndorfer

Germany – because Germany is our subject here – went to war with seventy million people and left behind two million dead, not quite 2.9 percent of the total population. At that time the Jews numbered 600,000 lives, and they left 12,000 of them on the battlefield – quite a respectable percentage for a breed of people so far removed from the craft of war . . . We do not even want to bother recalling that, in view of the generally anti-Semitic mood of the German army, the fifteen hundred Iron Crosses first class [awarded to Jews] are actually worth twice as much as the number of these medals awarded to non-Jews, and that the same applies to the approximately four thousand Jewish reserve officers . . . But since many countries, not only Germany, deny Jews this justice, harming themselves and demeaning their own state in the process, we need only point out here that as an organism the Jewish people suffered even more than others in the last war – actively because Jews were fighting in all the armies (at least 600,000, but probably 700,000 in the Russian army, 400,000 of them from the beginning of the war; over 100,000 among the German troops, or 17 percent of all Jews in Germany; over 300,000 in the Austrian army; and another 300,000 in all the other armies and expeditionary corps – for example, 3,000 in the South African army alone, or 6 percent of the total Jewish popula-

Right: Wilhelm Frankl, one of the most successful fighter pilots in World War I. 1916
A lieutenant, he was awarded the "Pour le Mérite" medal after converting. He was shot down in April 1917.
Below: Leo Loewenstein, the founder and first chairman of the Reichsbund jüdischer Frontsoldaten (Imperial League of Front-line Soldiers). Ca. 1918

tion); passively because from Lithuania to Romania, the war in the east, with its epidemics and famines, and the pogroms in its wake, took place where Jews lived in large numbers. The Jewish people consequently suffered a total loss of over a quarter of a million lives. If this terrible loss of living material is compared with the uncontrolled growth of enmity towards the Jews in the countries east of the Rhine, it is easy to understand our instinctive and fundamental opposition to war.
Arnold Zweig

The victorious armies of the Allied Great Powers of Germany and Austria-Hungary have, with God's help, moved into Poland. The war we are now waging is a war not against the population but against Russian tyranny. Russian despotism has collapsed under the heavy blows of our brave troops. Jews in Poland! We come to you as friends and saviors! Our flags bring you justice and freedom: equality and full civil rights, genuine freedom of belief and the right to unrestricted activity in all economic and cultural spheres. You have suffered far too long under the iron yoke of Moscow. We come to you as liberators. Foreign tyranny has been crushed, a new era is beginning for Poland.

We will demand and secure the liberation of all the Polish people with all our might. We will introduce full equality for the Jews in Poland according to the western European model, on secure foundations and guaranteed by law.
Do not let yourselves be dazzled by the false promises of the Russians. In 1905 Russia solemnly promised you equality. Need we remind you, tell you, how Moscow has kept its word? Think of Kischinew, Homel, Bialystok, Odessa, Siedlce, and hundreds of other bloody pogroms! Remember the mass expulsions and expatriations. Your tormentor has shown no mercy for human suffering and has driven and hounded you and your wives and children as if you were wild animals . . . Jews of Poland! The hour of retaliation has come . . .
Proclamation of the General Command of Austria-Hungary and the German Reich at the start of World War I

them. No stars shone. A dark, flat sky hung low and dismal over the town.
Joseph Roth

*G*erman Jews!
In this fateful hour it is once again time to show that, proud of our lineage, we Jews are among the best sons of our fatherland.
The noblesse of our millenia-old history obliges.
We expect our young to hasten to the colors voluntarily and with high hearts.
German Jews!
We appeal to you, in the spirit of the old Jewish rule of duty, to dedicate yourselves to the service of the fatherland with all your heart, all your soul and all your abilities.
Appeal of the "Reichsverein der Deutschen Juden" (Imperial Association of German Jews) and the "Zionistische Vereinigung für Deutschland" (Zionist Association for Germany) at the start of World War I

A lieutenant giving classroom instruction: "Recruit Teitelbaum, why should a soldier gladly sacrifice his life for Kaiser and country?" Teitelbaum: "Yes, honestly Lieutenant, why should he?"

*I*t was dusk by now and, since this was a Friday evening, candles, alight in all the little houses of the Jews, lit up the pavements. Every little house was like a sepulcher. Death himself had lit the candles. Louder than on other Jewish holidays came the chanting from the houses in which they prayed. They were ushering in an extraordinary, bloody Sabbath. They rushed out through the dusk in dark swarms over the pavements, and gathered together at the crossroads, where soon their lamentations rose for those among them who were soldiers and were going to war in the morning. They clasped each other's hands, they kissed one another on the cheek, and when two embraced, as if this parting were their last, their two red beards became entangled so that the men had to use their hands to separate their beards. The bells tolled above their heads. Bugles from the barracks cut across the bells and the lamentations of the Jews. They were sounding lights-out. The last lights-out. Night was upon

*F*all in by rank! It is time to honor the roster of the dead! "Oh, why don't you let us sleep," a mild voice broke in. "We were already lying so peacefully in the arms of the earth!" And the clerk replied: "The statistics ask how many of you Jews evaded the rest of the war by going to their graves." A great groan went up, as if the ground itself were grieving, and the voice called painfully: "Oh fatherland, it was for you that I wanted to die and go to my eternal rest!" But a drumroll brought the dead to their feet. They stood at the table, one behind the other, military and medical corps captains in front, then the lieutenants and doctors, sergeants and corporals. Noncommissioned officers, privates first class, and privates. And the clerk placed a brittle pen in every hand; the ink flowed like blood from a scratched finger. Each one wrote his Hebrew name in little red letters that shone like square seals. There the corpses stood waiting patiently, and whoever had written silently laid the insignia and decorations he had been wearing on the table and stepped back, one among many. There they lay: the thick shoulder boards of the captains of the medical corps and the silver ones of the officers, sword knots like silver eggs, the noncommissioned officers' fourragères, the little sword-of-Aesculapius staff badges, the large buttons of the privates first class; the Iron Crosses first class and oh, how many second class, other crosses and medals, and black-and-white ribbons in all colors. The pile on the table grew and grew.
Arnold Zweig

Left: War service at the Stadttempel (City temple) in Vienna. 1915
Below: The composer Arnold Schoenberg as a private at Bruck army camp on the Leitha (Lower Austria). 1916

Opposite page: Breslau rabbi Dr. Sali Lewi as an army chaplain. Ca. 1916

As burdensome as it may be, visiting all parts of the army is absolutely essential. That is the only way for many, if perhaps not all, to gain the personal impression and certainty that there is a rabbi among them. That the Jewish soldiers realize this is very important, that the Gentiles know it is equally so. It is of indisputable significance to the recognition of Judaism; and that acceptance of the Jews always depends on the recognition of Judaism goes without saying. It is also important to the Jewish soldier's position that his religion should stand visibly side by side with the others.
Leo Baeck

If we Jewish soldiers thought that by taking part in the war we would obtain the love of our fellow human beings, we were mistaken. Though there was no open anti-Semitism, the Jews, who had declared their solidarity with the workers, were opposed by a large number of people who hated the thought of a republic. These opponents already appeared to possess great economic strength and to be responsible for spreading the word that most Jews were shirkers. And as it was in my home town, so it was in the whole of the Empire. Even though the workers always defended the Jews, the Jewish front-line soldiers, for whom defense from that quarter constituted a kind of humiliation, banded together and, under the leadership of former officers, formed an association: the Reichsbund jüdischer Frontsoldaten (Imperial league of front-line soldiers).
Edwin Landau

Whenever a people asks itself a question, mankind must also have a say.
Leo Baeck

Moreover, the Jews have always constituted a minority, and a minority is constantly compelled to think; that is the blessing of their fate.
Leo Baeck

I first became acquainted with the works of Karl Marx when I was at university; and it was a relief to me, after all the abstract views of the world, like Hegel's and Schelling's, finally to get to know an intellectual work that looked directly at life and derived its material not from history but from the future. The marvelous, cogent logic, the relentless diagnostic method, and above all the prophetic manner of defining problems made a deep impression on me, and I grasped in my innermost soul the whole, explosive, time-unsettling force concentrated like ecrasite in those few hundred pages.
Stefan Zweig

And I, a powerless young Jew, rose up against the most terrible powers – alone against the world, against the powers of rank and the whole aristocracy, against the power of unbounded wealth, against the government, and against officials of all kinds, always the natural allies of rank and riches, against all possible prejudices.
Ferdinand Lassalle

As surely as we need to start a social revolution with respect to economic conditions, so surely do we need to start a social revolution with respect to love, the relationship of the sexes, and decency. The mark of modern times is that the human being wants to achieve free and unconditional personal fulfillment. But how can human beings be genuinely free . . . if not even that which is most unique and immediate to them – their feelings and bodies – are subject to this freedom . . .
Naturally the development of the notion of love most affects, oppresses, or exalts women, as they live only in this sphere, while men live in many others as well . . . German women used to be – and sometimes still are – born as housewives.
Ferdinand Lassalle

I swear by the Almighty under the stars and curse myself if I become unfaithful to my oath . . . I want to go before the German people and before all peoples, and exhort them in passionate words to join the battle for freedom.
Ferdinand Lassalle

Karl Marx (Trier 1818 – London 1883) had rabbis among his antecedents, but his father Heinrich converted to Protestantism with the whole family. On completing his university studies, Karl Marx became editor-in-chief of the liberal leftist *Rheinische Zeitung* (1842). In Paris from 1843, he became co-editor of the *Deutsch-Französischer Jahrbücher* (German-French Yearbooks). It was at this point that he and his friend Friedrich Engels took the step to revolutionary socialism, promulgating the historical materialism and scientific socialism now known as "Marxism." In the *Communist Manifesto* (1848) they leveled sharp criticism at the bourgeois social and economic order, at the same time summoning the workers to join the class struggle. By way of an analysis of revolution, Marx arrived at the analysis of the laws of economics (*Das Kapital*, 1867). In *Zur Judenfrage* (On the Jewish Question [1843]), he defined his view of Judaism from the Marxist perspective.
Above: Karl Marx during his London period. Ca. 1875

It is in the nature of prophetic religion to view the reform of existing conditions as its task and aim . . . It contains a ferment, something that again and again sets that which exists and is at rest in motion and unrest. From the moment prophetic religion entered the world, societal and social quiescence ceased.
Leo Baeck

Do you know what we were put on this earth for? To call every human countenance before Sinai. You do not want to go? If I do not call you, Marx will. If Marx does not call you, Spinoza will. If Spinoza does not call you, Christ will.
You want to die for an old world order? You will live for a new world order. And that world order will be a very simple one. It is not those of noble birth who are responsible for those of low birth; Kol Israel, the whole of Israel, is responsible for everyone, yes, everyone. But the whole of Israel is everyone who was created in the image of God; that means you and your colonel and your orderly and I and all of us.
Walther Rathenau

Only the struggle against general class injustice will ultimately guarantee justice for the Jews.
Arnold Zweig

Like a wild cry sweeping across the earth and like a hardly perceptible whisper in our innermost selves, an irrefutable voice tells us that the Jew can only be redeemed with the rest of humanity, and that it is one and the same thing to wait for the Messiah in exile and diaspora and to be the Messiah of the peoples.
Gustav Landauer

We were politically backwards, the most presumptuous and demanding of slaves; the calamity that consequently befell us with the inexorability of fate incited us to rise up in wrath against our masters, and drove us to revolution.
Gustav Landauer

Ferdinand Lassalle (Breslau 1825 – Geneva 1864) was a socialist who wanted to change prevailing social conditions by means of an evolutionary process, a view contradictory to the revolutionary ideas of internationally oriented *Karl Marx*. In 1863 he founded the "Allgemeiner Deutscher Arbeiterverein" (General German Worker's Association), the first social democratic organization in Germany. Lassalle also advocated the formation of production cooperatives and demanded universal suffrage, with voting by secret ballot. He died of wounds sustained in a duel.
Opposite page, below: Ferdinand Lassalle. Ca. 1860

Eduard Bernstein (Berlin 1850 – Berlin 1932) edited *Der Sozialdemokrat*, a periodical that first appeared in Zurich in 1879 and was published in London between 1887 and 1901. As a member of the moderate wing of the Social Democrats, he belonged to the Reichstag from 1902 to 1906, 1912 to 1918, and 1920 to 1928; between 1916 and 1920 he numbered among the independent social democrats. The leading revisionist theoretician, he was able to secure the upper hand for his faction in the SPD.
Above: Eduard Bernstein on his way to the Reichstag in Berlin. 1920

The bond that has united the Jews for thousands of years and that unites them today is, above all, the democratic ideal of social justice, coupled with the ideal of mutual aid and tolerance among all men. Even the most ancient religious scriptures of the Jews are steeped in these social ideals, which have powerfully affected Christianity and Mohammedanism and have had a benign influence upon the social structure of a great part of mankind.
Albert Einstein

Rosa Luxemburg (Za-mość 1871 – Berlin 1919) helped found the "Sozialdemokratische Partei des Königreiches Polen und Litauen" (Social Democratic Party of the Kingdom of Poland and Lithuania). In 1897 she moved to Germany, where she made her mark as a theoretician of the left wing of the SPD. She spent most of World War I in prison, fighting the SPD's policy of compromise from there. With Karl Liebknecht she created the Spartakusbund, which represented the radical left wing of the social democratic movement in the November revolution. She developed the program of the KPD (Communist Party of Germany), established in 1918/19. After the defeat of the Spartacist revolution in 1919, she was arrested and murdered.

Left: Rosa Luxemburg speaking at the Socialist Congress in Stuttgart in 1907.

Rosa Luxemburg is a unique blend of the German, Polish, and Russian characters and of the Jewish temperament.
Isaac Deutscher

Oh, the "lofty silence of eternity," where so many cries go unheard, resounds so strongly in me that I have no special corner in my heart for the ghetto; I feel at home in the whole world, wherever there are clouds and birds and human tears.
Rosa Luxemburg

Being human is far and away the main thing. And that means being resolute, clear, and serene; yes, serene despite everything, for whining is the business of the weak. Being human means throwing oneself joyfully onto the "great scales of destiny," one's whole life if need be, but at the same time enjoying every fine day and every beautiful cloud. Oh, I can offer no prescriptions for how to be human, I only know how it is done, and you used to know, too, when we walked together for hours in the Südender Feld and lay in the grain in the red glow of evening. The world is so beautiful despite its horrors, and it would be even more beautiful if there were no weaklings and cowards in it. Come, you get another kiss because you are an honest little fellow. Happy New Year!
Rosa Luxemburg

There are letters here that read like a chapter out of a novel by Flaubert, with more true poetry, more of the German character expressed in a few sentences by this "Polish Jewess" than can be found in nine tenths of German poetry. Because they are not invented, because they have been experienced. Open the volume anywhere: whether at a "trivial" postcard or a matter-of-fact account of an agitational trip, there is not a single empty phrase to be found in these one hundred letters.
Leo Lania

in the first year and month of the glorious German revolution! . . . Behind this buzz of rumors, ridiculous fantasies, lunatic stories, and shameless lies a very serious process is under way: there is method in it . . . The rumors are fabricated deliberately and spread among the public . . . in order to create a pogrom atmosphere . . . They scream murder, putsch, and similar nonsense when what they mean is socialism.
Rosa Luxemburg

Communism . . . the Devil take its practical application, but God preserve it as a constant threat looming over the heads of those who own property and, to protect it, want to drive everyone else – comforting them all the way with the thought that the material life is not the highest good – to the fronts of hunger and patriotic honor. God preserve it so these scoundrels, so brazen they hardly know what to do with themselves, do not become even more brazen, so that those of the exclusive society of the privileged . . . at least have to face night terrors as well! So that they at least lose their taste for sermonizing their victims and their pleasure in making jokes about them!
Karl Kraus

In southern Friedrichstadt stand a few mighty houses, old bulwarks of the spirit, renovated and extended, inviting with their ample window space, threatening with their stone balustrades, enticing and repelling, houses beautiful and dangerous. They belong to fabled kings and royal families.by the names of Ullstein, Mosse, and Scherl. When our last little revolution broke out, the newspaper kings were driven out of their palaces for a time along with the other kings. In the castle courtyards stood bivouac fires with pots of bacon and peas on them, there was shooting on the roofs, and spiked soldiers' boots thumped through the newspaper offices. But the newspaper kings returned much more quickly than other monarchs. Now their chariots with paper munitions stand in the courtyards again and ladies-in-waiting – light-footed secretaries and typists – dart through the newspaper offices.
Franz Hessel

Whenever a window shatters somewhere, or a tire bursts with a loud bang at the corner, the philistine, hair on end, goose flesh down his back, looks over his shoulder and says: "Aha, the Spartacus people must be coming!" . . . Various people have appealed to Lieb-knecht with the touching plea to spare their husband, nephew, or aunts from the Beth-lehemite murder of the innocents that the Spartacists are planning. This really happened

Above: Government troops with armored vehicle on Münzstrasse in Berlin during the March battles in 1919.
Below: The vandalized offices of Ullstein publications in Berlin in January 1919.
Opposite page: The Spartacus Revolution in Berlin in January 1919: Spartacist leader holding a speech from the balcony of the badly damaged Mosse publications building.

On the afternoon of July 10, 1934, Erich Mühsam was summoned to the guardroom, where, with sneering courtesy, SS officer Ehrat made the following disclosure: "So you're Herr Mühsam? Surely the Mühsam of the Räterepublik? Well, listen to what I have to tell you. You have until tomorrow morning to hang yourself. You understand what I mean? By the neck. If you don't carry out the order, we'll do it for you!"
Distraught, Mühsam returned to his fellow sufferers and explained the situation to them. He declared that, regardless of the suffering he had already experienced, he was by no means going to hang himself now. At 8:15 that evening, Mühsam was taken to the administration building. He never returned. He was later seen crossing the yard with SS officer Werner. The next morning he was found in latrine number four, a rope round his neck, his feet hanging down into the hole. The noose was too elaborately knotted for the half-blind Mühsam ever to have managed himself.
Karl Grünberg

*One morning the citizens of Munich woke up and, to their amazement, found themselves in a "Räterepublik" [republic governed by workers' councils] – even worse, in one established by "rogues," by "alien elements" (as any peasant calls any man born further away than he can spit). There they sat, behind their beer mugs, gaping at the world. It was a bitter time. If people are asked today what they actually had to endure then, most of them will give the same answer, namely, basically nothing at all. The Munich Räterepublik cost a total of fourteen lives – the ten hostages in the Luitpoldgymnasium (murders for which there are many explanations but no excuses) – plus, if some very fastidious calculations are undertaken, a further four lives to be set on the same bill. So much for the revolutionaries. Once Munich's narrow-minded bourgeois philistines had been liberated from outside, the "victorious" troops made their entry into the Bavarian state palace – and one hundred and eighty-four people on the opposing side paid with their lives in a multiplicity of ways: the victims of arbitrarily wielded martial law, of bestial murders (the way Landauer was slain by men in uniform one would not kill a dog: the corpse was plundered) – Revenge! Revenge!
Cold revenge was the order of the day. The "rogues" were brought up before People's Courts, special courts – and the Workers' Government of Munich paid a penalty of 519 years and 9 months of imprisonment for its crimes; one death sentence was pronounced*

(Leviné), three leaders were murdered by soldiers. (All of the supporters of the Kapp régime are free men.)
Kurt Tucholsky

Kurt Eisner (Berlin 1867 – Munich 1919) was appointed editor of the social democratic weekly *Vorwärts* (Forward) in 1899 but was fired for his revisionist views in 1905. From 1910 on he lived in Munich, writing feuilletons. When the party split in 1917, he joined the pacifist independent social democrats. During the November Revolution he proclaimed the "Freistaat Bayern" (Free State of Bavaria) and became its prime minister. He championed a radical peace program and a combination of workers' councils and parliamentarianism. On his way to the opening of the new Landtag (parliament), he was shot by *Anton Count Arco*. His death was the signal for the proclamation of a *Räterepublik* (republic governed by workers' councils).
Above: *Räterepublik* Munich, 1919: the poet Erich Mühsam speaking at a rally.
Right: Kurt Eisner, prime minister of Bavaria, driving up to the Imperial Chancellery in Berlin for the imperial conference of representatives of state governments. 1918

And my German self and my Jewish self do nothing against and a great deal for each other. Like two brothers, a first-born and a Benjamin, whose mother loves them in different ways but equally; like the harmony in which these two brothers can live, both where they are alike and where each goes his own way – that is how I experience this strange but familiar juxtaposition as something delightful, and find neither element in this relationship primary or secondary. I have never had the need to simplify myself or to unify myself by denial; I accept the complex entity that I am, and hope that I am even more varied than I know.
Gustav Landauer

Gustav Landauer (Karlsruhe 1870 – Berlin 1919) was Volksvertreter für Volksaufklärung (People's representative for people's enlightenment) in the government of the Bavarian *Räterepublik* in 1919. An opponent of both social democracy and communism, he advocated a radical though non-doctrinaire form of socialism and the institution of workers' councils. When the *Räterepublik* fell, he was imprisoned and killed. Apart from political works (*Die Revolution*, 1908), he also wrote stories and literary essays (*Vorträge über Shakespeare* [Lectures on Shakespeare], 1920).
Below: Gustav Landauer. 1916

Erich Mühsam (Berlin 1878 – Oranienburg concentration camp 1934) had earned his living as a freelance writer in Berlin since 1901. In 1909 he moved to Munich, where he put out a revolutionary literary periodical, *Kain – Zeitschrift für Menschlichkeit* (Cain – A Magazine for Humaneness). He participated in the establishment of the Bavarian *Räterepublik* in 1919. Convicted after its overthrow, he was pardoned in 1924. From 1926 to 1933 he edited the magazine *Fanal* (Beacon). After the Reichstag fire Mühsam was arrested by the SA and sent to Oranienburg concentration camp, where he was murdered. He made his mark as an essayist, dramatist, journalist, and writer of revolutionary songs with an anarchist bent.
Above: Erich Mühsam. Photograph by *Lotte Jacobi*. 1929

269

Victor Adler (Prague 1852 – Vienna 1918) started out as a German nationalist, but after working with the poor as a public-assistance doctor, became a social democrat. To prevent a schism between the reformists and the revolutionaries, he created the periodical *Gleichheit* (Equality) in 1886 and the *Arbeiter-Zeitung* (Workers' Paper) in 1889. He founded the Social Democratic Party of Austria at the party convention in Hainfeld in 1888/89. After the 1905 voting rights demonstrations in Vienna led to the introduction of universal male suffrage, Adler was elected to parliament in 1907 and became leader of the Social Democrats. In the years that followed he fought against the impending war and the rapid growth of nationalism in the poly-ethnic Austro-Hungarian Monarchy. In 1918, shortly before his death and the proclamation of the republic, he was appointed Secretary of State for Foreign Affairs.
Left: Victor Adler. Ca. 1910
Opposite page, right: Unveiling of the Lassalle monument in front of the Winarsky-Hof, one of the noteworthy municipal buildings of "Red Vienna." 1928

Compared with Adler, all socialist leaders, whether Bebel or Jaurès, are romantics, and one actually only wonders how a person whose greatest virtues are clarity and sobriety ever became leader of a (at least at one time) revolutionary party. His own party comrades often have an uncanny feeling when they think how cleverly and quickly this ever cool mind works. At the last party conference one of the popular leaders said about him: "Dr. Adler has the habit of swimming right through the difficult issues." Oh, and, of course, the others are so quickly out of their depth! How is it that despite all the "slaves' revolts" Adler remains so firmly in the saddle? Perhaps because he has, above all, a sure eye for his historic task. How much intelligence the man has, though he cannot really make complete use of it in the party! But he knows how to acquiesce and rein himself in; here is a man who knows when to remain silent! He has never been a dilettante. He does not like to let his all too expansive horizons frighten off his comrades; he knows how to restrict himself . . . The coarser spirits actually tend to have a stronger effect on the large masses. Pernerstorfer, for example, fires greater enthusiasm with those stentorian tones from a German breast. But Victor Adler knows the techniques of a democratic party! His effect is not so much on the masses as on the agitators arising from the masses, the mediators between party and people.
Stefan Grossmann

Austrian social democracy received its spiritual wealth and its intellectual and moral impulses above all from Jewish intellectuals, whose thinking habits did not quite coincide with the intellectual temperament of Alpine workers and the petit bourgeoisie.
Julius Braunthal

And the wealth of Jewish intelligence that had made itself available [to socialism] when [the movement] was still fighting, justified the struggle, even for the Jews themselves, as a defense of civilization. This was the secret meaning, welling forth from unconscious layers of collective experience, of the compact we Jewish intellectuals had made with the workers' parties.
Arnold Zweig

Otto Bauer (Vienna 1882 – Paris 1938), an exponent of the radical left wing of the Social Democratic Party of Austria, became Secretary of the socialist faction in the Austrian parliament in 1907 and was *Victor Adler*'s direct successor as Secretary of State for Foreign Affairs in 1918/19. A member of parliament until 1933, he was one of the leaders of the February battles in 1934. While the fighting was still going on, he emigrated to Czechoslovakia, where he founded the Foreign Branch of the Socialists in Brünn (Brno). He emigrated to Paris in 1938. Bauer, one of the co-founders of the periodical *Der Kampf* (The Fight) in 1907, authored fundamental works on Austro-Marxism (*Die Nationalitätenfrage und die Sozialdemokratie* [The nationality question and social democracy], 1907; *Bolschewismus oder Sozialdemokratie*, 1920).

Right: Otto Bauer at an election rally. Photograph by Lothar Rübelt. Ca. 1925

271

The Germans so long and so thoroughly demonstrated to us that our nationality is an obstacle to our "inner" emancipation that we ultimately believed it ourselves and did everything we could to prove ourselves worthy of the blond Germanic lineage by denying our origins. But apart from the masters of calculation, who traded their Judaism for a government job, all of our Jewish Germanomaniacs grossly miscalculated. That Meyerbeer fearfully avoided using Jewish subjects in his operas did not help him a bit; it did not preserve him from the hatred the Germans have for the Jews. Nor was it of any use to the German patriot Börne that he changed his last name from Baruch. He admits it himself: "As soon as my opponents run aground on Börne," he says somewhere in his writings, "they throw out Baruch as an emergency anchor." – I myself have found that in every personal quarrel, not only with my opponents but also with those who share my convictions, this weapon is employed, and it is a weapon that seldom misses its mark in Germany. I have resolved to make this convenient weapon even more convenient by henceforth adopting my Old Testament name, Moses; my only regret is that I am not called Itzig.
Moses Hess

The Jewish masses will participate in the great historic movement of modern mankind only once they have a Jewish homeland. But as long as the bulk of Jews remain in their special position, the relatively few Jews who will try vainly to do everything to make an individual escape from this invalid position will be far more painfully affected by it than the mass, who only feel unhappy but not dishonored. – Therefore the Jew, whether Orthodox or not, cannot evade the responsibility of working to promote an uprising of the whole of Jewry. – Every Jew, even the convert to Christianity, shares in the responsibility for the rebirth of Israel.
Moses Hess

Moses Hess (Bonn 1812 – Paris 1875) co-edited the liberal-democratic *Rheinische Zeitung* with *Karl Marx* in 1842/43. His theories of "true socialism" had strong ethical underpinnings (which is why Arnold Ruge called him the "communist rabbi"). Though he exercised an influence on Karl Marx and Friedrich Engels, their *Comunist Manifesto* took a more radical turn. Moses Hess became a precursor of Zionism with his work *Rom und Jerusalem: Die letzte Nationalitätenfrage* (Rome and Jerusalem: The final nationality question [1862]), in which he demanded an independent state for the Jews.
Above: Moses Hess. Ca. 1860

What ultimately made me decide to stand up for the national rebirth of my people was the infinite pain of your bereavement over a loved one. Only a Jewish heart is capable of such love, such unbounded familial love, which, like mother love, originates in the blood and yet is as pure as God's spirit. And this love is the natural well-spring of every intellectual love of God, which, according to Spinoza, is the very highest the mind can achieve. The redeemers of mankind spring from the inexhaustible source of Jewish family life.
"Through you," the divine genius of the Jewish family says in self-revelation, "all families of the earth are blessed."
Every Jewish man is a potential Messiah, every Jewish woman a potential mater dolorosa . . .
Moses Hess

It is not a question today of casting off our German identity, to which we have an inner affinity no German behavior towards us can alter – a fact unconnected with those loyalty oaths and declarations of love certain representatives of German Jewry occasionally make into the void – but of intensifying Judaism and, placing our hope in the Covenant, renewing the old bond. It is a question of making a great virtue out of necessity.
Martin Buber

Zionism is, on the contrary, a movement born of the terrible crisis in which Jews and Judaism are today, after a hundred years of development since they were first accepted (in France). The motive force of Zionism is to overcome this crisis, to solve the present-day "Jewish question."
Adolf Böhm

What good are delusions? – The peoples of Europe have never regarded the existence of the Jews in their midst as anything but an anomaly. We shall always remain strangers among nations; they may emancipate us out of a feeling of humanity and justice, but will never ever respect us until we accept "ubi bene ibi patria" as our maxim and dogma, and put our great individual national memories in second place.
Moses Hess

We are a people, "one" people. Everywhere we have sincerely endeavored to merge with the national communities surrounding us and to preserve only the faith of our fathers. We are not permitted to do so. In vain are we loyal patriots, in some places even extravagantly so; in vain do we make the same sacrifices of life and property as our fellow citizens; in vain do we strive to enhance the fame of our native countries in the arts and sciences, or their wealth through trade and commerce. In our native lands where, after all, we too have lived for centuries, we are decried as aliens, often by people whose ancestors had not yet come to the country when our fathers' sighs were already heard in the land. The majority can decide who the strangers are; like everything else in relations between peoples, this is a matter of power. I do not waive any part of our prescriptive right when I make this statement as an individual, one with no particular authority. In the world as it is now constituted and will probably continue to be for an indefinite period, might precedes right. So it avails us nothing to be good patriots everywhere, as were the Huguenots, who were forced to emigrate. If only we were left in peace. . . .
But I think we shall not be left in peace.
Theodor Herzl

Right: Theodor Herzl opening the
Second Zionist Congress in Basel.
1898

*The first congress came.
The reports were devoured. The
speeches by Theodor Herzl and
Max Nordau roused friends and
opponents alike. The miracle had
happened. The Jewish people had
awoken and found its tongue
again. There was a Jewish stand.
The immensity of the work involved in creating an organization
out of this heterogeneous mass of
people from all parts of the world
and representing all possible attitudes can be assessed only in re-
trospect, now that this organization, created in a few short days,
has seen so much progress.*
Sammy Gronemann

Herzl's step came substantially as a sort of response to the upsurge of Luegerite anti-Semitism at the time. But that was only an outward, incidental reason and, considering the dimensions and age of the whole problem, one is tempted to call it a minor one. In the pages of this pamphlet a proud, free human being awoke from the dream of assimilation so many noble and well-meaning Jews had dreamed since the days of Henriette Herz and Rahel Varnhagen. He saw the countless great achievements of the great men of his people in all countries and all fields, he saw the valuable, the precious contributions this people had made in all cultures, and saw the wall of hatred that had repulsed the Jews, the wall against which their most passionate endeavors had shattered.
He no longer wanted to court acceptance, which had again and again been sneeringly denied. As a student, Theodor Herzl had experienced the insults of the Waidhofener

Program, which repudiated the Jews' right to demand satisfaction by duel; he only saw the chasm becoming wider and deeper, and his idea was that there could be reconciliation only when the Jews acknowledged the traditions of their own people, their ancient heritage, and their ancient land.
Felix Salten

But it also bespeaks a very peculiar view held by the honorable representatives at the Congress if they want to portray all Jews as a single nation. That is as mistaken as wanting to portray everyone who professes the Catholic faith, for example all Frenchmen, Germans, Russians, Magyars, Negroes, as a single nation.
Israelitische Gemeindezeitung Prag (Jewish Community Paper, Prague), 1898

Only small-minded Zionism, whose political line can be followed effortlessly to its nearby end point of practical impossibility, has enabled these gentlemen, who were previously concerned exclusively with their nerves, to feel that they too are contemporaries. How amazingly quickly they have appropriated the pain of Judaism, the pain of a thousand years, which now helps them to attain a thousand undreamed-of new positions. It is certainly interesting to watch a poet whose words made everyone in the Town Hall Quarter prick up their ears now divest himself of all social ties. He parts with his exotic cravat, which might disturb the ensemble of "strange melancholy," orders a suit à la sackcloth and ashes from the most fashionable tailor, and has only one response when asked if he is in need of anything: A homeland . . . !
Karl Kraus

273

Judaism is a mass shelter for misery, with branches all over the world.
Theodor Herzl

Dreams are not so different from Deeds as some may think. All the Deeds of men are only Dreams at first. And in the end, their Deeds dissolve into Dreams.
Theodor Herzl

It was a singular day, a day in July, unforgettable to those who participated in the experience. Suddenly, to all the railroad stations of the city, by day and by night, from all realms and lands, every train brought new arrivals. Western, Eastern, Russian, Turkish Jews; from all the provinces and all the little towns they hurried excitedly, the shock of the news still written on their faces; never was it more clearly manifest what strife and talk

had hitherto concealed – it was a great movement whose leader had now fallen. The procession was endless. Vienna, startled, became aware that it was not just a writer or a mediocre poet who had passed away, but one of those creators of ideas who disclose themselves triumphantly in a single country, to a single people at vast intervals. A tumult ensued at the cemetery; too many had suddenly stormed to his coffin, crying, sobbing, screaming in a wild explosion of despair. It was almost a riot, a fury. All regulation was upset through a sort of elementary and ecstatic mourning such as I had never seen before nor since at a funeral. And it was this gigantic outpouring of grief from the depths of millions of souls that made me realize for the first time how much passion and hope this lone and lonesome man had borne into the world through the power of a single thought.
Stefan Zweig

Theodor Herzl (Budapest 1860 – Edlach 1904) wrote *Der Judenstaat* (The Jewish State [1896]) under the influence of the Dreyfus affair, which he experienced as Paris correspondent (1881–1895) of the Vienna paper *Neue Freie Presse.* This book created the impulse for political Zionism, the primary aim of which was the foundation of a Jewish state. Herzl's concern with the Jewish question dated from the appearance of modern anti-Semitism. Though he had originally favored total Jewish assimilation as the solution, his analysis of the position of the Jews in modern society gradually led him to the

realization that the Jewish question was a national question and could only be solved as such. The first expression of this insight was his play *Das neue Ghetto* (The New Ghetto, first version 1894). Herzl's road from assimilationism to Zionism is indicative: as Martin Buber saw it, Herzl underwent the development of a "disappointed liberal" who, affected by the irrationality of anti-Semitism, declared his belief in nationalism.
At the First Zionist Congress in Basel in 1897, Theodor Herzl founded the Zionist International, and it was at that congress that the so-called Basel Program was ac-

cepted: "Zionism strives to create for the Jewish people a home in Palestine secured by public law." In 1898 the Zionist bank, the "Jewish Colonial Trust," was set up; and in 1901 Herzl established the Jewish National Foundation (Keren Kajemet Lejisrael) to purchase land as the national property of the Jewish people. Herzl was president of all these organizations until he died. As an acknowledged representative of the Zionist organization, he tried to convince the Great Powers in particular of the idea of a Jewish state. He traveled to Constantinople in 1896 and, thanks to the good offices of the Grand

Duke of Baden, was received by Kaiser Wilhelm II in Constantinople and Jerusalem in 1898. The emperor suggested that a German protectorate might be possible. Herzl also negotiated with the Ottomans and the English, but negotiations failed. Next to his political activities, Herzl retained his post as arts editor of the *Neue Freie Presse* in Vienna and continued his literary writing, which was his secret love. In the novel *Altneuland* (Oldnewland [1902]) Herzl portrayed the future of an aristocratically governed Jewish state.
Right: Theodor Herzl at the Second Zionist Congress in Basel. 1898
Left: Theodor Herzl's funeral in Vienna on July 7, 1904.

Max Nordau (Pest 1849
– Paris 1923), originally Max Süd-
feld, studied medicine in Pest,
where he wrote feuilletons for the
Pester Lloyd and from 1876 for the
Neuer Pester Journal. He settled in
Paris for good in 1880. Thanks to
his broad education, he was much
in demand as a correspondent
(*Vossische Zeitung, Neue Freie
Presse, Die Welt*). Apart from historical-cultural and political-critical
treatises (*Konventionelle Lügen
der Kulturmenschheit* [Conventio-
nal Lies of Cultured Mankind],
1883), he also wrote novels and
plays. Fired by *Theodor Herzl*'s
ideas, he committed himself to political Zionism in 1895. A leading
figure at most of the Zionist con-
gresses until 1911, he came into
increasing political conflict with
other Zionist groups.
Right: Max Nordau. Ca. 1900
Below: The decision to begin practical development work in Palestine was made at the Sixth Zionist
Congress in 1903. Supervision was
entrusted to (from left): the agrarian reformers Franz Oppenheimer,
Otto Warburg (president of the
Zionist International from 1911 to
1920, director of the agricultural
institute in Rechowot from 1921
and at the Hebrew University in
Jerusalem from 1925), and Selig
Soskin.

*Zionism strives for a lasting solution to the
Jewish question by founding a refuge secured
by public law for those Jews who cannot or do
not want to remain in the country of their
birth. – Zionism strives for the return of a
large proportion of Jews to agriculture on the
historically consecrated soil of Palestine.
Zionism strives for a revival of Jewish self-
confidence, the upholding of Jewish ideals,
the cultivation of Jewish literature and history, the education of the young in the spirit
of the Jewish people . . .
"Assimilate, then things will improve!" they
summoned us with pathos. We did, we assimilated, except for our noses. We imitated all the
customs and habits of other peoples without
scrutinizing their value, we forgot our own
customs and neglected our own culture. What
good did it do us? In the others' eyes we have
remained Jews, which does not mean profess-
ing the Jewish faith but being children of a
different race . . . We have courted the favor
of the Aryan peoples long enough, even
giving up our own dignity in the process, but
the lady is very coy, and the more one
humiliates oneself in front of her, the smaller
her affection.*
Der Zionismus (Zionism), 1897

*I was still in the "Gymnasium" when this
short pamphlet, penetrating as a steel shaft,
appeared; but I can still remember the general astonishment and annoyance of the
bourgeois Jewish circles of Vienna. What has
happened, they said angrily, to this otherwise
intelligent, witty and cultivated writer? What
foolishness is this that he has thought up and
writes about? Why should we go to Palestine?
Our language is German and not Hebrew,
and beautiful Austria is our homeland. Are
we not well off under the good Emperor
Franz Josef? Do we not make a decent living,
and is our position not secure? Are we not
equal subjects, inhabitants and loyal citizens
of our beloved Vienna? Do we not live in a
progressive era in which in a few decades all
sectarian prejudices will be abolished? Why
does he, who speaks as a Jew and who wishes
to help Judaism, place arguments in the hands
of our worst enemies and attempt to separate
us, when every day brings us more closely and
intimately into the German world? The rabbis thundered passionately from the pulpits,
the head of the "Neue Freie Presse" forbade
the very mention of the word Zionism in his
"progressive" newspaper. Karl Kraus, the*

*Thersites of Viennese literature, the master of
invective, wrote a pamphlet called "The King
of Zion," and when Theodor Herzl entered a
theater, people whispered sneeringly: "His
Majesty has arrived!"*
Stefan Zweig

*A pithy answer to the question "What is
Zionism?" . . . was: "Zionism is when one
Jew encourages another Jew to donate money
to pay for a third Jew to go to Palestine."*
Wilma Iggers

*Modern Zionism originated in Austria, in
Vienna. An Austrian journalist founded it. It
could have been founded by no one else.*
Joseph Roth

Right: The German Pro-Palestina-Komitee (front row from right): chairman Heinrich Count Bernstorff, Prof. Chaim Weizmann, and Undersecretary of State Carl von Schubert. Behind Schubert (left), Albert Einstein; between Schubert and Weizmann, recording secretary Katharina von Oheimb; left, next to Bernstorff, the banker Oskar Wassermann; next to him, Kurt Blumenfeld, president of the German Zionist organization. 1928

It is true that as a political movement Zionism was immediately successful, but the bulk of German Jewry continued to reject it in the following years. Only a minority participated in the development of the Zionist organization and the great battles that took place within the movement up to and beyond Herzl's death. These battles were not always political in nature. Apart from the fierce argument that broke out at the Sixth Zionist Congress (1903) between the "territorialists" and the Zionists who insisted on a homeland in Palestine as opposed to the Uganda project (as a "temporary asylum" before acquiring Palestine), cultural issues tended to be points of contention. The politically and socially oriented direction represented by Herzl himself could not be enough for the champions of a Jewish rebirth. For them it was a matter of an inner renewal of the people, a synthesis of Zionism and the religious mission of Judaism, and thus the solution to questions independent of the goal of political Zionism. The ideas

of the spiritual Zionism founded by Achad Haam, who envisioned a Jewish Palestine as a spiritual center reflecting back on the diaspora, the concepts of Nathan Birnbaum, which were expressed in the thesis "Israel goes before Zion," the reawakening of the spirit of Hasidism through Martin Buber – all of these trends expressed forces rooted deep in Jewish history and pushing intensely for rebirth. That is the reason for the fierce struggles within the Zionist movement, which made themselves felt even in the non-Zionist world.
Franz Kobler

In my early childhood Zionist ideas and aspirations were already awake in Russian Jewry. My father was not yet a Zionist, but the house was steeped in rich Jewish tradition, and Palestine was at the center of the ritual, a longing for it implicit in our life. Practical

nationalism did not assume form till some years later, but the "Return" was in the air, a vague, deep-rooted Messianism, a hope which would not die. We heard the conversations of our elders, and we were caught up in the restlessness. But is was not for children; when one of us ventured a remark on the subject he was put down rather roughly. In particular I remember one Rebbi, himself an ardent nationalist, who thought it impious and presumptuous of a youngster to so much as mention the rebuilding of Palestine. He would say: "You keep quiet. You'll never bring the Messiah any nearer. One has to do much, learn much, know much and suffer much before one is worthy of that." He intimidated us so completely that we learned to keep our own counsel. Still, the dream was there, an ever-present background to our thoughts. And the Rebbi's words, uttered so brusquely, have remained permanently in my mind.
Chaim Weizmann

*R*ight after the war, Zionism began to play a growing role in Germany. It had not gained any followers in our quiet, conservative community yet, but under the influence of our active student group, a small but enthusiastic youth circle was formed . . . The members of the group we had organized were young people moved by the same ideas that moved us or at least sufficiently infected by our enthusiasm that they were ready to join us. Our "league," which was actually just a small, dedicated association of youths my age plus a few younger ones, was organized along the lines of the "Wandervogel" [German youth movement]. There was only one crucial difference: all the members of our group were Jews. To the old German folksongs we loved so much, and the "Landsknecht" songs we sang on our hikes, we now added plaintive, emotional Yiddish songs and the rousing early melodies of the "chaluzim." Every organization needs a banner to march under, a flag to show the world, a standard to follow. Our symbol – how else could it have been – was the Mogen David, the Star of David. We had a beautiful pennant that we took with us on our hiking tours.
Henry Buxbaum

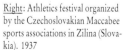

Right: Athletics festival organized by the Czechoslovakian Maccabee sports associations in Zilina (Slovakia). 1937

Above: Zionist worker's demonstration in Chelm (Poland). 1932

Right: Girls' group of the "Blau-Weiss" Zionist hiking club in Breslau. 1913

I first experienced my own Judaism in this group of optimistic people; filled with a romantic socialism of brotherhood and justice, they did a great deal of debating and even more singing. What they liked best were Landsknecht songs, the songs of the foot-soldiers of the "Zupfgeigenhansel": the same songs the non-Jewish youth organizations sang, the same songs we would later be appalled to hear bellowed by the followers of a political outsider named Adolf Hitler. Occasionally someone struck up one of the melancholy tunes of the eastern Jewish diaspora, or we formed a circle and stamped the "horah" as it was danced by the Zionist pioneers across the sea in Palestine. All this in those years when the illusion of allegedly successful Jewish-German assimilation reigned: it was a piece of recreated folklore – without particular involvement – like the Italian and French canons we hummed in the sparse shade of the pines of the Mark. As far as I can recall I saw the spiritual father of this branch of the Jewish youth movement, Ludwig Tietz, only once. He was spoken of with great respect. He was considered someone who had succeeded in recognizing "the best"

in host and guest nation, and in bringing them together. That two peoples who had so often confronted each other in enmity should enrich each other and intermingle seemed to us, in his spirit, happy progress. It would be a step to unite what had been separated and would lead out of the narrowness of national prejudice to a higher, more perfect synthesis.
Robert Jungk

For us, everything was connected: the almost militaristic posture during physical exercise, five-mile hikes, and the use of army terminology; the utterly free, endless discussions in which we talked ourselves hoarse, liberating ourselves from all pressures; the growing hostility toward war, toward anyone who profited from it, toward all bourgeois life and all authoritarianism; the martial marching songs and the melancholy Yiddish folk songs, the revolutionary songs of the Jewish and gentile labor movement and the "nigunim," the melodies crooned in the Hasidic homes and synagogues.
Manès Sperber

What did we want at the time? We considered ourselves unbourgeois, moderately revolutionary, hostile to the "mechanized," business- and pleasure-oriented world around us, and we viewed Zionism as the watchword for a basic renewal. To us, rationalism was a negative concept.
Robert Weltsch

The Zionists were the discontents then, the angry young men of the time. They considered Jewish existence in the Diaspora insignificant, empty, without a future, and staked everything on a single idea: reconstruction in Palestine, a radical and profound alteration of our way of life.
Max Brod

In mid-January my sister and some of her friends went to Lehnitz near Berlin. There was a so-called preparation camp there called Hachschara, where young people spent two weeks being prepared for their new surroundings, a kibbutz in Palestine. If they were "confirmed," they were allowed to embark on the journey to their new home. When my sister returned after two weeks, she had changed completely. She rhapsodized about the country on the east coast of the Mediterranean Sea; she had even picked up a few words of Hebrew, which she used whenever the proper occasion arose: if someone was to be quiet, she would only say "sheket" now, please was "bewakasha," and "toda raba" served as her thank you. My sister has always been very adaptable; she easily becomes enthusiastic about anything new, though the fires of enthusiasm can cool rapidly, too. The new way of life based on comradeship was very appealing to her; she was the focal point of her group and was, naturally, "confirmed," i.e. as early as late February or early March, she was to be allowed to join the transport from the diaspora to the Jewish homeland she called "Eretz."
Hans Winterfeldt

Left: Milking lessons in Hohenneuendorf/Berlin for Jewish women preparing to emigrate to Palestine. Photograph by *Abraham Pisarek*. 1936

Below: Agricultural training for prospective emigrants at Winkel, a teaching farm in Brandenburg. Photograph by *Tim Gidal*. Ca. 1935

At least as, if not more, important than industrial and commercial retraining was agricultural instruction. In this field the Jewish organizations were in the fortunate position of being able to send retrainees to long-standing Jewish agricultural estates, where they could receive thorough training under expert supervision in the various areas of farming, cattle-breeding, and market-gardening . . . The largest and best-known Jewish agricultural training center was the Neuendorf agricultural estate near Fürstenwalde, some 40 kilometers from the outskirts of the imperial capital. Under the supervision of the Jewish agronomist Moch, many hundreds of young Jews became perfect farmers, cattle-breeders, and market-gardeners.
Alexander Szanto

This policy of peace and reconciliation is the only right one for the Jews to exercise. It is consistent with the Jewish heart and the Jewish spirit, consistent with true, human precepts. Here, on the soil of their ancient home, the Jews are not permitted to act as eager European conquerors, not permitted to pit violence against violence. Nor would they be permitted to do so even had they the power to. For they will always live with the Arabs here, with the Arabs in Palestine and with the ones in all the large, neighboring countries. They are now putting down seeds in the soil and people's hearts for this eternal coexistence with the Arabs, and if they sow hatred or revenge now, they will never harvest love or even toleration. They must approach the Semitic Arabs, who are their brothers, in brotherhood. They must tell them that God has led them back to Palestine, that they have come back by God's will. And it is not enough merely to tell them that; they must prove by their attitude that the spirit of God is alive in them. Then the Arabs will believe them, and peace between them will gradually come. The Jews must always remember this. It is one of their greatest tasks here in Palestine and before the whole world. The success of all their work depends on the fulfillment of this task. "A very high price," some will say. But the price cannot be too high!
Felix Salten

Every responsible relationship with the others must begin with genuine, vivid imagination. If, as a sign of responsibility, we want to visualize what we are doing in Palestine, we must imagine viscerally and in all detail that we are the established population and the others are now coming into our country and want to take possession of more and more of it year after year! How would we feel about what was happening to us? How would we react to it? Only once we know that shall we learn not to do more injustice than we absolutely must to live. But living is not something we are permitted to do, it is something we should do. Because we live for the sake of the eternal task that we carry in ourselves.
Martin Buber

Above: Max Bodenheimer, chairman of the German Zionist organization, planting an olive tree as a symbolic gesture during a visit to a settlement in Palestine. 1904

Zionism triumphed – at least on the level of historical decisions in the history of the Jews – it owes its victory preeminently to three factors that left their imprint on its character: it was, all in all, a movement of the young, in which strong romantic elements inevitably played a considerable role; it was a movement of social protest, which drew its inspiration as much from the primordial and still vital call of the prophets of Israel as from the slogans of European socialism; and it was prepared to identify itself with the fate of the Jews in all – and I mean all – aspects of that fate, the religious and worldly ones in equal measure.
Gershom Scholem

Dear Mr. Sachs,
The distress of our Jewish fellow believers, particularly of the young, encourages me to comply with the wish of the people from the Werkbund (League for creativity in the applied arts) and warmly recommend to you, whom I know only as a generous art collector, the efforts of the Bund. We have been awakened all too rudely from the beautiful dream of assimilation. I see no hope for young Jews save going to Palestine, where they can grow up as free human beings and avoid the dangers of emigrant life.
Sadly, being in my 87th year, I am too old to go, but helping the rising generation of Jews to achieve freedom seems to me the most desirable way to help.
Max Liebermann

Reflections on one's Jewish heritage. The more the Jew is attacked because of his Judaism, the easier it is for him to turn away from imposed German nationalism and towards Judaism, which may have appeared disturbing, undesirable, alien, unimportant, old-fashioned, or restricted during his development. Now those who share his fate offer him comfort, understanding, encouragement, the strength to endure, and even a practical, usable liferaft: Palestine. The Zionist movement, born of German-speaking and Russian Judaism, advanced by men who – like Theodor Herzl, Max Nordau, and Martin Buber – were born in Vienna or Budapest, or – like Leon Pinsker, Uscher Ginsburg, and S. Dubnow – grew up in Russia, had always enjoyed the support of only a minority of German Jews. Our compatriots were afraid, and very wrongly so, that by excluding themselves from one-hundred percent German nationalism they would be risking emancipation and equal rights.
Arnold Zweig

Zionism is different from Jewish nationalism, for Zion is more than a nation. Zionism is an avowal of uniqueness . . . Nor is it a term linked solely with a geographical site, like Canaan or Palestine; it has always been a name for something that is to be at a certain geographical site; in the language of the Bible: the beginning of the Kingdom of God over all the human race.
Martin Buber

Joachim Riedl
SMOKE: THE GRAVE OF MILLIONS

There is a memorial on the site of the former concentration camp at Auschwitz now. A non-operational complex, a lifeless, shadowy inventory: unelectrified barbed wire, cold crematoriums, empty barracks. Grass grows over the tracks that once carried cattle wagon after cattle wagon crammed with human freight.

It is silent. There are reminders of the millions of deaths. Yet the tormented earth is still. Peace lies over the wounded land. The night and fog once rent by cold spotlight fingers have disappeared. No echo of shiny jackboots. No inmates' orchestra. No death rattle. The sharp panting of the bloodhounds has ceased, the barked commands and casual selection orders have yielded to deathly silence. A mute landscape; landscaped Auschwitz.

Where is the stone that marks the end of this historical journey? Stone is the material of our graves. Stone bears witness. Stone is the material of our purification. By erecting gravestones, the helpless expression of our longing to stay alive, we acknowledge the power of death. So it is in stone that we avow our humility toward life and the living.

There, where a corpse was no more than the by-product of a machine of human destruction. There, where a bastardization of death occurred long before the dying was over. There, where what remained after all the death and dying rose to heaven from

*S*ilence, the boundless silence of the unconcerned, of the pitilessly indifferent, accompanied the dull, distant grinding of the extermination machine. It devoured million upon million, more than lived in the country's largest cities, almost more than the Nazi era had minutes . . .

Above: Wedding rings of murdered prisoners at Mauthausen concentration camp (Upper Austria). 1945

Opposite page: A Jewish youth is forced by Nazis to paint "Jud" – Jew – on the façade of a shop in Vienna's Leopoldstadt, March 1938

the crematorium chimneys and dissolved into thin air, leaving not even the slightest tremor of a breeze. A heavy black pall of smoke hangs over this chapter of history. Smoke and helpless extinction. There are no stones to commemorate the dead who were robbed of death, the deathless dead, six million, seven million, no graves that might drag them out of oblivion into the terrifying images of memory.

The National Socialists had quickly realized that they needed only to strip the people of their humanity to the point where a mass of bodies re-

mained, soulless creatures whose fate could unhesitatingly be committed to dispassionate statistics. "Verjudet" – Jewified – before, "judenrein" – uncontaminated by Jews – afterwards. How easily that could be said, thought, read. Then.

That way the extermination camps could not be the death factories that are said to have been worse than all the hells and horrors any fire and brimstone preacher has ever described. What were those cyanide shower chambers and crematorium ovens? Nothing more than de-Jewification facilities, less disturbing than the slaughterhouses in the suburbs. Then.

And the blood that was shed there, did it stain? Did it mark those who had shed it? Did the neighbors pale when they met the de-Jewifier? On the stairs, perhaps, unexpectedly? Was sympathy expressed when the tailor's shop, when everything all around had been purified of Jews? Did people speak softly, or turn chalk-white, or whisper furtively about the harbinger of death? Were fingers pointed at him, did they pursue him? And what about his drinking companions? Then.

Did a wife freeze when she lay in the murderer's arms? And his breath; did the closeness make her shudder when the air from his lungs, which was the breath of murder, warmly, gently caressed her cheek? And the bloodstained hands that grasped her hips? Was she ashamed? Did she resist his embrace? Then.

It was silent. Soundless indifference accompanied what was happening. First they had abolished the human beings and then their death. What remained to be done was no more than insignificant routine; an organizational problem of enormous dimensions, but ultimately a technically solvable one. That is how it was then: a human being was no longer a human being who could have died a death, he was something (how revealing: *a thing*) that had to be disposed of, and the more disposed of, the better the execution reports read, production figures of a factory system that manufactured non-existence out of existence. Today bodies, tomorrow smoke.

Silence, the boundless silence of the unconcerned, of the pitilessly indifferent, accompanied by the dull, distant grinding of the extermination machine. It devoured million upon million, more than lived in the country's largest cities, almost more than the Nazi era had minutes.

And during all this time, not a sound. There is no keening for the dead, there are no funeral orations where there is no death, where there are no graves. "Silence, cooked like gold, in/ charred, charred hands./ Fingers smoke-thin, like crowns, crowns of air" (Paul Celan: *Chymisch*).

For what was one if one was a Jew and had ceased to be a human being? This sudden change from being to not-being, which still took place during physical existence and was cushioned between a pre- and a post-historic era, what caused it?

Was it no more than the heritage of anti-Semitism, the final murderous consequence? A thousand years and more it had blazed its bloody path without ever unleashing the fury of this hurricane of death.

They had burned the Jews alive. In Ancona the fires had smoldered at the stake, and in the torture chambers the Inquisitors had thrust at the Jewish heart; and in Vienna, where it is still called "Unter den Weissgerbern" (Among the Chamois-Dressers), it was a popular entertainment to listen to the stifled cries of the Jews as the flames licked at them and devoured them. Ghettos everywhere, flames everywhere, blood and torments. Numberless. Inescapable. A thousand years and more these Christians, who had crept out of the catacombs, had unceasingly persecuted the Jews – with whom they shared the *One God* – had hated and slandered them, had hounded them mercilessly from country to country. Popes, cossacks, despots, or even little village tyrants – all of them made the sign of the cross and then set upon them. The Catholic princes gave thanks to their Lord in Heaven and banished the Jews. It was their Christian duty. And this Christian occident, with its superabundance of moral precepts and doctrines of salvation, knew no mercy when the Jews got in the way.

Desecrators of the host, murderers of Christ, poisoners of wells, ritual murderers of Christian children "with multifarious concealment and destruction" – that remained the anti-Semitic creed until *Der Stürmer* [a violently anti-Semitic paper published by Julius Streicher between 1923 and 1945] rediscovered "the Jews' great hatred, vengeance, envy, and enmity toward the Christians" (*Flugschrift* [Pamphlet], Vienna, 1668). And, with panicky laments, gained the ear of the German people, who, whether Christian or not, were now to be "Aryan" in any case. And, defiling the language, extracted popular chauvinism from Christianity until only the fatal nakedness remained that makes a human being into a human being and a Jew what he is, an *Untermensch,* whose place is not *among* but *below* human beings. Probably among the rats that had carried the plague onto the medieval crusaders' ships – the plague for which the well-poisoning Jews had been blamed. No, they did not stint on fulsome language; by it shall ye recognize them.

In Christian Vienna, the Christian Socialist burgomaster Lueger possessed the veritable decency to tell his citizens: "What a Jew is, I decide."

The Frankish leader Streicher, on the other hand, who was only one mighty wordsmith among many, was not restrained by the niceties of Lueger's Jewish question. "What a human being is, I decide," he concluded.

The difference between the two men's arrogations amounted to six million.

At a single stroke the Jew had been exchanged for the human being, and the human being had become the stuff of history. Now it was no longer human history that demanded its sacrifices, it was history in general. But the actors had stepped out of history; they had objectified themselves and were now content to be villains, allowing themselves to become instruments and objects. Thus had the lofty Faustian spirit taken flight; and those whom the dream of the absolute drove to suspend the boundaries of life were cast out of the kingdom of life and death. They took the lives of others, but only at the expense of their own. Instead of shaping history they became the subject of the history they themselves had caused.

"The traces of my earthly days/ cannot perish down the eons." (J. W. Goethe: *Faust).* But there is no human trace, if it is historical fact, that cannot pass away, for it is "subject to all the flaws of the empirical, to change and passing away" (Hermann Broch: *Logik einer zerfallenden Welt*

[Logic of a disintegrating world]). What remains, and will remain until the end of time, is the huge black cloud of smoke that was the grave of millions. It is what obscures the heavens and cannot perish down the eons: the fog of history that shrouds every time of day in profound darkness.

Mass murder emerges from the abyss of hidden fears and passions: the blood it sheds is self-affirming. The mechanized obliteration of human beings, on the other hand, is an organized process, intent on efficiency, giving itself laws to operate by.

Cold and unfeeling, dehumanized and soulless, mechanized – with the machine directing the actions of the machinist (which instead of absolving him of guilt, redoubles it, for the machinist not only operates the machine, he also believes in it!) – thus proceeds the mechanized destruction of human beings. It does not want blood, nor does it revel in misery and torment. It wants far more. It wants the Absolute: Nothing.

For *it* happened. *There was* dying. *There was* life destroyed. Not: they were; no, *there was*. Therein lies the principle of Auschwitz: in the condemnation to absolute passiveness. Existence ceased to be: Here and There were decreed, and everyone who was either here or there was subject to that decree. That is the logic of mechanics. That is the way machines work, and according to its laws the machines of destruction can even produce Non-Being. "And everything happens to keep it in motion," writes Karl Kraus in *Die dritte Walpurgisnacht* [The third walpurgis night]; by their language alone he had recognized them.

I deny that there has ever been such a German-Jewish dialogue in any genuine sense whatsoever, i. e., as a historical phenomenon. It takes two to have a dialogue, who listen to each other, who are prepared to perceive the other as what he is and repre- sents, and to respond to him. Nothing can be more misleading than to apply such a concept to the discussions between Germans and Jews during the last 200 years. This dialogue died at its very start and never took place. It died when the successors of Moses Mendelssohn – who still argued from the perspective of some kind of Jewish totality, even though the latter was determined by the concepts of the Enlightenment – acquiesced in abandoning this wholeness in order to salvage an existence for pitiful pieces of it, whose recently popular designation as German-Jewish symbiosis re- veals its whole ambiguity. To be sure, the Jews attempted a dialogue with the Germans, starting from all possible points of view and situations, demandingly, imploringly, and en- treatingly, servile and defiant, with a dignity employing all manner of tones and a godfor- saken lack of dignity, and today, when the symphony is over, the time may be ripe for studying their motifs and for attempting a critique of their tones. No one, not even one who always grasped the hopelessness of this cry into the void, will belittle the latter's passionate intensity and the tones of hope and grief that were in resonance with it.
The attempt of the Jews to explain themselves to the Germans and to put their own creativi- ty at their disposal, even to the point of complete self-abnegation, is a significant phenomenon, the analysis of which in adequ- ate categories is yet to be accomplished and will perhaps become possible only now that it is at an end. In all this I am unable to perceive anything of a dialogue. Never did anything respond to that cry, and it was this simple and, alas, so far-reaching realization that affected so many of us in our youth and destined us to desist from the illusion of a "German-Judaism." Where Germans ven- tured on a discussion with Jews in a humane spirit, such a discussion, from Wilhelm von Humboldt to Stefan George, was always based on the expressed or unexpressed self- denial of the Jews, on the progressive atomi- zation of the Jews as a "community" in a state of dissolution, from which in the best case only the "individuals" could be received, be it as bearers of pure humanity, or be it even as bearers of a heritage that had in the mean- time become historical. It is that famous slogan from the battles of the Emancipation – "For the Jews as individuals, everything; for the Jews as a people (that is to say: as Jews) nothing" – which prevented a German-Jew- ish dialogue from getting started. The one and only partnership of dialogue which took the Jews as such seriously was that of the anti- Semites who, it is true, said something to the

Jews in reply, but nothing beneficial. To the infinite intoxication of Jewish enthusiasm there never corresponded a tone that bore any kind of relation to a creative answer to the Jews; that is to say, one that would have addressed them with regard to what they had "to give" as Jews, and not what they had to "give up" as Jews.
To whom, then, did the Jews speak in that much-talked-about German-Jewish dia- logue? They spoke to themselves, not to say that they outshouted themselves. Some felt uneasy, perhaps even dismal about it, but many acted as if everything were on the best

way to being settled, as if the echo of their own voice would be unexpectedly transmog- rified into that voice of the others they so eagerly hoped to hear. The Jews have always been listeners of great intensity, a noble legacy they brought with them from Mount Sinai. They listened to many kinds of voices, and one cannot say that this always served them well. When they thought they were speaking to the Germans, they were speaking to themselves. No one except Jews themselves, for example, was "spoken to" by the Jewish creativity of a thinker like Georg Simmel. And Simmel was indeed a truly symbolic phenomenon for all that of which I speak here, because he was that phenomenon of a man in whom the substance of Judaism still shows most visibly when the latter had arrived at the pure nadir of complete alienation. I will forgo the treatment of that deeply moving chapter that is designated by the great name of Hermann Cohen and the way in which this unhappy lover, who did not shun the step from the sublime to the ridiculous, was answered.

The allegedly indestructible community of the German essence with the Jewish essence consisted, so long as these two essences really lived with each other, only of a chorus of Jewish voices and was, on the level of historical reality, never anything else than a fiction, a fiction of which you will permit me to say that too high a price was paid for it. The Germans were mostly angered by this fiction and at best moved. Shortly before I went to Palestine, there appeared Jakob Wassermann's book, "Mein Weg als Deutscher und Jude" (My Way as German and Jew), certainly one of the most gripping documents of that fiction, a true cry into the void that knew itself to be such. The reply to him was in part embarrassment, in part sneer. One will look in vain for an answer on the level of the speaker, one that would thus have been a dialogue. And if once, directly before the onset of the catastrophe, it did indeed come to a dialogue in the form of a discussion, then it looked like that dialogue between the ex-members of the Wandervogel, Hans Joachim Schoeps and Hans Blüher, the reading of which even today causes the reader's hair to stand on end. But why heap up examples when, after all, the whole of that ghostlike German-Jewish dialogue ran its course in such an empty realm of the fictitious? I could speak of it endlessly, and I would nevertheless always be sticking to the same point.

It is true: the fact that Jewish creativity poured forth here is perceived by the Germans, now that all is over. I would be the last to deny that there is something genuine about that – at once gripping and depressing. But it no longer changes anything about the fact that no dialogue is possible with the dead, and to speak of an "indestructibility of this dialogue" strikes me as blasphemy.
Gershom Scholem

We were Germans; otherwise all that came later would not have been so terrible, so shattering. We spoke the cherished German language, in the truest sense of the word our mother tongue, in which we had received all the words and values of life, and language is, after all, almost more than blood. We knew none but the German fatherland, and we loved it with the same love of fatherland that would later be so fatal.
Margarete Susman

We do not wish to foist anything more on a country that has given us so much and that we gratefully strove to repay two- and threefold, for it does not value our thanks. Our relationship to Germany is that of an unhappy love affair: we finally want to be man enough to tear our mistress resolutely out of our hearts instead of endlessly pining away for her – though a piece of that heart be left behind.
Moritz Goldstein

The two springs – they are Judaism and German culture. When a man acts, it is from these two that his thoughts and feelings flow. I have never felt the conflict between the Jew and the German in me. In an overanalytical mind a gap might open up between them, but the emotions – which are decisive here – perceive them as a unity. And if ever I felt proud of anything, it was of being: a German and a Jew.
Jakob Loewenberg

Father and Grandfather were aware that if the poison that had contaminated Russian Poland was not to spread throughout Europe, the question of the eastern Jews, and not only those in Russia, had to be solved, not just in the philanthropic sense but in the cultural, economic, and perhaps even Jewish-national direction as well. I already realized then that I was a Jew in the religious-ethical sense and that this Judaism was as "katholos," in other words as "worldwide," as Roman Catholicism or one of the Protestant churches, but that I was politically and culturally a German, and there was no such thing as a specifically Protestant, Catholic, or Jewish way of being German. In other words, one had to render unto Caesar what was Caesar's and unto God what was God's. At least that is what I thought then, and prayed never to have to decide whether I wanted to be a German or a Jew.
Georg Tietz

Germany is neither a Christian theocratic state nor a Teutonic racial state; it is a community in spirit. We Jews are not Teutons, we are Semites, but that does not make us any less German. We shall always consider it the most galling effrontery if someone claims to be a better German simply because he is a blond, blue-eyed Schulze rather than a dark-haired, dark-eyed Cohn. Being German is a matter of temperament, not blood. A German is someone who wants to be a German.
Benno Jacob

We feel ourselves to be members of the same tribe and faith as all the Jews on the earth. We empathize deeply with their suffering and will never fail them in their distress; but we German Jews are and will remain Jewish by religion and German by nationality. What other nation could we belong to, what other country could be our fatherland if not the one in which our cradle stood and the graves of our fathers lie, whose air we have breathed since our birth, whose education we have absorbed, whose language we speak – the nation that feeds us and protects us, and for which we have now once again bled and suffered?
Benno Jacob

To the love of the Jews for Germany there corresponded the emphatic distance with which the Germans encountered them. We may grant that with "distant love" the two partners could have managed more kindness, open-mindedness, and mutual understanding. But historical subjunctives are always illegitimate. If it is true, as we now perceive, that "distant love" was the right Zionist answer to the mounting crisis in the relations between Jews and Germans, it is also true that the Zionist avant-garde hit upon it too late. For during the generations preceding the catastrophe, the German Jews – whose critical sense was as famous among Germans as it was irritating to them – distinguished themselves by an astounding lack of critical insight into their own situation.
Gershom Scholem

Generally speaking, the Jews' love affair with Germany remained one-sided and unrequited; at best it roused something like sentiment . . . and gratitude. Gratitude the Jews frequently encountered, but the love they sought, hardly ever.
Gershom Scholem

Few observers in the world seem to have genuinely considered precisely what the book burning, the expulsion of Jewish writers, and all of the Third Reich's other demented attempts to destroy the spirit mean . . .
In these times, with the smoke of our burned books ascending to heaven, we German writers of Jewish descent must above all recognize that we have been defeated. Let us who formed the first wave of soldiers to fight under the banner of the European spirit fulfill the noblest task of the warrior vanquished with honor; let us admit our defeat. Yes, we have been beaten . . .
In a time when His Holiness the infallible Pope of Christianity makes a peace pact called the "concordat" with the enemies of Christ, when the Protestants found a "German Church" and censor the Bible, we remain descendants of the ancient Jews, of the ancestors of European culture, and the only legitimate German representatives of this culture . . .
The incontestable achievement of Jewish writers in the domain of German literature consists in their discovery and literary exploitation of urbanism. The Jews discovered and described the cityscape and the city-dweller's soulscape. They unveiled urban civilization in all its diversity. They discovered the coffee-house and the factory, the bar and the hotel, the bank and the petit bourgeoisie of the capital, the meeting places of the rich and the slums, sin and vice, the city by day and the city by night, the character of the people who live in the big cities. Talented Jews were predestined for this because of the urban environment in which most of them grew up and into which society had driven their parents, but also because of their more highly developed sensibilities and the cosmopolitan gift characteristic of the Jews. The majority of non-Jewish German writers limited themselves to describing the landscape that was their home.
Joseph Roth

Drunken hordes at the palace and in the streets. Now they are still drinking wine, soon they will be swilling blood; now the torches still light their way, soon their roofs will burn and blaze, burn, burn, burn. And the books will go up in smoke as well.
Hermann Broch

What do you suppose you will do with the two rooms that contained my library? Books, I have been told, are not very popular in the Reich in which you live, Herr X, and whoever deals with them soon runs into trouble. I, for example, read the book by your "Führer" and harmlessly noted that his 140,000 words are 140,000 violations of the spirit of the German language. As a result of that statement, you are now sitting in my house. I sometimes wonder what bookcases could be used for in the Third Reich.
Lion Feuchtwanger

The German cataclysm, which we have been witnessing with astonished eye and ear for two years now, has even reached grammar. Reduced to a concise phrase, its basic statute says: abolish subject and predicate.
Anton Kuh

Asphalt literature and regional/sentimental art, the division is clear. It corresponds approximately to the division of people into healthy and sick "national comrades": the healthy ones being those who march in rank and file, do not ponder authority, and refresh themselves at Ganghofer's fragrant fountain, whereas the ones considered sick are those who cannot suppress an inclination to probe the context of things and to ask themselves about the meaning of life.
Anton Kuh

Austria is the cradle of the Germanic world. It is the place where both the good and the evil of the central European spirit were born, point and counterpoint; it was the birthplace of anti-Semitism and of Zionism, of the First Reich and the Third Reich, of Hitler and Mozart. It is where the German language first saw the light of the day in the "Nibelungenlied" (in Pöchlarn on the Danube). It is where the German language died several hundred years later (in Braunau on the Inn).
Anton Kuh

Below: SA officers in Hamburg confiscating literature for the book burning. Photograph by Joseph Schorer. May 15, 1933

As, I believe, I have said already, I am always being torn against my will from environments which I have thoughtfully, lovingly moulded to my tastes and my needs. Again and again I have surrounded myself with things that I enjoyed owning; again and again I have set up a very ample writing table at a place from which I could look out over a beautiful landscape; again and again I have ranged a few thousand books about me; again and again I have reared a number of cats and each time thought they were devoted to me for my own sake; again and again I

have bought a number of turtles and watched their slow, antediluvian movements; again and again I have put by a few bottles of choice wine in an air-conditioned room. And however often circumstances over which I had no control compelled me to forsake abodes that I had furnished with so much solicitude, I never learned my lesson. I would always begin building over again, then cling spiritually and literally to what I had built, confident that this time I must surely be able to keep it.
Lion Feuchtwanger

Above: Burning "un-German writings and books" on Opernplatz in Berlin. May 10, 1933

Yes, we love this country.
And now let me tell you something: it is not true that those who call themselves "nationalists" and are nothing more than little bourgeois patriots have a monopoly on this country and its language.
Not only the honorable government representative in his frock coat, and the distinguished professor, and the gentlemen and ladies of the steel helmet are Germany. We are still here, too. They make grandiloquent statements and proclaim "in the name of Germany . . . !" They shout: "We love this country, we and only we love it." That is not true.
. . . And the way the nationalist associations beat their own drum – we have the same right, the very same right, we who were born here, we who write and speak German better than the majority of nationalist jackasses – we have the selfsame right to appropriate river and forest, beach and house, clearing and meadow for ourselves: it is our country.
. . . Germany is a divided country. Part of it is us. And despite the differences, what remains – unswerving, with neither flag nor hurdy-gurdy, neither sentimentality nor drawn sword – is that quiet love of our homeland.
Kurt Tucholsky

Your homeland was called Germany. Their homeland is called Germany. That is where they have lived for centuries, where they have worked and become verifiably creative. The book you so kindly wished to read, "Bilanz der deutschen Judenheit 1933" (German Jewry 1933: a balance sheet), described this process . . .
You did not believe the Germans capable of it. Neither did I. You did not believe that the Germans would swallow that garbage. Neither did I. But lo and behold, they swallowed it enthusiastically . . . That we were so wrong, that we so overestimated the people we grew up with does us no honor, but it does not discredit us either . . . We were mistaken about the Germans' degree of civilization and the Europeans' passion for their culture.
Arnold Zweig

I knew nothing, least of all about myself, but I had the constant feeling: this cannot last.
Hans Mayer

To bring alive for future generations this terrible time of waiting and transition, the darkest Germany had experienced since the Thirty Years' War. For it will be impossible for those future generations to understand why we could bear that kind of life for so long, incomprehensible to them that we waited so long before drawing the only sensible conclusion, namely that the reign of violence and absurdity had to be stopped by means of violence on our side and that a sensible order had to be established in its stead. Why we did not do it, why most did not even want to, why even the few who realized what was happening went on living from day to day in such a strange and inexplicable way: to make this wretched, bitter, insane, heroic existence in the long period of waiting and transition comprehensible to generations to come, that is what the cycle of novels "Der Wartesaal" (The waiting-room) attempts to accomplish.
Lion Feuchtwanger

It is time to destroy some dangerous illusions. Not only democrats, but socialists and communists, too, are inclined to feel that Hitler should be allowed to govern because that would be the quickest way for him to "make a mess of things." What they forget is that the National Socialist Party is characterized by its will to power and retaining power. Of course they will put up with democracy as a means of coming to power, but they will never let democracy take that power away from them again.
Ernst Toller

We watched with growing concern as the "Gleichschaltung" (imposed conformity) of public opinion in Germany began to succeed. We had to accept that the hopes many people harbored of seeing National Socialist policies moderated were futile. Accordingly, emigration activity increased in all Jewish circles, including our own.
Kurt Baumann

Left: Organized Nazi vandalism in Berlin; the sign urges the public to boycott Jewish businesses ("Germans Defend yourselves. Do not buy from Jews"). Summer 1933

Opposite page: Z.b.V. (zur besonderen Verwendung – for special use) police squad raid in Berlin's Scheunenviertel: the Jewish occupants of a house on Grenadier-strasse have been driven into the courtyard, and are being checked for weapons and forced to produce proof of identification. April 5, 1933

If the German nationalists did not possess the almost ruminant barnyard torpor of nineteenth-century Pomeranian roughriders, they would long ago have discarded the slogan "Finish off the Jews," despite its admittedly populist appeal – in which case three quarters of today's Jews would be sitting where they belong from the standpoint of class: in the German People's Party. That they are not is because its anti-Semitism repels them; and some of them, in fact, are because they have a greater fondness for their bank accounts than for a religion that is no more to them than its Christmas celebration and the "Frankfurter Zeitung."
Kurt Tucholsky

I cannot get over the fact that people whose fathers were born on Markish soil, fought valiantly and bled in the wars of 1864 and 1866, who were themselves soldiers, saw active service, went off to war as reservists, should no longer be acknowledged as Germans. It is an unbearable thought to me that the banners of the old regiments under which I myself and my fathers served may no longer be a symbol for me.
Central-Verein Zeitung (Central-Verein Paper), 1933

The death of my mother, the execution of the six young people in Cologne (the youngest 18, the oldest 28), the murder of my friends – each death is a legacy. Wild animals kill when they are hungry, these barbarians murder out of satiated vengeance and take pleasure in that vengeance. That they should be ripped out of the soil of Europe leaf and root, that is something for me to live for. I have occasionally considered mustering the emigrants with the strict discipline of a legion – it would be a futile attempt. The emigrants of 1933 are a desolate heap of chance outcasts, including a great many Jewish Nazis manqués, weaklings with vague ideas, virtue-mongers whom Hitler prevents from being pigs, and only a very few men with convictions. Germans all too German.
Ernst Toller

A sense of the situation there is better conveyed by the totality of the cultural state of affairs than by the particulars of individual acts of terror. It is difficult to obtain absolutely reliable information about the latter. Without any doubt there are countless cases of people being dragged from their bed in the middle of the night, and tortured or murdered. . . .

In my case it was not these conditions – more or less foreseeable for some time – that prompted me barely one week ago to transform what were ill-defined wishes to leave Germany into a hard and fast decision. Rather, it was the almost mathematical simultaneity with which every conceivable office returned manuscripts, broke off negotiations either in progress or in the final stages, and left inquiries unanswered. Every attitude or manner of expression that does not fully conform to the official one is terrorized – a reign of terror that has reached virtually unsurpassable heights.

Walter Benjamin

Above: Jew-baiting on the display window of a Jewish clothing store. ("Don't you think I'm a good Tschoiman?") Photograph by Heinrich Hoffmann. 1938
Below: Boycott propaganda against Jewish store-owners. SA and SS officers in front of a women's wear store in Berlin. April 1, 1933
Opposite page: "Kohn Isaak and Co . . . . To Jerusalem": Nazi vandalism and boycott signs in two languages on the window of a women's wear store in Berlin. April 1, 1933

Dear friends, we are turning to you in a very pressing and confidential matter. In view of the current situation in Germany, we have decided to insure our property in Berlin – both movable effects and realty – against damage by pogroms; against destruction of the house, the furniture, and the machinery as well as against fire resulting from riots. We are considering taking out this insurance with Lloyds. For reasons you will understand, we have decided that you, the Zionist Executive, should apply for and effect the insurance on our behalf, naming us as the insured party. We request you to let us know immediately whether you are prepared to take over the matter. As soon as we receive your basic assent, we will send you a detailed draft of our proposal to be forwarded to Lloyds. Hoping for your immediate reply, we are thankfully and with Zionist regards, Zionistische Vereinigung für Deutschland (Zionist Association for Germany)
Dr. Georg Landauer

Let us beware of weaklings who preach restraint at a time like this, and let us unwaveringly hold fast to what emancipation has achieved! We should not and will not voluntarily retreat a single step from our equal rights as citizens! . . . We believe in the forces of good among the German people, we believe that these forces will soon awaken, even in the right-wing camp. We will remain as we are, and because we remain so, we will do credit to both the Jewish and the German spirit in us.
Central-Verein Zeitung, 1932

The Jewish community drew closer together. The optimistic articles in the Zionist "Jüdische Rundschau" (Jewish review) did a great deal to raise people's spirits. We tried to start a Jewish school in Hanau, but the government refused to grant its consent. Businesses were harassed . . . The pressure on customers to stay away from Jewish shops became stronger. The NS-Handels-Organisation (Nazi commercial organization) did meticulous work.
Carl Schwabe

Above: "500,000 unemployed/ 400,000 Jews/Solution very simple": anti-Semitic Nazi propaganda for the city council election in Vienna. Photograph by Lothar Rübelt. 1932

Right: Terror and humiliation–no realm was too intimate: SA officers pillory a woman and her Jewish boyfriend in front of local Nazi headquarters in Cuxhaven ("I am the greatest pig in town and only have affairs with Jews" / "As a Jewboy I *always* take only German girls up to my room!"). July 27, 1933

*W*e, on the contrary, knew that whatever was the most monstrous was the natural thing to expect. Everyone of us had the vision of a slain friend, a tortured comrade in our mind's eye, hence had harder, sharper, more pitiless eyes. The proscribed, the hunted, the expropriated knew that no pretext was too absurd or false when robbery and power were concerned.
Stefan Zweig

*I*t had to be the liberator of the stenotypists [Hugo Bettauer] that the young German moralist and his heroic mentality took a fancy to. A nationalist paper splashed a denunciatory headline about him across the front page, and below it, in equally large letters, the exhortation: "Our blond girls as fair game for lecherous Jewish rascals" – a phrase that, apart from a graceful grouping of plural s's, distinguishes itself only through the naive admission of where the heart of German nationalism actually lies . . .
Anton Kuh

We of the new generation who have learned not to be surprised by any outbreak of bestiality, we who each new day expect things worse than the day before, are markedly more skeptical about a possible moral improvement of mankind. We must agree with Freud, to whom our culture and civilization were merely a thin layer liable at any moment to be pierced by the destructive forces of the "underworld." We have had to accustom ourselves gradually to living without the ground beneath our feet, without justice, without freedom, without security. Long since, as far as our existence is concerned, we have denied the religion of our fathers, their faith in a rapid and continuous rise of humanity. To us, gruesomely taught, witnesses of a catastrophe which, at a swoop, hurled us back a thousand years of humane endeavor, that rash optimism seems banal. But even though it was a delusion our fathers served, it was a wonderful and noble delusion, more humane and more fruitful than our watchwords of today; and in spite of my later knowledge and disillusionment, there is still something in me which inwardly prevents me from abandoning it entirely. That which, in his childhood, a man has drawn into his blood out of the air of time cannot be taken from him. And in spite of all that is daily blasted into my ears, and all that I myself and countless other sharers of my destiny have experienced in trials and tribulations, I cannot completely deny the faith of my youth, that some day things will rise again – in spite of all. Even in the abyss of despair in which today, half-blinded, we grope about with distorted and broken souls, I look up again and again to those old star patterns that shone over my childhood, and comfort myself with the inherited confidence that this collapse will appear, in days to come, as a mere interval in the eternal rhythm of the onward and onward.
Stefan Zweig

Above: Making a mockery of the Jewish inhabitants of Baden-Baden: they are being driven through the streets of the city by the SS, carrying the sign "God will not desert us." November 1938

Below: Humiliating the Jewish inhabitants of Vienna: after Hitler's entrance into Vienna, they are forced, under the scrutiny of Hitler Youths – and with the derisive participation of the population – to join so-called "Reibpartien", scrubbing parties, and clean the Schuschnigg government's Austria slogans off the streets on their hands and knees. March 1938

Right: "Jews enter this park at their own risk." Jews were only warned not to enter parks, they had already been forbidden to sit on park benches for years: sign on the gate of a public park in Vienna. Vienna 1938

Juden
betreten diese
Parkanlage auf
eigene Gefahr.

Above: Farewell celebration for a group of youths who, with the help of the Youth Alijah, were given the opportunity to emigrate to Palestine in 1938. Photograph by *Abraham Pisarek*. 1938

Below: Spanish course for emigration-minded members of the Jewish community in Berlin. Photograph by *Abraham Pisarek*. 1935

*O*ur B'nai Brith women's group also succeeded in organizing school meals for needy school children. We did what we could, but we could not help the families that had fallen into the hands of the Gestapo; in those cases we were totally powerless. The Gestapo did not even acknowledge the objections of Jewish lawyers, and Christian attorneys were afraid to represent Jews.

If God did not help, there was no help for us anymore. No one could be certain he would not disappear behind the electrically charged barbed wire of a concentration camp the following day and either never come back, or if he did, then only broken under the cruel torture of body and soul.
Marta Appel

*I*n self-defense we once demanded: Do not allow yourselves to get used to it! Namely to the way Jews are systematically being stripped of their rights in Germany and to the fact that this has become an everyday occurrence without much ado. The chronological occasion for that exhortation was the half-year anniversary of the existence of the Third Reich; in the meantime, only another few months and it will have reached the five year mark, which makes it the most gigantic source of anti-Semitism on this earth. Do not get used to it: to revocation of rights, humiliation, the stream of vituperation constantly being poured out over us Jews there, to the hardships of emigration and the collapse of a healthy branch of the Jewish people.
Hans Lichtwitz

*H*is parents registered him at a Jewish school. One of his new classmates took him along to a meeting of a Jewish youth group. There he discovered a new world. Up to now being a Jew had brought him nothing but trouble and grief. Now he learned to be proud of his Judaism. When they were together in the group, he felt free and happy. He read a lot now, dipping into 3,500 years of Jewish history, learning about the heroes of Jewish liberation like the Maccabees, about the fearlessness of the prophets, and about the religious counter-world of Hasidism. Friedrich joined a Zionist group. He went to lectures that invoked the end of the history of Jewish suffering and the beginning of a new era. He dreamed the dream of Theodor Herzl and Martin Buber. Friedrich decided to go to Palestine as a farmer and pioneer. There were violent quarrels with his parents. "We are Germans," his father had informed him, "what do we care about a desert in Palestine. We were and we are Germans. We speak German and we feel German! I won't let some riff-raff of a Mustachekowski (by which he meant Hitler) and some drunken beer-hall rabble in uniform dispute my Germanhood."

"And where," countered Friedrich, "are your Germans? Where are your friends, where are your fellow war veterans? If the Germans don't want us, we don't need them. Stand up for your own people. Germany isn't your home, Eretz Israel is." They were distressing quarrels, not only because of their violence but because of the apparent impossibility to understand each other.
Günther B. Ginzel

Dear fellow citizens! Our young people are at stake, the future of Judaism! Young Jews are as oppressed economically and mentally as the old and have no possibility, under the given circumstances, of getting together privately with people of similar age to unburden themselves in convivial surroundings and forget the cares and worries of everyday life. Young people occasionally need to relax and be allowed to be cheerful and happy. Young people should not constantly be trapped in thoughts of their fate. New strength to live arises only from the will to shape one's life. Those who only ponder the cares that surround them lose their will to live and forget how to be cheerful and happy. This is where we want to help! We want to give our young people the opportunity to meet unencumbered by the troubles of the time, to get to know each other and unburden themselves. We want to create this possibility far away from all religious, ideological, or political controversy, purely on the basis of a feeling of belonging together, which has brought us together and keeps us together. And so we let the young people laugh and dance, and do not raise a threatening finger of admonition and warn them of the seriousness of the time. Think instead of your own youth, of all the happy hours you were able to spend in your home surroundings.
To accomplish the goal we have set ourselves, we need your help: bring your young people to us, invite your children and your grandchildren to come to our events. Notify us on the enclosed card of the addresses of our young fellow citizens, so we can invite them to join us. We do not want to form youth groups, we want our young people to come to our gatherings and spend a few hours together, free of the burdens of the time. Our young people are at stake, the future of Judaism!
Verband Jüdischer Heimatvereine (League of Jewish local associations)

Right: Morning prayers on board a refugee ship bound for South America. Photograph by B. Federmeyer. 1938

Apart from all our other obligations, we had been busy for weeks preparing a large number of young people for their departure for Palestine. The young Jews were as passionately enthusiastic about the idea of building a new home in Palestine as the young Germans were about building a new Germany. They flocked to register, and everyone tried to get onto the first transports. This zeal was not born only of the wish to escape the defamation and hatred of Germany, but equally of the vision of finding a great and holy task in Palestine that was worth living for. In no other country had the idea of rebuilding Palestine encountered as many [Jewish] opponents as in Germany, in no other country had so fierce a stand been taken against the Zionists. The older generation still firmly rejected Zionism. "By religion we are Jews, but politically we are Germans," was the principle firmly rooted in the German Jews' thinking. Hatred and persecution could not destroy our love for our homeland. That is why young Jews' enthusiasm for Palestine caused such grave conflicts in many families.
Marta Appel

Left: The dream of emigrating. Even the remotest, most exotic countries were considered, the most grotesque plans forged, but few were able to obtain, let alone afford, the visa that would save them. Photograph by *Abraham Pisarek*. Ca. 1938

Below: Jewish emigrants' bureau in Berlin. 1935

Opposite page: Jewish parents at the Anhalter railroad station in Berlin, saying good-bye to their children, who were being sent to Palestine under the auspices of the Youth Alijah. Some 4,000 children were able to be saved this way up to autumn 1939. Photograph by *Abraham Pisarek*. 1936

If I am permitted already at this point to give a first and tentative answer to the question of how much home a person needs, I would say: all the more, the less of it he can carry with him. For there is, after all, something like a transportable home, or at least an ersatz for home. That can be religion, like the Jewish one. "Next year in Jerusalem," the Jews have promised themselves for generations during their Passover ritual, but it wasn't at all a matter of really getting to the Holy Land; rather it sufficed to pronounce the formula together and to know that one was united in the magic domain of the tribal God Yahweh.
Jean Améry

I see I will always be alone. jewish, german-speaking, in france; jew without god and without knowledge of our past; german-speaking but, unlike my countrymen and like-tongued people, not prepared to let the german language go to wrack and ruin. in france, i.e. without readers . . . i will never be at home in french literature; for i dream and reflect in german. so now, through Hitler, i have been condemned to total homelessness and alienation.
Carl Einstein

*You all know that I have never done anything that could harm Germany. You know that even before I embarked on my trip to the United States, I had written to my American friends that I would talk neither publicly nor unofficially about Germany, on the one hand because I am no longer authorized to represent German cultural affairs and on the other because I cannot bring myself to make disparaging statements about the country where my family has lived for 225 years.
You know that I have always had unshakable faith in the victory of the good in human nature and have lived for it. I will continue in the same way, "according to the law to which I am pledged."*
Alice Salomon

There is no "new home." Home is the land of one's childhood and youth. Whoever has lost it remains lost himself, even if he has learned not to stumble about in the foreign country as if he were drunk, but rather to tread the ground with some fearlessness.
Jean Améry

*O*n the other hand, I also had telling proof of the Aryan population's seething hatred for the present "brown" regime. An old farmer's wife could not restrain herself from roundly cursing the "brown" plague so loudly that I had to beg her to be more careful in the future. While I was talking to this woman, more and more farmers and their wives joined us. When they heard I was emigrating to America, they were absolutely silent at first, but then the tallest of them said: "Who will see to it from now on that we can sell our wine every year?" They all invited me to their homes for a last glass of wine. Because time was so short, I had to decline, but within a quarter of an hour eight women came, and each had a farewell gift under her apron – butter, eggs, bread, kirsch, and a freshly slaughtered chicken. I was very touched by their kindness, and when I had already said good-bye and thanked them and was about to climb into the car, the mayor's daughter appeared with a large bouquet of fresh lilies of the valley for my wife. I still like to think back on that hour, when the old Germany wanted to show me once more what it was really like!
Friedrich Weil

*F*or me emigration was only the confirmation of not belonging, something I had experienced since earliest childhood. I had never possessed home ground.
Peter Weiss

*A*t the time there was an anecdote circulating among the emigrants about the Jew who was planning to emigrate to Uruguay. When his friends in Paris were astonished that he wanted to go so far away, his response was: Far away from where?
Peter Szondi

*A*ll my pulses hammer.
From the shouts: up and away!
And I obey and weep
Weep, because the heart is orphaned
Because a millenium has iced over.
Karl Wolfskehl

*L*et us not deceive ourselves about the following three crucial facts: firstly, that the majority of German emigrants are Jews; secondly, that there is latent anti-Semitism in most countries; thirdly, that of all the reproaches made against the Third Reich, the charge of bestial anti-Semitism will have the least effect.
The contrary is more likely to be true: the anti-Semitism of the Third Reich is among its most effective propaganda weapons. It strikes at the heart of the latent bestial instinct of every plebeian outside the Third Reich.
Joseph Roth

*W*e were expelled from Germany because we are Jews. But hardly had we crossed the border to France than we were made into "krauts" . . . For seven years we played a ridiculous role in the attempt to become French or at least ordinary . . . We were the first "prisonniers volontaires" history has ever seen. After the German invasion, the French government only needed to change the name of the company; we had been imprisoned because we were Germans, now we were not freed because we were Jews.
Hannah Arendt

*O*nly one thing remained reachable, close and secure amid all losses: language. Yes, language. In spite of everything, it remained secure against loss. But it had to go through its own lack of answers, through terrifying silence, through the thousand darknesses of murderous speech. It went through. It gave me no words for what was happening, but went through it. Went through and could resurface, 'enriched' by it all.
In this language I tried, during those years and the years after, to write poems: in order to speak, to orient myself, to find out where I was, where I was going, to chart my reality.
Paul Celan

Die Synagoge wird abgebrochen

Komm lieber Mai und mache   von Juden uns jetzt frei.

Above: "We take leave of our big, beautiful house of God. Taking leave has become the overwhelming Jewish fate of our days": on April 15, 1939, the Jews of the "free city of Danzig" gathered for a last time in their large synagogue at the Reitbahn. It was torn down on June 9, 1939. The signs read: (on the building) "This synagogue is to be torn down" and (in the foreground) "Come lovely May and make us free of Jews." Photograph by Douglas Alcombe.

Below: Interior of the synagogue on Fasanenstrasse in Berlin after the so-called "Reichskristallnacht." November 9, 1938

And now to the Jewish people, this people to whom ordinary rules do not apply. It has experienced unparalleled suffering and has as a whole, though specific individuals may have failed, shown an unparalleled greatness that promises a future. The Jewish people has often been torn apart and scattered in many a country, but it has never capitulated. It has always, or at least in its best times, been an apolitical people, but for that a people with an idea, a faith.
Leo Baeck

That is truly what Judaism had been and was alone to continue being: the un-classical element in the Classical world, the un-modern in the modern world. That is how the Jew had to be as a Jew: the great nonconformist in history, the great dissenter. That is what he was there for. That was the reason the battle for religion was always a battle for self-preservation. There was no thought of power in it, that would have been a contradiction – not power, but individuality, personality for the sake of the eternal, not power but strength. Jewish existence in the world lives as strength. And strength is greatness.
Leo Baeck

Religion? I am an atheist. Jewish nationalism? I am an internationalist. In neither sense am I, therefore, a Jew. I am, however, a Jew by force of my unconditional solidarity with the persecuted and exterminated. I am a Jew because I feel the Jewish tragedy as my own tragedy; because I feel the pulse of Jewish history; because I should like to do all I can to assure the real, not spurious, security and self-respect of the Jews.
Isaac Deutscher

Right: Waiting for deportation – from 1940/41 on, there was no other alternative for the German Jews: Laibisch Banach, a well-known Zionist functionary from Bendzin.

We wanderers,
At every crossroads a door awaits us
Behind it the doe, the orphan-eyed Israel of
the animals
Disappears in its rustling woods
And the lark rejoices above the golden fields.
A sea of loneliness stands motionless with us
Wherever we knock.
Oh, you guardians with flaming swords,
The dust under our wandering feet
Is already beginning to rouse the blood of our
grandchildren –
Oh, we wanderers outside the doors of the
world,
Our hats already have stars pinned on
Souvenirs of greetings from afar.
Like yardsticks our bodies lie on the ground
And measure out the horizon –
Oh, we wanderers,
Crawling worms for shoes to come,
Our deaths will lie like thresholds
Before your locked doors!
Nelly Sachs

At assembly points, human beings were reduced to mere numbers, with cardboard signs round their necks, and forced to wait for hours or even days. Under the pretext of a luggage check, virtually everything they had with them was confiscated. Their "destination," which no one knew but many suspected, was extermination.

Below: Assembly point for deportation at the Grossmarkthalle in Wiesbaden. 1942

Opposite page: After the so-called "Reichskristallnacht," SS and police drive the Berlin Jews who have been arrested to assembly points to be transported to Sachsenhausen concentration camp. November 10, 1938

But the longer one of them had placed trust in Germany, the greater his reluctance to wrench himself from his beloved home, the more severely he had been punished. First the Jews had been deprived of their professions; they were forbidden the theaters, the movies, the museums, and scholars lost the use of the libraries; they had stayed because of loyalty or of indolence, cowardice or pride. They preferred being humiliated at home to humiliating themselves as beggars abroad. They were not permitted to have servants, radios and telephones were removed from their homes, then the homes themselves were taken; the star of David was forced on them so that they might be recognized, avoided and mocked like lepers expelled and proscribed. Every right was withdrawn from them, every spiritual and physical cruelty was practiced on them with playful sadism.
Stefan Zweig

Above: Even children had to wear the "Judenstern," the Jewish star: unidentified girl from Berlin. After 1941

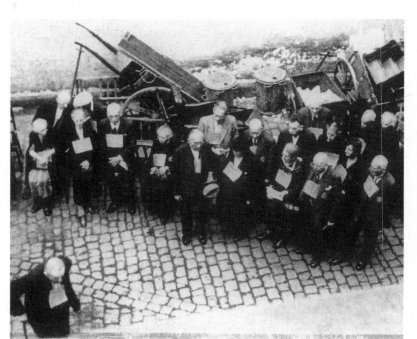

In those hours I frequently spoke with Freud about the horror of Hitler's world and the war. The outburst of bestiality deeply shocked him as a humanitarian, but as a thinker he was in no way astonished. He had always been scolded as a pessimist, he said, because he had denied the supremacy of culture over the instincts; but his opinion that the barbaric, the elemental destructive instinct in the human soul was ineradicable, has become confirmed most terribly. Not that he got any satisfaction in being right. Perhaps coming centuries might find a formula to control those instincts, at least as regards the common concerns of people; in everyday life, however, and deep within man they survived ineradicably, perhaps as useful energizing agents. The problem of Judaism and its present tragedy occupied him even more in those days but his science provided no formula and his lucid mind found no solution. Shortly before that he had published his work on Moses in which he presented Moses as a non-Jew, an Egyptian, thus giving offense by this allocation of dubious scientific worth to devout Jews and to those holding the nationalist ideal. He had come to regret having published the book right in the most terrible hour of Jewry, "now that everything is being taken from them, I had to go and take their best man." I could not but agree with him that by now every Jew's sensitiveness had increased sevenfold for even in the midst of the world tragedy they were the real victims, everywhere the victims, because, already dispersed before the blow, they knew that whatever evil was to come would touch them first and with sevenfold force, and that the most hate-maddened man of all times wished to humiliate them especially and to harry them to the end of and under the earth.
Stefan Zweig

Right: "I saw a mountain . . . made of Jewish glasses in Mauthausen." 1945

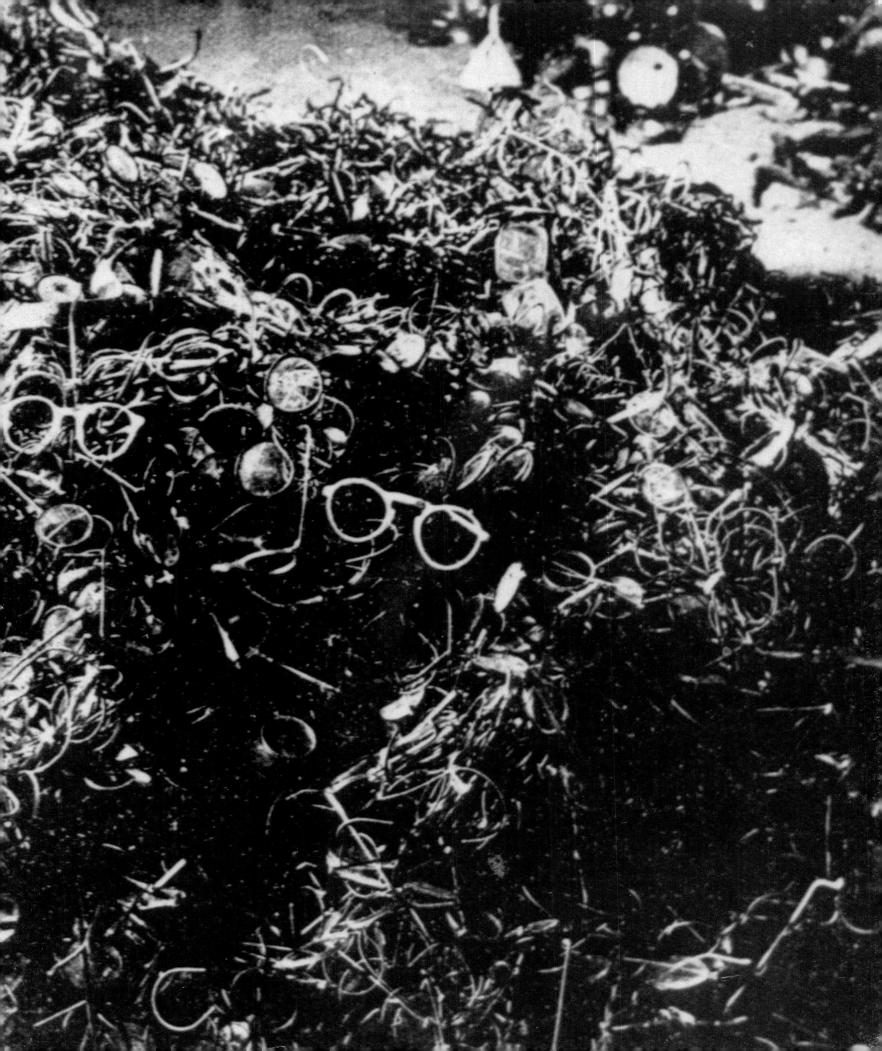

Moische Schulstein
CH'HOB GESEJN A BARG / I SAW A MOUNTAIN

Ch'hob gesejn a Barg –
is er hecher gewejn fun
    Montblanc,
un heiliger fun'em Barg Sinai,
nischt in Trojm – ojf der Wahr, ojf
    der Erd
is er geschtanen –
asa Barg, asa Barg hob ich gesejn
fun jidische Schich in Majdanek.

Asa Barg, asa Barg hob ich gesejn.

Un pluzzem, wie s'wollt durch a
    Wunder geschejn,
ch'hob dersejn
wie er riert sich un riert fun'em Ort,
un die tojsenter Schich schtelln ojs
    sich allejn
zu der Moß, zu der Poor,
un in Reijen –
un geijen . . .

Hert-ojs, hert-ojs dem Marsch, hert
    ojs dem Hymen
fun Schich varbliebene – dem letzten
    Simen
fun Klein un Grojs, fun Kind-und-
    Keit.
A Ware far die Reijen, far die Pooren,
a Ware far die Dojres, far die Johren! –
Die Schich-Armee, sie geijt und geijt.

Mir sennen Schich, mir sennen letzte
    Eides,
mir sennen Schich fun Einiklech und
    Seides,
fun Prag, Paris un Amsterdam.
Un weil mir sennen blojß fun Stoff un
    Leder –
un nischt fun Blut un Fleisch – hot
    jeder
gemittn dem Gehennim-Flamm.

Hert-ojs, hert-ojs dos ojsgemischte
    Trettn
fun alle Geng! Fun Rebbns
    Schtiwelettn,
und Schtiwl proste un gemein,
fun proste Jidn, fun Kazojwim-
    Schinder,
un fun geschtrickte Schichelech fun
    Kinder,
wus heibn nor-wos un zu geijn.

Mit Klangen allerlei die Sojln
    raschen:
Gescharrech fun Chussns gemsene
    Kamaschn,
der Kalles Letschelech fun Seid, –
si sennen zu der Chupe nischt
    dergangen,
itzt jammern noch sei die Chupe-
    Stangen,
varlosn ergetz, in a Seit.

Mir, Schich fun Jass, fun Munkacz un
    fun Athen,
wos flegn geijn zu Merk un zu
    Warschtattn,
un geijn bescholem unser Weg,
in Kram, Fabrik, in Kinder-Schul, in
    Cheder.
Itzt geijn mir – Jerusche fun an Eide,
wos is fun uns aweg, aweg . . .

Weil s'hot Gebein un Fleisch dem
    Flamm gesteijet,
hot uns der Feier-Pisk varsucht un
    nischt verdeijet,
un ojsgeschpign in a Seit, –
itzt hert, itzt hert in unser Sojln-
    Skrippen,
s'zescheid-gewein un dos Millionen
    Chlippen,
wos geijt uns noch wie a Bagleit.

Mir, Schich, wos flegn geijn in Park
    spaziern,
un Chussn-Kalle zu der Chupe fiern,
un geijn asoi Dor-ojs, Dor-ein
ojf Simches, Chassenes, un gejn zu
    Kimpet,
un hojch a Tanz-geijn, full mit Rasch
    un Impet,
un ruig of Leweijes gejn.

Bis einmul in a Trojer-Zug a langen,
ojf eigener Leweije schtill gegangen,
zescheid mit Gang fun Alt un Jung,
wenn Lebn is aweg fun uns varborgn,
hot uns der Sam geschojnt un nischt
    geworgn,
wojl mir – ohn Harz, ohn Kehl, ohn
    Lung.

Ohn Apru geijen mir un klappn,
    klappn . . .
s'hot nischt bawisn uns
    areinzuchappn
der Talion in sein Rojber-Sack, –
itzt geijen mir zu ihm, s'soll jeder
    hern
die Tritt, wos geijen wie der Fluß fun
    Trern,
die Tritt, wos klappn ojs dem Psak.

Un hert, un hert, wer s'flegt amul
    nischt welln
derhern unser Geijn durch Tojtn-
    Schwelln,
itzt hert, Schtadt-ojs, Schtadt-ein, –
mir geijn – tojter Abhilch fun a Lebn –
mir welln keinmul eich kein Ru
    nischt gebn
un geijn, un geijn, un geijn . . .

I saw a mountain –
it was higher than Mont Blanc
and holier than Mount Sinai, not
in a dream – in reality, on earth
it stood –
such a mountain, such a mountain
    did I see
of Jewish shoes in Majdanek.

Such a mountain, such a mountain
    did I see.

And suddenly, as if a miracle had
    happened,
I saw
how it stirred and moved away,
and the thousands of shoes arranged
    themselves
by size, in pairs,
and in rows –
and walked . . .

Listen, listen to the march, listen to
    the anthem
of the shoes left behind – the last
    remains
of young and old, kith and kin.
Wares for the rows, wares for the
    pairs,
wares for the sexes, for the years! –
The shoe army, it walks and walks.
We are shoes, we are the last wit-
    nesses,
we are the shoes of grandchildren and
    grandparents,
from Prague, Paris and Amsterdam.
And because we are only of cloth and
    leather –
and not of flesh and blood – each one
avoided the flames of hell.

Listen, listen to the combined tread
of all the steps: of the rabbi's ankle-
    boots,
and the simple, ordinary boots
of simple Jews, of butchers
and the knitted booties of babies,
who had just begun to walk.

The soles tread with so many noises:
the scraping of the bridegroom's
    chamois spats,
the silk shoes of the bride –
they did not reach the wedding
    canopy,
now forsaken in a corner
the poles of the canopy lament them.

We shoes from Jassy, from Munkacz
    and from Athens,
that used to walk in marketplaces and
    workshops,
and went our way in peace,
in grocery stores, factories, kinder-
    gartens, schools.
Now we go – legacy of a witness
who has gone from us, has gone from
    us.

Because the flames savored only
    bones and flesh,
the fiery jaws tasted but did not
    digest us,
and spat us out into a corner, –
now listen, listen to the creaking of
    our soles
the weeping farewells and the mil-
    lion-fold whimpers,
that follow us like companions.

We shoes that used to stroll in the
    park,
and led the bride and bridegroom
    under the canopy,
and from generation to generation
went to celebrations and weddings
    and to the childbed,
and strode loudly to the dance-floor,
    full of vivacity and noise,
and went quietly to funerals.

Until once, in a long funeral proces-
    sion,
we went silently to our own funeral,
separated into the gaits of old and
    young,
when life secretly walked away from
    us,
the poison spared and did not choke
    us,
oh, happy we – who have no hearts,
    throats, lungs.

Ceaselessly we walk and clatter,
    clatter . . .
he did not manage to catch us,
the hangman, in his booty-sack, –
now we go to him, everyone shall
    hear
the steps that move like flowing tears,
the steps that pass judgment.

And listen, and listen, whoever may
    one day not want to hear us as we
        walk across the thresholds of the
            dead,
now listen, everywhere we go, –
we walk – the dead echo of a life –
we will never give you peace,
and walk and walk and walk . . .

BIBLIOGRAPHY

Rachel Salamander in a displaced persons camp in Föhrenwald near Munich. 1954

ADLER, Hans G. *Die Juden in Deutschland: Von der Aufklärung bis zum Nationalsozialismus.* Munich, 1987.

ADLER, Jankel. *Jankel Adler.* Cologne, 1984.

ADLER-RUDEL, S. *Jüdische Selbsthilfe unter dem Naziregime 1933–1939.* Tübingen, 1974.

ADORNO, Theodor W. *Kulturkritik und Gesellschaft. Prismen. Ohne Leitbild. Gesammelte Schriften.* Frankfurt, 1976.

ADORNO, Theodor W. *Minima Moralia: Reflexionen aus dem beschädigten Leben.* Frankfurt, 1986.

AGNON, Samuel Josef. *Der Verstossene.* Translated from Hebrew by N. Glatzer and M. Spitzer. Frankfurt, 1988.

ALTENBERG, Peter. *Peter Altenberg: Leben und Werk in Texten und Bildern.* Frankfurt, 1980.

AMÉRY, Jean. *At the Mind's Limits: Contemplations by a survivor on Auschwitz and its realities.* Translated by Sidney Rosenfeld and Stella P. Rosenfeld. Bloomington, 1980.

ANDICS, Hellmut. *Die Juden in Wien.* Cologne, 1988.

ANGRESS, Werner. *Generation zwischen Furcht und Hoffnung: Jüdische Jugend im Dritten Reich.* Hamburg, 1985.

ARENDT, Hannah. *Men in Dark Times.* New York, 1968.

ARENDT, Hannah. *Rahel Varnhagen: Lebensgeschichte einer deutschen Jüden aus der Romantik.* Munich, 1984.

ARENDT, Hannah. *Die verborgene Tradition: Acht Essays.* Frankfurt, 1984.

ARENDT, Hannah. *Zur Zeit: Politische Essays.* Berlin, 1986.

ARENDT, Hannah, and JASPERS, Karl. *Hannah Arendt/Karl Jaspers: Briefwechsel.* Munich, 1985.

ASCH, Schalom. *Moses: Der Gott hat gegeben. Roman.* German translation by R. Jordan. Zurich, 1986.

ASCH, Schalom. *Mottke der Dieb. Roman.* Edited by V. Hacken, translated from Yiddish by G. Richter. Zurich, 1985.

ASSALL, Paul. *Juden im Elsass.* Elster, 1984.

BAB, Julius. *Leben und Tod des deutschen Judentums.* Edited by H. Haarmann and K. Siebenhaar. Berlin, 1988.

BACH, Hans I. *Jacob Bernays: Ein Beitrag zur Emanzipationsgeschichte der Juden und zur Geschichte des deutschen Geistes im 19. Jahrhundert.* Tübingen, 1974.

BAECK, Leo. *The Essence of Judaism.* Translated by Victor Grubwieser and Leonard Pearl. London, 1936.

BAHR, Erhard. *Nelly Sachs.* Munich, 1980.

BARNER, Wilfried. *Von Rahel Varnhagen bis Friedrich Gundolf: Juden als deutsche Goethe-Verehrer.* Heidelberg, 1988.

BAUMANN, Guido. *Erinnerungen an Paul Celan.* Frankfurt, 1986.

BAUSCHINGER, Sigrid. *Else Lasker-Schüler: Ihr Werk und ihre Zeit.* Heidelberg, 1980.

BECKER, Heinz. *Giacomo Meyerbeer.* Reinbek, 1980.

BECKERMANN, Ruth. *Die Mazzesinsel: Juden in der Wiener Leopoldstadt 1918–1938.* Vienna, 1984.

BEIN, Alex. *Die Judenfrage: Biographie eines Weltproblems.* Stuttgart, 1980.

BELKE, Ingrid. *In den Katakomben: Jüdische Verlage in Deutschland 1933–1938.* Marbach/Neckar, 1985.

BEN-CHORIN, Schalom. *Mein Glaube—mein Schicksal: Jüdische Erfahrungen.* Freiburg, 1984.

BEN-CHORIN, Schalom. *Zwiesprache mit Martin Buber.* Gerlingen, 1978.

BEN-SASSON, Hayim Hillel. *Geschichte des jüdischen Volkes.* Vol. 1: *Von den Anfängen bis zum 7. Jahrhundert.* Munich, 1981. Vol. 2: *Das Mittelalter: Vom 7. bis zum 17. Jahrhundert.* Munich, 1979. Vol. 3: *Vom 17. Jahrhundert bis zur Gegenwart: Die Neuzeit.* Munich, 1979.

BENJAMIN, Walter. *Benjamin über Kafka—Texte, Briefzeugnisse, Aufzeichnungen.* Frankfurt, 1981.

BENJAMIN, Walter. *Berliner Kindheit um Neunzehnhundert.* Frankfurt, 1987.

BENJAMIN, Walter. *The Correspondence of Walter Benjamin and Gershom Scholem 1932–1940.* Edited by Gershom Scholem, translated by Gary Smith and Andre Lefevre. New York, 1989.

BENJAMIN, Walter. *Gesammelte Schriften.* Vol. 6: *Fragmente vermischten Inhalts: Autobiographische Schriften.* Frankfurt, 1985.

BENZ, Wolfgang, and GRAML, Hermann, eds. *Biographisches Lexikon zur Weimarer Republik.* Munich, 1988.

BERGELSON, David. *Das Ende vom Lied. Roman.* Translated from Yiddish by A. Eliasberg, revised by V. Hacken. Munich, 1988.

BERMANN-FISCHER, Gottfried. *Lebendige Gegenwart: Reden und Aufsätze.* Frankfurt, 1987.

BERTHELSEN, Detlef. *Alltag bei Familie Freud.* Hamburg, 1987.

BEST, Otto F. *Mameloschen—Jiddisch, eine Sprache und ihre Literatur.* Frankfurt, 1988.

Biographisches Handbuch der deutschsprachigen Emigration nach 1933. Institut für Zeitgeschichte. Vol. 1: H. A. Strauss. *Politik, Wirtschaft, Öffentliches Leben.* Munich, 1980. Vol. 2: H. A. Strauss, et al. *Sciences, Arts and Literature.* Munich, 1983. Vol. 3: *Gesamtregister/Index.* Munich, 1983.

BLOCH Ernst. *Werkausgaben in 17 Bänden.* Frankfurt, 1985.

BLUMBERG, H. M. *Chaim Weizmann: His Life and Times.* Berlin, 1975.

BOEHLICH, Walter, ed. *Der Berliner Antisemitismusstreit.* Frankfurt, 1988.

BÖRNE, Ludwig, and HEINE, Heinrich. *Ludwig Börne und Heinrich Heine: Ein deutsches Zerwürfnis.* Nördlingen, 1986.

BORRIES, Achim von. *Selbstzeugnisse des deutschen Judentums 1861–1945.* Frankfurt, 1988.

BREUER, Mordechai. *Jüdische Orthodoxie im Deutschen Reich 1871–1918: Die Sozialgeschichte einer religiösen Minderheit.* Frankfurt, 1986.

BROCH, Hermann. *Briefe von 1929 bis 1951.* Frankfurt, 1957.

BROCH, Hermann. *Hugo von Hofmannsthal and His Time: The European Imagination.* Translated and edited by Michael P. Steinberg. Chicago, 1984.

BROCKE, Michael, ed. *Die Erzählungen des Rabbi Nachmann von Bratzlaw.* Reinbek, 1989.

BROD, Max. *Der Prager Kreis.* Frankfurt, 1979.

BROCH, Hermann. *Streitbares Leben: Autobiographie.* Frankfurt, 1979.

BRONSEN, David. *Joseph Roth und die Tradition: Eine Aufstatz- und Materialsammlung.* Cologne, 1975.

BUBER, Martin. *Begegnung: Autobiographische Fragmente.* Heidelberg, 1986.

BUBER, Martin. *Die Erzählungen der Chassidim.* Stuttgart, 1987.

BUBER, Martin. *Ein Land und zwei Völker: Zur jüdisch-arabischen Frage.* Frankfurt, 1983.

BUBER, Martin. *The Origin and Meaning of Hasidim.* Edited and translated by Maurice Friedman. New York, 1960.

BUBER, Martin. *Pfade in Utopia: Über Gemeinschaft und deren Verwirklichung.* Edited by A. Schapira. Heidelberg, 1985.

BUBER, Martin. *Tales of the Hasidim: The early masters.* Translated by Olga Marx. New York, 1947.

BUBER, Martin. *Tales of the Hasidim: The later masters.* Translated by Olga Marx. New York, 1948.

BUNZL, John. *Sportklub Hakoah: Jüdischer Sport in Österreich 1909–1987.* Vienna, 1987.

BUNZL, John. *Der Weg des Menschen nach der chassidischen Lehre.* Heidelberg, 1981.

BUNZL, John, and MARIN, Bernd. *Antisemitismus in Österreich: Sozialhistorische und soziologische Studien.* Innsbruck, 1987.

CALIMANI, Ricardo. *Die Kaufleute von Venedig: Die Geschichte der Juden in der Löwenrepublik.* Düsseldorf, 1988.

CANETTI, Elias. *Das Augenspiel: Lebensgeschichte 1931–1937.* Munich, 1985.

CANETTI, Elias. *Die Fackel im Ohr: Lebensgeschichte 1921–1931.* Munich, 1982.

CANETTI, Elias. *Die gerettete Zunge: Geschichte einer Jugend.* Munich, 1983.

CANETTI, Elias. *The Play of the Eyes.* Translated by Ralph Manheim. New York, 1986.

CANETTI, Elias. *Die Provinz des Menschen: Aufzeichnungen 1942–1972.* Frankfurt, 1986.

CANETTI, Elias. *The Tongue Set Free: Remembrance of a European Childhood.* Translated by Joachim Neugroschel. New York, 1979.

CARROLL, Lewis. *The Complete Works.* Vol. 33. London, 1965.

CELAN, Paul. *Collected Prose.* Translated by Rosemarie Waldrop. Manchester, 1986.

CHAGALL, Bella. *Brenendike Likht.* New York, 1945. Translated by Norbert Guterman, under the title *Burning Lights.* New York, 1946.

CHALFEN, Israel. *Paul Celan: Eine Biographie seiner Jugend.* Frankfurt, 1983.

CLAUSSEN, Detlev. *Vom Judenhass zum Antisemitismus.* Cologne, 1987.

COHEN, Hermann. *Religion of Reason: Out of the Sources of Judaism.* Translated by Simon Kaplan. New York, 1972.

DAHM, Volker. *Das jüdische Buch im Dritten Reich.* Vol. 1: *Die Ausschaltung der jüdischen Autoren, Verleger und Buchhändler.* Frankfurt,

1979.

DAWIDOWICZ, Lucy S. *Der Krieg gegen die Juden: 1933–1945*. Wiesbaden, 1975.

DER NISTER (Pinchas Kahanowitsch). *Unterm Zaun: Jiddische Erzählungen*. Edited by D. Mantovan-Kromer. Frankfurt, 1988.

DEUTSCHER, Isaac. *The Non-Jewish Jew: Essays*. Edited by Tamara Deutscher. London, 1968.

DEUTSCHKRON, Inge. *Berliner Juden im Untergrund*. Berlin, 1980.

DIEDERICHS, Ulf, ed. *Ostjüdische Geschichten*. Illustrated by Ephraim Mose Lilien. Munich, 1988.

DINSE, Helmut. *Die Entwicklung des jiddischen Schrifttums im deutschen Sprachgebiet*. Tübingen, 1974.

DINSE, Helmut, and LIPTZIN, Sol. *Einführung in die jiddische Literatur*. Tübingen, 1978.

DÖBLIN, Alfred. *Ausgewählte Werke in Einzelbänden: Autobiographische Schriften und letzte Aufzeichnungen*. Olten, 1980.

DÖBLIN, Alfred. *Briefe*. Munich, 1988.

DÖBLIN, Alfred. *Reise in Polen*. Olten, 1968. Translated by Joachim Neugroschel, under the title *Journey to Poland*. Edited by Heinz Graber. New York, 1991.

DREWITZ, Ingeborg. *Berliner Salons: Gesellschaft und Literatur zwischen Aufklärung und Industriezeitalter*. Berlin, 1984.

DUBNOW, Simon. *Geschichte des Chassidismus*. Translated from Hebrew by A. Steinberg. Frankfurt, 1981.

DUBNOW, Simon. *Weltgeschichte des jüdischen Volkes*. 3 vols. Jerusalem, 1971.

DUBROVIC, Milan. *Veruntreute Geschichte: Die Wiener Salons und Literatencafés*. Vienna, 1985.

EBAN, Abba. *Das Erbe: Die Geschichte des Judentums*. Berlin, 1986.

EBAN, Abba. *Ein Ghetto im Osten: Wilna*. Foreword by H. A. Strauss. Berlin, 1985 (1931).

EINSTEIN, Albert. *Ausgewählte Texte*. Munich, 1986.

EINSTEIN, Albert. *The Born-Einstein Letters: Correspondence between Albert Einstein and Max and Hedwig Born from 1916–1955*. Translated by Irene Born. London, 1971.

EINSTEIN, Albert. *Mein Weltbild*. Zurich, 1986.

EINSTEIN, Albert. *Out of My Later Years*. New York, 1950.

EINSTEIN, Albert, and FREUD, Sigmund. *Warum Krieg? Ein Briefwechsel*. Zurich, 1972.

ELBOGEN, Ismael, and STERLING, Eleonore. *Die Geschichte der Juden in Deutschland*. Frankfurt, 1988.

ELOESSER, Arthur. *Vom Ghetto nach Europa: Deutsche Juden im geistigen Leben des 19. Jahrhunderts*. Berlin, 1988.

ENGELMANN, Bernt. *Deutschland ohne Juden: Eine Bilanz*. Berlin, 1988.

ERICH, Renata M., and HÖFER, Edmund. *Ojtser: Das Schtetl in der Moldau und Bukowina heute*. Vienna, 1988.

ESCHWEGE, Helmut. *Die Synagoge in der deutschen Geschichte: Eine Dokumentation*. Wiesbaden, 1988.

Exilforschung: Ein internationales Jahrbuch. Edited by T. Koebner et al. Vol. 4: *Das jüdische Exil und andere Themen*. Munich, 1986.

FEUCHTWANGER, Lion. *The Devil in France*. Translated by Elisabeth Abbott. New York, 1941.

FEUCHTWANGER, Lion, and ZWEIG, Arnold. *Briefwechsel 1933–1958*. Frankfurt, 1986.

FIEDLER, Leonhard M. *Max Reinhardt*. Reinbek, 1981.

Der Fiedler vom Ghetto: Jiddische Gedichte aus Polen. Translated from Yiddish by H. Witt. Berlin, 1985.

FITTKO, Lisa. *Mein Weg über die Pyrenäen: Erinnerungen 1940/41*. Munich, 1988.

FLADE, Roland. *Die Würzburger Juden: Ihre Geschichte vom Mittelalter bis zur Gegenwart mit vielen Fotos und Augenzeugenberichten*. Würzburg, 1987.

FLESCH-BRUNNINGEN, Hans. *Die verführte Zeit: Lebenserinnerungen*. Edited by M. Mixner. Vienna, 1988.

Flucht und Exil. Edited by Peter Strelka. With texts by M. Brod, H. Broch, M. Sperber, T. Mann, A. Polgar, H. Sahl, and others. Frankfurt, 1988.

FRAENKEL, Joseph, ed. *The Jews of Austria*. London, 1967.

FREEDEN, Herbert. *Die jüdische Presse im Dritten Reich*. Tübingen, 1987.

FREEDEN, Herbert. *Jüdisches Theater in Nazideutschland*. Berlin, 1964.

FREUD, Sigmund. *Briefe 1873–1939*. Frankfurt, 1980.

FREUD, Sigmund. *Gesammelte Werke: Texte aus den Jahren 1885–1935*. Frankfurt, 1987.

FREUD, Sigmund. *Sein Leben in Bildern und Texten*. Frankfurt, 1985.

FREUD, Sigmund. *The Standard Edition of the Complete Psychological*

Works. Translated by James Strachey and Anna Freud. Vol. 8: *1905*. London, 1960. Vol. 13: *1913/14*. London, 1955.

FREUD, Sigmund. *Studienausgabe*. 10 vols. Frankfurt, 1981.

FREUD, Sigmund, and ZWEIG, Arnold. *Sigmund Freud/Arnold Zweig: Briefwechsel*. Frankfurt, 1984.

FREUND, Gisele. *Photographien*. Munich, 1985.

GAY, Peter. *Freud, Juden und andere Deutsche: Herren und Opfer in der modernen Kultur*. Munich, 1988.

GAY, Peter. *Die Republik der Aussenseiter: Geist und Kultur in der Weimarer Zeit 1918–1933*. Frankfurt, 1987.

GEIGER, Ludwig. *Geschichte der Juden in Berlin*. Berlin, 1986.

Geschichten aus dem Ghetto: Eine Anthologie deutschsprachiger Ghetto-Geschichten aus dem 19. Jahrhundert. Edited by J. Hermand. Frankfurt, 1987.

Gesichter einer verlorenen Welt: Fotos aus dem Leben des polnischen Judentums 1864–1939. New York, 1982.

GIDAL, Nachum T. *Die Juden in Deutschland von der Römerzeit bis zur Weimarer Republik*. Munich, 1988.

GILBERT, Martin. *Endlösung: Die Vertreibung und Vernichtung der Juden. Ein Atlas*. Reinbek, 1982.

GINZEL, Günter B. *Jüdischer Alltag in Deutschland 1933–1945: Fotografierte Zeitgeschichte*. Düsseldorf, 1984.

GOLDSTEIN, Walter B. *Der Glaube Martin Bubers*. Jerusalem, 1969.

GOLDSTEIN, Walter B. *Tausend Jahre Europa und die Juden*. Jerusalem, 1983.

GOMBRICH, Ernst H. *Aby Warburg: Eine intellektuelle Biographie*. Frankfurt, 1984.

GORION, Micha Josef. *Born Judas*. Part 1: *Legenden, Märchen und Erzählungen*. Edited by E. bin Gorion. Frankfurt, 1959.

GRAB, Walter. "Deutsche Aufklärung und Judenemanzipation." *Jahrbuch des Inst. f. Dt. Geschichte*. Third supplement. Tel Aviv, 1980.

GRAETZ, Heinrich. *Volkstümliche Geschichte der Juden*. 6 vols. on cassette. Munich, 1985.

GRAF, Oskar Maria. *Gelächter von aussen: Aus meinem Leben 1918–1933*. Munich, 1985.

GREIVE, Hermann. *Grundzüge der Geschichte des modernen Antisemitismus in Deutschland*. Stuttgart, 1983.

GRIMM, Gunter E., and BAYERDÖRFER, Hans-P. *Im Zeichen Hiobs: Jüdische Schriftsteller und deutsche Literatur im 20. Jahrhundert*. Frankfurt, 1984.

GSTREIN, Heinz. *Jüdisches Wien*. Vienna, 1984.

HAAS, Willy. *Die literarische Welt: Lebenserinnerungen*. Fischer, 1983.

HABERMAS, Jürgen. *Philosophisch politische Profile*. Frankfurt, 1981.

HAMBURGER, Ernest. *Juden im öffentlichen Leben Deutschlands: Regierungsmitglieder, Beamte und Parlamentarier in der monarchischen Zeit 1848–1918*. Tübingen, 1968.

HÄUSLER, Wolfgang. *Das galizische Judentum in der Habsburger Monarchie: Im Lichte zeitgenössischer Publizistik und Reiseliteratur von 1772 bis 1848*. Munich, 1981.

HEER, Friedrich. *Gottes erste Liebe: Die Juden im Spannungsfeld der Geschichte*. Berlin, 1986.

HEILBORN, Ernst. *Die gute Stube: Berliner Geselligkeit im 19. Jahrhundert*. Berlin, 1987.

HEILBUT, Anthony. *Kultur ohne Heimat: Deutsche Emigranten in den USA nach 1930*. Weinheim, 1987.

HEMPEL, Henri Jacob. *"Wenn ich schon ein Fremder sein muss . . ."*: *Deutsch-jüdische Emigranten in New York*. Berlin, 1984.

HERZ, Henriette. *Berliner Salon: Erinnerungen und Porträts*. Berlin, 1984.

HERZL, Theodor. *The Jewish State*. Translated by Harry Zohn. New York, 1970.

HERZL, Theodor. *The Old-New Land*. Translated by Lotta Levensohn. New York, 1960.

HERZL, Theodor. *"Wenn ihr wollt, ist es kein Märchen": Altneuland—der Judenstaat*. Frankfurt, 1985.

HETMANN, Frederik. *Rosa L.: Die Geschichte der Rosa Luxemburg und ihrer Zeit*. Frankfurt, 1987.

HEUER, Renate. *Bibliographica Judaica: Verzeichnis jüdischer Autoren deutscher Sprache*. Vol. 1: *A–K*. Frankfurt, 1982. Vol. 2: *L–R. Mit Nachträgen, Pseudonymen- und Ortsverzeichnis*. Frankfurt, 1985. Vol. 3: *S–Z*. Frankfurt, 1988.

HEYWORTH, Peter. *Otto Klemperer: Dirigent der Republik 1885–1933*. Berlin, 1988.

HILBERG, Raul. *Die Vernichtung der europäischen Juden: Die Gesamtgeschichte des Holocaust*. Berlin, 1982.

HILLER, Kurt. *Leben gegen die Zeit: Erinnerungen*. Reinbek, 1973.

HIRSCH, Helmut. *Marx und Moses: Karl Marx zur "Judenfrage" und zu Juden*. Hamburg, 1980.

HOFFMANN, Hilma, and SCHOBERT, W. *Von Babelsberg nach Hollywood: Filmemigranten aus Nazideutschland*. Exponatenverzeichnis. Exhibition catalogue. Frankfurt, 1987.

HORCH, Hans Otto, ed. *Judentum, Antisemitismus und europäische Kultur*. Tübingen, 1988.

HORKHEIMER, Max. *Dialektik der Aufklärung und Schriften 1940–1950*. Frankfurt, 1987.

HORKHEIMER, Max. *Notizen 1950–1969 und Dämmerung*. Frankfurt, 1974.

IGGERS, Wilma, ed. *Die Juden in Böhmen und Mähren: Ein historisches Lesebuch*. Munich, 1986.

JÄCKEL, Eberhard, and ROHWER, Jürgen. *Der Mord an den Juden im Zweiten Weltkrieg: Entschlussbildung und Verwirklichung*. Stuttgart, 1985.

JACOBI, Lotte. *Russland 1932/33*. Edited by M. Beckers and E. Moortgat. Berlin, 1988.

JACOBI, Ruth. *Heinrich Heines jüdisches Erbe*. Bonn, 1978.

JANOUCH, Gustav. *Conversations with Kafka*. Translated by Goronwy Rees. New York, 1971.

JERSCH-WENZEL, Stefi. *Deutsche—Polen—Juden: Ihre Beziehungen von den Anfängen bis ins 20. Jahrhundert. Ein Tagungsbericht*. Berlin, 1987.

Jiddische Sprichwörter: Je länger ein Blinder lebt, desto mehr sieht er. Jidd. in lateinischen Buchstaben und in dt. Translated by H. C. Artmann. Frankfurt, 1965.

Juden in der deutschen Literatur: Ein deutsch-israelisches Symposium. Frankfurt, 1985.

Die jüdische Emigration aus Deutschland 1933–1941: Die Geschichte einer Austreibung. Frankfurt, 1985.

JUNGK, Peter S. *Franz Werfel: Eine Lebensgeschichte*. Frankfurt, 1987.

KAFKA, Franz. *Briefe an Milena*. Frankfurt, 1986.

KAFKA, Franz. *The Diaries of Franz Kafka*. Edited by Max Brod. New York, 1948–49.

KAFKA, Franz. *Eine innere Biographie in Sebstzeugnissen*. Frankfurt, 1983.

KAFKA, Franz. *Letter to his Father*. Translated by Ernst Kaiser and Eithne Wilkins. New York, 1966.

KAFKA, Franz. *Letters to Felice*. Edited by Erich Heller and Jürgen Born; translated by James Stern and Elisabeth Duckworth. New York, 1973.

KAFKA, Franz. *Letters to Friends, Family, and Editors*. Translated by Richard and Clara Winston. New York, 1977.

KAFKA, Franz. *Tagebücher 1910–1923*. Frankfurt, 1984.

KAMPF, Abraham. *Jüdisches Erleben in der Kunst des 20. Jahrhunderts*. Weinheim, 1987.

KANTOROWICZ, Alfred. *Exil in Frankreich: Merkwürdigkeiten und Denkwürdigkeiten*. Hamburg, 1983.

KARPELES, Gustav. *Geschichte der jüdischen Literatur*. Graz, 1963.

KAUFFELDT, Rolf. *Erich Mühsam: Literatur und Anarchie*. Stuttgart, 1984.

KEDOURIE, Eli. *Die jüdische Welt: Offenbarung, Geschichte und Prophetie*. Frankfurt, 1980.

KESSLER, Harry Graf. *Walther Rathenau: Sein Leben und sein Werk*. Edited by C. Blasberg. Frankfurt, 1988.

KLÜSENER, Erika. *Else Lasker-Schüler*. Reinbek, 1985.

KNOBLOCH, Heinz. *Herr Moses in Berlin: Ein Menschenfreund in Preussen. Das Leben des Moses Mendelssohn*. Berlin, 1987.

KOESTER, Rudolf. *Joseph Roth*. Reinbek, 1982.

KOESTLER, Arthur. *Als Zeuge der Zeit: Die Abenteuer meines Lebens*. Frankfurt, 1983.

KOLITZ, Zvi. *Jossel Rackower spricht zu Gott*. Translated from Yiddish by A. M. Joki. Neu-Isenburg, 1985.

Konzentrationslager Dachau 1933–1945. Dachau, 1978.

KÖPCKE, Wulf. *Lion Feuchtwanger*. Munich, 1983.

KRINSKY, Carol Herselle. *Europas Synagogen: Architektur, Geschichte und Bedeutung*. Translated from English by B. Witsch-Aldor. Stuttgart, 1988.

KROHN, Claus D. *Wissenschaft im Exil: Deutsche Sozial- und Wirtschaftswissenschaftler in den USA und die New York School for Social Research*. Frankfurt, 1987.

KÜHNER, Hans. *Der Antisemitismus der Kirche: Genese, Geschichte und Gefahr*. Zurich, 1976.

KWIET, Konrad, and ESCHWEGE, Helmut. *Selbstbehauptung und Widerstand: Deutsche Juden im Kampf um Existenz und Menschenwürde 1933–1945*. Hamburg, 1984.

LAQUEUR, Walter. *Der Weg zum Staat Israel: Geschichte des Zionismus.* Vienna, 1972.

LASKER-SCHÜLER, Else. *"Was soll ich hier?": Exilbriefe an Salmann Schocken.* Heidelberg, 1986.

LASSALLE, Ferdinand. *Reden und Schriften.* Berlin, 1987.

LESSING, Theodor. *Der jüdische Selbsthass.* With an essay by B. Groys. Munich, 1984.

LICHARZ, Werner. *Leo Baeck—Lehrer und Helfer in schwerer Zeit.* Frankfurt, 1983.

LIEBERMANN, Max. *Die Phantasie in der Malerei.* Frankfurt, 1978.

LIEBESCHÜTZ, Hans. *Von Georg Simmel zu Franz Rosenzweig: Studien zum jüdischen Denken im deutschen Kulturbereich.* Tübingen, 1970.

LILIEN, Ephraim M. *Briefe an seine Frau.* Frankfurt, 1985.

LÖWITH, Karl. *Mein Leben in Deutschland vor und nach 1933: Ein Bericht von 1940.* Stuttgart, 1986.

LUETZELER, Paul Michael. *Hermann Broch: A Biography.* Translated by Janice Furness. London, 1987.

LUXEMBURG, Rosa. *Ich umarme Sie in grosser Sehnsucht: Briefe aus dem Gefängnis 1915–1918.* Berlin, 1986.

MAHLER, Gustav. *Im eigenen Wort—im Worte der Freunde: Selbstbildnis.* Zurich, 1958.

MAHLER, Gustav, and BLAUKOPF, H. *Briefe.* Munich, 1983.

MAIMONIDES, Moses (Moses ben Maimon). *Eine Abhandlung zur jüdischen Ethik und Gotteserkenntnis.* Hamburg, 1981.

MANGER, Itzik. *Das Buch fun Gan Eden (Das Buch vom Paradies).* Genf/Hamburg, 1963.

MAOR, Maimon. *Max Horkheimer.* Berlin, 1981.

MARCUSE, Ludwig. *Ludwig Börne: Aus der Frühzeit der deutschen Demokratie.* Zurich, 1986.

MARCUSE, Ludwig. *Sigmund Freud: Sein Bild vom Menschen.* Zurich, 1986.

MARWEDEL, Rainer. *Theodor Lessing 1872–1933: Eine Biographie.* Darmstadt, 1987.

MATTENKLOTT, G. "Die Exotik der Ostjuden in Deutschland." In *Die andere Welt.* Edited by T. Koebner and G. Pickerodt. Frankfurt, 1987.

MATTENKLOTT, Gert, and SCHLAFFER, Hannelore and Heinz, eds. *Deutsche Briefe 1750–1950.* Frankfurt, 1988.

MAURER, Trude. *Ostjuden in Deutschland 1918–1933.* Hamburg, 1986.

MAYER, Hans. *Ein Deutscher auf Widerruf: Erinnerungen.* Frankfurt, 1984.

MAYER, Hans. *Wir Aussenseiter: Grazer Rede 1981.* Frankfurt, 1983.

MEHRING, Walter. *Die verlorene Bibliothek: Autobiographie einer Kultur.* Berlin, 1978.

MEIER-UDE, Klaus, and SENGER, Valentin. *Die jüdischen Friedhöfe in Frankfurt.* Frankfurt, 1985.

MELCHER, Peter. *Weissensee: Ein Friedhof als Spiegelbild jüdischer Geschichte in Berlin.* Berlin, 1986.

MENDELE, Mojcher Sforim. *Die Mähre. Ein Roman.* Edited by V. Hacken. Stuttgart, 1984.

MENDELSOHN, Erich. *Erich Mendelsohn: Das Gesamtschaffen des Architekten: Skizzen, Entwürfe, Bauten.* Berlin, 1988.

MENDELSSOHN, Moses. *Gesammelte Schriften: Jubiläumsausgabe.* 20 vols. Stuttgart, 1970.

METZGER, Heinz-K., and RIEHN, Rainer. *Mendelssohn-Bartholdy.* Munich, 1980.

METZGER, Heinz-K., and RIEHN, Rainer, eds. *Gustav Mahler.* Munich, 1988.

MICHALSKI, Gabrielle. *Der Antisemitismus im deutschen akademischen Leben in der Zeit nach dem 1. Weltkrieg.* Bern, 1980.

MOSSE, George. *Ein Volk, ein Reich, ein Führer: Die völkischen Ursprünge des Nationalsozialismus.* Königstein, 1979.

MOSSE, Werner E. *Entscheidungsjahr 1932: Zur Judenfrage in der Endphase der Weimarer Republik.* Tübingen, 1966.

MÜHSAM, Erich. *In meiner Posaune muss ein Sandkorn sein: Briefe 1900–1934.* Edited by Gerd Jungbluth. Ruggell, 1984.

MÜLLER, Hartmut. *Stefan Zweig.* Reinbek, 1988.

MYNONA (Salomo Friedlaender). *Briefe aus dem Exil 1933–1946.* Edited by H. Geerken. Mainz, 1982.

NA'AMAN, Schlomo. *Emanzipation und Messianismus: Leben und Werk des Moses Hess.* Frankfurt, 1981.

NATHORFF, Hertha. *Das Tagebuch der Hertha Nathorff: Berlin—New York. Aufzeichnungen 1933 bis 1945.* Edited by W. Benz. Frankfurt, 1988.

OLSVANGER, Immanuel. *Rosinkess mit Mandlen: Schwänke, Erzählungen, Sprichwörter, Rätsel.* Zurich, 1965.

OPATOSCHU, Josef. *Bar Kochba: Der letzte Aufstand. Roman.* Translated from Yiddish by E. Hacken. Stuttgart, 1985.

PASCHELES, Jacob Wolf. *Sippurim: Eine Sammlung jüdischer Volkssagen, Erzählungen, Mythen, Chroniken. Mit Biographien berühmter Juden.* Hildesheim, 1976.

PAUCKER, Arnold, and GILCHRIST, Sylvia, et al. *Die Juden im nationalsozialistischen Deutschland. The Jews in Nazi Germany 1933–1945.* Tübingen, 1986.

PAZI, Margarita. *Fünf Autoren des Prager Kreises: Oskar Baum, Paul Kornfeld, Ernst Sommer, Ernst Weiss, Ludwig Winder.* Hildesheim, 1978.

PEREZ, Isaac Leib. *Die Seelenwanderung einer Melodie: Erzählungen.* Translated from Yiddish by J. Schajowicz, et al. Munich 1988.

PETUCHOWSKI, Jakob J. *Feiertage des Herrn: Die Welt der jüdischen Feste und Bräuche.* Freiburg, 1984.

POLGAR, Alfred. *Lieber Freund! Lebenszeichen aus der Fremde.* Vienna, 1981.

POLIAKOV, Léon. *Geschichte des Antisemitismus.* 8 vols. Vol 5: *Die Aufklärung und ihre judenfeindliche Tendenz.* Worms, 1983. Vol. 6: *Emanzipation und Rassenwahn.* Worms, 1987. Vol. 7: *Zwischen Assimilation und "jüdischer Weltverschwörung."* Frankfurt, 1988. Vol 8: *Am Vorabend des Holocaust.* Frankfurt, 1988.

POLIAKOV, Léon, and WULF, J. *Das Dritte Reich und die Juden.* Berlin, 1983.

POLLACK, Martin. *Nach Galizien: Von Chassiden, Huzulen, Polen und Ruthenen. Eine imaginäre Reise durch die verschwundene Welt Ostgaliziens und der Bukowina.* Vienna, 1984.

PRATER, Donald A. *Stefan Zweig: Das Leben eines Ungeduldigen.* Frankfurt, 1983.

PRINZ, Arthur. *Juden im deutschen Wirtschaftsleben: Soziale und wirtschaftliche Struktur im Wandel 1850–1914.* Edited by A. Barkai. Tübingen, 1984.

RANSMAYR, Christoph, ed. *Im blinden Winkel: Nachrichten aus Mittel-europa.* Vienna, 1985.

REICH-RANICKI, Marcel. *Über Ruhestörer: Juden in der deutschen Literatur.* Stuttgart, 1989.

REICHMANN, Eva G. *Grösse und Verhängnis deutsch-jüdischer Existenz.* Heidelberg, 1974.

REUTER, Fritz. *Warmaisa: 1000 Jahre Juden in Worms.* Frankfurt, 1987.

RICHARZ, Monika. *Jüdisches Leben in Deutschland: Selbstzeugnisse zur Sozialgeschichte.* Vol. 1: *1780–1871.* Stuttgart, 1976. Vol. 2: *Im Kaiserreich.* Stuttgart, 1978. Vol. 3: *1918–1945.* Stuttgart, 1982.

ROBERT, Marthe. *Einsam wie Franz Kafka.* Frankfurt, 1985.

ROSENSTRAUCH, Hazel, ed. *Aus Nachbarn wurden Juden.* With photographs by Abraham Pisarek. Berlin, 1988.

ROTH, Joseph. *Briefe 1911–1939.* Cologne, 1970.

ROTH, Joseph. *1894–1939: Ein Austellungskatalog.* Frankfurt, 1979.

ROTH, Joseph. *Job: The Story of a Simple Man.* Translated by Dorothy Thompson. Woodstock, 1982.

ROTH, Joseph. *Juden auf Wanderschaft.* Cologne, 1985.

ROTH, Joseph. *The Radetzky March.* Translated by Eva Tucker. New York, 1974.

ROTH, Joseph. *The Silent Prophet.* Translated by David le Vay. Woodstock, 1980.

ROZENBLIT, Martha L. *Die Juden Wiens: Assimilation und Identität 1876 bis 1914.* Cologne, 1986.

RUBINSTEIN, Mordechai. *Die Greinizraisser: Unser "umlegaler" Weg fun Goles kein "Isroel."* Jerusalem, 1986.

RÜRUP, Reinhard. *Emanzipation und Antisemitismus: Studien zur "Judenfrage" der Bürgerlichen Gesellschaft.* Frankfurt, 1987.

SACHS, Nelly. *Briefe der Nelly Sachs.* Frankfurt, 1984.

SALOMON, Erich. *Der unsichtbare Photograph: Ermanox-Aufnahmen 1928–1932.* Nördlingen, 1987.

SAUDER, Gerhard. *Die Bücherverbrennung: 10 May 1933.* Berlin, 1985.

SCHEBERA, Jürgen. *Damals im Romanischen Café.* DDR, 1988.

SCHLÖSSER, Manfred. *Karl Wolfskehl—Biographie.* Berlin, 1970.

SCHNELTING, Karl B. *Zwischen Diktatur und Literatur: Marcel Reich-Ranicki im Gespräch mit Joachim Fest.* Frankfurt, 1987.

SCHNITZLER, Arthur. *Arthur Schnitzler: Sein Leben—sein Werk—seine Zeit.* Frankfurt, 1981.

SCHNITZLER, Arthur. *Briefe 1875–1912.* Frankfurt, 1981.

SCHNITZLER, Arthur. *My Youth in Vienna.* Translated by Catherine Huller. New York, 1970.

SCHNITZLER, Arthur. *The Road to the Open.* Translated by Horace Samuel. New York, 1923.

SCHNITZLER, Arthur. *Tagebuch 1879–1931.* Edited by W. Welzig. Vol 1: *1909–1912.* Vol. 2: *1913–1916.* Vol. 3: *1917–1919.* Vol. 4: *1879–1892.* Frankfurt, 1978–85.

SCHOENBERNER, Gerhard. *Der gelbe Stern: Die Judenverfolgung in Europa 1933–1945.* Frankfurt, 1985.

SCHOENBERNER, Gerhard, ed. *Wir haben es gesehen: Augenzeugenberichte über Terror und Judenverfolgung im Dritten Reich.* Wiesbaden, 1988.

SCHOEPS Julius H. *Theodor Herzl: Wegbereiter des politischen Zionismus.* Frankfurt, 1975.

SCHOEPS, Julius H., ed. *Zionismus: Text zu seiner Entwicklung.* Wiesbaden, 1983.

SCHOLEM, Betty. *Briefe an Werner Kraft.* Frankfurt, 1986.

SCHOLEM, Betty, and SCHOLEM, Gershom. *Betty Scholem/Gershom Scholem: Mutter und Sohn im Briefwechsel 1917–1946.* Edited by I. Shedletzky. Munich, 1989.

SCHOLEM, Gershom. *Judaica 1: Essays.* Frankfurt, 1981. *Judaica 2: Essays.* Frankfurt, 1982. *Judaica 3: Essays.* Frankfurt, 1987. *Judaica 4.* Frankfurt, 1984.

SCHOLEM, Gershom. *Major Trends in Jewish Mysticism.* New York, 1954.

SCHOLEM, Gershom. *On Jews and Judaism in Crisis.* Edited by Werner Dannhauser. New York, 1976.

SCHOLEM ALEJCHEM. *Menachem Mendel: Briefe von Menachem Mendel an seine Frau Scheine Scheindel.* Nördlingen, 1987.

SCHOLEM ALEJCHEM. *Tewje, der Milchmann.* With lithographs by Anatoli L. Kaplan. Translated by A. Eliasberg and M. Reich. Wiesbaden, 1987.

SCHRADER, Bärbel, and SCHEBERA, Jürgen. *Die "Goldenen" zwanziger Jahre: Kunst und Kultur der Weimarer Republik.* East Berlin, 1987.

SCHULIN, Ernst. *Walther Rathenau: Repräsentant, Kritiker und Opfer seiner Zeit.* Göttingen, 1979.

SCHULTHEIS Herbert A. *Die Reichskristallnacht in Deutschland nach Augenzeugenberichten.* Würzburg, 1986.

SCHÜTZ Hans J. *Ein deutscher Dichter bin ich einst gewesen: Vergessene und verkannte Autoren des 20. Jahrhunderts.* Munich, 1988.

SCHWARBERG, Günther, ed. *Das Getto: Geburtstagsspaziergang in die Hölle.* Göttingen, 1988.

SELIG, Wolfram, ed. *Synagogen und jüdische Friedhöfe in München.* Munich, 1988.

SERKE, Jürgen. *Böhmische Dörfer: Wanderungen durch eine verlassene literarische Landschaft.* Vienna, 1987.

SERKE, Jürgen. *Die verbrannten Dichter: Berichte—Texte—Bilder einer Zeit.* Frankfurt, 1983.

SHAKED, Gershon. *Die Macht der Identität: Essays über jüdische Schriftsteller.* Frankfurt, 1986.

SILBERMANN, Alphons. *Der ungeliebte Jude.* Cologne, 1981.

SILBERMANN, Alphons. *Mahler-Lexikon.* Bergisch-Gladbach, 1986.

SILBERNER, Edmund. *Moses Hess: Geschichte seines Lebens.* Berlin, 1966.

SIMON, Ernst. *Aufbau im Untergang: Jüdische Erwachsenenbildung im nationalsozialistischen Deutschland als geistiger Widerstand.* Tübingen, 1959.

SIMON, Ernst. *Entscheidung zum Judentum: Essays und Vorträge.* Frankfurt, 1980.

SINGER, Isaac Bashevis. *In My Father's Court.* New York, 1966.

SINGER, Israel J. *Yoshe Kalb.* Translated by M. Samuel with an introduction by Irving Howe. New York, 1988.

SKIRECKI, Ingetraut, ed. *Die Wunder von Chanukka: Geschichten zu jüdischen Fest- und Feiertagen.* Hanau, 1989.

SOMOGYI, Tamar. *Die Scheijnen und die Prosten: Untersuchungen zum Schönheitsideal der Ostjuden.* Berlin, 1982.

SPERBER, Manès. *Ein politisches Leben: Gespräche mit L. Reinisch.* Stuttgart, 1984.

SPERBER, Manès. *God's Water Carriers.* Translated by Joachim Neugroschel with a foreword by Elie Wiesel. New York, 1987.

SPIEL, Hilde. *Glanz und Untergang: Wien 1866–1938.* Munich, 1987.

SPIEL, Hilde. *Die hellen und die finsteren Zeiten: Erinnerungen 1911–1946.* Munich, 1989.

SPIEL, Hilde. *Rückkehr nach Wien: Ein Tagebuch.* Berlin, 1989.

SPIERO, Claude. *Und wir hielten die für Menschen: Jüdisches Schicksal während der Emigration.* Frankfurt, 1987.

STEINHARDT, Wolfgang O. *Mein Vater—Deutscher Bürger jüdischen Glaubens.* Berlin, 1986.

STERN, Fritz. *Gold and Iron: Bismarck, Bleichröder, and the Building of the German Empire.* New York, 1977.

STERNBURG, Wilhelm v. *Lion Feuchtwanger: Eine Biographie.* Frankfurt, 1984.

TAUSK, Walter. *Breslauer Tagebuch.* Berlin, 1988.

TAYLOR, John R. *Fremde im Paradies: Emigranten in Hollywood 1933–1950.* Berlin, 1984.

THALMANN, Rita, and FEINERMANN, Emmanuel. *Die Reichskristallnacht.* Frankfurt, 1987.

TOLLER, Ernst. *I was a German.* Translated by Edward Crankshaw. New York, 1970.

TORBERG, Friedrich. *In diesem Sinne . . . Briefe an Freunde und Zeitgenossen.* Berlin, 1981.

TOURY, Jacob. *Die jüdische Presse im Österreichischen Kaiserreich: Ein Beitrag zur Problematik der Akkulturation 1802–1918.* Tübingen, 1983.

TOURY, Jacob. *Soziale und politische Geschichte der Juden in Deutschland 1847–1871: Zwischen Revolution, Reaktion und Emanzipation.* Düsseldorf, 1977.

TRABER, Habakuk, and WEINGARTEN, Elmar. *Verdrängte Musik: Berliner Komponisten im Exil.* Berlin, 1987.

TROLLER, Georg Stefan. *Selbstbeschreibung.* Hamburg, 1988.

TUCHOLSKY, Kurt. *Briefe aus dem Schweigen: Briefe an Nuuna.* Reinbek, 1978.

TUCHOLSKY, Kurt. *1890–1935: Ein Lebensbild.* Weinheim, 1987.

TUCHOLSKY, Kurt. *Die Q-Tagebücher 1934–1935.* Reinbek, 1978.

TUCHOLSKY, Kurt. *Unser ungelebtes Leben: Briefe an Mary.* Reinbek, 1983.

UEXKÜLL, Gösta v. *Ferdinand Lassalle.* Reinbek, 1979.

VARNHAGEN, Rahel. *Gesammelte Werke.* Munich, 1983.

VIERTEL, Salka. *Das unbelehrbare Herz: Ein Leben mit Stars und Dichtern des 20. Jahrhunderts.* Frankfurt, 1987.

VISHNIAC, Roman. *Verschwundene Welt: Photographien 1933–1939.* Munich, 1983.

VÖLKER, Klaus. *Fritz Kortner: Schauspieler und Regisseur.* Berlin, 1987.

VRIES, S. Philipp de. *Jüdische Riten und Symbole.* Wiesbaden, 1986.

WAGNER, Renate. *Arthur Schnitzler: Eine Biographie.* Frankfurt, 1984.

WALK, Joseph. *Kurzbiographien zur Geschichte der Juden 1918–1945.* Munich, 1988.

WALK, Joseph. *Das Sonderrecht für die Juden im NS-Staat: Eine Sammlung der gesetzlichen Massnahmen und Richtlinien.* Heidelberg, 1981.

WALL, Renate. *Verbrannt, verboten, vergessen: Kleines Lexikon deutschsprachiger Schriftstellerinnen 1933–1945.* Cologne, 1988.

WASSERMANN, Jakob. *Mein Weg als Deutscher und Jude.* Berlin, 1987.

Wegweiser durch das jüdische Berlin: Geschichte und Gegenwart. Mit Berlin-Plan von 1936. Berlin, 1987.

WEINZIERL, Ulrich. *Alfred Polgar: Eine Biographie.* Vienna, 1984.

WEIZMANN, Chaim. *Trial and Error: The Autobiography of Chaim Weizmann.* New York, 1949.

WELTSCH, Robert. *Tragt ihn mit Stolz, den gelben Fleck: Eine Aufsatzreihe der "Jüdischen Rundschau" zur Lage der deutschen Juden.* Edited by H. M. Broder and H. Recher. Nördlingen, 1988.

WIESEL, Elie. *Chassidische Feier: Geschichten und Legenden.* Translated from French by M. Venjakob. Freiburg, 1988.

WIESENTHAL, Simon. *Recht, nicht Rache: Erinnerungen.* Berlin, 1988.

WIZNITZER, Manuel. *Arnold Zweig: Das Leben eines deutsch-jüdischen Schriftstellers.* Frankfurt, 1983.

WOLFF, Kurt. *Briefwechsel eines Verlegers: 1911–1963.* Frankfurt, 1980.

WOLFF, Theodor. *Die Juden.* Edited by B. Sösemann. Frankfurt, 1984.

WOLFSKEHL, Karl. *Briefwechsel aus Neuseeland 1938–1948.* Darmstadt, 1988.

Zeugnisse einer tragischen Begegnung. Foreword by H. Gollwitzer. Heidelberg, 1974.

ZOCH-WESTPHAL, Gisela. *Aus den sechs Leben der Mascha Kaléko: Biographische Skizzen, Tagebuch, Briefe.* Berlin, 1987.

ZOHN, Harry. *. . . bin ein Sohn der deutschen Sprache nur: Der jüdische Anteil an der österreichischen Literatur.* Berlin, 1985.

ZUCKERKANDL, Bertha. *Österreich intim: Lebenserinnerungen.* Berlin 1988.

ZWEIG, Stefan. *Tagebücher.* Frankfurt, 1988.

ZWEIG, Stefan. *The World of Yesterday: An Autobiography.* Lincoln, Neb., 1964.

TEXT SOURCES

ADORNO, Theodor W. In *Frankfurter Beiträge zur Soziologie,* 1967, no. 18–20.　　　　　　　　　　　　　　　　　　　　p. 233

AGNON, Samuel Josef. "Das Licht der Tora." In *Das Buch von den polnischen Juden.* Berlin, 1916.　　　　　　　　　　　　pp. 41, 71

ALLERHAND, Jakob, and Claudio Magris. *Studien zur Literatur der Juden in Osteuropa.* Eisenstadt, 1977.　　　　　　　　　　p. 195

ALTENBERG, Peter. In *Gesammelte Werke,* edited by Werner J. Schweiger. Frankfurt am Main, 1987.　　　　　　　　　pp. 136, 149

AMÉRY, Jean. *At the Mind's Limits: Contemplations by a Survivor on Auschwitz and its Realities.* Bloomington, 1980.　　　　p. 300 (2)

ANZ, Thomas, and Michael Stark, eds. *Expressionismus: Manifeste und Dokumente zur deutschen Literatur 1910–1920.* Stuttgart, 1982.　p. 184

APPEL, Marta. "Memoirs." In Monika Richarz, ed., *Jüdisches Leben in Deutschland 1918–1945.* Stuttgart, 1982.　　　　pp. 298, 299

ARENDT, Hannah. In *Die verborgene Tradition: Acht Essays.* Frankfurt am Main, 1976.　　　　　　　　　　　　　　　　p. 184

ARENDT, Hannah. "Hermann Broch 1886–1951." In *Men in Dark Times.* New York, 1968.　　　　　　　　　　　　　　　　p. 190

ARENDT, Hannah. "On Humanity in Dark Times." In *Men in Dark Times.* New York, 1968.　　　　　　　　　　　　　　p. 190

ARENDT, Hannah. *Rahel Varnhagen: Lebensgeschichte einer deutschen Jüdin aus der Romantik.* Munich, 1959. Reprint. Munich, 1987.　p. 190

ARENDT, Hannah. In *Zur Zeit: Acht Essays.* Munich, 1989.　p. 301

ASCH, Schalom. *Der Trost des Volkes.* Zurich, 1934.　　　p. 28

ASCH, Schalom. "Hohes Gras." In *Kinder in der Fremde.* Amsterdam, 1935.　　　　　　　　　　　　　　　　　　　　p. 66

AUERBACH, Berthold to Jakob Auerbach, 4 October 1862. In Franz Kobler, *Jüdische Geschichte in Briefen aus Ost und West.* Vienna, 1938. p. 42

AUERBACH, Berthold to Jakob Auerbach, 28 December 1867. In Franz Kobler, *Juden und Judentum in deutschen Briefen aus drei Jahrhunderten.* Vienna, 1935.　　　　　　　　　　　　　　　　p. 171

Aufruf [Proclamation] des Reichsvereins der Deutschen Juden and the *Zionistischen Vereinigung für Deutschland.* Berlin, 1914.　p. 260

AUSLÄNDER, Rose. "Bukowina." In Rose Ausländer, *Gesammelte Werke,* edited by Helmut Braun. Frankfurt am Main, 1985–88.　p. 79

BAB, Julius. *Das Theater der Gegenwart.* Leipzig, 1928.　p. 224

BAECK, Leo. *Das Wesen des Judentums.* Berlin, 1905. Reprint. Wiesbaden, 1988.　　　　　　　　　　　　　　　　pp. 302

BAECK, Leo. *The Essence of Judaism,* translated by Victor Grubweiser and Leonard Pearl. London, 1936.　　　　　　　pp. 15, 22, 261

BAECK, Leo. "Israel und das deutsche Volk." In *Merkur 6,* No. 56/10 (1952).　　　　　　　　　　　　　　　　pp. 261, 302

BAECK, Leo. In *Juden in Berlin: Ein Lesebuch.* Berlin, 1988.　p. 261

BAECK, Leo. "Wohlfahrt, Recht und Religion. 1930." In *Wege im Judentum.* Berlin, 1933.　　　　　　　　　　　　　p. 262

BAMBERGER, Ludwig. "Deutschtum und Judentum." In *Unsere Zeit,* 1880 annual.　　　　　　　　　　　　　　　　　p. 170

BAUM, Oskar. "Das Geheimnis der jüdischen Energie." In *Jüdischer Almanach 5686 (1925/26).* Prague, 1925.　　　　　pp. 100, 184

BAUMANN, Kurt. "Memoiren." In Monika Richarz, ed., *Jüdisches Leben in Deutschland 1918–1945.* Stuttgart, 1982.　　　p. 290

BEER-HOFMANN, Richard, to Martin Buber, 3 April 1913. In Martin Buber, *Briefwechsel aus sieben Jahrzehnten.* Heidelberg, 1972–75.　p. 174

BEER-HOFMANN, Richard. *Der Tod Georgs.* Berlin, 1900. Reprint. Ditzingen, n.d.　　　　　　　　　　　　　　　　p. 102

BEER-HOFMANN, Richard. In Harry Zohn, *. . . ich bin ein Sohn der deutschen Sprache nur.* Vienna/Munich, 1986.　　　　p. 174 (2)

BENJAMIN, Walter. *The Correspondence of Walter Benjamin and Gershom Scholem.* New York, 1989.　　　　　　　　p. 292

BENJAMIN, Walter. "Die Wiederkehr des Flaneurs." In *Die literarische Welt 5,* No. 40 (1929).　　　　　　　　　　　　p. 207

BENJAMIN, Walter. *Gesammelte Schriften,* edited by Rolf Tiedemann and Hermann Schweppenhäuser, under the direction of Gershom Scholem and Theodor W. Adorno. Frankfurt am Main, 1980.　　pp. 182, 191

BENJAMIN, Walter, to Max Rychner. In *Walter Benjamin: Briefe,* edited by Gershom Scholem and Theodor W. Adorno. Frankfurt am Main, 1987.　　　　　　　　　　　　　　　　　　p. 191

BENJAMIN, Walter, to Gershom Scholem, 22 October 1917. In *Walter Benjamin: Briefe,* edited by Gershom Scholem and Theodor W. Adorno. Frankfurt am Main, 1987.　　　　　　　　　　　p. 191

BENN, Gottfried. "Rede auf Else Lasker-Schüler." In *Der Tagesspiegel,* 24 February 1952. In *Gesammelte Werke in vier Banden,* edited by Dieter Wellershoff. Wiesbaden, 1987–89.　　　　　　　　p. 186

BERNSTEIN, Daniel. "Handel und Industrie." In Siegmund Kaznelson, ed., *Juden im deutschen Kulturbereich.* Berlin, 1962.　p. 239

BERNSTEIN, Daniel. "Wirtschaft I: Finanzwesen." In Siegmund Kaznelson, ed., *Juden im deutschen Kulturbereich.* Berlin, 1962.　　p. 161

BERNSTEIN, S. "Das Wesen des Judentums." In *Jüdischer Almanach 5663 (1902/03).* Berlin, 1902.　　　　　　　　　p. 42

BILLROTH, Theodor, to Joseph Joachim, 20 January 1890. In Franz Kobler, *Juden und Judentum in deutschen Briefen aus drei Jahrhunderten.* Vienna, 1935.　　　　　　　　　　　　　　　p. 219

BLOCH, Ernst. *Geist der Utopie.* Munich, 1918. In Ernst Bloch, *Gesamtausgabe in 16 Bänden.* Frankfurt am Main, 1975.　　p. 233

BLOCH, Ernst. In Silvia Markun, *Ernst Bloch.* Reinbek, 1985.　p. 233

BLUMENFELD, Kurt. In Carl Seelig, ed., *Helle Zeit—Dunkle Zeit: In memoriam Albert Einstein.* Frankfurt am Main/Stuttgart/Vienna, 1956.　　　　　　　　　　　　　　　　　　　　　p. 237

BLUMENTHAL, Hermann. *Knabenalter* (second part of the trilogy *Der Weg der Jugend*). Berlin, 1908.　　　　　　　　　　p. 96

BÖHM, Adolf. "Die zionistische Bewegung." In *Vom Judentum: Ein Sammelbuch.* Leipzig, 1913.　　　　　　　　　　pp. 82, 272

BORN, Max, to Albert Einstein, 2 June 1933. *The Born—Einstein Letters: The Correspondence between Albert Einstein and Max and Hedwig Born from 1916–1955,* with commentaries by Max Born, translated by Irene Born. London, 1971.　　　　　　　　　　　　p. 237

BÖRNE, Ludwig. In *Börnes Werke,* edited by Helmut Bock and Walter Dietze. East Berlin, 1986.　　　　　　　　　　　p. 171

BRAUNTHAL, Julius. In *Auf der Suche nach dem Millennium.* Nuremberg, 1948–49.　　　　　　　　　　　　　　　　p. 270

BROCH, Hermann. *Hugo von Hofmannsthal and His Time.* Chicago, 1984.　　　　　　　　　　　　　　　　　pp. 157, 383

BROD, Leo. *Geschichten aus dem Böhmerwald.* Munich, n.d. Reprint. Fürstenfeldbruck, 1976.　　　　　　　　　　　p. 96

BROD, Max. *Streitbares Leben.* Munich, 1960. Reprint. Frankfurt am Main, 1979.　　　　　　　　pp. 22, 184, 229, 279

BUBER, Martin. "Aus der Rede zur Wiedereröffnung des Frankfurter jüdischen Lehrhauses." In *Die Stunde und die Erkenntnis.* Berlin, 1936.　　　　　　　　　　　　　　　　　　pp. 235, 272

BUBER, Martin. *Briefwechsel aus sieben Jahrzehnten,* edited by Grete Schaeder. Heidelberg, 1972–75.　　　　　　　pp. 70, 235 (2)

BUBER, Martin. *The Origin and Meaning of Hasidim.* New York, 1960.　　　　　　　　　　　　　　　　　　　　p. 70

BUBER, Martin. *Tales of the Hasidim: The Early Masters,* translated by Olga Marx. New York, 1947. pp. 41, 48, 51, 93, 103

Buber, Martin. *Tales of the Hasidim: The Later Masters,* translated by Olga Marx. New York, 1948. pp. 41, 76, 100

Buxbaum, Henry. "Erinnerungen." In Monika Richarz, ed., *Jüdisches Leben in Deutschland 1918–1945.* Stuttgart, 1982. pp. 126 (2), 278

Canetti, Elias. *Die gerettete Zunge: Geschichte einer Jugend.* Munich/Vienna, 1977. p. 170

Canetti, Elias. *The Play of the Eyes.* New York, 1986. p. 215

Canetti, Elias. *The Tongue Set Free.* New York, 1979. pp. 19, 24, 109, 242

Canetti, Elias. *The Torch in My Ear.* New York, 1982. pp. 53, 137, 147

Carroll, Lewis. *The Complete Works: Journal of a Tour in Russia.* New York, 1965. p. 38 (2)

Celan, Paul. *Collected Prose.* Manchester, 1987. p. 301

Celan, Paul. "Und mit dem Buch aus Tarussa." In *Paul Celan: Gesammelte Werke,* edited by Beda Allemann and Stefan Reichert. Frankfurt am Main, 1983. p. 170

"Central-Verein, Satzung aus dem Jahr 1893." In Gunter E. Grimm and Hans-Peter Beyerdörfer, eds., *Im Zeichen Hiobs.* Frankfurt am Main, 1986. p. 252

Central-Verein Zeitung, 5 August 1932. p. 292

Central-Verein Zeitung, 30 March 1933. p. 291

Chagall, Bella. *Burning Lights,* translated by Norbert Guterman. New York, 1962. pp. 22–23

Cohen, Hermann. *Religion of Reason Out of the Sources of Judaism,* translated by Simon Kaplan. New York, 1972. pp. 17, 19, 28, 48, 74

Daniel, Max. "Meine Familiengeschichte." In Monika Richarz, ed., *Jüdisches Leben in Deutschland 1871–1918.* Stuttgart, 1979. p. 102

Deutscher, Isaac. *The Non-Jewish Jew.* London, 1968. pp. 82, 95, 108, 135, 202 (2), 245, 265, 302

Dinse, Helmut, and Sol Liptzin. *Einführung in die jiddische Literatur.* Stuttgart, 1978. p. 195 (2)

Döblin, Alfred. *Berichte und Kritiken 1921–1924.* Olten/Freiburg, 1976. p. 229

Döblin, Alfred. *Journey to Poland.* New York, 1991. pp. 29, 31, 32, 49, 74, 76, 85 (2), 91, 99

Döblin, Alfred. *Schicksalsreise, Bericht und Bekenntnis.* Frankfurt am Main, 1949. p. 188 (2)

Ehrenstein, Albert. In *Werke,* edited by Hanni Mittelmann. Munich, 1988. p. 177

Einstein, Albert. In *Albert Einstein als Philosoph und Naturforscher,* edited by Paul Arthur Schilpp. Stuttgart, 1955. p. 237

Einstein, Albert. *Mein Weltbild,* edited by Carl Seelig. Zurich/Stuttgart/Vienna, 1953. p. 237 (3)

Einstein, Albert. *Out of My Later Years.* New York, 1950. pp. 237 (2), 263

Einstein, Albert. In Carl Seelig, ed., *Helle Zeit—Dunkle Zeit: In memoriam Albert Einstein.* Zurich/Stuttgart/Vienna, 1956. p. 237

Einstein, Carl. "Pariser Nachlass." In *Gesammelte Werke,* edited by Sibylle Penkert. Reinbek, 1973. p. 300

Eliasberg, Alexander. "Reb Jajnkew-Mejer." In *Sonderheft der Süddeutschen Monatshefte "Ostjuden,"* February 1916. p. 15

Eljashoff, J. "Über Jargon ('Jüdisch') und Jargonliteratur." In *Jüdischer Almanach* 5663 (1902/03). Berlin, 1902. p. 120

Epstein, Jehudo. *Mein Weg von Ost nach West: Erinnerungen.* Stuttgart, 1929. pp. 15, 19, 27, 76, 80

Feuchtwanger, Lion. "Centum opuscula." 1929. In a collection compiled by Wolfgang Berndt. Rudolstadt, 1956. Reprint. Frankfurt am Main, 1984. p. 192 (2)

Feuchtwanger, Lion. *The Devil in France.* New York, 1941. p. 289

Feuchtwanger, Lion. *Exil.* Berlin, 1956. Reprint. Frankfurt am Main, 1989. p. 290

Feuchtwanger, Lion. "Offener Brief an den Bewohner meines Hauses Mahlerstrasse 8 in Berlin." In Heinz Knobloch, *Der Berliner zweifelt immer: Feuilletons von damals.* East Berlin, 1978. p. 288

Fischer, Brigitte B. *Sie schrieben mir oder Was aus meinem Poesiealbum wurde.* Zurich/Stuttgart, 1978. Reprint. Munich, 1989. p. 194

Flake, Otto. "Juden in der Literatur." In Die Weltbühne 19, no. 12 (1923). In *Werke in Einzelausgaben,* edited by Rolf Hochhuth and Peter Härtling. Frankfurt am Main, 1974–76. p. 217

Fraenkel, Joseph, ed. *The Jews of Austria.* London, 1967. p. 245

Frank, Fritz. "Verschollene Heimat." In Monika Richarz, ed., *Jüdisches Leben in Deutschland 1871–1918.* Stuttgart, 1979. pp. 79, 126, 199

Frank, Julius. "Reminiscences of days gone." In Monika Richarz, ed., *Jüdisches Leben in Deutschland 1871–1918.* Stuttgart, 1979. p. 48

Franzos, Karl Emil. *Der Pojaz.* Stuttgart, 1893. Reprint. Frankfurt am Main, 1988. p. 135

Franzos, Karl Emil. *Die Juden von Barnow.* Leipzig, 1877. p. 69

Frei, Bruno. "Der blinde Bettler von der Produktenbörse." In *Jüdisches Elend in Wien: Bilder und Daten.* Vienna, 1920. p. 118

Freud, Martin. "Who was Freud." In Josef Fraenkel, *The Jews of Austria.* London, 1967. p. 245

Freud, Sigmund. *Briefe 1873–1939,* edited by Ernst L. Freud. Frankfurt am Main, 1980. pp. 244(2), 245

Freud, Sigmund. "Briefe an Arthur Schnitzler," edited by Heinrich Schnitzler. In *Neue Rundschau* 66 (1955). p. 173

Freud, Sigmund. "Die Widerstände gegen die Psychoanalyse." In *Imago.* 1925. In *Gesammelte Werke.* Frankfurt am Main, 1974. p. 244

Freud, Sigmund. *The Standard Edition of the Complete Psychological Works,* translated by James Strachey and Anna Freud. Vol. 8 (1905). London 1960. pp. 92, 242, 244–45

Freud, Sigmund. *The Standard Edition of the Complete Psychological Works,* translated by James Strachey and Anna Freud. Vol. 13 (1913/14). London 1955. p. 244

Friedell, Egon. *Ecce poeta.* Berlin, 1912. p. 177

Friedell, Egon. In *Meine Doppelseele: Taktlose Bemerkungen zum Theater,* edited by Herbert Illig. Vienna, 1985. p. 173

Friedländer, Otto. *Letzter Glanz der Märchenstadt.* Vienna, 1948. Reprint. Vienna, 1985. p. 137

Fromer, Jacob. "Eine Hochzeit im Ghetto." In Artur Landsberger, *Das Volk aus dem Ghetto.* Berlin/Vienna, 1921. p. 26

Frýd, Norbert. *Muster ohne Wert und der Herr Bischof.* Prague, 1966. In Wilma Iggers, ed., *Die Juden in Böhmen und Mähren.* Munich, 1986. p. 74

Fuchs, Vilém. In Johannes Urzidil, *Die Prager Juden.* Radio Bremen, 15 September 1976. p. 182

Genée, Pierre, and Hans Veigl. *Fritz Grünbaum: Die Schöpfung und andere Kabarettstücke.* Vienna, 1985. pp. 230 (2), 231

Ginzel, Günther B. "Aus Friedrich wurde Chajim: Alltag eines jüdischen Kindes." In *Jüdischer Alltag in Deutschland 1933–1945.* Düsseldorf, 1984. p. 298

Goldschmidt, Levin, to Heinrich von Treitschke, 4 May 1881. In Franz Kobler, *Jüdische Geschichte in Briefen aus Ost und West.* Vienna, 1938. p. 128

Goldstein, Moritz. "Deutsch-jüdischer Parnass." In *Kunstwart* 25 (1 March 1912). p. 287

Gottlieb, Moritz, to an editor, 1876. In Franz Kobler, *Jüdische Geschichte in Briefen aus Ost und West.* Vienna, 1938. p. 202

Granach, Alexander. *Da geht ein Mensch: Roman eines Lebens.* Stockholm, 1945. Reprint. Munich, 1987. pp. 15, 78, 79, 227

Graupe, Heinz Mosche. *Die Entstehung des modernen Judentums: 1650–1942.* Hamburg, 1977. p. 235

Gronemann, Sammy. Erinnerungen. In Monika Richarz, ed., *Jüdisches Leben in Deutschland 1871–1918.* Stuttgart, 1979. pp. 122, 127, 273

Grossmann, Stefan. "Wiener Köpfe, dritter Teil: Victor Adler." *Die Zeit,* 1898, no. 177. p. 270

Grünberg, Karl. In Jürgen Serke, *Die verbrannten Dichter.* Frankfurt am Main, 1983. p. 268

Grunwald, Max. "Chanukka." In Friedrich Thieberger, ed., *Jüdisches Fest—jüdischer Brauch.* N.p., 1937. Reprint. Frankfurt am Main, 1985. p. 23

Hamburger, Ernest. *Juden im öffentlichen Leben Deutschlands: 1848–1918.* Tübingen, 1968. p. 252

Hamerow, Theodore S. From *Commentary,* April 1984. In *Die versunkene Welt,* edited by Joachim Riedl. Vienna, 1984. p. 110

Hauschner, Auguste. *Die Familie Lowositz.* Berlin, 1908. p. 86

Havel-Ornstein, Alfred M. "Autobiographie des Adolf Ornstein." In Wilma Iggers, ed., *Die Juden in Böhmen und Mähren.* Munich, 1986. p. 120

Heine, Heinrich. *Heines Briefe in einem Band,* edited by Fritz Mende. Weimar, 1989. p. 171

Heine, Heinrich. *Reisebilder.* Stuttgart, n.d. In *Atta Troll.* Klagenfurt, 1984. p. 161

Herben, Jan. *Itzig Wolf, Gemischte Waarenhandlung.* Telč, 1892. In Wilma Iggers, ed., *Die Juden in Böhmen und Mähren.* Munich, 1986. p. 80

Herrmann, Hugo. *In jenen Tagen.* Jerusalem, 1938. pp. 126, 199

Herzfeld, Ernst. "Lebenserinnerungen." In Monika Richarz, ed., *Jüdisches Leben in Deutschland 1871–1918.* Stuttgart, 1979. p. 253

Herzfelde, Wieland. "Else Lasker-Schüler." In *Sinn und Form: Beiträge zur Literatur* 21, no. 6 (1969). p. 186

Herzl, Theodor. *Briefe und Tagebücher 1866–1895,* edited by Alex Bein and Hermann Greive. Berlin/Frankfurt am Main/Vienna, 1983–88. p. 255

Herzl, Theodor. "Die Menora." In Friedrich Thieberger, ed., *Jüdisches Leben—jüdischer Brauch.* N.p., 1937. Reprint. Frankfurt am Main, 1985. p. 23

Herzl, Theodor. *The Jewish State.* New York, 1970. p. 272

Herzl, Theodor. *The Old-New Land.* New York, 1960. p. 274 (2)

Herzl, Theodor. *Theodor Herzls Tagebücher 1895–1904.* Berlin, 1922–23. p. 274

Hess, Moses. *Rom und Jerusalem: Die letzte Nationalitätenfrage.* Leipzig, 1862. p. 272 (4)

Hessel, Franz. *Ein Flaneur in Berlin.* Leipzig/Vienna, 1929. Reprint. Berlin, 1984. p. 266

Hille, Peter. "Pastellbilder der Kunst." In *Kampf,* 1904, No. 7. p. 186

Hirschfeld, Isidor. "Tagebuch." In Monika Richarz, ed., *Jüdisches Leben in Deutschland 1871–1918.* Stuttgart, 1979. pp. 139, 252

"Hochzeitsfeier im Sadagorer Rabbihaus." *Czernowitzer Allgemeine Zeitung,* 4 June 1904. p. 70

Höllriegel, Arnold. "Die Fahrt auf dem Katarakt, Autobiographie ohne einen Helden." In Monika Richarz, ed., *Jüdisches Leben in Deutschland 1871–1918.* Stuttgart, 1979. p. 137 (2)

Hofmannsthal, Hugo von. "Aufzeichnungen." In *Gesammelte Werke in 10 Einzelbänden,* edited by Bernd Schoeller. Frankfurt am Main, 1985. p. 172

Horkheimer, Max. *Die Sehnsucht nach dem ganz Anderen: Ein Interview mit Kommentar von Helmut Gumniar.* Hamburg, 1970. In *Gesammelte Schriften,* edited by Gunzelin Schmid-Noerr. Frankfurt am Main, 1988. p. 233

Horkheimer, Max. In Thilo Koch, ed., *Porträts deutsch-jüdischer Geistesgeschichte.* Cologne, 1961 p. 233

Horkheimer, Max. *Zur Kritik der instrumentellen Vernunft.* Frankfurt am Main, 1986. p. 233 (2)

Iggers, Wilma, ed. *Die Juden in Böhmen und Mähren.* Munich, 1986. p. 276

Israelitische Gemeindezeitung. Prague, 1898. In Wilma Iggers, ed., *Die Juden in Böhmen und Mähren.* Munich, 1986. p. 273

Israelitische Wochenschrift, 1887. In Ernest Hamburger, *Juden im öffentlichen Leben Deutschlands 1848–1918.* Bulletin des Leo-Baeck-Institutes. New York, 1968. p. 252

Jacob, Benno. *Rede im Centralverein deutscher Staatsbürger jüdischen Glaubens,* 1919. In *Aus Geschichte und Leben der Juden in Westfalen: Eine Sammelschrift,* edited by Hans Chanoch Mayer. Frankfurt am Main, 1962. p. 287 (2)

Jacobsohn, Egon, and Leo Hirsch. *Jüdische Mütter.* Berlin, 1936. p. 76

Jens, Walter. "1966." In Hilde Domin, *Zusätzliche Informationen zu Leben und Werk von Nelly Sachs.* In *Text und Kritik.* Munich/Hannover, 1979. p. 187

Jonas, Hans. In Wolfgang Heuer, *Hannah Arendt.* Reinbek, 1987. p. 191

Jüdische Rundschau, 7 April 1933. p. 225

Jungk, Robert. In *Mein Judentum,* edited by Hans Jürgen Schultz. Stuttgart, 1978. pp. 235, 279

Kafka, Franz. *Conversations with Kafka,* edited by Gustav Janouch. New York, 1971. p. 87

Kafka, Franz. *The Diaries of Franz Kafka,* edited by Max Brod. New York, 1948–49. p. 77

Kafka, Franz, to Max Brod, 1921. In *Franz Kafka: Briefe von 1902 bis 1924,* edited by Max Brod. Frankfurt am Main, 1983. pp. 178, 182

Kafka, Franz, to Oskar Pollak, 27 January 1904. In *Franz Kafka: Briefe von 1902 bis 1924,* edited by Max Brod. Frankfurt am Main, 1983. p. 197

Kafka, Franz. *Letter to his Father.* New York, 1966. pp. 182–84

Kafka, Franz. *Tagebücher 1910–1923,* edited by Max Brod. Frankfurt am Main, 1989. pp. 93, 182

Kahler, Ottilie von. *Ein Beitrag zu einer Familiengeschichte des Hauses M. B. Teller.* Svinaře, 1930. In Wilma Iggers, ed., *Die Juden in Böhmen und Mähren.* Munich, 1986. p. 124

Kaléko, Mascha. "Die frühen Jahre." In Gisela Zoch-Westphal, *Aus den sechs Leben der Mascha Kaléko.* Berlin, 1988. p. 187

Kästner, Erich. In Bernt Engelmann, *Deutschland ohne Juden.* Cologne, 1988. p. 188

Kerr, Alfred. In *Werke in Einzelbänden,* edited by Hermann Haarmann and Günther Rühle. Berlin, 1989. p. 177

Kesten, Hermann. "Der Mensch Joseph Roth." In *Joseph Roth: Leben und Werk. Ein Gedächtnisbuch,* edited by Hermann Linden. Cologne/The Hague, 1949. p. 194

Kirchheim, Rafael, to Leopold Löw, 17 December 1865. In Franz Kobler, *Jüdische Geschichte in Briefen aus Ost und West.* Vienna, 1938. p. 252

Kisch, Bruno. *Wanderungen und Wandlungen.* Cologne, 1966. pp. 103, 201

Klapheck, Anna. *Mutter Ey: Eine Düsseldorfer Künstlerlegende.* Düsseldorf, 1958. p. 203

Kobler, Franz. *Juden und Judentum in deutschen Briefen aus drei Jahrhunderten.* Vienna, 1935. p. 277

Kobler, Franz. *Jüdische Geschichte in Briefen aus Ost und West.* Vienna, 1938. p. 151, 215

Kohn, Salomon. "Der Kaddisch von Kol Nidre in der Altneusynagoge." In Artur Landsberger, *Das Volk aus dem Ghetto.* Berlin/Vienna, 1921. p. 31

Kohn, Salomon. *Prager Ghettogeschichten.* Leipzig, n.d. p. 94

Kortner, Fritz. *Aller Tage Abend.* Munich, 1959. Reprint. Munich, 1986. p. 228

Kosta, Oskar. "Der Weg in die Vergangenheit." In Wilma Iggers, ed., *Die Juden in Böhmen und Mähren.* Munich, 1986. p. 35

Kraus, Karl. "Credo." In *Die Fackel* 19. Vienna, May 1917. p. 266

Kraus, Karl. *Die demolirte Literatur.* Vienna, 1897. p. 136

Kraus, Karl. In *Die Fackel* 2, no. 5. Vienna, 1899. p. 199

Kraus, Karl. In *Die Fackel* 10, no. 254–55. Vienna, 1908/09. p. 245

Kraus, Karl. *Eine Krone für Zion.* Vienna, 1898. In Karl Kraus, *Frühe Schriften 1892–1900,* edited by Johannes J. Braakenburg. Frankfurt am Main, 1979.

Kraus, Karl. In Harry Zohn, *. . . . ich bin ein Sohn der deutschen Sprache nur.* Vienna/Munich, 1986. p. 256

Kuh, Anton. "Asphalt und Scholle." In *Prager Tagblatt* 58, no. 101 (1933). p. 288

Kuh, Anton. "Central" und "Herrenhof." In *Der unsterbliche Österreicher.* Munich, 1931. pp. 136, 177

Kuh, Anton. "Die 'blonden Mädels' und die 'Tante'." In *Die Stunde* 3, no. 647 (6 May 1925). p. 294

Kuh, Anton. "Eisenbach." In *Von Goethe abwärts: Aphorismen, Essays, kleine Prosa.* Vienna/Hannover/Bern, 1963. p. 231 (3)

Kuh, Anton. "Pallenberg plappert." In *Der unsterbliche Österreicher.* Munich, 1931. p. 213

Kuh, Anton. *Physiognomik: Aussprüche.* Munich, 1931. pp. 182, 252.

Kuh, Anton. "Prag: Eine Vision der Wirklichkeit." In *Der unsterbliche Österreicher.* Munich, 1931. pp. 86, 87

Kuh, Anton. "Von Pöchlarn bis Braunau." In *Die Neue Weltbühne* 13 (1935). p. 288 (2)

Kuh, Anton. "Wörterbuch des Fremdenverkehrs." In *Prager Tagblatt* 58, no. 130 (1933). p. 242

Kunert, Günter. Foreword to Eike Geisel, *Im Scheunenviertel.* Berlin, 1981. p. 110

Landau, Edwin. "Mein Leben vor und nach Hitler." In Monika Richarz, ed., *Jüdisches Leben in Deutschland 1918–1945.* Stuttgart, 1982. p. 261

Landau, Philippine. "Kindheitserinnerungen." In Monika Richarz, ed., *Jüdisches Leben in Deutschland 1871–1918.* Stuttgart, 1979. pp. 22, 32

Landau, Saul Raphael. *Unter jüdischen Proletariern: Reiseschilderungen aus Ostgalizien und Russland.* Vienna, 1898. p. 90

Landauer, Gustav. *Aufruf zum Sozialismus.* Berlin, 1919. p. 262

Landauer, Georg. In *Dokumente zur Geschichte des deutschen Zionismus 1882–1933,* edited by Jehuda Reinharz. Tübingen, 1981. p. 292

Landauer, Gustav. "Sind das Ketzergedanken." In *Der werdende Mensch,* edited by Martin Buber. Potsdam, 1921. pp. 262, 268

Landsberger, Artur. *Das Volk aus dem Ghetto.* Berlin/Vienna, 1921. p. 75

Langer, Frantisek. *Sie waren und es war.* Prague, 1963. In Wilma Iggers, ed., *Die Juden in Böhmen und Mähren.* Munich, 1986. pp. 103, 126

Lania, Leo. In *Die Weltbühne* (Berlin), 19 (1923). p. 265

Lasker-Schüler, Else. *Der Wunderrabbiner von Barcelona.* Berlin, 1921. In *Gesammelte Werke.* Munich, 1986. p. 186.

Lasker-Schüler, Else. "Ernst Toller." In *Die Weltbühne* (Berlin), 21, no. 1 (1925). p. 185

Lasker-Schüler, Else. *Ich räume auf!* Zurich, 1925. In *Gesammelte Werke.* Munich, 1986. p. 186

Lasker-Schüler, Else. "Jankel Adler." In Anna Klaphek, *Jankel Adler.* Recklinghausen, 1966. p. 203

Lasker-Schüler, Else. "Mein Volk." In *Der siebente Tag.* Berlin, 1905. In *Gesammelte Werke.* Munich, 1986. p. 186

Lassalle, Ferdinand. *Nachgelassene Briefe und Schriften,* edited by Gustav Mayer. Stuttgart, 1921–25. p. 262

Lassalle, Ferdinand. *Reden und Schriften, Tagebuch: Seelenbeichte.* Vienna, 1911. p. 262 (2)

Lazarus, Moritz. In Nahida Lazarus, *Ein deutscher Professor in der Schweiz.* Berlin, 1924 p. 235

Lessing, Theodor. *Gesammelte Schriften.* Vol. 1: *Einmal und nicht wieder: Lebenserinnerungen.* Prague, 1935. p. 234

Levin, Schemarja. *Kindheit im Exil.* Berlin, 1931. p. 66

Lichtwitz, Hans. In *Jüdischer Almanach* 5699 (1938/39). Berlin, 1938. p. 298

Liebermann, Max. In *Central-Verein Zeitung,* 5 November 1933. p. 201

Liebermann, Max, to Carl Sachs, 28 February 1934. In *Deutsche Briefe 1750–1950,* edited by Gert Mattenklott et al. Frankfurt am Main, 1988. p. 281

Liebermann, Max. *Siebzig Briefe,* edited by Franz Landsberger. Berlin, 1937. p. 201

Liebermann, Mischket. *Aus dem Ghetto in die Welt.* East Berlin, 1977. pp. 95, 109

Loewenberg, Jakob. In *Jüdisch-liberale Zeitung,* 16 October 1925. p. 287

Löwenfeld, Philipp. "Memoiren." In Monika Richarz, ed., *Jüdisches Leben in Deutschland 1871–1918.* Stuttgart, 1979. p. 110

Lützeler, Paul Michael. *Hermann Broch.* London, 1987. p. 190

Luxemburg, Rosa. *Briefe an Freunde,* edited by Benedikt Kautsky. Hamburg, 1950. Reprint. Frankfurt am Main, 1986. p. 265 (2)

Luxemburg, Rosa. *Gesammelte Werke,* edited by Georg Adler et al. Berlin 1979–83. p. 266

Magris, Claudio. *Weit von wo? Verlorene Welt des Ostjudentums.* Vienna, 1974. pp. 132, 253

Mauthner, Fritz. In Walter Muschg, *Von Trakl zu Brecht.* Munich, 1961. p. 232

Mauthner, Fritz, to Gustav Landauer, 10 October 1913. In Franz Kobler, *Juden und Judentum in deutschen Briefen aus drei Jahrhunderten.* Vienna, 1935. p. 232

Mauthner, Fritz. *Erinnerungen: Prager Jugendjahre.* Frankfurt am Main, 1969. p. 232

Mayer, Hans. *Ein Deutscher auf Widerruf: Erinnerungen.* Frankfurt am Main, 1982. Reprint. Frankfurt am Main, 1987. pp. 187, 290

Mayer, Louis, to his son, 10 July 1868. In Franz Kobler, *Jüdische Geschichte in Briefen aus Ost und West.* Vienna, 1938. p. 38

Mayer, Paul. "Maximilian Harden." In Gustav Krojanker, *Juden in der deutschen Literatur.* Berlin, 1922. p. 199

Mehring, Walter, to Kurt Tucholsky. In *Kurt Tucholsky hasst—liebt,* edited by Mary Gerold-Tucholsky. Reinbek, 1962. p. 187

Mendelssohn, Peter de. Afterword to Jakob Wassermann, *Der Fall Maurizius.* Munich, 1981. p. 180

Mischne, Tora. "Der Richter." In Maimonides, *Gesammelte Werke,* edited by Valerio Verra. Hildesheim, 1965–71. p. 27

Morgenstern, Soma. "Dichten, denken, berichten: Gespräche zwischen Roth und Musil." In *Frankfurter Allgemeine Zeitung,* 1975, no. 79. p. 184

Mühsam, Paul. "Ich bin ein Mensch gewesen." In Monika Richarz, ed., *Jüdisches Leben in Deutschland 1871–1918.* Stuttgart, 1979. p. 128

Neuhaus, Leopold. "Barmizwa." In Friedrich Thieberger, ed., *Jüdisches Fest—jüdischer Brauch.* N.p., 1937. Reprint. Frankfurt am Main, 1985. p. 24

Niemirower, J. "Rebb Aphikomen und der Prophet Elijahu." In Artur Landsberger, *Das Volk aus dem Ghetto.* Berlin/Vienna, 1921. p. 71

Ostrovsky, Bruno. "Erinnerungen und Betrachtungen." In Monika Richarz, ed., *Jüdisches Leben in Deutschland 1918–1945.* Stuttgart, 1982. pp. 137, 153

Peretz, Jizchak Leib. In Otto F. Best, *Mameloschen: Jiddisch, eine Sprache und ihre Literatur.* Frankfurt am Main, 1988. p. 195 (2)

Peretz, Jizchak Leib. In *Das Buch von den polnischen Juden.* Berlin, 1916. p. 62

Pinski, David. "Das Erwachen." In *Jüdischer Almanach* 5663 (1902/03). Berlin, 1902. p. 52

Piscator, Erwin. *Das Politische Theater.* Berlin, 1929. Reprint. *Das Politische Theater und weitere Schriften von 1915 bis 1966.* Reinbek, n.d. p. 225

Polgar, Alfred. "Das Wiener Feuilleton." In *Der Weg* I (17), 20 January 1906. p. 177

Polgar, Alfred. "Der Theaterdichter Schnitzler." In *Die Weltbühne* (Berlin) 27/2, no. 44 (1931). p. 172

Polgar, Alfred. "Habima." In *Der Morgen,* 7 June 1926. p. 229

Polgar, Alfred. "Sonnenthal." In *Wiener Sonn- und Montags-Zeitung,* 26 December 1904. p. 226

Politzer, Heinz. *Das Schweigen der Sirenen: Studien zur deutschen und österreichischen Literatur.* Stuttgart, 1968. p. 173

Rathenau, Walther. In Franz Kobler, *Juden und Judentum in deutschen Briefen aus drei Jahrhunderten.* Vienna, 1935. p. 257 (2)

Rathenau, Walther. *Briefe: Neue Folge.* Dresden, 1928. p. 262

Rathenau, Walther. "Staat und Judentum." In *Zur Kritik der Zeit.* Berlin, 1912. p. 256

Reiner, Max. "Mein Leben in Deutschland vor und nach dem Jahr 1933." In Monika Richarz, ed., *Jüdisches Leben in Deutschland 1918–1945.* Stuttgart, 1982. p. 198

Reinhardt, Max, to Einar Nilson, 18 October 1934. In *Schriften,* edited by Hugo Fetting. Berlin, 1974. p. 225

Rosegger, Peter, to Berthold Auerbach, 27 June 1870. In Franz Kobler, *Jüdische Geschichte in Briefen aus Ost und West.* Vienna, 1938. p. 171

Rosenstein, Conrad. "Der Brunnen, eine Familienchronik." In Monika Richarz, ed., *Jüdisches Leben in Deutschland 1871–1918.* Stuttgart, 1979. pp. 24, 38, 85, 122, 137

Rosenstock, Werner. In *Gegenwart im Rückblick, Festgabe für die jüdische Gemeinde zu Berlin,* edited by Herbert A. Strauss and K. Grossmann. Heidelberg, 1970. p. 132

Rosenzweig, Franz. *Briefe und Tagebücher,* edited by Rachel Rosenzweig and Edith Rosenzweig-Scheinmann. The Hague, 1978. pp. 41, 252

Rosenzweig, Franz. In Josef Ehrlich, *Schabbat.* Munich, 1982. p. 85

Roth, Joseph. *Briefe 1911–1939,* edited by Hermann Kesten. Cologne/Berlin, 1970. pp. 194 (3), 199

Roth, Joseph. "Das Autodafé des Geistes." In Gerhard Sonder, ed., *Die Bücherverbrennung 10. Mai 1933.* Berlin, 1985. pp. 170, 288

Roth, Joseph. "Das Moskauer jüdische Theater." In *Das Moskauer jüdische akademische Theater.* Berlin, 1928. In *Werke,* edited by Hermann Kesten. Cologne, 1975–76. p. 229 (2)

Roth, Joseph. *Die Kapuzinergruft.* Bilthoven, 1938. Reprint. Cologne, 1987. pp. 66, 98

Roth, Joseph. "Döblin im Osten." In *Frankfurter Zeitung,* 31 January 1926. p. 188

Roth, Joseph. "Einstein, der 'Fall'." In *Freie Deutsche Bühne,* 5 September 1920. p. 237

Roth, Joseph. "Emigration." Typescript, 1937. In *Werke,* edited by Hermann Kesten. Cologne, 1975–76. p. 301

Roth, Joseph. *Job.* New York, 1982. p. 35

Roth, Joseph. *Juden auf Wanderschaft.* Berlin, 1927. Reprint. Cologne, 1985. pp. 21, 28, 29, 35, 43, 54, 57, 68, 72, 89, 92, 96, 99, 104, 107 (2), 110, 111, 117, 136, 194

Roth, Joseph. In Egon Erwin Kisch, *Hetzjagd durch die Zeit: Reportagen.* Frankfurt am Main, 1974. p. 177

Roth, Joseph. "Lemberg die Stadt." In *Frankfurter Zeitung,* 22 November, 1924. In *Werke in sechs Bänden.* Cologne, 1989. p. 97

Roth, Joseph. *The Radetzky March,* translated by Eva Tucker. New York, 1974. p. 260 (2)

Roth, Joseph. In Hartmut Scheible, *Arthur Schnitzler in Selbstzeugnissen und Bilddokumenten.* Reinbek, 1976. p. 172

Roth, Joseph. *The Silent Prophet.* Woodstock, N.Y., 1980. p. 147

Roth, Joseph. "Wassermanns letzter Roman." In *Das Neue Tage-Buch* 39, No. 2 (1934). p. 178

Saar, Ferdinand von. "1894." In Rudolf Holzer, *Villa Werheimstein.* Vienna, 1960. p. 151

Sachs, Nelly. In Ruth Dinesen and Helmut Müssener, eds., *Briefe der Nelly Sachs.* Frankfurt am Main, 1985. p. 187

Sahl, Hans. *Memoiren eines Moralisten.* Zurich, 1983. pp. 178, 224, 225

Salomon, Alice. *In Juden in Berlin: Ein Lesebuch.* Berlin, 1988. p. 300

Salten, Felix. "Aus den Anfängen." In *Jahrbuch deutscher Bibliophiler und Literaturfreunde* 18/19 (1932). p. 172

Salten, Felix. *Geister der Zeit.* Vienna, 1924. p. 217

Salten, Felix. *Neue Menschen auf alter Erde.* Berlin/Vienna/Leipzig, 1925. Reprint. Frankfurt am Main, 1986. pp. 75, 78, 174, 273, 281

Sandler, Aron. "Aus der Frühgeschichte des Zionismus." In Monika Richarz, ed., *Jüdisches Leben in Deutschland 1871–1918.* Stuttgart, 1979.

SAPHIR, Moritz Gottlieb. *Gesammelte Schriften.* Stuttgart, 1832. p. 171

SCHERLAG, Lorenz. "Der Musikant." In Artur Landsberger. *Das Volk aus dem Ghetto.* Berlin/Vienna, 1921. p. 93

SCHILDE, Kurt, ed. "Spurensicherung: Jüdischer Sport in Berlin 1933–1938." In Felix Simmenauer, *Die Goldmedaille: Erinnerungen an die Bar Kochba-Makkabi Turn- und Sportbewegung 1898–1938.* Berlin, 1989. p. 140

SCHIVELBUSCH, Wolfgang. *Intellektuellendämmerung.* Frankfurt am Main, 1982. p. 150

SCHNITZLER, Arthur. *Briefe 1875–1912,* edited by Therese Nickl and Heinrich Schnitzler. Frankfurt am Main, 1981. pp. 82, 172

SCHNITZLER, Arthur. *Gesammelte Werke in Einzelbänden.* Frankfurt am Main, 1981. p. 217

SCHNITZLER, Arthur. *Jugend in Wien.* Vienna/Munich/Zurich, 1968. Reprint. Frankfurt am Main, 1988. p. 172

SCHNITZLER, Arthur. *My Youth in Vienna.* New York, 1970. p. 172

SCHNITZLER, Arthur. *The Road to the Open.* New York, 1923. pp. 136, 173, 253 (2), 255

SCHOENBERG, Arnold. *Ausgewählte Briefe,* edited by Erwin Stein. Mainz, 1965. pp. 217, 218 (2)

SCHOLEM Alejchem. *Die Geschichte Tewjes des Milchhändlers.* Berlin, [1921]. Reprint. Frankfurt am Main, 1964. p. 91

SCHOLEM Alejchem. "Pessach im Dorfe." In *Ostjüdischer Erzähler.* Weimar, 1916. Reprint. Langen, 1963. p. 76

SCHOLEM, Gershom. In *Deutsche und Juden: Beiträge von Nahum Goldmann, Gershom Scholem, Golo Mann, Salo W. Baron . . .* Frankfurt am Main, 1967. pp. 129, 287

SCHOLEM, Gershom. "Ernst Bloch." In *Der Spiegel* 29, No. 28 (1975). p. 233

SCHOLEM, Gershom. In *Judaica 4.* Frankfurt am Main, 1984. pp. 131 (2), 134, 140

SCHOLEM, Gershom. *Major Trends in Jewish Mysticism.* New York, 1954. pp. 48, 72

SCHOLEM, Gershom. *On Jews and Judaism in Crisis.* New York, 1976. pp. 128, 281 (2), 286–87, 287

SCHOLEM, Gershom. In *Ostjüdische Geschichten,* edited by Ulf Diederichs. Munich, 1988. p. 73

SCHOLEM, Gershom. "Walter Benjamin." In *Neue Rundschau* (Frankfurt am Main) 76 (1965). In *Judaica 2.* Frankfurt am Main, 1970. p. 191

SCHORSCH, Emil. "Die zwölf Jahre vor der Zerstörung der Synagoge in Hannover." In Monika Richarz, ed., *Jüdisches Leben in Deutschland 1918–1945.* Stuttgart, 1982. pp. 28, 47

SCHULSTEIN, Moische. *Ch'hob gesejn a Barg.* Warsaw, 1954. p. 308

SCHWABE, Carl. "Mein Leben in Deutschland vor und nach dem 30. Januar 1933." In Monika Richarz, ed., *Jüdisches Leben in Deutschland 1918–1945.* Stuttgart, 1982. p. 292

SCHWARZ, Karl. Kunstsammler. In Siegmund Kaznelson, ed., *Juden im deutschen Kulturbereich.* Berlin, 1962. p. 206

SCHWIND, Moritz von, to Eduard von Bauernfeld, 25 May 1866. In Franz Kobler, ed., *Jüdische Geschichte in Briefen aus Ost und West.* Vienna, 1938. p. 151

SELIGSBERGER-WHITE, Philip. "Memoirs of my youth in Fürth, Bavaria." In Monika Richarz, ed., *Jüdisches Leben in Deutschland 1918–1945.* Stuttgart, 1982. p. 20

SICHER, Gustav. "Dringende Kapitel." In *Jüdischer Kalender 1924/25.* Prague, 1924. In Wilma Iggers, ed., *Die Juden in Böhmen und Mähren.* Munich, 1986. pp. 32, 38

SIMMENAUER, Felix. *Die Goldmedaille: Erinnerungen an die Bar Kochba-Makkabi Turn- und Sportbewegung 1898–1938.* Berlin, 1989. pp. 140, 144

SINGER, Isaac Bashevis. *In My Father's Court.* New York, 1966. p. 106

SPERBER, Manès. *God's Water Carriers.* New York, 1987. pp. 41, 51, 61, 81 (2), 108, 279

SPIRO, Samuel. "Jugenderinnerungen aus hessischen Judengemeinden." In Monika Richarz, ed., *Jüdisches Leben in Deutschland 1871–1918.* Stuttgart, 1979. p. 126

SUSMAN, Margarete. *Ich habe viele Leben gelebt: Erinnerungen.* Stuttgart, 1964. p. 287

SVOBODA, Emil. *Über die reale Teilung der Häuser auf dem Gebiet des gewesenen Prager Ghettos.* Prague, 1909. In Wilma Iggers, ed., *Die Juden in Böhmen und Mähren.* Munich, 1986. p. 87

SWARSENSKY, Manfred. "Rosch Haschana." In Friedrich Thieberger, ed., *Jüdisches Fest—jüdischer Brauch.* N.p., 1937. Reprint. Frankfurt am Main, 1985. p. 20

SZANTO, Alexander. "Im Dienste der Gemeinde 1923–1939." In Monika Richarz, ed., *Jüdisches Leben in Deutschland 1918–1945.* Stuttgart, 1982. p. 280

SZONDI, Peter. In Claudio Magris, *Weit von wo? Verlorene Welt des Ostjudentums.* Vienna, 1974. p. 301

TAL, Josef. *Der Sohn des Rabbiners.* Berlin, 1985. p. 19

TAU, Max. *Das Land, das ich verlassen musste.* Hamburg, 1961. p. 194

TEIGE, Josef, Ignát Hermann, and Zikmund Winter. "Das Prager Ghetto." 1903. In Wilma Iggers, ed., *Die Juden in Böhmen und Mähren.* Munich, 1986. p. 87 (2)

THEILHABER, Felix A. In Arnold Zweig, *Bilanz der deutschen Judenheit.* Amsterdam, 1934. pp. 241, 243

TIETZ, Georg, and Hermann Tietz. *Geschichte einer Familie und ihrer Warenhäuser.* Stuttgart, 1965. p. 287

TOLLER, Ernst, to Emil Ludwig, 2 January 1943. Deutsches Literaturarchiv Marbach/Neckar. p. 291

TOLLER, Ernst. "Eine Jugend in Deutschland." In *Gesammelte Werke,* edited by John M. Spalik and Wolfgang Frühwald. Munich, 1978. p. 185

TOLLER, Ernst. "Ferdinand und Isabella." In *Das Neue Tage-Buch IV,* 25 January 1936. In *Gesammelte Werke,* edited by John M. Spalek and Wolfgang Frühwald. Munich, 1978. p. 184

TOLLER, Ernst. *I was a German.* New York, 1934. pp. 184–85

TOLLER, Ernst. "Reichskanzler Hitler." In *Die Weltbühne* 26, No. 2 (1930). In *Gesammelte Werke,* edited by John M. Spalek and Wolfgang Frühwald. Munich, 1978. p. 290

TORBERG, Friedrich. *Die Tante Jolesch oder der Untergang des Abendlandes.* Munich, 1975. Reprint. Munich, 1989. pp. 136, 138, 139, 177, 182, 228, 231 (2)

TORBERG, Friedrich, to Max Brod, 15 March 1955. In *In diesem Sinne . . . Briefe an Freunde und Zeitgenossen,* edited by David Axmann, Marietta Torberg and Hans Weigel. Munich/Vienna, 1981. p. 184

TORBERG, Friedrich. "Warum ich stolz darauf bin." In *50 Jahre Hakoah 1909–1959.* Tel Aviv, 1959. p. 142

TRAMER, Hans. "Der Beitrag der Juden zu Geist und Kultur." In Werner E. Mosse/Arnold Paucker, *Deutsches Judentum in Krieg und Revolution 1916–1923.* Tübingen, 1971. p. 170

TUCHOLSKY, Kurt. *Briefe an eine Katholikin.* Reinbek, 1970. p. 291

TUCHOLSKY, Kurt. *Gesammelte Werke.* Reinbek, 1975. pp. 187, 188, 268, 290

TUCHOLSKY, Kurt, to Hans Reichmann, 4 May 1929. In *Kurt Tucholsky hasst—liebt,* edited by Mary Gerold-Tucholsky. Reinbek, 1962. p. 187

TUCHOLSKY, Kurt. *Panther, Tiger und andere.* Berlin, 1957. pp. 180, 222, 231

TUCHOLSKY, Kurt. "Prozess Harden." In *Deutschland, Deutschland—unter anderem.* Berlin, 1957. p. 178

TUCHOLSKY, Kurt. *Q-Tagebücher 1934–1935.* Reinbek, 1985. p. 245

TUCHOLSKY, Kurt. In Richard von Soldenhoff, *Kurt Tucholsky 1890–1935: Ein Lebensbild.* Weinheim, 1985. pp. 187, 188

"Verband jüdischer Heimatvereine, 9 November 1935." In Günther B. Ginzel, *Jüdischer Alltag in Deutschland 1933–1945.* Düsseldorf, 1984. p. 299

VIERTEL, Berthold, to Hermann Wlach, 1908. *In Jugend in Wien: Literatur um 1900.* Exhibition catalogue. Deutsches Literaturarchiv Marbach/Neckar, 1974. p. 136

Die Wahrheit: Wochenschrift für Leben und Lehre im Judenthume, 18 August 1871. p. 252

WASSERMANN, Jakob. *Deutscher und Jude: Reden und Schriften 1904–1933,* edited by Dierk Rodewald. Heidelberg, 1984. p. 180

WASSERMANN, Jakob, to Thomas Mann. In Martha Karlweiss, *Jakob Wassermann: Bild, Kampf und Werk.* Amsterdam, 1935. p. 255

WEIL, Friedrich. "Mein Leben in Deutschland vor und nach dem 30. Januar 1933." In Monika Richarz, ed., *Jüdisches Leben in Deutschland 1918–1945.* Stuttgart, 1982. p. 301

WEISEL, Georg Leopold. "Träger." In Wilma Iggers, ed., *Die Juden in Böhmen und Mähren.* Munich, 1986. p. 91

WEISS, Gittel. *Ein Lebensbericht.* East Berlin, 1982. pp. 37, 47

WEISS, Peter. *Abschied von den Eltern: Erzählung.* Frankfurt am Main, 1980. p. 301

WEIZMANN, Chaim. *Trial and Error.* Vol. 1: *Earliest Days.* New York, 1949. p. 277

WELTSCH, Robert. *An der Wende des modernen Judentums: Betrachtungen aus fünf Jahrzehnten.* Tübingen, 1972. pp. 174, 279

WERFEL, Franz. "Pogrom." In *Gesammelte Werke: Erzählungen aus zwei Welten,* edited by Adolf Klarmann. Frankfurt am Main, 1952–53. p. 184

WERTHEIMER, Willi. "Erinnerungen." In Monika Richarz, ed., *Jüdisches Leben in Deutschland 1871–1918.* Stuttgart, 1979. p. 92

WILBRANDT, Adolf. *Erinnerungen.* Stuttgart, 1905. p. 151

WINTERFELDT, Hans. "Deutschland: Ein Zeitbild 1926–1945." In Monika Richarz, ed., *Jüdisches Leben in Deutschland 1918–1945.* Stuttgart, 1982. p. 280

WITTGENSTEIN, Ludwig. *Werkausgabe in acht Bänden.* Frankfurt am Main, 1989. p. 232

WITTLIN, Józef. *Erinnerungen an Joseph Roth.* In Joseph Roth, *Leben und Werk: Ein Gedächtnisbuch,* edited by Hermann Linden. Cologne/The Hague, 1949. p. 194

WOLFENSTEIN, Alfred. "Jüdisches Wesen und Dichtertum." In *Der Jude* 6, no. 7 (1922). p. 185

WOLFSKEHL, Karl. "An die Deutschen." In *Gesammelte Werke.* Hamburg, 1960. p. 301

ZECHLIN, Egmont. *Die deutsche Politik und die Juden im Ersten Weltkrieg.* Göttingen, 1969. p. 257

Der Zionismus. Erste Schrift der Zionistischen Vereinigung gleichen Namens 1, no. 1 (1897). p. 276

ZONDEK, Hermann. *Auf festem Fusse: Erinnerungen eines jüdischen Klinikers.* Stuttgart, 1973. p. 108

ZÜRNDORFER, Josef. In Günther B. Ginzel, *Jüdischer Alltag in Deutschland 1933–1945.* Düsseldorf, 1984. p. 259

ZWEIG, Arnold. *Bilanz der deutschen Judenheit.* Amsterdam, 1934. pp. 145, 153, 163, 164 (2), 178, 197, 199, 201, 205, 214, 224, 234, 239, 242, 246, 259, 262, 271, 281

ZWEIG, Arnold. *Das ostjüdische Antlitz.* Berlin, 1922. Reprint. Wiesbaden, 1988. p. 99

ZWEIG, Arnold. In *Die Weltbühne* (Berlin) 18, no. 31 (1922). p. 257

ZWEIG, Arnold. *Herkunft und Zukunft: Zwei Essays zum Schicksal eines Volkes.* Vienna, 1929. p. 106

ZWEIG, Arnold. *Mein Weltbild.* Zurich, 1954. p. 192

ZWEIG, Arnold. "Öffentlicher Brief an Kurt Tucholsky, 16 January 1936." *Neue Weltbühne,* 6 February 1936. pp. 103, 187, 290

ZWEIG, Arnold. In Georg Wenzel, ed., *Arnold Zweig 1887–1968, Werk und Leben in Dokumenten und Bildern: Mit unveröffentlichten Manuskripten und Briefen aus dem Nachlass.* Berlin/Weimar, 1978. pp. 192, 260

ZWEIG, Stefan. "Antwort auf eine Umfrage der 'Internationalen Literatur'." *Moskau* 3 (1933). p. 262

ZWEIG, Stefan. *Briefe an Freunde,* edited by Richard Friedenthal. Frankfurt am Main, 1984. pp. 178, 181 (2)

ZWEIG, Stefan. *Die Welt von gestern.* Stockholm, 1944. Reprint. Frankfurt am Main, 1988. p. 245

ZWEIG, Stefan. *Europäisches Erbe.* Frankfurt am Main, 1986. p. 181

ZWEIG, Stefan. *The World of Yesterday.* Lincoln, Neb., 1964. pp. 156, 158, 202, 206, 274, 276, 294, 296, 304, 306

TEXT AND PICTURE CREDITS

The copyright of the quotations has been obtained from copyright-licensed authors. They are represented by the following publishers whom we thank for their permission.

PROF. DR. J. ALLERHAND, Vienna (Jakob Allerhand); VERLAG ALLERT DE LANGE, Amsterdam (Salomon Asch); VERLAG ALLERT DE LANGE, Amsterdam, and VERLAG KIEPENHEUER & WITSCH, Cologne (Joseph Roth); AMANN VERLAG, Zurich (Hans Sahl), AMS PRESS, INC., New York (Ernst Toller); ARANI-VERLAG, Berlin (Mascha Kaléko); ARGON VERLAG, Berlin (Alfred Kerr); AUFBAU VERLAG, Berlin (Lion Feuchtwanger, Felix Theilhaber, Arnold Zweig); LEO BAECK INSTITUTE, New York (Monika Richarz, Margarete Susman, Hans Tramer, Robert Weltsch); THE BALKIN AGENCY, New York (Martin Buber); MR. THOMAS BARRY-BRAUNTHAL, Linkebeek, Belgium (Julius Braunthal); VERLAG CH. H. BECK'SCHE VERLAGSBUCHHANDLUNG, Munich (*Die Juden in Böhmen und Mähren*, edited by Wilma Iggers); BLOCH PUBLICATIONS AND HERZL PRESS, New York (Theodor Herzl); DR. KLAUS BOER VERLAG, Munich (Albert Ehrenstein); PETER BROD, Fürstenfeldbruck (Leo Brod); HELMUT BUSKE VERLAG, Hamburg (Heinz Mosche Graupe); CARCANET PRESS LTD., Manchester, Mass. (Paul Celan); WERNER CLAASSEN VERLAG, Zurich (Brigitte B. Fischer, Karl Wolfskehl); EUGEN DIEDERICHS VERLAG, Munich (Samuel Josef Agnon); SONJA DOBBINS, London (Stefan Zweig); DROSTE VERLAG GMBH. Düsseldorf (Günther B. Ginzel, Anna Klapheck, Josef Zürndorfer); ECON VERLAGSGRUPPE, Düsseldorf (Karl Wolfskehl); EUROPA VERLAG, Zurich (Carl Seelig); FARRAR, STRAUS & GIROUX, INC., New York (Elias Canetti, Isaac Bashevis Singer); S. FISCHER VERLAG, Frankfurt am Main (Peter Altenberg, Rose Ausländer, Richard Beer-Hofmann, Paul Celan, Brigitte B. Fischer, Otto Flake, Sigmund Freud, Karl Grünberg, Hugo von Hofmannsthal, Max Horkheimer, Franz Kafka, Jakob Wassermann, Franz Werfel, Stefan Zweig); FOURIER VERLAG, Wiesbaden (Leo Baeck); MRS. MARGARETHE FRANKENSCHWERTH, London (Alfred Wolfenstein); HAMLYN PUBL. INC., c/o OCTOPUS PUBLISHING GROUP, London (Lewis Carroll); CARL HANSER VERLAG, Munich (Ernst Toller); HARCOURT, BRACE AND WORLD c/o HARCOURT, BRACE, JOVANOVICH, INC., New York (Hannah Arendt); HARPER COLLINS, Scranton, Pa (Chaim Weizmann); THE HEBREW UNIVERSITY c/o AMERICAN FRIENDS OF THE HEBREW UNIVERSITY, New York (Albert Einstein); EDITION HENTRICH, Berlin (Felix Simmenauer, Kurt Schilde); VERLAG F. A. HERBIG VERLAGSBUCHHANDLUNG GMBH., Munich (Alexander Granach, Friedrich Torberg); HERZL PRESS, SUBST. OF WORLD ZIONIST ORGANIZATION, New York (Theodor Herzl); THE HOGARTH PRESS, LTD., London (Sigmund Freud); HOLMES & MEIER PUBL. INC., New York (Manès Sperber); HOLT, REINHART & WINSTON INC. DIVISION OF HARCOURT, BRACE, AND JOVANOVICH, INC., New York (Arthur Schnitzler); INDIANA UNIVERSITY PRESS, Bloomington, Ind. (Jean Améry); INSEL VERLAG, Frankfurt am Main (Otto Best, Wolfgang Schivelbusch); PROFESSOR DR. WALTER JENS, Tübingen (Walter Jens); PROFESSOR ROBERT JUNGK, Salzburg (Robert Jungk); VERLAG KIEPENHEUER & WITSCH, Cologne (Joseph Roth); KINDLER VERLAG, Munich (Fritz Kortner); KNOPF, New York (Arthur Schnitzler); KÖSEL-VERLAG GMBH. & Co., Munich (Else Lasker-Schüler); LANGEN MÜLLER/HERBIG, Munich (Peter de Mendelssohn, Friedrich Torberg); ERHARD LÖCKER VERLAG, Vienna (Bruno Frei, Egon Friedell, Pierre Genée, Fritz Grünbaum, Anton Kuh, Alfred Polgar); MACMILLAN PUBL., LTD., Basingstoke, UK (Max Born, Albert Einstein); MARTINUS NIJHOFF UITGEVERIJ, The Hague (Franz Rosenzweig); J. B. METZLER VERLAG GMBH., Stuttgart (Helmut Dinse, Sol Liptzin, Heinz Politzer); J. C. B. MOHR, Tübingen (Ernest Hamburger, Georg Landauer); MUSIKVERLAG B. SCHOTT'S SÖHNE, Mainz (Arnold Schönberg); MRS. ELISABETH NEUMANN-VIERTEL, Vienna (Berthold Viertel); NEW DIRECTIONS PUBLISHING CORP., New York (Gustav Janouch); NIEDIECK LINDER AG, Zurich (Claudio Magris); OPEN COURT PUBL. Co., Peru, IL. (Albert Einstein); THE OVERLOOK PRESS OF WOODSTOOK, N.Y. (Joseph Roth); OXFORD UNIVERSITY PRESS, Oxford, UK (Isaac Deutscher); PARAGON HOUSE PUBL., New York (Alfred Döblin); MR. MARK PATERSON, Wivenhoe, Essex, UK (Sigmund Freud); PHILOSOPHICAL LIBRARY INC., New York (Albert Einstein); R. PIPER & CO., Munich (Hanna Arendt: *Lebensgeschichte einer deutschen Jüdin aus der Romantik)*; QUADRIGA VERLAG, Weinheim (Josef Tal); QUARTET BOOKS, London (Paul Michael Luetzeler); PROF. GOTTFRIED REINHARDT, Los Angeles (Max Reinhardt); ROTBUCH VERLAG, Berlin (Hannah Arendt); ROWOHLT VERLAG GMBH., Reinbek (Walter Mehring, Erwin Piscator, Kurt Tucholsky); VERLAG LAMBERT SCHNEIDER, Heidelberg (Martin Buber); SCHOCKEN BOOKS, INC., DIV. OF RANDOM HOUSE, INC., New York (Walter Benjamin, Martin Buber, Bella Chagall, Franz Kafka, Gershom Scholem); SEABURY PRESS, INC., DIVISION OF HARPER & ROW PUBLICATIONS, San Francisco (Elias Canetti); WOLF JOBST SIEDLER VERLAG GMBH., Berlin (Günter Kunert); SUHRKAMP VERLAG, Frankfurt am Main (Walter Benjamin, Max Brod, Karl Kraus, Nelly Sachs, Gershom Scholem); JOSEF TAL, Jerusalem (Josef Tal); VERLAG ULLSTEIN, Berlin (Albert Einstein); THE UNGAR PUBLISHING GROUP, New York (Hermann Cohen); THE UNIVERSITY OF CHICAGO PRESS, Chicago (Hermann Broch); VALLENTINE, MITCHELL AND CO., LTD., London (*The Jews of Austria*, edited by Josef Fraenkel); VANDENHOECK & RUPRECHT VERLAGSBUCHHANDLUNG, Göttingen (Egmont Zechlin); VIKING PRESS, New York (Lion Feuchtwanger, Stefan Zweig); WALTER-VERLAG, Olten (Alfred Döblin); MRS. JACQUELINE WASSERMANN, Toronto (Jakob Wassermann); MRS. MARIA WHITE, Northport, N.Y. (Max Liebermann); GEORGE WYLAND, Zurich (Wieland Herzfelde); DR. VEIT WYLER, Zurich (Felix Salten).

The editors and publisher thank all private collectors, archives, and institutions for their assistance in compiling the pictures for this book. Special thanks are due Eike Geisel, Berlin, and the Salomon-Ludwig-Steinheim-Institut, Duisburg.

AKADEMIE DER KÜNSTE, Berlin, p. 227 l.
ALLGEMEINE JÜDISCHE WOCHENZEITUNG, Düsseldorf, p. 303
ALLGEMEINER DEUTSCHER NACHRICHTENDIENST, Zentralbild, Berlin, p. 291
AMT DER BURGENLÄNDISCHEN LANDESREGIERUNG, Eisenstadt, pp. 26 b., 27 b., 47 b.
PETER BADEL, Berlin, for copyright for Hans Thormann, pp. 110 b., 120 l.
LEO-BAECK-INSTITUTE, New York (Jim Strong, New York), pp. 43 t. r., 126 (2), 127, 131 r., 134 (2), 148 r., 160 t. r., 232 t., 235 t., 239 b., 259 l., 269 l.
BERLINISCHE GALERIE, Berlin, p. 205 b.
BETH HATEFUTSOTH, Tel Aviv, pp. 81, 104 b., 111, 122, 125
THE CENTRAL ARCHIVES OF THE HISTORY OF THE JEWISH PEOPLE, Jerusalem, pp. 48 b., 91
CENTRAL ZIONIST ARCHIVES, Jerusalem, pp. 73, 254/255, 273, 274, 276 b., 277, 280 r.
CHRISTIAN BRANDSTÄTTER COLLECTION, Vienna, pp. 54 t., 86 (2), 118 b., 119, 129 l., 129 t. r., 133 t., 159 l., 171 b. l., 172, 178 b., 214, 214/215, 225 t., 226 r., 260 t., 262 (2)
DEUTSCHES THEATERMUSEUM, Munich, p. 228 b.
DOKUMENTATIONSARCHIV DES ÖSTERREICHISCHEN WIDERSTANDES, Vienna, pp. 283, 306/307
DOKUMENTATIONSSTELLE FÜR NEUERE ÖSTERREICHISCHE LITERATUR, Vienna, p. 190 t.
S. FISCHER VERLAG, Frankfurt am Main, p. 196
SIGMUND FREUD COPYRIGHTS, LTD., Colchester, pp. 138/139, 245, 246
GISÈLE FREUND, Paris, p. 191 t.
EIKE GEISEL COLLECTION, Berlin, pp. 109 b., 117 b., 124 b.
GESELLSCHAFT DER MUSIKFREUNDE, Vienna, p. 219
LI HANDLER COLLECTION, Perchtoldsdorf, p. 87 l.
CARL HANSER VERLAG, Munich, see ROMAN VISHNIAC
ANDRÉ HELLER COLLECTION, Vienna, p. 194
HISTORISCHES MUSEUM, Vienna, pp. 176, 215, 217
HANS HOFFMANN, Berlin, p. 124 t.

FRANZ HUBMANN COLLECTION, Vienna, pp. 6/7, 7 c., 14, 21, 31 b., 33, 34/35, 34 t. l., 34 t. r., 38 b., 43 t. c., 49, 60, 64 t., 76 b., 78, 80 b., 82 b., 87 t., 94/95, 99 b., 102 t., 103 (2), 104 t., 136, 138 b., 139 b., 154/155, 157 c., 159 b., 200, 202 b., 256, 275, 300 b.
INSTITUT FÜR DIE GESCHICHTE DER MEDIZIN, Vienna, pp. 242, 243 (2)
THE LOTTE JACOBI ARCHIVE, Media Services, Dimond Library, University of New Hampshire, p. 223 (2)
JEWISH LABOUR MOVEMENT, Bund Archives, New York, pp. 15 (2), 17, 24 b., 28, 29 (2), 41, 66, 92 b. l.
THE JEWISH MUSEUM, New York, p. 43 b. c.
JEWISH NATIONAL AND UNIVERSITY LIBRARY, Jerusalem, pp. 160 c. r., 197 b.
LOTTE KÖHLER, New York, p. 191 b.
LANDESARCHIV BERLIN, pp. 37, 157 t.
LANDESBILDSTELLE BERLIN, p. 302 b.
THE LIBRARY OF CONGRESS, Washington, D.C., p. 107
MUSEUM FÜR KUNST UND GEWERBE, Hamburg, pp. 128, 147, 201
ÖSTERREICHISCHE NATIONALBIBLIOTHEK, Bildarchiv, Vienna, pp. 20 b., 32, 36, 46, 68 b., 71 t., 88/89, 117 t., 122/123, 132 b. r., 146, 150, 151 t., 154 t., 158 (2), 159 t., 163 t., 174, 175, 177 t., 178 t., 181, 182, 184 b., 190 b., 203, 206 t., 207 b., 216, 218/219, 220 (4), 221, 222 (2), 225 b., 226 l., 227 r., 231 b., 232 r., 234 t. l., 241, 244, 247 l., 257, 260 b., 270, 276 t., 297
ÖSTERREICHISCHES FILMMUSEUM, Vienna, pp. 211 (2), 212 t. l.
ÖSTERREICHISCHES INSTITUT FÜR ZEITGESCHICHTE, Vienna (Albert Hilscher, Vienna), pp. 177 t., 271 t. l., 282
ÖSTERREICHISCHES MUSEUM FÜR VOLKSKUNDE, Vienna, pp. 11, 52 t. r., 72, 75, 97 (2)
ÖSTERREICHISCHES STAATSARCHIV/KRIEGSARCHIV, Vienna, pp. 56, 68 t., 82 t., 101
FRIEDRICH PFÄFFLIN, Marbach/Neckar, p. 186 l.
ABRAHAM PISAREK, Berlin, pp. 20 b., 23, 25, 27 t., 34 t. c., 47 t., 52 b. r., 53 (2), 64/65, 70, 79 b., 110 t., 144 t., 298 t., 300 t., 301, 304 t.
PPS GALERIE F. C. GUNDLACH, Hamburg, for copyright for Herbert List, p. 286
PREUSSISCHER KULTURBESITZ, Bildarchiv, Berlin, pp. 19 (2), 31 t., 38 t., 39, 42, 43 b. c., 45 b., 69, 121, 122, 125, 131 l., 133 t., 140 t., 153, 162/163, 165, 199 t. (Friedrich Seidenstücker), 235 b. (Abraham Pisarek), 239 t., 248, 255, 259 t., 263, 266 t. (Abraham Pisarek), 288, 289, 290, 292 t. (Hans

Hoffmann), 296 (2), 298 b., 299, 302 t., 304 b.
PRIVATE COLLECTION, Vienna, p. 148 t. l.
WILLY PUCHNER COLLECTION, Vienna, pp. 30, 54 b., 62/63
ROWOHLT VERLAG, Reinbek bei Hamburg, p. 188
LOTHAR RÜBELT, Vienna, pp. 140 b., 141, 142 (2), 143, 151 b., 154 t., 230, 271 r., 294
RACHEL SALAMANDER COLLECTION, Munich, pp. 135 b., 310
GUNTHER SANDER, USA, for copyright for August Sander, p. 202 t.
SCHILLER-NATIONALMUSEUM, Deutsches Literaturarchiv, Marbach/Neckar, p. 197 t. l.; Lotte Jacobi, Manchester, 179, 180, 183, 184 t., 187, 189, 192, 193, 197 t. r., 209, 233, 234 t. r., 269 r.
PETER SCHNITZLER COLLECTION, Vienna, p. 173
LILLY SCHOEN COLLECTION, Haifa, pp. 144 b., 278 r.
WERNER J. SCHWEIGER COLLECTION, Vienna, pp. 205 r., 206 b.
STADTARCHIV FRANKFURT, p. 161
STADTARCHIV MANNHEIM, p. 253 r.
STADTMUSEUM FRANKFURT, p. 130
STADTMUSEUM KÖLN, p. 272
STÁTNÍ ŽIDOVSKÉ MUZEUM, Prague, pp. 9, 43 t. l., 43 b. r., 44/45, 213 b.
SALOMON-LUDWIG-STEINHEIM-INSTITUT, Duisburg (Nachum Tim Gidal, Jerusalem), p. 129 t. (Elishewa Cohen, Jerusalem), 152/153 (Eric Warburg, Hamburg), 164 (Alex Bein, Jerusalem), 166 (Heinrich-Heine-Institut, Düsseldorf), 170 (Peter Hunter, The Hague), 207 t., 210 b., 229 t., 234 b. l. (Ruth Gorny-Lessing, Hannover), 240/241 (Bernhard Witkop, Washington, D.C.), 258 (Ursula Liebstädter, Jerusalem), 268 b., 279 t. r., 296 b., 309 r., 355 b., 370 l., 378 t. r., 378 t. r., 414 b. l.
ALBERT STERNFELD COLLECTION, Vienna, p. 26 t.
THEATERMUSEUM DER UNIVERSITÄT KÖLN, p. 231 t.
ULLSTEIN BILDERDIENST, Berlin, pp. 16, 24 t., 64 b., 80 t., 84, 85 (2), 145, 156, 157 b., 185, 186 r., 198, 199 b., 204, 228 t., 236/237, 238, 264/265, 266 b., 267, 268 (2), 292 b., 293, 294/295, 305
NIKOLAUS VIELMETTI COLLECTION, Vienna, p. 138 t.
ROMAN VISHNIAC, New York, pp. 40, 41, 83, 89, 92 t. r.
YAD VASHEM, Jerusalem, p. 49
YIVO, New York, pp. 18, 22 (2), 43 b. l., 48 t., 50, 51, 52 l., 55, 57, 61, 67, 71 b., 74 (2), 76 t., 77, 79 t., 90 (2), 93, 96 t., 98, 99 t., 100, 104/105, 106, 108, 132 t., 135 t., 139 t., 148 b. l., 149, 195 (2), 213 t., 229 (2), 261, 278 l.

All other pictures are from the archive of Brandstätter Verlag.